DATE			

∞ *By the Grace of Guile* ∞

By the Grace
∽ of Guile ∾

The Role of Deception
in Natural History and
Human Affairs

LOYAL RUE

New York   Oxford
OXFORD UNIVERSITY PRESS
1994

for Marilyn

Oxford University Press

Oxford   New York   Toronto
Delhi   Bombay   Calcutta   Madras   Karachi
Kuala Lumpur   Singapore   Hong Kong   Tokyo
Nairobi   Dar es Salaam   Cape Town
Melbourne   Auckland   Madrid

and associated companies in
Berlin   Ibadan

Copyright © 1994 by Loyal D. Rue

Published by Oxford University Press, Inc.
200 Madison Avenue, New York, New York 10016

Oxford is a registered trademark of Oxford University Press, Inc.

Library of Congress Cataloging-in-Publication Data

Rue, Loyal D.
By the grace of guile : the role of deception in
natural history and human affairs / Loyal Rue.
p. cm.   Includes bibliographical references and index.
ISBN 0-19-507508-0
1. Deception.   I. Title.
BD171.R8   1994
302'.1—dc20   93-32877

I am grateful to the publishers listed below for permission to reprint the following:

Dylan Thomas, "Do Not Go Gentle into That Good Night," *The Collected Poems of Dylan Thomas*.
Copyright 1952 by Dylan Thomas. Reprinted by permission of New Directions Publishing Corp.
From *The New English Bible*. © The Delegates of the Oxford University Press and the Syndics of the
Cambridge University Press, 1961, 1970, 1989. Reprinted by permission.
From "Hypocrite Auteur," *Collected Poems, 1917–1982* by Archibald MacLeish. © 1985 by The Estate of
Archibald MacLeish. Reprinted by permission of Houghton Mifflin Company. All rights reserved.

1 3 5 7 9 8 6 4 2

Printed in the United States of America
on acid-free paper

∽ *Acknowledgments* ∽

A T SOME unremembered point in my youth I was forced to give serious consideration to the problematic distinction between appearance and reality. This book has its ultimate origins in the wonder of that moment.

More immediate stimulation has come from dozens of individuals with whom I have shared the pleasure of conversations about deception, and especially those who inquired about my intentions to write a book on the subject. I cannot recall when I stopped answering these queries in the negative, but at some point the frequency of the question finally convinced me that a book was in order.

I have been helped along the way by insights and observations from many friends and colleagues. To the following I express my thanks for especially helpful conversations and suggestions: Eric Chaisson, Don Cupitt, Langdon Gilkey, James Hippen, Sol Katz, Gordon Kaufman, Alan Lerstrom, Ann Loades, Martha Nussbaum, Harley Refsal, Norma Refsal, John Sieber, Robert Sussman, Robert Trivers, and Bruce Willis.

Special thanks go to those generous colleagues who agreed to read portions or all of the manuscript and to give me valuable responses. I am especially grateful to David Bishop, Mihaly Csikszentmihalyi, Eugene d'Aquili, Neil Elgee, Ursula Goodenough, Philip Hefner, William Irons, Werner Nitschke, Max Oelschlaeger, David Olds, Phillip Reitan, Conrad Røyksund, Michael Ruse, C. R. Snyder, Tex Sordahl, and John Whelan.

Jami Dueland, Matthew Maker, and Aaron Knight provided valuable assistance during the early stages of research. Jennifer Martinson Pierce assisted me for three years, performing tedious research tasks and preparing draft after draft of the manuscript. Her contributions have been indispensable. Thanks also to Cynthia Read and Peter Ohlin at Oxford University Press for helping the press live up to its excellent reputation; and to Barbara Salazar for her expertise in copy editing the manuscript.

Finally, to my wife, Marilyn, and our children, Carl, Anna, and Elena, I am deeply indebted for the love and support that bring meaning to my life and work.

July 1993   L.R.
Decorah, Iowa

❦ *Contents* ❦

∞ *By the Grace of Guile* ∞

∞ *Introduction* ∞

*To recognize untruth as a condition of life: that is certainly to
impugn the traditional ideas of value in a dangerous manner,
and a philosophy which ventures to do so, has thereby alone
placed itself beyond good and evil.*

Friedrich Nietzsche

WHEN Charles Darwin's revolutionary thesis began to work its way
through the halls and streets of London, a lady of the period is reputed
to have remarked, "It cannot be true; but if it is let us hope it does not become
generally known." I must confess that something of the spirit of this woman's
remark has been at work in motivating this book. A dangerous thesis has been
growing in our midst for the past two centuries or so, one I feel has become
too generally known. This book will not contest the truth of the thesis, for it is
one to which I myself subscribe. Yet it is a thesis which I hope this book may
ultimately help to obscure from general view. The thesis has been articulated
in many ways and by various advocates, but basically it comes to this: The
universe is blind and aimless; it has no value in and of itself; it is unenchanted
by forces, qualities, characteristics that might objectively endorse any particular human orientation toward it. The universe is dead and void of meaning; its
significance is not demonstrably one thing or another. The universe *just is*.

This thesis—sometimes called "nihilism"—is not something that one can
argue away by showing that it results from fallacious thinking. Nor can it be
dismissed by a display of indisputable facts. It is logically and empirically
secure. But I have no interest in refuting the nihilistic thesis. I shall not bother
much about its origins or whether it is true. On the contrary, I will assume its
truth. What I shall bother about is what can be done to defeat its appeal, to
submerge it out of sight, to make it appear beside the point. The question is
whether we can find the resources sufficient to reenchant the universe despite
the truth of nihilism.

What are the means by which nihilism—or any other truth, for that
matter—might be defeated? There are, I think, only two possibilities: force
and guile. The first option is abhorrent to me and I will not discuss it. But the
second option I will defend against any further advance of the nihilistic thesis.
The ultimate purpose of this book, therefore, is to oppose a monstrous truth
with a noble lie.

But such an aim, many will say, is no less abhorrent than suppressing truth
by means of force. Therefore much of this book—most of it, actually—will be
preoccupied with a sort of preface to a noble lie. Deceit as a means to any

3

end, however noble, is met with such aversion in Western culture that it will take some doing to make a case for its use. So the first four chapters of this book are given over to an examination of the phenomena of deception to see how far it deserves the demonic imagery we have come to associate with it.

Human beings hate to be deceived. It makes us feel violated, used, and stupid, as if something essential had been taken from us (deceive = *de* + *capere* = to take from). Deception is a foul business, we say. Nothing good can come of it. So we immortalize honest George Washington and quote the Ten Commandments to each other. And yet every human practices deception in a multitude of ways. We conceal information, we distort and exaggerate, we rationalize, we bluff. We even tell tall tales about George Washington's honesty and fabricate laws that we attribute to God. So we simultaneously fear and practice deception. This fundamental human duplicity regarding the realities of deception will characterize the general tone of this book.

The reader should be forewarned that several layers of argument are being played out in the pages ahead. I discovered very early in my research for this book that to say something significant about deception would involve saying many things about a wide range of topics. To understand deception well, I realized, one must appreciate its role within history, nature, personality, and society. This role was sufficiently large and central to warrant the conclusion that one cannot adequately understand history, nature, personality, and society without also understanding the nature and functions of deception. The topic of deception gradually reared up before me in the manner of Lord Tennyson's "Flower in the Crannied Wall":

> Little flower—but *if* I could understand
> What you are, root and all, and all in all,
> I should know what God and man is.

In the process of resolving these issues, I found myself pressed to articulate general perspectives on history, nature, personality and society, with the result that this book approaches the dimensions of a broad philosophical outlook, complete with a utopian agenda for the future.

In chapter 1 I argue that the intellectual and moral traditions of Western culture have been shaped and driven by an explicit and consistent fear of deception. The fundamental values of Western culture—as expressed in religious doctrines, philosophical principles, theories of mental health and social progress, and even the scientific method—have found legitimation in their perceived power to safeguard humans against the danger of being deceived.

In chapter 2 the focus shifts from a cultural bias against being deceived to a biological bias favoring traits for deceiving. I first develop a general theory and typology of deception and then illustrate these principles with examples drawn from nature in order to show that deception operates as a fundamental dynamic in the process of evolution. Nature, I argue, provides niches for effective deceivers at every level in the organization of life, from one-celled creatures to human beings.

In chapters 3 and 4 I apply this thesis on the adaptive value of deception to the realm of human affairs, both individual and collective. In chapter 3 I attempt to answer three questions: What is a person? What constitutes personal wholeness? What is the role of deception in the achievement of personal wholeness? In chapter 4 I adopt the same approach to collective human experience. Here I ask: What is a society? What constitutes social coherence? What is the role of deception in the achievement of social coherence?

The argument for a noble lie is taken up in chapter 5. Here I argue that our culture is caught up in a *Kulturkampf*, with nihilists promoting radical intellectual and moral relativism while realists defend objective and universal truths. The option of the noble lie introduces a third voice into the debate, one which first agrees with the nihilists that universal myths describing the origins, nature, and destiny of human existence are pretentious lies but then insists, against the nihilists, that without such lies humanity cannot survive.

∞ 1 ∞

Deception in Historical
Perspective

T HE TASK before us is to assess the manner in which deception has been
regarded within the context of Western intellectual and moral traditions, both religious and secular. A thorough examination of this topic
might easily occupy an intellectual historian for the better part of a long
career. But since the scope of this book is more broadly defined, our survey of the historical dimension must be restricted. In particular, the focus
of this chapter is limited to Western attitudes toward the dangers of *being
deceived*, quite aside from the evils of *deceiving*. At first sight this restric-
tion might seem to exclude half the story, since the topic of deceiving others has held a prominent place in Western culture. Yet on reflection it
becomes obvious that the cultural bias against acts of deceiving is derived
from the more fundamental belief that one is harmed by being deceived. It
is our profound fear of being deceived that gives moral substance to prohi-
bitions against deceiving.

Western culture has feared nothing quite so much as it has feared deception. This concern over deception has played a fundamental role—I believe a
directive role—in the formulation of our doctrines of sin and salvation, our
definitions of philosophical problems, our conceptions of mental health, and
even our justifications of the scientific enterprise. It would not be excessive to
claim that in the Western tradition deception has commanded as much aversion as death itself. Perhaps it is mere quibbling to say that the Western
tradition developed more as a flight from deception and falsehood than as a
quest for certainty and truth, but it might also be said that much can be
learned by a slight change in emphasis.

My plan is to sift through the ancient, medieval, modern, and contemporary periods to see what the major figures of Western cultural history have had
to say about deception. It may be objected that I am far too selective in my
coverage of relevant material. In particular, I pay very little attention here to
works of imaginative literature. This omission represents neither an oversight
nor a judgment that the influence of such works on Western values is unimportant. My only defense is that one must of necessity work within limits of time
and competence. If my conclusions are distorted by these omissions, I wel-
come the efforts of others to correct them.

6

THE ANCIENT PERIOD

The Biblical Record

The Old Testament

The Old Testament is dominated by the idea of covenant, which is nothing more, finally, than a distinctively biblical version of the universal principle of moral retribution. The principle of moral retribution says simply that moral excellence will be rewarded and moral failure will be punished. The essential features of the Old Testament version of the principle are well known. From their beginnings, the people of the covenant community believed that they were the special concern of Yahweh, the god who delivered them from slavery in Egypt and called them into a special relationship with himself. The relationship was defined and controlled by the terms of Yahweh's will for the people, expressed in the laws given to Moses. The biblical record includes several variants on the covenant model, but the essential features of the idea remain constant throughout: The covenant is an expression of the conditions of Israel's existence. If the people of God fulfill their obligations to the covenant, they will be blessed with survival and prosperity; but if they fail, they will cease to exist:

> See, I have set before you this day life and good, death and evil. If you obey the commandments of the Lord your God which I command you this day, . . . then you shall live and multiply, and the Lord your God will bless you in the land you are entering to take possession of it. But if your heart turns away, and you will not hear, but are drawn away to worship other gods and serve them, I declare to you this day, that you shall perish; you shall not live long in the land which you are going over the Jordan to enter and possess. (Deut. 30:15–18)

The options could not be more clear: obedience brings life and good, disobedience brings death and evil. This retributive principle was so deeply imprinted on the Hebrew psyche that disobedience came to be regarded as both necessary and sufficient for the existence of evil. Thus the covenant idea, while providing normative moral substance for Hebrew society, also provided a solution to the problem of evil. Not only could the Hebrews expect evil as a consequence of moral failure, but they could also regard evil as decisive evidence of moral failure. If and *only* if the Hebrews disobeyed would they suffer as a nation. And suffer they did. The record shows, for the most part, a chronic disposition for being led astray to do "what was wrong in the eyes of the Lord."

The reader of this dismal record might well ask for an explanation. In the light of the covenant's clear options for good and evil, Israel's chronic disobedience appears almost inconceivable. Just how do the Old Testament writers account for such a record of sin? In other words, what does the Old Testament say about the *cause* of sin? One might hope for a consistent response to this question, but in fact the Old Testament does not provide one. Instead, when we investigate the nature and origin of sin in the Old Testament, we get a confusing picture. Part of the difficulty is that the Old Testament speaks of sin with a profusion of terminology. Sin to the Hebrews is rather what snow is to the Eskimos—it is ubiquitous. And as in the case of the Eskimos amid the snowfields, the Hebrews have an abundance of names for sin. A selection of English equivalents includes: "to miss," "to stumble," "to wander" or "stray," "to defy," "revolt," "rebel," "transgress," "to be wicked," "do wrong," "perversity," "profanity," and so on. Frequently the Old Testament simply heaps together synonyms for sin.[1] And often the character of sin is simply left to its results: "death," "toil," "mischief," "trouble," "slavery," "humiliation," and so on.

One should be wary of seeking a consistent Old Testament doctrine of sin in the face of such diversity. Yet behind the diversity one finds a fairly consistent understanding that sin is a weakness of human nature which threatens to separate the sinner from God, the source of existence. To argue that the Old Testament offers a psychology of sin would be misleading; to ask it to do so is to bring contemporary standards of theological sophistication to bear upon ancient texts. Nevertheless, we are justified in asserting that the Old Testament regards sin as a universal condition, somewhat akin to illness. In fact, the similarities between rituals for sin and rituals for illness encourage this view.[2]

One of the bewildering facts about the Old Testament is that though it is preoccupied with sin, it pays relatively little attention to its origins. And even though the story of the fall is prominently placed at the beginning of Genesis, much of the Old Testament appears to be unfamiliar with it. Nevertheless, it might be argued that the fall narrative is especially important just because it is the one place where a serious attempt is made to account for the origin of sin. Certainly later traditions found it so, for no other biblical passage has been more influential in shaping Judeo-Christian doctrines of sin.

The decisive act of disobedience in the Garden of Eden is plausible to the reader because it results from a universal human experience, the experience of being deceived: "Then the Lord God said to the woman, 'What is this that you have done?' The woman said, 'The serpent tricked me, and I ate.' " (Gen. 3:13) There is nothing to suggest that the woman is attempting to displace responsibility (as Adam has done); she is giving an honest account of her behavior: She was genuinely taken in by the serpent. The reading to be favored here is that sin is a possibility precisely because human beings are vulnerable to deception. Unlike God, human beings can be deceived, and herein lies an explanation for the universal weakness of the human condition. The important point is that the controlling theme of the Old Testament (fidelity to the covenant) is linked to a recognition that human beings are vulnerable to deceit. To remain faithful is, in the most fundamental sense, to avoid being deceived, and thus to preclude disobedience. To be deceived is to be damned. And ultimately, as the prophets were to declare, the age of salvation will be brought forth when deception ends.[3] To the extent that the Old Testament offers a plausible and consistent account of sin, this is it.

The idea that being deceived ultimately leads to disobedience is brought to the surface in the numerous Old Testament admonitions against the worship of false gods, where the tendency to go astray is attributed to the deceits of false prophets and visions:

> Take heed lest your heart be deceived, and you turn aside and serve other gods and worship them. (Deut. 9:6)

> I am against the prophets, says the Lord, who dream lies and retail them, misleading my people with wild and reckless falsehoods. (Jer. 23:32)

> These, then, are the words of the Lord God: Because your words are false and your visions a lie, I am against you, says the Lord God. I will raise my hand against the prophets whose visions are false, whose divinations are a lie. (Ezek. 13:8–9)

It is not my purpose here to argue that the Old Testament consistently and unambiguously attributes sin to the state of being deceived. It is sufficient to show that it does so frequently and explicitly enough to justify the conclusion that the Old Testament expresses a strong bias against being deceived. This conclusion is reinforced by the observation that the Old Testament never once allows that being deceived can be beneficial.

The New Testament

If the Old Testament is somewhat less than univocal in the identification of sin with the state of being deceived, there can be no doubt that this was the understanding carried forward by New Testament traditions. In the New Testament the mechanics of sin must be viewed under the influence of the apocalyptic worldview, which is both dualistic and deterministic. It describes world history as unfolding in epochs, according to a predetermined divine plan. The present age is dominated by the cosmic powers of sin and evil, but this age is being drawn toward a tragic climax, at which time God will intervene to conquer his foes and establish a new age beyond history. Central to apocalyptic thinking is its ethical dualism. Humanity, living out the final throes of history, is offered the choice of moral alignment with either the forces of good or the forces of evil. Those who stand with the powers of evil on the final day of judgment will be banished to eternal punishment along with Satan, but those who stand with the righteous will be ushered into the age of everlasting peace.

The nuances of apocalyptic thinking vary among the New Testament writers, but a fundamental orientation of historical and ethical dualism remains constant. And it is within the polarities of this dualistic symbolism that we can detect the role of deception. In the letters of Paul the dualism of apocalyptic thinking is expressed in the fundamental opposition of "flesh" and "spirit." To live "according to the flesh" is to live according to human nature; it is the life of this world, the life governed by the law of sin (Rom. 7:25). Alternatively, to live "according to the spirit" is to live the life of faith, the life of a new nature, the life "in Christ" (Rom. 8:10). For Paul humanity's options are fairly clear: one can follow the life of the spirit (faith, life, truth) or the life of the flesh (sin, death, falsehood). It is within the dynamics of these two options that we can see the importance of deception for Paul's thought.

It is tempting to hear Paul to be saying that the life of the flesh and the law is not really life at all, but merely the illusion of life. But this would be somewhat misleading. The world, the body, the law, and such things are not illusions in the strong, gnostic sense. Paul's meaning seems to be that while the life of the world is real enough, it is not sufficient for our true existence. This is the sense in which we might construe the polarity of flesh and spirit as parallel to the opposition of appearance and reality. To live in the flesh is to be deceived not in the strong sense of mistaking an unreality for a reality but rather in the weak sense of mistaking a contingent reality for the ultimate reality. This is precisely what Paul means by sin. Sin is the condition which prevails when humans think and act as if this world and the law were sufficient for righteousness. But this is to take the penultimate for the ultimate; it is "to exchange the truth about God for a lie" (Rom. 1:25).

Paul grants an element of plausibility to the view that the law is sufficient. After all, the law carries a certain authority insofar as it is from God. And indeed, before God's act in the person of Christ, the law was everything. But *since* the coming of Christ the law has been relativized (Gal. 3:23–25). Now the law can be seen for what it is: God's instrument (Gal. 3:19). Now that God himself has intervened directly in history, the reality of the law must be seen as derivative. But the reality of Christ is constitutive; the law comes *from* God, but Christ *is* God. This Christological claim does not erase the presence of the law, but it does remove its ultimacy. And now, of course, the law can become an instrument of sin—that is, it can still be held in our regard as an absolute, even though its present status is displaced to the relative. In relation to the *world* the law may have ultimate authority, but in relation to the presence of God himself in Christ it is without authority. Thus can the law be the occasion for sin: "Sin found its chance, and by means of the commandment it deceived me and killed me" (Rom. 7:11).

It is very difficult to understand Paul's thinking because on the one hand he suggests that nothing has changed, but on the other hand everything has changed. What has not changed is that we are still accountable to God's will. But what has changed is that the law has been superseded as the standard by which we are deemed righteous. Before Christ, righteousness was defined by the law, but now it is defined by the life in Christ. To continue, then, as if the law were the standard of righteousness is equivalent to the primordial disobedience of Adam and Eve, or to the historic disobedience of the Jews. In all cases, such disobedience can be attributed to a vulnerability to deception: "And if indeed our gospel be found veiled, the only people who find it so are those on the way to perdition. Their unbelieving minds are so blinded by the god of this passing age, that the gospel of the glory of Christ, who is the very image of God, cannot dawn upon them and bring them light" (2 Cor. 4:4). Paul therefore goes to extremes in reiterating his admonitions against being deceived,[4] because it is the vulnerability to deception, whether by the evil one or by oneself, that represents the greatest danger for humanity.

The ultimate danger of being deceived is no less evident in the Deutero-Pauline corpus. Here, too, deception is identified as the mechanics of sin. In Ephesians, for example: "Do not let anyone deceive you with foolish words; it is because of these very things that God's anger will come upon those who do not obey him" (Eph. 5:6). The life of faith is characterized by its maturity and invulnerability to deception: "Then we shall no longer be children, carried by the waves and blown about by every shifting wind of the teaching of deceitful men, who lead others into error by the tricks they invent" (Eph. 4:14). The letters to Timothy give eschatological warnings against deceptive agents: "The Spirit says clearly that some people will abandon the faith in later times; they will obey lying spirits and follow the teachings of demons. Such teachings are spread by deceitful liars, whose consciences are dead, as if burnt with a hot iron" (1 Tim. 4:1–2). And again: "[A]nd evil persons and impostors will keep on going from bad to worse, deceiving others and being deceived themselves" (2 Tim. 3:13). Similar eschatological warnings are included in the Petrine letters, especially the second one, which is devoted to combating the deceptions of false teachers. In the letter to the Hebrews, Christians are encouraged to fortify one another against being deceived: "My fellow believers, be careful that no one among you has a heart so evil and unbelieving that he will turn away from the living God. Instead, in order that none of you will be deceived by sin and become stubborn, you must help one another every day" (Heb. 3:12–13).

The synoptic gospels (Matthew, Mark, Luke) represent the coming together of various strands of Hellenistic Christian tradition to create a new literary form: the gospel. The chief characteristic of the gospel form is the kerygma, the proclamation that in the person of Jesus God was acting directly and decisively to bring to fulfillment his promise of salvation for the people of the covenant. With the appearance of Jesus the terms of the covenant had changed. Now righteousness before God was identified by an attitude toward the person of Jesus as God's son and a willingness to follow his teachings. The synoptic gospels are dominated by common eschatological, moral, and Christological themes, and these themes are treated within the context of an apocalyptic worldview. Jesus was God's son, sent to inaugurate the New Age. His authority was vindicated by his death and exaltation. Jesus would return shortly to bring creation to its final state in the kingdom of God. The kingdom, therefore, was "at hand," and was soon to be consummated with the triumphant second coming of Jesus. Until that time, however, the faithful must respond to the call to discipleship—to relinquish the security of the world, to confess his lordship, and to follow his teachings. Upon Jesus' return his disciples would be the remnant to accompany him into the kingdom of God. The gospel form originated in a time when this proclamation was in danger of being lost or distorted after the death of original eyewitnesses. The major impulse for the appearance of the synoptic gospels, then, was to preserve the Christian proclamation against loss or distortion.

The synoptics have no common theme focused on the nature and origin of evil or sin, and the gospel form itself provides no occasion for dwelling upon anthropological issues. Clues to such matters are found in the manner in which the gospel writers identify specific threats to the faith. Such threats are identified in the so-called apocalyptic discourses.[5] In these discourses Jesus describes the preordained cataclysmic events that will signal the end of history. It is in the context of these apocalyptic discourses that the evangelists warn their readers to be alert to attempts to deceive them:

> Jesus answered: "Watch out, and do not let anyone fool you. Many men, claiming to speak for me, will come and say, 'I am the Messiah!,' and they will fool many people. . . .
>
> "Many will give up their faith at that time; they will betray one another and hate one another. Then many false prophets will appear and fool many people. Such will be the spread of evil that many people's love will grow cold. But whoever holds out to the end will be saved. . . .
>
> "Then if anyone says to you, 'Look, here is the Messiah!' or 'There he is!'—do not believe him. For false Messiahs and false prophets will appear; they will perform great miracles and wonders in order to deceive even God's chosen people, if possible." (Matt. 24:4–5, 10–13, 23–24)[6]

The dualism of apocalyptic thinking is even more pronounced in the gospel of John, where the evangelist's expressed purpose is to provoke belief in the reader (20:31). The rhetorical supposition appears to be that when the options are made clear, a faith response will be forthcoming. And in John's gospel the options are, if anything, clear. He offers only two possibilities: the life of belief and the death of unbelief (3:16). To believe or not to believe—that is the question. And to accentuate both the virtues and the urgency of belief, the gospel presents a clearly defined cosmic and religious dualism. Believers belong to the realm of light, spirit, life, truth, and goodness, whereas unbelievers belong to the realm of darkness, flesh, death, falsehood, and evil. Nowhere in the New Testament are the possibilities for humankind more acutely delineated.

And yet, in the context of a black-and-white religious vision, the evangelist employs a device (a series of "signs") which is notable for its ambiguity.[7] For John the analogue for religious faith is perception—one comes to the life of faith by "seeing" or "hearing." The reality that is seen or heard is, of course, the reality of God as disclosed in Jesus. Whoever has seen Jesus has seen God (14:9). But as always, there is seeing and then there is *seeing*, and this is the ambiguity that John plays upon in his presentation of the signs. The signs in John's gospel are manifestations of God's power, and these signs, when properly *seen*, have the power to provoke faith. But not all who behold the signs are moved to faith; the signs are ambiguous and are therefore open to misapprehension. The dualism of appearance and reality could hardly be more explicit.

John's point is that the faithful see the reality of God in Jesus, while the unfaithful do not. And wherein lies the difference? The difference is that some people are open to the faith-provoking power of the signs, while others are closed to the power. And those whose eyes and ears are closed have been deceived into a state of unbelief.

To see this more clearly we turn to the evangelist's treatment of the Jews. In John's gospel the Jews come in for special attention. They are almost always the villains: they persecute Jesus (5:16), they misunderstand him (8:27), they try to stone him (8:59), they arrange for his arrest and execution (18:12). But behind these offenses is the source of their evildoings: they are the ones who refuse to accept Jesus as the Messiah. Such Jew-bashing might tell us something about the state of Jewish-Christian polemics during the evangelist's lifetime, but it is clear that John's treatment of the Jews takes on a somewhat larger meaning. The Jews of the fourth gospel are stylized types who represent all people who fail to believe. They, like Adam and Eve, provide a metaphor for sin, so if we want to find the source of disbelief, we must look to John's account of the Jews.

John presents the Jews as a symbol for those who cannot properly apprehend the signs. They are the ones whose eyes and ears are closed to the divine self-disclosure. And the reason is that they have been blinded by the deceits of the devil:

> Why do you not understand my language? It is because my revelation is beyond your grasp. Your father is the devil and you choose to carry out your father's desires. He was a murderer from the beginning, and is not rooted in the truth; there is no truth in him. When he tells a lie he is speaking his own language, for he is a liar and the father of lies. But I speak the truth and therefore you do not believe me. (John 8:43–45)

The central preoccupation of the Johannine epistles is the threat of false teaching. Under the terms of apocalyptic expectation, the New Testament Christians came to associate the appearance of widely divergent variants of the gospel message with the impending end of time. Heresy, therefore, was thought to be instigated by various false prophets and antichrists. Grave dangers lurked for the believing Christians. Such concerns about false teachings can make sense only on the assumption that human beings are vulnerable to trading God's truth for a lie. Thus it is the human vulnerability to deceit that ultimately prompts John to warn his readers about the dangers and to help them to unveil the disguise of the deceivers: "I am writing this to you about those who are trying to deceive you" (1 John 2:26). The first letter of John makes a fundamental distinction between the spirit of truth and the spirit of error. Those who follow the spirit of truth will be known by their fulfillment of the commandment to love one another. The distinction appears in the second letter as well, where the deceived have themselves become deceivers (2 John 1:7).

The book of Revelation is the most vivid example of apocalyptic thinking in the entire New Testament. This book was written in the final decade of the first century, at a time when the Christians of Asia Minor were becoming victims of Roman persecution. The purpose of the book is to provide encouragement to those who face the prospect of martyrdom. As frightening as the author's visions of the future appear to be, he is in fact writing a message of hope and consolation to the faithful, for they will endure the crisis of the end times and live as kings forever (Rev. 22:5).

The author of Revelation explicitly identifies Satan with the serpent in Genesis, whose principal weapon against faith is deception: "The huge dragon was thrown out—that ancient serpent, named the Devil, or Satan, that deceived the whole world" (Rev. 12:9). Satan claims dominion over the earth and deputizes two beasts (the Roman emperor and his local authority) to capture the people of the world. The beasts complete the conquest only because Satan has bestowed upon them his powers to deceive the world (Rev. 13:2–4, 13–14; 19:20). But the beasts (Roman authorities) and the dragon (Satan) are defeated by Christ. The beasts are thrown into a lake of fire, and Satan is imprisoned in the abyss for a thousand years, "so that he could not deceive the nations any more" (Rev. 20:3). After a thousand years Satan and his powers of deceit are again set loose upon the world, only to be defeated again in a final encounter with the powers of heaven:

> After the thousand years are over, Satan will be set loose from his prison, and he will go out to deceive the nations scattered over the whole world, that is Gog and Magog. Satan will bring them all together for battle. . . . But fire came down from heaven and destroyed them. Then the Devil who deceived them, was thrown into the lake of fire and sulphur, where the beast and the false prophet had already been thrown; and they will be tormented day and night forever and ever. (Rev. 20:7–10)

Biblical texts are not works of philosophy, and it would be misleading to suggest that they present an explicit and systematic epistemology of sin. Yet epistemological assumptions are embedded in the thinking of biblical writers. What I have been arguing in this brief survey is that the state of being deceived plays a central role in these assumptions. The general elements are these: God's self-disclosure is the ultimately real, to which humanity can respond appropriately (in faith and obedience) or inappropriately (in sin and disobedience). Those who respond in faith and obedience are in possession of the truth, while all others are in possession of a lie. Whether the delusions of the unfaithful are attributed directly to the agency of the Devil or to false prophets or to personal weakness is of only relative importance. The significant point is that all humans, according to the biblical view, are vulnerable to deception; they can be led astray, misperceive, ignore, confuse, or deny the divine self-disclosure. And it is this vulnerability to deception that is decisive in accounting for evil.

The Philosophical Tradition

The Presocratics

The emergence of philosophy in Greece in the sixth century B.C. has often been described as a movement from *mythos* to *logos*; that is, a movement away from perceiving the world through anthropomorphic images toward a worldview generated by depersonalized principles of order. In the view of the earliest speculative philosophers, order and regularity in human experience was explained more satisfactorily by concepts of substance, process, and form than by episodic accounts of ambition, jealousy, and revenge among the gods of Mount Olympus. By the sixth century B.C. mythological accounts of the world around were becoming threadbare, as these rather skeptical observations by Xenophanes reveal:

> Mortals believe that the gods are begotten, and that they wear clothing like our own, and have a voice and a body. . . . The Ethiopians make their gods snub-nosed and black; the Thracians make theirs gray-eyed and red-haired . . . and if oxen and horses and lions had hands and could draw with their hands and do what man can do, horses would draw the gods in the shape of horses, and oxen in the shape of oxen, each giving the gods bodies similar to their own . . . . The gods have not revealed all things from the beginning to mortals; but by seeing, men find out, in time, what is better. . . . No man knows the truth, nor will there be a man who has knowledge about the gods and what I say about everything. For even if he were to hit by chance upon the whole truth, he himself would not be aware of having done so, but each forms his own opinions.[8]

This radically new intellectual mood soon began to flourish into a lively tradition of speculative philosophy. These early philosophers, convinced that they had inherited mere subjective opinion from the mythological past, set out to find what was better. They were bent on discovering the *archē*, the original Ur-principle of reality. For some, the secret was in some primal substance. Thales, for example, thought that the *archē* was water, that all reality was derived from and could ultimately be reduced to water. Water was the one permanent reality underlying the diversity of forms. Anaximander thought the Ur-substance was *apeīron*, a boundless invisible material that took on various forms. Anaximenes believed that air was the final principle of reality, that the multiplicity of forms could be explained by the condensation and rarefaction of air.

Other pre-Socratic philosophers thought that the substance undergoing transformation was less important than the process of transformation itself. Thus Heraclitus declared that there really was no permanent substance to be found. Permanence, he thought, was a mere illusion resulting from the deceptive character of sense experience, whereas in reality everything is in a constant state of flux. The illusion of permanence is a function of the differential patterns of change in nature—a stone appears more permanent than a storm only because the two vary in their rate of transformation. So all of nature is characterized by the process of change, or variable patterns of transformation, all of which are governed by the only permanent reality: the rational laws of change (i.e., the *logos*). The transformations of nature are not random and chaotic, they are rather orderly and programmed by a certain inherent logic.

Still other philosophers believed that forms were more ultimately real than either substance or process. The Pythagorean school, for example, taught that all of reality was ultimately derived from the forms of mathematics. Numbers were represented by shapes, and these numerical shapes imposed limits or boundaries on unlimited material substance. Objects of knowledge were therefore constructed by the aggregation of these elementary numerical forms, and to understand reality was to apprehend its essential numerical formation.

As this speculative tradition developed, later philosophers attempted to combine concepts of substance, process, and form to produce ever more sophisticated cosmologies. Empedocles offered four essential substances (air, earth, fire, water), which were mixed by the forces of attraction and repulsion to form the various objects of the world around. Anaxagoras proposed an all but infinite number of material substances that were variously mixed in elementary forms, or seeds, by a process of *mind*. The atomists proposed atomic units that varied in their forms, thus giving rise, under the influence of natural laws, to variations in observable characteristics.

The tradition of pre-Socratic philosophy eventually produced an impressive diversity of speculation about the ultimate nature of reality. But underlying these various attempts was the explicit recognition of a distinction between appearance and reality. So fundamental was this distinction that we may say it is constitutive of the philosophical enterprise itself. The pre-Socratics' concern over questions of unity versus diversity and permanence versus change were variations on the more fundamental distinction, namely, appearance versus reality. Some philosophers argued for the essential unity of reality against an apparent diversity. Others argued for an essential plurality behind an apparent unity. Some said change was real and permanence was apparent, while others said change was illusory and permanence real. But whatever positions the pre-Socratics took, they were convinced that their opponents were victims of illusion. Thus the fundamental metaphysical distinction between appearance and reality found a parallel epistemological distinction between knowledge and opinion. One had knowledge if one apprehended the truth about reality, but one had mere opinion if one were deceived by appearances. And around these fundamental distinctions emerged various theories to explain the mechanics of knowledge and opinion. The rationalists were those who trusted reason over the deceptive influence of the senses, and the empiricists were those who trusted sense experience over the deluded fantasies of the imagination. The foundations of the Western philosophical tradition are so intimately linked to a concern about deception that one can readily concur with Michel Despland's observation that "the life of the philosopher is a struggle against delusion, outside and inside."[9]

The range of diversity generated by the pre-Socratic tradition eventually gave way to an emergent skepticism about the ability of philosophy to attain a final, objective vision of truth. If philosophy cannot produce a consensus, then it may well be that truth is essentially subjective, that humanity and not some objective reality is the measure of truth. This was the conviction of the Sophists, who launched an educational movement in Athens during the fifth century B.C. The Sophists were itinerants who taught that knowledge is relative to the knower, that all claims to knowledge are finally no more than opinion. In reducing knowledge to opinion the Sophists also reduced value to social convention, justice to political power, and virtue to the skill of rhetorical manipulation. The Sophists were therefore teachers of expedience. They gave lessons in rhetoric, not for the intellectual and moral edification of students but rather to equip them to compete successfully in the Athenian pastime of litigation. It was a dog-eat-dog world out there, a circus of appearances only, and those who were practiced in the arts of verbal manipulation would prevail.

The Socratic School

Socrates appeared on the scene in the mid–fifth century to oppose the teachings of the Sophists. He countered the Sophist notion that humanity is the measure of truth with the idea that truth is the measure of humanity. Against the skepticism of the Sophists, Socrates taught that objective truth exists, that we can know it, and that we can communicate it. If opinion and appearances prevail, he thought, the implication is not that there is no truth but only that people are deceived. Adherents to Socratic doctrine were convinced that the relativism of the Sophist movement had put Athens on the path toward a degenerate society. Their conviction was that a just society required knowledge of the good, on the assumption that a person who truly knew what was good would behave in such a way as to serve it. For the Socratics it was inconceivable that one might act against the good while truly knowing it. Human beings naturally seek the good, or what they perceive to be good, so that if one acts against the known good, one has, *ipso facto*, misperceived the good. These basic Socratic doctrines were given their full systematic expression in the works of Plato and Aristotle.

Plato was a dualist. He divided reality into two distinct realms: the sensible world of temporal, multiple, mutable, physical, imperfect *things* and the intelligible world of eternal, universal, permanent, ideal, and perfect *forms*. The sensible world is the realm of appearances, and our understanding of it is never more than mere opinion. The intelligible world, however, is objectively real, and of it we may have true knowledge. Plato's metaphysical dualism implies an anthropological dualism. The distinction between the sensible world and the intelligible world carries with it a distinction between body and soul. The body is physical, temporal, and mutable, and thus properly belongs to the sensible world of things. Indeed, it is equipped with sense organs to enable it to manage itself within the realm of things. But the soul is immaterial, eternal, and rational, and thus belongs to the realm of intelligible forms. The eternal soul is nevertheless intimately associated with a temporal body. As Plato puts it, the soul is ensnared by or imprisoned within the body: "The lovers of knowledge are conscious that the soul was simply fastened and glued to the body—until philosophy received her, she could only view real existence through the bars of a prison."[10]

The eternal soul, by its nature, seeks the good, but so long as it is associated with the sensuous body, it tends to accept as good what the sensuous body regards as good. That is, when the soul is in union with the body, it is all too easily deceived by the senses and their conventions into accepting the appearance of good in place of the real, eternal good, which transcends the sensible world. And to be thus deceived is to admit falsehood into the soul, a state which Plato regards as the greatest evil of all: "But I am only saying that deception, or being deceived or uninformed about the highest realities in the highest part of themselves, which is the soul, and in that part of them to have and hold the lie, is what mankind least like;—that, I say, is what they utterly detest."[11]

All of these features of Plato's thought are brought together in the famous allegory of the cave (*Republic*, bk. vii). Plato pictures the human condition by analogy to a group of men chained in a cave where their experience is limited to the apprehension of shadows projected upon a wall from behind them. The prisoners see only shadows, never the figures themselves or the fire that projects the shadows. Clearly they are living in a realm of appearance and illusion. And since they have no direct experience of the objects, they assume that the shadows are real. In their ignorance the prisoners mistake mere appearances for reality; their "knowledge" is no more than mere opinion. But if one of these prisoners were to escape and turn around to behold the fire and the figures themselves, and if the prisoner were to emerge from the cave to behold the full splendor of the world outside, then surely he would disparage his previous condition of bondage to the world of appearance and illusion.

Plato is suggesting that most people, in fact, live out their lives in the realm of appearances, never transcending the state of being deceived to achieve true knowledge. For to do so is an arduous and painful process of undoing the habits and conventions of thought that have been fixed upon the soul by the senses. Plato pictures human life as a pilgrimage from the world of illusion to the world of truth, a pilgrimage that is advanced by the therapy of philosophy. With the aid of philosophy it is possible for the soul to extricate itself from the cavelike realm of appearances and apprehend eternal truth. It is important to recognize that for Plato this process of coming to know the good is a process not of acquisition but rather of reversing the deceiving effects of the body upon the soul. The soul, being eternal and perfect, is not deficient in its knowledge. It is in full possession of the truth, but because of the hindrances of the sensuous body, the soul has forgotten what it has known from eternity. In order to achieve the good, therefore, the soul must recollect the truth, or better, the soul must unforget the truth through the undeceiving care of philosophy.

The Socratic doctrines concerning the knowability of good and the natural predisposition of humans to do the good (unless they are deceived) are brought to point by Aristotle, but in the final analysis he remains faithful to the Socratic teachings. For Aristotle, nature is a realm of objects that are subject to motion. And all motion, he says, tends by nature to some end. Living things are "purpose built" to actualize innate potential to achieve an end that is appropriate to their particular nature. To achieve these natural ends is to achieve the good: "Every art and every inquiry, and similarly every action and pursuit, is thought to aim at some good; and for this reason the good has rightly been declared to be that at which all things aim." In contrast to Plato, Aristotle did not conceive of the good in terms of a comprehensive, universal idea. The good, he says, is relative to the nature or to the proper function of the living being. And since human beings have certain functions in common with lower forms of life (i.e., plants and animals), it follows that there is a hierarchy of goods for humans. But the goods relative to these lower functions must be regarded as subsidiary to the chief aim of human life, which is desired for its own sake and the knowledge of which is essential for the good life: "If, then, there is some end of the things we do, which we desire for its own sake, . . . clearly this must be the good and the chief good. Will not the knowledge of it, then, have a great influence on life?"[12]

Aristotle regards happiness as the chief aim of human life; it is the final and self-sufficient end of all human actions. To the extent that a particular act is conducive to happiness it is "right," and to the extent that an act precludes happiness it is "wrong." And just as logic is the science of determining true and false thinking, so ethics is the science of determining right and wrong conduct. To know the good is therefore to know what actions are conducive to genuine happiness. But recognition of these principles does not greatly simplify the moral life, for the relative circumstances in which humans find themselves tend to relativize their perceptions of happiness. If one is ill, then happiness is perceived to consist in health; or if one is poor, then happiness consists in wealth. Aristotle, unlike Plato, does not dismiss such perceptions of the good (pleasure, health, wealth, honor) as mere appearances. Such ends are legitimate and we are not deceived in perceiving them to be worthwhile. We are deceived, however, if we take them to represent the final end of human life. The final good for human life consists in the actualization of potential for reason, and for Aristotle this amounts to the life of philosophical contemplation: "That which is proper to each thing is by nature best and most pleasant for each thing; for man, therefore, the life according to reason is best and pleasantest, since reason more than anything else *is* man. This life therefore is also the happiest."[13] Any perception of the ultimate good that falls short of the life of reason is in error because it misconstrues the true nature of humanity.

The similarity of logic and ethics shows up in Aristotle's analysis of moral behavior. An individual desires an end and then establishes a syllogistic series of intermediate ends until the implication for an immediate choice becomes clarified. Thus, for example, an individual may desire happiness and then subsequently perceive health as a means to happiness, and exercise as a means to health. The individual may then perceive a brisk walk as an immediate option that will activate the moral syllogism. With each link of a moral syllogism there appears an occasion for error. One may be in error if one fails to see that a brisk walk is a suitable form of exercise, or if one fails to see that exercise is conducive to health, or health to happiness, and so on. The moral life is therefore contingent both on knowledge regarding the ultimate good for humanity and on the ability of an individual to construct an effective moral syllogism. If one is deceived either about the ultimate end or about the appropriate means, then the good will not follow: "[F]or the syllogisms which deal with acts to be done are things which involve a starting point, viz. 'since the end, i.e., what is best, is of such and such a nature' . . . and this is not evident except to the good man; for wickedness perverts us and causes us to be deceived about the starting points of action. Therefore it is evident that it is impossible to be practically wise without being good."[14] For Aristotle, then, as for Socrates and Plato, one can achieve the good life if and only if one is undeceived about the nature of the good.

Greco-Roman Schools

At the time of Aristotle's death some profound social and political developments were transforming the way of life within the Greek city-states. For an Athenian citizen the city-state had been a compact and all-embracing source of identity. The ancient loyalties to clan and tribe had been completely transferred to the city. Art, entertainment, law, religion, the moral life—all were sustained by the autonomous city. For the Athenian the good life was inconceivable apart from the beloved city. It is unlikely that any society, either before or since the golden age of Greece, has achieved so thorough an identity of private morality and public virtue.

But all of this changed dramatically with the emergence of the Alexandrian empire. Alexander the Great had inherited the Macedonian empire in 332 B.C., and by the time of his death in 323 he had extended his realm to include the ancient empires of Persia and Egypt. Under the conditions of the new imperial order the independent city-state ceased to function as a unit of social organization. The institutions and life patterns that had once forged a unity of individual and collective identity were now irrelevant. The Greeks were stripped of their ability to manage their own destiny. Events were now taking place at a rate and on a scale and according to principles that Greek citizens were not prepared to comprehend. In this "world grown too suddenly large" the Greeks were reduced to the status of foreigners in their own land.

Under the conditions of a rapidly expanding and incomprehensible sociopolitical order the personal lives of Greek citizens became unpredictable and fraught with anxiety. And these were the conditions that generated a wave of new schools of pop philosophy—popular schemes that offered cognitive resources for coping with the stress and anxiety of life within the new imperial order. The most influential of these schemes were Stoicism, Skepticism, and Epicureanism. Each of these therapeutic schools persisted throughout the Hellenistic period, and each was generated by the view that deception was the source of debilitating anxiety.

These new schools were typically eclectic in their use of philosophical resources to build up a cosmology, which then legitimated their own peculiar forms of psychotherapy. The cosmology of Stoicism, for example, was an amalgam of Heraclitean and Aristotelian principles. The Stoics taught that the natural order is a deterministic system governed by a set of immutable natural laws. These rational laws drive the cosmos through an infinite series of successive "worlds," each one identical to the others in every minute detail. Each successive world begins in fire and will end in fire, giving rise to the next, and the next, *ad infinitum*. The moral life is the life of reason, the life that conforms to the necessarily determined flow of events. Unhappy is the one who is deluded by the illusion of freedom. Ignorance of the determined nature of the cosmos leaves the individual with the false impression that things might be otherwise than they are. And this illusion of freedom disturbs the minds of those who harbor ambitions contrary to the actual and necessarily determined state of affairs. Serenity of mind comes when one takes an attitude of acquiescence to necessity: "Ask not that events should happen as you will, but let your will be that events should happen as they do, and you shall have peace."[15] One need not be aware of the precise details of the providential laws of nature (for who can comprehend the machinations of the empire?) but it is essential to recognize that there are such laws and that all attempts to resist them are utterly futile. A positive understanding of the truths of nature is less important than becoming undeceived. Ignorance of the details is perfectly consistent with serenity of mind, but the illusion of freedom is not.

The Skeptics agreed with the Stoics that philosophy was ultimately therapeutic, and that its goal was to help the individual achieve serenity of mind: "The originating cause of Skepticism is, we say, the hope of attaining quietude."[16] And the Skeptics agreed that disquietude was ultimately the result of being deceived. But they disagreed with the Stoics on the matter of what the anxious mind was deceived *about*. The Skeptics believed that the anxious mind was a product of dogmatism, the view that a certain account of appearances is better than some other account. Thus for the Skeptic there was no advantage in becoming disabused of a particular doctrine if the end result was only to become ensnared by the opposing doctrine. The point, for the Skeptics, was to become disabused of *all* doctrines.

Unlike most philosophical orientations, Skepticism does not worry about the inferiority of appearances. It accepts appearances for what they are. But it refuses to take the dogmatic leap from appearances to some doctrine of reality or essence which pretends to explain the appearances. To make this leap, as the dogmatic mind does, is to establish the conditions for mental anguish. The dogmatist reasons beyond appearances to capture the truth about things. But it is this impulse that ultimately deceives: "We do not propound such arguments with the intention of abolishing appearances, but by way of pointing out the rashness of the Dogmatists; for if reason is such a trickster as to all but snatch away the appearances from under our very eyes, surely we should view it with suspicion in the case of things non-evident so as not to display rashness by following it."[17] As soon as the individual forms dogmatic opinions about something, an endless snare of perturbations of the mind is set in place. The only way to escape this perpetual state of strife is to avoid making the leap from appearances to some dogmatic account of what they ultimately mean. All such dogmatic positions on the nature of things are suspect. In the end, say the Skeptics, there are no adequate grounds in reason or sense for preferring theory X to theory not-X, or vice versa. The Skeptics eventually honed their agnostic arguments to a pair of fundamental points: first, nothing can be rendered certain through itself, and second, nothing can be rendered certain through anything else. And it follows that nothing whatsoever can be known to be certain; all "truths" are pretentious lies to be avoided lest they ensnare the mind in perpetual disquietude. As soon as we form an opinion—even, so it happens, on the principle of Skepticism—we are ensnared by a lie. One achieves serenity of mind, therefore, by suspending judgment concerning all appearances.

Of all the Hellenistic schools of philosophy, Epicureanism was perhaps the most blatantly practical and eclectic. For this school philosophy was clearly and simply therapy for the soul, and any philosophical principles that might help to clarify the nature and plight and deliverance of the soul were acceptable on those grounds alone. Thus the Epicureans appear to have had little use for the likes of mathematics, as its value for undisturbing the soul was far from evident. They did, however, find value in the metaphysical views of the ancient atomists. The atomists taught that the entire universe was constructed of tiny seeds, or atoms, which varied in size and shape. Nothing exists but atoms and empty space. Even the human soul is an atomic construct, formed of exceedingly small and smooth particles, which explain its delicacy and its sensitivity to perturbations. It appears to follow from the atomistic view that most of everyday human discourse travels in the realm of sheer illusion, for what we claim to see (rocks, trees, whatever) is not really what is there. Such illusions, the Epicureans thought, were entirely tolerable unless they produced the conditions for disturbances of the soul. But in some cases "the idle and empty imaginings of men" do create disturbances, and in these cases philosophy may intervene to undeceive the troubled mind: "For soon as thy philosophy issuing from a godlike intellect has begun with loud voice to proclaim the nature of things, the terrors of the mind are dispelled."[18]

The Epicureans thought that there were two principal sources of the mind's disturbance: desires and fears. Philosophy, then, could provide therapy to the mind by revealing the illusory nature of these debilitating desires and fears. Desires are of two types: natural and unnatural. The mind is not much troubled by natural desires (e.g., for food, drink, sleep), for one can straightforwardly put their disturbances to rest by satisfying them. But the unnatural desires (e.g., for wealth, status, power) are more problematic, for they can never be sufficiently satisfied. Indeed, attempts to satisfy them merely increase their intensity. Unnatural desires must therefore be put to rest by the sober, undeceiving influence of reasoning: "For it is not continuous drinkings and revellings, nor the satisfaction of lusts, nor the enjoyment of fish and other luxuries of the wealthy table, which produce a pleasant life, but sober reasoning, searching out the motives for all choice and avoidance, and banishing mere opinions, to which are due the greatest disturbance of the spirit."[19]

In addition to the deceptive influence of unnatural desires there were two types of fear which disturbed the mind: fear of death and fear of the gods. The Epicureans sought to dispel these fears by revealing their delusive nature. According to the Epicurean interpretation of atomist doctrine, death implies the complete dissolution of the soul and the deliverance of the individual into a state of absolute nothingness. But nothingness is certainly not to be feared: "Become accustomed to the belief that death is nothing to us. For all good and evil consists in sensation, but death is deprivation of sensation. . . . For there is nothing terrible in life for the man who has truly comprehended that there is nothing terrible in not living."[20] The Epicureans taught that fear of the gods was also an irrational fear to be dispelled by the power of reason. This fear arises from the illusion that the gods have something to gain or lose by interaction with humans. But how could this be? The gods occupy their own realm of immortal bliss and have no need for or interest in the affairs of humans. The notion that the gods might descend to the mortal realm with resulting disadvantage to humans is nothing but an illusion that deceives the unfortunate. All such "groundless terrors" must be rooted out before the mind can achieve serenity.

The Early Church

As the early church extended its mission into the Hellenistic world, it encountered external challenges to the plausibility of its proclamation as well as internal challenges to the integrity of its teachings. Criticism of the gospel from without the church was equaled only by distortion of it within. It was only natural, then, that the church would seek the rational and rhetorical means to combat paganism on the one hand and heresy on the other.

The unavoidable practice of polemicizing with pagan adversaries had the effect of emphasizing intellectual dimensions of the faith, and under these conditions the distinction between moral and intellectual failure began to fade—orthodoxy was increasingly the measure of faith. Sin, therefore, came to mean intellectual error. And as this development advanced, the role of deception as the source of sin became even more pronounced.

Among the earliest surviving works of the church fathers are the letters of Ignatius of Antioch, an early second-century figure who wrote seven letters to various churches while en route to martyrdom in Rome. Among Ignatius' chief concerns were the heretical movements that threatened the unity of the church. In his letter to the Ephesians, Ignatius congratulates them for their orthodoxy and warns them against the "mad dogs" of heresy who will prey upon them and bite them on the sly. And he praises them for resisting such deceits in the past: "Let no one mislead you, as, indeed, you are not misled, being wholly God's. For when you harbor no dissention that can harass you, then you are indeed living in God's way. . . . I have heard that some strangers came your way with a wicked teaching. But you did not let them sow it among you. You stopped up your ears to prevent admitting what they disseminated."[21]

Ignatius' other letters go on in the same manner. He warns his readers against "outmoded tales," "stupid ideas," "foreign fare," "false pretenses," "deadly poisons," "specious wolves," "shams," "fancies," and "wild beasts in human shapes." These are the "devil's wiles," or "the wicked tricks and snares of the prince of this world."[22] And those who fall prey to the deceits of heresy are lost: "Make no mistake, my brothers, if anyone joins a schismatic, he will not inherit God's kingdom."[23]

The anonymous *Epistle to Diognetus*, attributed to the late second century, represents a similar view with respect to the role of deception. The writer wants to bring his reader to recognize the superiority of Christian "knowledge" over the "aimlessness and trickery" of the Jews and Greeks. And throughout the letter he assumes that he can achieve this end by undeceiving the reader: "Now, then, clear out all the thoughts that take up your attention, and pack away all the old ways of looking at things that keep deceiving you." The religion of the Jews is presented as superstitious folly, no more plausible than Greek philosophy, which is "just quackery and deceit practiced by wizards." In contrast to the illusions of the Jews and Greeks, Christian knowledge reveals reality: "If you too yearn for this faith, then first of all you must acquire full knowledge of the Father. . . . And when you have acquired this knowledge, think with what joy you will be filled! . . . Then you will condemn the fraud and error of the world, once you really understand the true life in heaven, once you look down on the apparent death here below." The author appears to assume that "true" knowledge is innate and has been destroyed by deception: "It was because the first men did not use this knowledge with clean hearts that they were stripped of it by the deceit of the serpent."[24]

The central role of deception in Christian thought was extended by Justin Martyr, the great second-century apologist. The *First Apology* of Justin was written to the emperor Titus as a plea for toleration of Christians, but the aim of conversion was also most certainly a motivating factor. Himself a convert, Justin was familiar with various ancient schools of philosophy and had come to view Christianity as the one true philosophy. As a product of Greek culture, Justin held reason in high regard—so high, in fact, that it became the foundation of his Christology: Christ was Reason incarnate. This identification of reason with the divine, having ancient roots in pre-Socratic philosophy, had already been formulated in John's gospel, and it became pervasive in the early church as Hellenization continued. By Justin's time the idea was very much in the air. But also in the air was the view that the world was infested with hostile, demonic forces. In Justin's thought these demons, led by Satan, are the enemies of reason, moving about in the world to deceive and thus to deprive God's children of their natural, God-given powers of reason. The natural state of human existence is to live in harmony with reason: "In the beginning he made the race of men endowed with intelligence, able to choose the truth and do right, so that all men are without excuse before God, for they were made with the powers of reason and observation." But this natural state of reason was disrupted by demons, who deceived individuals into lives of irrationality and wrongdoing. For Justin, then, salvation consists in removing the deception caused by demons and returning individuals to the path of reason. These are the terms which frame his plea to the emperor for tolerance: "We warn you in advance to be careful, lest the demons whom we have attacked should deceive you and prevent your completely grasping and understanding what we say."[25]

Justin's primary concern was to defend Christianity against criticisms originating outside the church. But as the church extended its reach to embrace people of diverse backgrounds, internal controversy inevitably arose. Evidence of such controversy appears in the writings of Irenaeus, an associate of Justin's: "Certain men, rejecting the truth, are introducing among us false stories and vain genealogies, which serve rather to controversies, as the apostle said, than to God's work of building up the faith."[26]

The great worry of Irenaeus and of Tertullian, who followed him, was that theological diversity would undermine the integrity of the church. And both of these writers attacked the problem by exposing the origins of heresy in deception. Irenaeus makes this point clear in his preface to *The Refutation and Overthrow of the Knowledge Falsely So Called*:

> By their craftily constructed rhetoric they lead astray the minds of the inexperienced, and take them captive, corrupting the oracles of the Lord, and being evil expounders of what was well spoken. For they upset many, leading them away by the pretense of knowledge from Him who constituted the universe, as if they had something higher and greater to show them than the God who made the heaven and the earth and all that is in them. By skillful language they artfully attract the simple-minded into their kind of inquiry, and then crudely destroy them by working up their blasphemous and impious view about the Demiurge. Nor can their simple hearers distinguish a lie from the truth.[27]

But it was the strident voice of Tertullian that was most clearly heard, especially with respect to the deceptive character of speculative philosophy. Whereas Justin found Christianity to be the epitome of philosophy, Tertullian found philosophy to be the bane of a unified Christianity. Philosophy is the father of heresy, and it preys upon human weakness by extolling the virtues of truth-seeking: "Notorious, too, are the dealings of heretics with swarms of magicians and charlatans and astrologers and philosophers—all, of course, devotees of speculation. 'Seek and ye shall find,' they keep reminding us." Under the guise of seeking, philosophy deceives the faithful by falsifying Scripture: "But in fact it is only for the sake of deceiving us that they pretend to be still seeking. . . . What sort of faith are they arguing when they come with deceit? What truth are they vindicating when they introduce it with a lie?"[28]

Tertullian follows Justin in seeing the ultimate source of deception as the devil. The devil can create nothing, but can only destroy what God has created. And the devil finds his opportunity by using philosophy to distort God's truth:

> Indeed, when I read that heresies must be, I think I may say without fear of contradiction that by the will of God the Scriptures themselves were so arranged as to furnish matter for the heretics. For without Scripture there can be no heresy. . . .
>
> It shall be asked next, Who interprets the meaning of those passages which make for heresy? The devil, of course, whose business it is to pervert truth.[29]

The cosmopolitan city of Alexandria was vastly different in composition and culture from either the Lyons of Irenaeus or the Carthage of Tertullian. Alexandria was one of the major commercial and intellectual centers of the Hellenistic world, a heady environment teeming with ideas drawn to it from all corners of the civilized world. Such an arena was sure to produce eclectic and syncretistic movements such as the Alexandrian school of Christianity, of which Clement and Origen were the principal exponents. Though the Alexandrian style of theology was anathema to the likes of Tertullian, the role of deception was no less central to it.

Clement, a contemporary of Irenaeus, offers a good example of the eclectic spirit of Alexandria. He draws upon Gnostic, Stoic, and Platonic sources to render a highly sophisticated interpretation of the Christian faith. For Clement, the goal of the religious life is to enjoy harmony with God, and one is to achieve it by acquiring knowledge of spiritual reality. The true God is perceived by the mind, not by the senses, as the deluded pagans assume. Originally humankind enjoyed perfect harmony with heaven, but this harmony was disrupted by the intrusion of ignorance into the world. The extreme forms of ignorance are atheism and idolatry, which have their origins in deception. Clement identifies seven forms of idolatry, but these "ways of deception" have a common theme— erroneous veneration of that which is base, material, sensuous: "But opinions that are mistaken and deviate from the right . . . turned aside man . . . inducing him to give heed to things formed out of earth." Our preference for the pleasures of the flesh and our propensity to turn away from the supreme object of the mind are accounted for in Clement's allegorical interpretation of Genesis 3. The serpent of Genesis 3 represents pleasure. Humanity was created in perfect innocence and freedom, but fell victim (as innocent children do) to the lure of immediate pleasures. And this attraction to objects of sense was an error which then flourished in the "deceitful arts" of idolatry: "I cannot help wondering, therefore, what delusive fancies could have led astray those who were the first to be themselves deceived, and the first also . . . to proclaim their superstitions to mankind. . . . We must not then be surprised that, once daemon worship had somewhere taken a beginning, it became a fountain of insensate wickedness."[30]

Humankind therefore suffers from the "deceitful dreams" of ignorance and must be saved by knowledge of divine reality. To this end, God took on human flesh in the form of a teacher who brings the perfect wisdom which can undeceive us and restore us to the original state of harmony with heaven.

Origen takes the Alexandrian school to even greater speculative heights than did his teacher, Clement. Origen's theology is both systematic and dramatic, and at every point is supported by his Platonized allegorical exegesis. The central drama of Origen's theology is the passage of the human soul from its fallen state back to its original condition of contemplative union with God. In the beginning, God created a finite number of rational beings, or intellects, which were perfectly free to continue in their contemplation of divine unity or to turn aside in the direction of multiplicity. This turning away, led by the devil, results in the fall and subsequent creation of the physical world, as the stage upon which rational beings have a second chance to use their freedom properly, and thus to return to their original unity with God. As a result of the fall, all rational beings are left in a weakened state of reason that leaves them vulnerable to the deceptions of demons. Thus was Eve an easy mark for the devil's deceit: "Eve's easy deception and the unsoundness of her reasoning did not come about when she listened to the serpent and disobeyed God, but was in existence before she was tested. And this is why the serpent approached her, since he perceived by his own subtle judgment her weakness."[31]

For Origen genuine freedom implies a vulnerability to deception. Life is therefore a series of temptations, and each temptation is an occasion for the devil to sustain the fallen creation by deceiving rational souls. To counteract the devil's power to deceive, the Word was made flesh as a source of illumination for souls. Thus the Bible is a divinely inspired resource for the return of souls to their union with God. But the Bible is also an occasion for further deceptions, and must be read carefully for its true spiritual meaning. Jews and heretics, for example, fall further into error because in their weakness they are deceived by superficial meanings. On account of these deceptions the Jews failed to recognize Jesus as the Messiah, and the Marcionites failed to see the continuity of the Old and New Testaments. For Origen, then, the journey of the soul toward God is like a trek through a minefield of deceptions, where the only sure guide for the traveler is the Scripture properly understood.

The point I have been trying to make so far is simply this: According to the ancient sources of the Western intellectual and moral traditions, the vulnerability of human beings to deception is the central feature of the human condition, which accounts for the ultimate evils which may befall humanity. Vulnerability to deception is vulnerability to evil. It is in this sense that these traditions may be said to fear nothing so much as they fear being deceived.

THE MEDIEVAL PERIOD

St. Augustine

St. Augustine was a pivotal figure between the ancient world and the medieval world. His theological vision, which was to become the orthodoxy of the medieval church, was braided together with strands from both primitive Christianity and the ancient pagan classics. It can hardly be disputed that deception plays a major role in the thought of St. Augustine. In one way or another the topic receives attention in most of his major works.

For Augustine, evil is introduced into the world by an act of free will. But he is impatient with demands to identify the ultimate origin of an evil will. Such inquiry can lead only to an infinite regress: "An evil will, therefore, is the cause of all evils. . . . But you ask what is the cause of this root. How then will it be the root of all evils? If it has a cause, that cause will be the root of evil. And if you find a cause, as I said, you will ask for a cause of that cause, and there will be no limit to your inquiry."[32]

Augustine feels it is unnecessary to settle the issue of the ultimate origin of sin. It is enough to recognize that since Adam and Eve the human condition has been a sinful condition. To the extent that Augustine is willing to speculate on the ultimate origin of sin, he resorts to the phenomenon of deception: "I do not know why you should want to inquire further, but here is a further point. . . . Whatever be the cause of willing, if it cannot be resisted no sin results from yielding to it. If it can be resisted, and it is not yielded to, no sin results. Possibly it may deceive a man when he is off his guard? Let him then take care not to be deceived."[33]

However the question of ultimate origins is resolved, Augustine is satisfied to assert, as the Scriptures do, that a sinful condition resulted from the willful act of Adam and Eve in turning away from God. And after their fall the condition of sin was transmitted sexually to all humanity.

What, precisely, is the sinful condition? Augustine tells us that sin is a penalty: "In fact there are for every sinful soul these two penal conditions, ignorance and difficulty. From ignorance springs disgraceful error, and from difficulty comes painful effort."[34] Under the penal condition of ignorance humanity is engulfed in a mental abyss of darkness and confusion. As G. R. Evans observes, "Everything Augustine has to say about evil must be read in the light of one central principle: that the effect of evil upon the mind is to make it impossible for the sinner to think clearly, and especially to understand higher, spiritual truths and abstract ideas."[35]

We are not wrong if we suggest that sin is the condition of being vulnerable to deception. Sin is the state of being predisposed to perceptual and cognitive error. There is no question that for Augustine sin is a matter of the perverted will, but the will is perverse by virtue of a clouded mind, a mind that is too bollixed up to perceive truth by its own powers. The sinful mind in its ignorance has turned from the unchangeable to the changeable, whereby it becomes habituated in the world of appearances. What we can know in this state is limited to the temporal, the material, the apparent. We are deceived into accepting the truths of this realm as genuine wisdom. Nor do we possess the will to love God, for we can love only that which we know: "But unless we already love him, we shall never see him. Yet how can we love what we do not know?"[36]

Salvation is ultimately a matter of perception. We cannot know and love God because we live in a world of deceptive appearances, unable to lift ourselves to apprehend the eternal and unchangeable. It was therefore necessary, says Augustine, that God should enter into the realm of appearances in order to clear the mind:

> Since, then, we were not fit to take hold of things eternal, and since the foulness of sins weighed us down, which we had contracted by the love of temporal things, and which were implanted in us as it were naturally, from the root of mortality, it was needful that we should be cleansed. But cleansed we could not be, so as to be tempered together with things eternal, except it were through things temporal, wherewith we were already tempered together and held fast.[37]

This is the act of grace. God enters into the temporal realm of appearances so that he can become known and therefore loved. God brings illumination into the realm of darkness and ignorance in order to undeceive the mind and free the will. Sin, for Augustine, is the state of inescapable vulnerability to deception, and grace is God's act of self-disclosure which frees the mind to see eternal truth.

Monasticism

Just as the Roman Empire was fading there was a flourish of monastic communities. The popularity of monastic life in the West had many causes—social and economic factors as well as religious ones. In complex times alternative lifestyles attract recruits for a wide variety of reasons. Some men fled to monasteries to avoid taxation and legal obligations, others found the monastery a safe refuge in the absence of Roman law enforcement, others came searching for a secure livelihood as the Roman economy flagged. Whatever the precise nexus of material causes may have been, we will certainly fail to understand the monastic movement unless we reckon with the theological inspiration which justified, promoted, and sustained it. In fact, it may be argued that the theology which inspired monasticism is the key to understanding medieval religious life in general, since the monks were the religious heros who provided inspiration for lay believers.

Much of the inspiration for the Western monastic movement came from popular biographies of Eastern heros of the ascetic life. Accounts such as the *Life of St. Anthony* and the *Historia monachorum in Aegypto* extolled the virtues of Egyptian monks who renounced the world and escaped into the desert to achieve the holy life of divine contemplation. These works were translated into Latin and used as propaganda for the development of monasticism in the West. The role of deception in these accounts helped to shape the religious sensitivities of medieval Europe.

The *Life of St. Anthony*, normally attributed to the pen of Athanasius, was written soon after Anthony's death in 356 and was quickly translated into Latin. It was probably the most influential work in a series of lives of the saints. The *Life of St. Anthony* narrates the struggle of the saint to withstand the temptations of the devil. The following passage is typical of the experiences of St. Anthony:

> But the devil, who hates and envies what is noble, would not endure such a purpose in a youth: but attempted against him all that he is wont to do; suggesting to him the remembrance of his wealth, care for his sister, relation to his kindred, love of money, love of glory, the various pleasures of luxury, and the other solaces of life; and then the harshness of virtue, and its great toil; and the weakness of his body, and the length of time; and altogether raised a great dust-cloud of arguments in his mind, trying to turn him back from his righteous choice. But when the enemy saw himself to be too weak for Antony's determination, then he attacked him with the temptations he is wont to use against young men; but Antony protected his body with faith, prayers and fastings. At last, when the evil one could not overthrow Antony even thus, as if beside himself, he appeared to the sight as a black child, and falling down before him, no longer tempted him to argue, but using a human voice,

said, "I have deceived many; I have cast down many. But now I have been worsted in the battle."[38]

The explosive popularity of the *Life of St. Anthony* encouraged others to visit Egypt and witness the ascetic life at firsthand. The *Historia monachorum* is the result of one such expedition. The *Historia* reflects the same monastic ideal as the *Life of St. Anthony*. The good life is understood to be the life of communion with God. The monks were seen to have achieved a sort of heavenly life while still on earth. As the prologue claims,

> I saw new prophets who have attained a Godlike state of fulfillment by their inspired and wonderful and virtuous way of life. For they are true servants of God. They do not busy themselves with any earthly matter or take account of anything that belongs to this transient world. But while dwelling on earth in this manner they live as true citizens of heaven. Some of them do not even know that another world exists on earth or that evil is found in cities.[39]

One could achieve this ideal of living as a true citizen of heaven only by renouncing the world and disciplining oneself to withstand the devil's deceits. We are given the sense that sin can be avoided only by the most heroic feats of spiritual concentration, as if the life of faith is a shell game played upon humans by a relentless deceiver. The monk could not drop his guard for an instant, lest the devil find his mark. The *Historia* warns the reader with an example of one who failed:

> There was a monk who lived in a cave in the nearer desert and had given proof of the strongest ascetic discipline. He obtained his daily bread by the work of his own hands. But because he persevered with his prayers and made progress in the virtues, he came eventually to trust in himself, placing his reliance on his good way of life. Then the Tempter asked for him, as he did with Job, and in the evening presented him the image of a beautiful woman lost in the desert. Finding the door open she darted into the cave, and throwing herself at the man's knees begged him to give her shelter since darkness had overtaken her. He took pity on her, which he should not have done, and received her as a guest in his cave. Moreover, he asked her about her journey. She told him how she had lost her way and sowed in him words of flattery and deceit. She kept on talking to him for some time, and somehow gently enticed him to fall in love with her. The conversation became much freer, and there was laughter and hilarity. With so much talking she led him astray. Then she began to touch his hand and beard and neck. And finally she made the ascetic her prisoner. As for him, his mind seethed with evil thoughts as he calculated that the matter was already within his grasp, and that he had the opportunity and the freedom to fulfil his pleasure. He then consented inwardly and in the end tried to unite himself with her sexually. He was frantic by now, like an excited stallion eager to mount a mare. But suddenly she gave a loud cry and vanished from his clutches, slipping away like a shadow. And the air

resounded with a great peal of laughter. It was the demons who had led him astray with their deception. . . .

In the morning he got up, dragging behind him the miserable experience of the night. He spent the whole day in lamentation, and then, despairing of his own salvation, which is something he should not have done, he went back to the world. For this is what the evil one generally does: when he overcomes someone he makes him lose his judgement, that afterwards he should no longer be able to raise himself up.[40]

The lesson is clear: "I have narrated these things to you, my children, that whether you consider yourselves to be among the little ones or the great ones you may make humility your chief aim in the ascetic life—and that you may not be deceived by the demons, who raise up images before you."[41] One could achieve the good life, the heavenly life, only to the extent that one was able to avoid being deceived. And the life of renunciation, though not a guarantee, could make this avoidance possible.

The attitude toward women is especially noteworthy here. Throughout the Middle Ages women were generally regarded as the devil's principal instruments of deception. Any man who cared for the eternal destiny of his soul would do well to remove himself from the company of women. Chastity became a measure of piety, to the extent that Jerome, for example, could think of only one justification for marriage: It produced more virgins. Even Augustine refused to meet with any woman without the security of a third party in attendance.

The monastic movement in the West came to maturity as the influence of these popular biographies was both ratified and mitigated by Augustinian theology. That Augustine approved of the monastic life is clear; he had himself been influenced by the *Life of St. Anthony*, and he had organized his own monastery at Hippo. But the Eastern form of asceticism was too hermitlike in practice to be approved by the increasingly bureaucratic and sacramental Western church. In time Western monasticism came to reflect the Augustinian model of an isolated community of charitable and obedient scholars rather than the austere and fiercely independent asceticism typical of the East. Yet in spite of institutional adjustments, the fundamental perspective of Western monasticism did not depart from its Eastern sources of inspiration. Indeed, it was a perspective that found confirmation in the emergent orthodoxy of the West: the City of Man was rife with tempters and deceivers, and the City of God, represented by the institutions and ministrations of the church, was the only safe refuge for the vulnerable soul.

Scholasticism

The transition from the monastic ideal characteristic of the Dark Ages to the scholastic ideal of the high Middle Ages is as complex as it is fascinating. But what stands out clearly amid the complexity is a radical shift both in the manner in which the threat of deception is perceived and in the discipline deemed appropriate for avoiding deception. Deception remains the source of evil, but it is experienced differently and combated with new strategies. In the monastic period, deeply influenced as it was by the dramatic *Life of St. Anthony,* the devil was expected to work his wiles in the forms of phantoms and demons. Security against such onslaughts could be achieved by the disciplines of isolation and spiritual exercise. But as the mentality of religious leaders was gradually transformed by the reinstitutionalization of learning, evil deceits came to be expected in the more subtle forms of linguistic trickery. And under such conditions the disciplines of the ascetic life were far less effective than the discipline of *dialectic*.

In its largest sense, "Scholasticism" refers simply to the tradition of thought that was developed in the medieval schools. But this tradition had a peculiar purpose and pattern, which together give us a more descriptive sense of the term. Scholasticism, then, is a tradition of understanding, clarifying, and defending the philosophic truth of Christian faith by means of a dialectic based on Aristotelian logic. And this tradition is further characterized by its distinctive pattern of presentation, which consists of question, argument, and conclusion. In the eleventh century this Scholastic method was beginning to develop among a new class of itinerant professional masters. These independent scholars elevated logic from the status of a perfunctory memory exercise to its new role as a powerful weapon for distinguishing truth from falsehood. Eventually controversies emerged as dialectic came to rival the authority of received theological dogma.

St. Anselm represents the first systematic attempt to apply the discipline of dialectic to every aspect of dogma, and for this effort Anselm has been called the father of Scholasticism. Anselm believed, with Augustine, that the religious life was a process of "faith seeking understanding." With Anselm it is abundantly clear that rational inquiry is in no way discontinuous with faith. Indeed, dialectic is part of the life of meditation, and in this respect it is identified with divine illumination: "That what at first I believed through Your giving, now by Your enlightening I so understand."[42] Anselm says the purpose of human life is to love God, but one comes to love God only by understanding God, and this understanding comes by way of dialectic:

> Therefore nothing is clearer than that the rational creature was made for this end, viz., to love above all other goods the Supreme Being, which is the Supreme Good. . . . Yet, the rational creature cannot love the Supreme Being without striving to remember and understand it. Clearly, then, the rational creature ought to devote his entire ability and will to the end of remembering, understanding, and loving the Supreme Good.[43]

Anselm's connection of faith and dialectic draws its strength from the idea that rationality is the substance of likeness between divine and human. For Anselm, then, dialectic is the means by which faith proceeds toward certitude. And it is also the means by which the truth-seeker can avoid the deceptiveness of language. Anselm was concerned that verbal improprieties could interfere with the dialectical process to the point of disturbing faith. Such was the case with heretics:

But by the neglect of good conscience even the understanding which has already been given is sometimes removed and faith itself is over-turned. . . . Therefore let no one plunge rashly into complex questions concerning divine things—lest running through a misleading mass of sophistries with frivolous lack of care, he be ensnared by some persistent falsehood. . . . Indeed, in the souls of these [heretical] dialecticians, reason—which ought to be the ruler and judge of all that is in man—is so covered over by corporeal images that it cannot extricate itself from them and cannot distinguish from them those things which it ought to contemplate purely and in isolation.[44]

There are no demonic phantoms here to endanger Anselm's faith. The danger is not that one can be deceived by visions but rather that one can be flawed in one's reasoning process or be deceived by verbal improprieties: "But we ought not to cling to the verbal impropriety concealing the truth as much as we ought to attend to the true propriety hidden beneath the many types of expression." To guard against these linguistic threats to the faith, one must reason with care: "It is not surprising [that you are confused]. For in our common way of speaking many things are said improperly. But when it is necessary to search out the very core of truth, it is necessary to analyse the troublesome impropriety as far as the subject matter requires and allows."[45]

As the Scholastic tradition matured, the role of reason expanded to be-come a judge of theological discourse rather than merely its handmaiden. There also emerged the view, sometimes called *Sprachlogik*, that words bear a direct and real correspondence to things in themselves. This view, held by Peter Abelard and others, strengthened the claim of dialectic upon theological utterances: "[A] *fortiori*, the theological expression of religious truths must conform to dialectical practice; only so could any discussion or explanation of the mysteries of the faith be practicable."[46] Dialectical disputes therefore became the substance of Scholastic theology. Abelard gave formative expres-sion to the *disputatio* in his *Sic et non*, in which he juxtaposed a long series of conflicting statements by theological authorities and then resolved the dis-putes by the rules of logic. In this method, which was to become standard Scholastic procedure, dialectic comes to replace monastic meditation as the essential religious discipline.

Scholasticism reached its fullest expression in the universities, where the focus of excitement became the *ars nova*, or "new logic," which emerged as a consequence of the rediscovery of some long-lost logical works of Aristotle. Of immediate interest to the logicians of the twelfth century was the transla-tion of Aristotle's *De sophisticis elenchis*, because its focus on the detection and refutation of linguistic fallacies was germane to the now-established prac-tice of *disputatio*. Even before the spread of the *ars nova*, fascination with sophisms was evident in the work of Adam of Balsham, who declared that the study of logic was essential because it enabled a mastery of language that could prevent one's being deceived by sophistry.[47] But now with the new logic firmly established in the universities, the systematic development of *soph-*

ismata as the heart of dialectic began to move forward rapidly. Virtually every logic text for the next two centuries contained an important and usually very lengthy section on sophistics, the assumption being that the purpose of logic was to prevent verbal deception.[48] The study of sophistics became the anvil of discipline upon which scholastics formed their understanding of the faith. As scholasticism progressed, it came closer to the view that faith amounted to the adequation of human thought to divine reality, and this adequation was clearly to be facilitated by the discipline of logic. The undialectical mind was therefore the most vulnerable to linguistic deception, and ultimately to sin.

It is interesting to note that the supreme expression of Scholastic thought, in the works of St. Thomas Aquinas, mitigates the central doctrine of Scholasticism. It is true that Aquinas accepted the Scholastic notion that truth amounts to the conformity of thought to reality, and that reason is the means to this adequation. But he did not allow that the whole of divine knowledge falls within the realm of the intellect, or that reason is the final judge of faith. Thus, dialectic or not, the human intellect is never, in this life, adequate to divine reality.

According to Aquinas, each thing seeks by the means appropriate to its nature to achieve the purpose for which it was created. Intelligent beings are by essence directed toward a perfection of the intellect. That is, they are ordered by eternal law to seek knowledge of the universal Good, to know God—insofar as he is knowable—according to their nature and by the means at their disposal. But in the case of human beings much more is to be said on the matter. Human beings, created in the image of God, are created as free moral agents. Therefore their movement toward universal good must be voluntary. That is, the intellect must be directed by the will toward its ultimate goal of knowing God. But according to Aquinas, the will takes action only with respect to objectives presented to it by the intellect.[49] That is, the will's perception of its goal depends on the understanding of the good brought to it by the intellect.

So here we have the human condition, one wherein intellect and will are mutually dependent: the will sends the intellect toward the intellect's own apprehension of the good. Now these matters appear to be rather straightforward and well in hand—until one discovers that the intellect is fairly unreliable in its apprehension of the good because of its dependence on the senses and appetites of the body. And when the shortcomings of the intellect are appreciated, we come away with a vision of the human condition which appears downright comic. Imagine two blind men (intellect and will) attempting to navigate their way toward an unknown destination (the ultimate good) on the advice of those (senses and appetites) who believe the destination has already been reached! This caricature is not far off the mark. Thomas believed that in this life the intellect is capable of understanding God only by indirection, by using the apparatus of the body as a resource with which to reason toward an approximation of divine truth. And on the strength of this approximate truth the will is directed to act. But the intellect is easily drawn off by the senses and appetites of the body because they are fixed on the particular goods appropriate to the corporeal nature of the body. As a result, the intellect directs the will toward particular goods and not toward its true goal in the universal good. This misdirection of the will by the deluded intellect violates eternal law by creating a discrepancy between the will and its goal, and this discrepancy, according to Aquinas, is the nature of sin. Sin results when the will is deprived by the intellect of its true purpose of serving God.

It is worth noting that the occasions for sin are manifold. The intellect may receive distorted reports from the senses, or it may be swayed by the emotions, or it may be flawed in its reasoning process, or it may be distracted by the wiles of demons.[50] In each of these instances the intellect is deceived with respect to its understanding of the good. And even when the intellect is not deceived, it is impossible for it to come to an adequate understanding because certain divine truths are beyond its scope, which is limited to the realm of natural law. And thus it was ordained that the divine law of Scripture would be revealed (a braille map for the navigators?) in order that the will might be undeceived and restored to its true object.

Mysticism

Two years before his death St. Thomas Aquinas experienced some form of mystical insight that prompted him to discontinue his prodigious writing career, which he thenceforth considered to be nothing but straw. Aquinas' assessment of his own work as a scholastic was prophetic in a way, for the next two centuries were swept by a wave of mystical writings which represented a fundamental departure from the central impulse of the Scholastic movement.

The Scholastic movement was premised on the assumption that divine reality could be approximated in the human intellect. And it is precisely this adequation of thought to divine reality that was denied by the mystical tradition of the late medieval period. The Scholastics believed that dialectic was essential as a hedge against deception, but for the mystics the discursive reasoning of dialectic was closer to being a *source* of deception. The mystics took particular issue less with the theology of Scholasticism than with its piety, its style, and its epistemology of faith. Where the Scholastics sought clarity of intellect, the mystics sought transformation of spirit. Where the scholastics insisted upon coherence and precision in theological formulation, the mystics were drawn to rhapsodic and often paradoxical expression. Where the scholastics scrutinized faith at the bar of reason, the mystics were suspicious of reducing faith to dialectic.

The mystics did not deny the possibility that humans could apprehend divine reality. Far from it. In fact, they insisted upon this possibility against the teachings of St. Thomas Aquinas, who said the beatific vision must await the afterlife. The mystics affirmed that true faith is not an intellectual achievement but rather an experiential event, an immediate and intimate union of the soul with God. Meister Eckhart, the thirteenth-century German mystic, speaks of mystical union as "a noble birth" that takes place "in the core of the soul." The fourteenth-century Flemish mystic John Ruysbroeck refers to the faith event as a unifying embrace: "In this embrace, in the essential Unity of

God, all inward spirits are one with God in the immersion of love; and are that same one which the Essence is in Itself, according to the mode of eternal bliss."[51] St. Teresa of Avila compares the mystical experience to the glory of heaven: "This instantaneous communication of God to the soul is so great a secret and so sublime a favour, and such a delight is felt by the soul, that I do not know with what to compare it, beyond saying that the Lord is pleased to manifest to the soul at that moment the glory that is in Heaven."[52] The anonymous fifteenth-century author of *The German Theology* writes, "And if a man would do this a thousand times a day, each time a fresh and true union would come about; and in this sweet and divine work stands the truest and purest union that may be in this temporal world. For he who has attained thereto, asks nothing further: he has found the Kingdom of Heaven and Eternal Life on earth."[53]

There can be no doubt that the medieval mystics believed that the spiritual *summum bonum* could be attained in this life; that divine reality could be apprehended in the human soul. But unlike the Scholastics, they insisted that the divine apprehension was not an intellectual achievement. In fact, they consistently made the point that the authentic faith experience transcends both the images of the senses and the subtleties of the intellect. The apprehension of divine reality is decisively without the mediations of sense and intellect. As Eckhart says, "And that indicates that within itself the soul is free, innocent of all instrumentalities and ideas, and that is why God can unite with it, he, too, being pure and without idea or likeness. . . . He acts in the soul without instrument, idea or likeness. He acts in the core of the soul, which no idea ever penetrated." And John Ruysbroeck states, "This contemplation sets us in purity and clearness above our understanding. . . . And to it none can attain through knowledge and subtlety, neither through any exercise whatsoever." Similarly, St. John of the Cross writes, "This consideration should make it clearer why a soul can not dispose itself for this union by either understanding, or sensory apperception, or inner feelings and imaginings, or by any other experiences relating either to God or to anything else, but only by purity and love, that is, by perfect resignation and total detachment from all things for the sake of God alone."[54]

The clear implication of these claims is that any and all attempts to mediate divine reality through intellectual means are to be regarded as deceptive. This is an important feature of mystical thought, though it does not receive much explicit comment from the mystics themselves. We must bear in mind, however, that the writings of the mystics are not polemical treatises; rather they are attempts to describe and interpret the spiritual experiences of devout men and women. Even so, there is sufficient evidence to support the view that the mystics regarded overintellectualization of the faith as a serious source of deception. Meister Eckhart, who was more sympathetic to the Scholastic tradition than most mystics, was careful to distinguish between discursive knowledge (i.e., knowledge of words) and direct knowledge (i.e., knowledge of love). A faith that is generated by a knowledge of words is vulnerable to deception, but faith based on the experience of God's love in the soul cannot be deceived: "This certainty [of love] is far greater, more complete and more true than the first and it cannot deceive. But words might deceive and might easily be a false enlightenment. But one feels [love] in all the powers of the soul and it cannot deceive those who truly love Him."[55]

The author of *The German Theology* makes essentially the same point in his distinction between True Light and False Light. The True Light is God, and the False Light is everything pertaining to nature:

> In short: All that can be deceived, must be deceived by this False Light. Now since all is deceived by this False Light that can be deceived, namely all that is creature and nature, and all that is not God nor divine, and since this False Light itself is nature, it is possible for it to be deceived.
>
> And therefore it becomes and is deceived, by itself, into rising and climbing to such a height that it imagines itself to be above nature.[56]

Anything which pertains to nature is deluded by the False Light, including cognition, even when, or especially when, this cognition purports to make reference to God. The issue here is that intellectual means are out of point for the mystic when it comes to true faith. To rely upon the well-coached intellect or the well-turned theological formulation as relevant to the apprehension of divine reality is to be utterly deceived.

To this point I have been arguing that the medieval mystics insist that the apprehension of divine reality is possible, and that it is an experiential apprehension in the depths of the soul, not a cognitive apprehension in the intellect. If one thinks that God can be approximated in the intellect by means of theological subtleties, then one has been deceived. All genuine apprehensions of God are experiential. But how can one know whether all so-called experiences of God are genuine? It might be granted to the mystic that all apprehensions of divine reality are profoundly experiential, but it does not follow that all profound experiences are apprehensions of divine reality, even when they appear to be. That is, it may be possible that the mystic himself has been deceived, and that the "experience of God" has in reality been induced by the devil. This was certainly the judgment of the pope who condemned Eckhart posthumously, saying he was "deceived by the father of lies" into "sowing thorns and thistles among the faithful and even the simple folk."[57]

Nor did this possibility escape the concern of the mystics themselves, as we see in the case of St. Teresa: "In such straights [*sic*] do I find myself at such a time that very often I should be glad to resist, and I exert all my strength to do so, in particular at times when it happens in public and at many other times in private, when I am afraid that I may be suffering deception." St. Teresa was given to raptures and visions of great diversity, and she worried at length over the authenticity of these momentous experiences. It concerned her that she could not easily discern which experiences came from God and which were caused by the deceits of the devil. As a result, it is important to be cautious or even skeptical in matters of the spirit: "I consider it quite certain that the devil will not deceive, and that God will not permit him to deceive, a soul which has no trust whatever in itself."[58] And because the soul cannot be left to trust itself, Teresa sought to identify objective criteria that could be relied upon to authenticate her spiritual experiences.

Teresa proposes three strategies for coping with the threat of spiritual deception. One is to secure the guidance of an objective spiritual director, some learned person who might judge reports of spiritual experience against the doctrines of the church: "None the less, the devil can play many tricks; and so there is nothing so certain as that we must always preserve our misgivings about this, and proceed cautiously, and choose a learned man for our director, and hide nothing from him." Another strategy is to reflect upon the experiences and judge them according to their practical effects. A third strategy is to judge spiritual experience by the standard of Scripture: "For, as far a I can see and learn by experience, the soul must be convinced that a thing comes from God only if it is in conformity with Holy Scripture; if it were to diverge from that in the very least, I think I should be incomparably more firmly convinced that it came from the devil than I previously was that it came from God, however sure I might have felt of this."[59]

Mysticism, it may be argued, takes us full circle with respect to the objective-cognitive and subjective-emotive standards of the religious life. Whereas Scholasticism may become arid and eventually drive the believer toward a more authentic subjective experience, mysticism soon becomes idiosyncratic and seeks validation in the objectivity of text and community. Whatever this paradox may suggest about the polar dynamics of a religious tradition, one is tempted to conclude that beneath these tendencies lies an abiding concern about deception, for felt deficiencies in either extreme find common expression in the fear that one is being deceived.

THE MODERN PERIOD

The Renaissance

Most historians would agree on the futility of bringing precision to the term "Renaissance." Yet it remains a useful term for the purpose of identifying a constellation of intellectual movements characteristic of the period from 1350 to 1600. The most important of these movements included the development of vernacular literary traditions, the emergence of a secular learning class, a shift from the military virtues of feudalism toward those associated with courtly life, and a recovery of Greco-Roman influences in art, literature and philosophy. If this complex period has a single feature that can speak for its unity, it is certainly a preoccupation with the task of developing human resourcefulness. And for many of the artists and thinkers of the Renaissance the key to the development of human personality lay in recovering the genius of classical culture.

The most influential scholar of the early Renaissance was Francesco Petrarch (1304–1374), whose disdain for the irrelevance of arid scholastic debates drew his attention toward the practical mind and edifying tongue of

Cicero. Petrarch would write of Cicero "O great father of Roman eloquence! I am not alone in offering you my gratitude; with me are all those who deck themselves with the flowers of Latin speech. We sprinkle our meadows with water from your fountains; you are our guide; it is you who sustain and enlighten us."[60]

It was a general adulation of this sort that put the Ciceronian ideal at the center of Renaissance learning. What attracted the Renaissance most about Cicero was his unique combination of rhetorical power and philosophical insight. Here was the complete intellect, the manifestation of excellence in both thought and expression. Here was a man whose interior life had all the clarity and range to be found in a great philosopher and whose external presentation had all the grace and splendor of the poets. In the early Renaissance Cicero was regarded as the embodiment of his very own ideal of learning: "No man has ever succeeded in achieving splendor and excellence in oratory, I will not say merely without training in speaking, but without taking all knowledge for his province as well."[61] In the view of Petrarch this dictum expressed the ideal of the learned person: one who combined the philosophical life of private contemplation with the rhetorical art of public edification. Wisdom without eloquence was irrelevant to civic life (e.g., Scholasticism), and eloquence without wisdom was degenerate (e.g., Sophism). The key to developing human potential was to achieve excellence in both philosophy and rhetoric.

Petrarch himself managed to keep the twin ideals of substance and form, wisdom and eloquence, in balance during his own career, but as the Renaissance advanced, a tendency to separate the disciplines of philosophy and rhetoric developed. The Ciceronian model called for a delicate balance, but it was eventually destabilized by the tendency of many Renaissance figures to take sides either with philosophy against rhetoric or with rhetoric against philosophy. The element of mutual suspicion that emerged was fueled, I suggest, by a fear of deception.

Just a generation after Petrarch, Colluccio Salutati took a position which effectively subordinated rhetoric to philosophy. Salutati was concerned that some of his younger friends were so enamored of eloquent speech and so desirous of the admiration it could earn them that they had become careless about the content of their rhetoric. The literary arts, he saw, were indiscriminate and could serve the interests of falsehood as well as the interests of truth. He warned his young friends not to be deceived by the flora of rhetoric:

Don't follow too closely that excessive and tendrilous style of your teacher, which he counts as flowery. According to him all things are divine, superb, and in brief such, that when you come to examine the truth of the matter, none of the things he says stands up. Swim through the sea of eloquence in such a way that you don't desert the truth. For the ocean of eloquence becomes infinite and impassible if you lose sight of truth.[62]

Salutati did not abandon the Ciceronian model of learning, but he did attempt to hedge it against deception by putting rhetoric in the service of philosophy. Rhetoric was the means of pursuing and expressing the end, which was wisdom: "The best thing is for wisdom and eloquence to join together, so that the second expounds what the first comprehends. In a contest over which was to be preferred, give the palm to wisdom . . . so that the pursuit of eloquence is a means to the end of seeking wisdom."[63]

Lorenzo Valla took the opposing position, favoring rhetoric over philosophy. In Valla's judgment the Ciceronian model would be achieved when rhetoric was placed in the service of Christian virtue. One could have the eloquence of the ancients without being bound to receive pagan philosophy as well: "To antiquity I concede the merit of letters, of studies, of learning, and of that which always had greater value, rhetoric; however, I deny that it arrived at wisdom or the knowledge of true virtue."[64]

It was inevitable that the Ciceronian model would begin to break down in its new Christian context, for Cicero had been a pagan, and his view of philosophical wisdom was destined to conflict with Christian dogma. Thus Valla, a loyal Christian, would take a position similar to Tertullian's, and would use the power of rhetoric in defense of Christian doctrine against the power of philosophy to inspire heresy. Philosophy, he argued, had nothing to offer but sophistry and self-deception because it was constantly departing from the natural forms of common speech. An example of the absurdities that result from philosophy is Aristotle's claim that a vessel is never really empty as long as it contains some air. Such deceptive wisdom, Valla thought, polite society could do without. The language of philosophy and dialectic reflects no common reality, but only the artificial and abstract delusions of the philosophers themselves: "After this let not dialecticians and philosophers persist in their ignorance of certain of their terms, but let them turn to a speech which is natural and commonly used by learned men. . . . The people speak better than the philosopher, and the best authors agree with them."[65]

Valla's attitude toward the ancient philosophical tradition may have been extreme, but nevertheless it became common among Christian humanists to emulate his restraint in the embrace of classical culture. For Christian humanists the literary heritage of classical culture was not an end in itself but rather a resource for exploring the origins and the essence of the Christian faith and for achieving moral reform within the church.

The most influential of the Christian humanists was Erasmus, a great admirer of Valla. Erasmus shared Valla's enthusiasm for scholarship and eloquence as allies of the Christian life, and he also shared a concern for a more practical, communal approach to theology. But Erasmus was less hostile toward the wisdom of the ancients. He lived at a time when the influence of classical skepticism was coming to bear upon the Renaissance, and the wisdom of the Skeptics played no small part in his regard for the dogmatic disputes of theologians. Erasmus became quite suspicious of the confidence, even arrogance, of theology. His own vast scholarship had convinced him that theologians often made dubious dogmatic leaps from the obscurity of their sources to the clarity of their doctrines. For his part, Erasmus was content to remain a theological minimalist, emphasizing moral and spiritual development over dogmatic certainty. Erasmus was deeply ambivalent about the religious issues of his day. With the intellectual bearing of a skeptic he remained aloof and satirical in his regard for the deluded self-confidence of theology, yet with the heart of a Christian moralist he engaged seriously in the task of edifying the church. In his two most influential works, the *Enchiridion* and *The Praise of Folly*, we can see Erasmus taking both roles: as a moral guide for the Christian laity and as a satirist of contemporary European culture. And in both works we can see the extent to which his thinking was shaped by the theme of deception.

In the *Enchiridion* Erasmus tells the reader it is his purpose to "propose a number of fundamental rules or norms that will guide us through the labyrinth of this world into the pure light of the spiritual life."[66] The image of the world as a labyrinth is a familiar one in Erasmus, and he leaves us no doubt that human life is a constant struggle against deception:

> To begin with we must be constantly aware of the fact that life here below is best described as being a type of continual warfare. . . . Yet in this matter the great majority of mankind is often deceived, for the world, like some deceitful magician, captivates their minds with seductive blandishments, and as a result most individuals behave as if there had been a cessation of hostilities. . . . It is amazing to see in what false security these people live and in what a complacent manner they close their minds to reality. In the meantime the vices, our armored enemies, attack us unceasingly; we are entrapped by their espionage and assaulted by their endless deceptions.[67]

The entire *Enchiridion* is thus intended to safeguard the Christian laity against the deceits of the world and against their own self-deception. To them he commends the virtues of faith and learning, prayer and knowledge, patience and reason. Erasmus could be deeply serious when he considered common, hardworking, unpretentious Christian folk. He regarded these humble Christians as the true elite; in them he invested his hope for genuine reform. But when he considered the supposed elite—*The Praise of Folly* was composed in the wake of a trip to Rome—he could be caustic and derisive. In *The Praise of Folly* Erasmus shows his reader how the labyrinth of deception appears in the absence of genuine faith and learning. Here reigns Folly, parented by wealth and youth, nursed by drunkenness and ignorance, and served by self-love, flattery, laziness, pleasure, madness, sensuality, intemperance, and sloth. In the world of Folly it is the deceived who are wise: "However, I seem to hear the philosophers disagreeing. They say that it is misery itself to live in folly, to err, to be deceived, and to be ignorant. On the contrary, however, this is what it is to be human." And in this world the deceived are happy: "But they say it is an unhappy thought to be deceived. To this I say no, for the unhappiest thought is not to be deceived. . . . Finally the mind of man is so constructed that it is far more susceptible to accepting falsehoods than realities. If anyone wants to make a convincing and easy test of this, let him go to church and listen to the sermons."[68]

Erasmus is having fun here, but a serious and fundamental point underlies the good humor, and it is the same point made in the *Enchiridion*; namely, that human beings are vulnerable to deception in many forms, and to the extent that they are deceived they fail to realize their capacity for personal and moral development. But if they avoid deception by the means of true faith, genuine learning, and sound reason, they have to that extent achieved the good.

As the Renaissance developed, the influence of the classical Skeptical tradition became increasingly evident. The views of the Skeptics were known to the early Renaissance through the works of Cicero and Diogenes Laertes, but it was not until midway through the sixteenth century that the works of Sextus Empiricus became widely known. Erasmus, as we have noted, was already influenced by the Skeptical tradition, but it was not until Montaigne that the full impact of Skepticism was felt. Montaigne was a transitional figure, representing the culmination of Renaissance ideals and at the same time laying the foundations for the new departure in philosophy normally associated with Descartes.

Montaigne lived in the thick of the reformation wars, and he was particularly discouraged by the dogmatic fanaticism of the French Protestants. To a fanatical age the Skeptic's gospel of serenity of mind must have had a special appeal. Or so, at least, it did for Montaigne. He found in skepticism a way out of the passion-fed troubles of his day. In his "Apology for Raymond Sebond" Montaigne worked out the elements of a full-blown Christian skepticism. At some length Montaigne guides the reader through the whole range of skeptical arguments and finally concludes that human beings are incapable of knowing truth. All human claims to know the truth result either from the deceptive influence of the unruly imagination (also "trickster reason") or from the deceptive influence of the senses. The reason and the senses feed deception to each other, jading the mind into a chimerical darkness: "This same deception that the senses convey to our understanding they receive in their turn. Our soul at times takes a like revenge; they compete in lying and deceiving each other. . . . It seems as though the soul draws the powers of the senses inward and occupies them. Thus both the inside and the outside of man is full of weakness and falsehood."[69]

Montaigne thus concludes that no knowledge is forthcoming from the powers of intellect or sense. And herein lies the ultimate condition of human existence: "In case this deception escapes my sight, at least it does not escape my sight that I am very deceivable."[70] But it is not Montaigne's purpose to abandon his reader to the absolute despair of unredeemed skepticism. That he is an extreme skeptic is clear enough, but his skepticism is strategic. He employs it as a purgative, to undeceive the mind so that it will be receptive to revelation. Skepticism, then, has immense value for the religious life:

There is nothing in man's invention that has so much verisimilitude and usefulness. It presents man naked and empty, acknowledging his natural weakness, fit to receive from above some outside power; stripped of human knowledge, and all the more apt to lodge divine knowledge in himself, annihilating his judgment to make more room for faith . . . ; a sworn enemy of heresy, and consequently free from the vain and irreligious opinions introduced by the false sects. He is a blank tablet prepared to take from the finger of God such forms as he shall be pleased to engrave on it."[71]

The Reformation

Whether the Protestant reformation was ultimately the result of theological disputes, or of political, social, and economic changes in the late medieval period is one of the most interesting and vexing problems of historical scholarship. But this problem will not detain us here. Most scholars now insist upon including all these factors in an adequate account of the reformation, but for our purposes it is important to focus on the theological dimension, for it is there that we will encounter the reformers' rationale. If there is a single theme upon which the reformers agreed it is this: that the Roman church was responsible for distorting the true proclamation and practice of Christianity. And the ultimate explanation given for this distortion involves the reformers' belief that the Roman church was deluded in its understanding of the faith. And for its part, the Roman church volleyed the same charge back at the reformers. At the level of theological discourse, then, the reformation was all about who was and who was not deceived, and why.

Martin Luther

At the heart of Martin Luther's critique of the Roman church is a fundamental distinction between two kinds of righteousness, the righteousness of faith and the righteousness of the law. The righteousness of faith is passive, infused in the soul by the grace of God. The righteousness of the law is active, manifested in the works performed by individuals. Luther believed it was absolutely essential that these forms of righteousness should not be confused: "This is our divinity, whereby we teach how to put a difference between these two kinds of righteousness, active and passive: to the end that manners and faith, works and grace, policy and religion should not be confounded, or taken the one for the other."[72]

Luther became convinced that this fundamental distinction between the two forms of righteousness was at the core of the gospel proclamation. And to fail to recognize the distinction is to distort the gospel and obstruct God's work. Luther did not disparage the righteousness of the law, he only insisted that this form of righteousness be seen in its proper perspective; that is, as ultimately dependent upon the other form of righteousness, the righteousness of faith. The critical point stressed by Luther is that righteousness is genuine if and only if it proceeds from faith. If it does not proceed from faith, then it is a perverse, sham, or counterfeit righteousness, proceeding from the deluded impression that human beings can please God by virtue of their own resources. Thus whenever humans attempt to achieve righteousness on their own (i.e., apart from faith), their counterfeit righteousness stands in opposition to the righteousness of God: "For when we act thus—and this is the greatest perversion—righteousness works against righteousness, wisdom against wisdom, power against power."[73] And here we see the absoluteness of the distinction Luther makes between faith-generated works and self-generated works. The former are genuinely righteous, whereas the latter are sinful, no matter how good they may appear: "It follows that what is done in the absence of faith on the one hand, or in consequence of unbelief on the other, is naught but falsity, self-deception, and sin, no matter how well it is gilded over."[74]

Human beings, therefore, are vulnerable to the belief that they possess the resources for righteousness. But to believe this is to be deceived by the appearances of counterfeit works. And once so deceived, humans will perpetuate the deception: "We do not condemn [good works] for their own sake but on account of this godless addition to them and the perverse idea that righteousness is to be sought through them; for that makes them appear good outwardly, when in truth they are not good. They deceive men and lead them to deceive one another like ravening wolves in sheep's clothing."[75]

Luther believed that the only defense against this avalanche of deceit was the Word, God's self-disclosure, which restores believers to faith by undeceiving them: "Our faith in Christ does not free us from works but from false opinions concerning works, that is, from the foolish presumption that justification is acquired by works. Faith redeems, corrects and preserves our consciences so that we know that righteousness does not consist in works."[76] And herein lies Luther's charge against the Roman church. The Roman church, he thought, was the victim of deception. The church itself engaged in "the greatest perversion" by teaching the doctrine of works apart from faith. In particular, the church had perverted the sacrament of penance, which had become, in Luther's opinion, one of the devil's snares. And in so doing, the Roman church was both deceived and a purveyor of deceit:

> If the influence of custom is added and confirms the perverseness of nature, as wicked teachers have caused it to do, it becomes an incurable evil and leads astray and destroys countless men beyond all hope of restoration. Therefore, although it is good to preach and write about penitence, confession, and satisfaction, our teaching is unquestionably deceitful and diabolical if we stop with that and do not go on to teach about faith.[77]

The result of this fundamental deception is that the church has placed its awesome power and authority in the service of the devil. The church has strayed away from the Word, its only true source of authority, and imagines itself to have some authority of its own. And in so doing it has perverted the gospel by exchanging God's truth for a lie. The whole point of the reformation was therefore to undo this great perversion by undeceiving the church.

John Calvin

Calvin agreed with Luther that a general disregard for the gospel had come to be a serious source of delusion in the church. In their disregard for the Scriptures the "ungodly men" in the church had fallen prey to the "subtleties of the sophists" and the "squabbles of the dialecticians."[78] And under these conditions the church could become disabused of its errors only by returning to the testimony of the Scriptures under the guidance of the Holy Spirit. The task of the reformers, then, was to undeceive the church. Calvin, in fact, placed this ministry of undeceiving at the center of his theology.

Calvin believed that human beings are naturally endowed with the capacity to apprehend God. This natural sense of God is evidenced by the fact that no culture, however uncivilized or barbarous, is without its own conception of God. And to this inherent sense is added an abundance of external evidence for the existence and majesty of God: "But upon his individual works he has engraved unmistakable marks of his glory, so clear and so prominent that even unlettered and stupid folk cannot plead the excuse of ignorance." Both this instinctive sense and the external evidence are available, so that all people must acknowledge that the means for divine apprehension are at hand: "They have within themselves a workshop graced with God's unnumbered works, and, at the same time, a storehouse overflowing with inestimable riches."[79]

Yet despite all these advantages, humanity has made a mess of things and falls short of an original likeness of God created to his glory. As a result of the devil's deceits, human beings turned away from God and began falsely to credit their created worth and excellence to themselves. Such was the origin of sin, which has since left all of humanity in a state of darkness and confusion: "But however great such commendation of human excellence is that teaches man to be satisfied with himself, it does nothing but delight in its own sweetness; indeed it so deceives as to drive those who assent to it into utter ruin."[80]

The result of original sin is human self-reliance, the error of errors, which renders humanity incapable of beholding God's truth either in the internal workshop of the soul or in the external storehouse of nature. And yet "the seed of religion" that has been planted in the soul propels us to seek God. But under the conditions of original sin this seeking for God can produce nothing but gross superstition and falsehood. Under the conditions of original sin, "the human heart has so many crannies where vanity hides, so many holes where falsehood lurks, is so decked out with deceiving hypocrisy, that it often dupes itself."[81]

It was in response to universal superstition and falsehood that God bestowed his Word upon the world. Calvin's doctrine is that the Word is sent for the purpose of undeceiving a fallen humanity: "Despite all this, it is needful that another and better help be added to direct us aright to the very Creator of the universe . . . so Scripture, gathering up the otherwise confused knowledge of God in our minds, having dispersed our dullness, clearly shows us the true God."[82]

But Calvin was not content to leave everything to the Scriptures alone. He was keenly aware of the Renaissance debates about rhetoric and realized that the written Word was itself vulnerable to the distortions of the sophists. He insisted, therefore, that the teachings of the Scriptures must be confirmed in the human heart by the Spirit: "God did not bring forth his Word among men for the sake of a momentary display, intending at the coming of his Spirit to abolish it. Rather, he sent down the same Spirit by whose power he had dispensed the Word, to complete his work by the efficacious confirmation of the Word."[83] Calvin's doctrine of the Word, therefore, combines the testimony of the Scriptures with the work of the Spirit. The gospel, then, is not merely taught externally by the Scriptures but also demonstrated inwardly by the Spirit.

It is as if Calvin constructed his doctrine of the Word to combat the deceptive influences in the church of Scholastic theology on the one hand and fanatical mysticism on the other. These are the chief dangers that lurk within the church. The Scholastics are likely to be drawn away from the gospel by the delusion that human reason is sufficient for the elucidation of scriptural teachings. Against this delusion Calvin sets the Spirit. But there are also fanatical elements within the church that are likely to be deceived by any gust of frenzy into believing that it is God's Spirit that has moved them. Against these tendencies Calvin sets the standard of Scripture. Calvin thus regarded true salvation as God's act of undeceiving humanity through the knowledge of Scripture and the inspiration of the Holy Spirit. And the work of the reformation was parallel to God's; that is, to reform the church by undeceiving it.

The Catholic Reformation

From the point of view of the Roman church the reformation was nothing short of a calamity. Much of Rome's influence was lost, not to mention huge tracts of land and material wealth. And all at the hands of heretics! The church responded militantly by reasserting its authority as the sole custodian of the deposit of faith. The response of the Roman church to the reformation grew out of its traditional attitudes toward heresy. Heresy (literally, "choice") was considered an error of the intellect resulting in the will to follow false doctrine. It was, simply put, the state of being deceived about divine truths. And since the medieval mind could not conceive of morality apart from true religion, the appearance of heresy amounted to the thin end of the wedge of anarchy. Informed by such thinking, the church sensed an urgency to articulate clearly the errors of the reformers with respect to true doctrine and to enforce its doctrine through appropriate measures of discipline.

On the theological front several polemicists emerged to expose the errors of the reformers. Especially worrisome was the reformation doctrine concerning the absolute and exclusive authority of Scripture. Indeed, the reformation itself tended to confirm Origen's warning that heresy springs from a misguided reading of Scripture. Apart from the guidance of the Catholic church, therefore, there could be no "living and efficacious propagation of the word, but only the tyranny of the letter that kills and deceives."[84] Thus Cochlaeus attempted to expose the Protestant error by demonstrating the extent to which one might be deceived once the Scriptures had been wrested from the church. By the free examination of scattered texts, he showed how one might be led to believe that Satan must be obeyed, that Jesus Christ is not God, and that Mary was not a virgin.[85] The reformers' view of *sola scriptura* was therefore the master delusion that had led them into manifold errors.

The centerpiece of the Catholic reformation was the Council of Trent (1545–63), which was convened to address the Protestant challenge but also to respond to demands within the church for wholesale reform. It was quickly decided, however, that the need was not to reform Catholic doctrine but only to clarify its truth against Protestant heresy. Each of the Protestant theses was thoroughly considered by the council, and canons were formulated to clarify in exactly what sense they were heretical. Thus there were canons against Protestant views on the authority of Scripture and tradition, the role of faith and works, the nature of the sacraments, and so on. The documents of the council left no room for doubt that the reformers had indeed counterfeited the faith and were therefore a menace to the gospel. The council also made provisions for stiffening moral and spiritual discipline within the church. Simony, absenteeism, pluralism, violations of chastity vows, and ignorance among the clergy would no longer be tolerated. The council also considerably strengthened the power of the pope as disciplinarian of the revitalized church. Thus the Roman church came out of council with its structure taut and with firm resolve to adhere to its traditional doctrine.

This militant spirit of obedience was also characteristic of the Society of Jesus (Jesuits) and the Inquisition, the two principal instruments of discipline in the Catholic reformation. Though these institutions were distinct, they often worked in concert to identify heretics and to attempt to disabuse them of their deception. Ignatius Loyola, founder of the Jesuits, stressed the importance of submission to ecclesiastical authority as the only sure defense against being deceived: "How great a deception it is, and how dangerous for those who think it lawful to withdraw from the will of their superior."[86] Ignatius wanted the members of his society to be exemplary in their obedience. The faithful should assume, says Ignatius, that their spiritual superiors are themselves incapable of being deceived, and on this assumption the obedient servant, too, can avoid being deceived:

> The first is that . . . you do not behold in the person of your superior a man subject to errors and miseries, but rather him whom you obey in man, Christ, the highest wisdom . . . who, you know, cannot be deceived and does not wish to deceive you. And because you are certain that you have set upon your shoulders this yolk of obedience . . . , be assured that his most faithful charity will ever direct you.
>
> Then to proceed blindly, without inquiry of any kind, to the carrying out of the command, with a kind of passion to obey.[87]

With such resolve the Jesuits went forth as the shock troops of the Roman church to countervail the effects of the Protestant heresy through their efforts in preaching, teaching, converting the heathen in distant lands, and pamphleteering. In these efforts it was typical of the Jesuits to turn the reformers' strategies against them to undermine their deceits: "The heretics write a large number of books and pamphlets, taking all authority from the Catholics . . . and set up their false dogmas. It would seem expedient, therefore, that ours here also write answers in pamphlet form. . . . These works should be modest, but lively; they should point out the evil that is abroad and uncover the evil machinations and deceits of the adversaries."[88]

In addition to fostering discipline by the founding of the Jesuit order, the Roman church revived the Inquisition and made it a churchwide tribunal for the detection and suppression of heresy. The Inquisition employed various devices, including intimidation, public humiliation, exclusion from civil rights, fines, confiscation of goods, imprisonment, torture, and ultimately death to halt the spread of the Protestant heresy. Such enormities were justified within the context of the sacramental system. In fact, the Inquisition *just was* the sacrament of penance in its most extreme form, a form suitable to the sin of heresy. In order to be undeceived of their sinful errors the heretics first had to be brought to a state of contrition and then forced to confess their errors. If the circumstances called for duress, then so be it. The means were justified by the end of preserving God's truth against the influence of noxious lies. If a heretic refused to comply with the proceedings, then the case might be abandoned to the secular arm, which usually meant the stake. The Inquisition, then, proved its effectiveness against deception on two fronts. First, it disabused the heretic of errors, and second, it prevented both repentant and unrepentant heretics from deceiving others.

The Rise of Modern Science

The transition from medieval mentality to modern mentality can be best described by the diffusion of authority that took place between the fourteenth century and the seventeenth century. In the early fourteenth century the Roman church was still the center of intellectual and moral authority in Western culture. But as the Renaissance and the reformation developed, this centralized authority began to break down. The Renaissance elevated the classical tradition to a status of authority alongside the church. The reformation introduced new ecclesiastical organizations based on the independent authority of the Scriptures. And at the same time, ambitious monarchs were asserting the independent authority of their secular states. It was in this context of pluralizing authorities that science, too, began to assert itself.

While the early modern scientists might have drawn courage from the examples set by Renaissance scholars and reformers, there were risks in proposing new ideas that contradicted the teachings of the militant Roman church. Nor did the reformation ease the struggles of the new science, for the reformed churches themselves were not exactly tolerant of views that appeared to contradict the Scriptures. Yet in spite of the difficulties, the new science made its way into the expanding arena of authority, and it did so partly on the strength of its claim to be an effective hedge against deception.

The basis for this claim lay in the ancient distinction between reality and appearance, which Johannes Kepler and Galileo Galilei construed as the distinction between primary and secondary qualities. This distinction, revived along with the ancient Skeptics during the sixteenth century, held that there was a fundamental difference between those characteristics of things that could be reduced to mathematical formulation (e.g., size, shape, weight, density, velocity) and those that could not (e.g., color, taste, smell, sound). The former were construed as primary characteristics, the latter as secondary. For Kepler and Galileo the primary characteristics, the quantifiable ones, were fundamentally real, whereas the secondary characteristics were derivative and conducive to deception. Differences and similarities in the world that could be shown to conform to mathematical order were real; differences and similarities that were not quantifiable could be discarded as illusory. Mathematics was the language of reality, and without it we might easily be deceived: "Philosophy is written in that great book which ever lies before our eyes—I mean the universe—but we cannot understand it if we do not first learn the language and grasp the symbols, in which it is written. This book is written in the mathematical language, and the symbols are triangles, circles, and other geometrical figures, without whose help it is impossible to comprehend a single word of it; without which one wanders in vain through a dark labyrinth."[89]

Galileo was convinced that the primary qualities were independent of human perception, that they would remain in the absence of perceivers, whereas the secondary qualities would not. It was henceforth argued, by Galileo and others, that a consideration of secondary qualities should be systematically expunged from all reasoning about nature to safeguard knowledge from the deceptive influence of the senses. And science, so it was argued, was just the method for doing the job.

But it was not only the reports of the senses that had to be scrutinized. The same was true of the testimony of all traditional authorities. Thus when it became clear that the findings of science occasionally contradicted the Scriptures, Galileo defended the authority of science by pointing out that a superficial and literal reading of the Bible was likely to deceive:

> I think in the first place that it is very pious to say and prudent to affirm that the holy Bible can never speak untruth—whenever its true meaning is understood. But I believe nobody will deny that it is often very abstruse, and may say things which are quite different from what its bare words signify. Hence in expounding the Bible if one were always to confine oneself to the unadorned grammatical meaning, one might fall into error. Not only contradictions and propositions far from true might thus be made to appear in the Bible, but even grave heresies and follies."[90]

Galileo thought that the Bible was written for "rude and unlearned" people, and it was written for the sake of their salvation, not for the sake of understanding nature. When it comes to physical realities, therefore, the Bible has no authority whatsoever, and worse, may well be a source of deception.

Galileo's suspicion of uncritical testimony from the senses and from traditional authorities was shared completely by Francis Bacon. Bacon, like so many others of his day, was somehow aware that he was living at the dawn of a new era. And to his mind a new age called for a comprehensive reorientation of human knowledge, away from the fallacious procedures that were commonly followed and toward the more reliable methods of the new science. Bacon identified four classes of fallacious ideas which had the effect of deceiving the mind and thus preventing the pursuit of true knowledge. These he called the four idols: "Idols are the deepest fallacies of the human mind. For they do not deceive in particulars, as the others do, by clouding and ensnaring the judgment; but by a corrupt and ill-ordered predisposition of mind, which as it were perverts and infects all the anticipations of the intellect."[91] The first of the idols are the *idols of the tribe*. These idols include those preconceptions and tendencies toward error that are inherent in human nature. For example, humans are naturally predisposed to accept the testimony of the senses, to proceed by force of habit, and to see what they expect to see. Such predispositions, if not carefully resisted, will lead us into error. In the second group are the *idols of the cave*. Among these idols are included all the personal idiosyncrasies that might lead one into falsehood, such as a peculiar temperament, or neurosis, or the special character of one's education, habits, or life experiences. These factors of chance may well obstruct the mind. In the third group are the *idols of the marketplace*. Here Bacon had in mind the tyranny of common discourse. Our thinking is shaped by words, which are, in turn, begat by other words. But the common stock of verbiage is notoriously imprecise, prejudicial, and vulgar, leading us unawares into fuzzy and ill-defined habits of thought. The last group, the *idols of the theater*, include philosophical systems and dogmas that are uncritically received through the authority of tradition. Bacon subdivided this group of idols into the sophistical (e.g., Aristotle), the empirical (e.g., alchemists and astrologers), and the superstitious (e.g., Plato and the mystics). Bacon's point in describing these systematic fallacies was to suggest that most of human thought is ensnared by deception. The first order of business is therefore to undeceive the mind so that it can reorient itself according to the methods of science.

Modern Philosophy

Modern philosophy began to develop in the seventeenth century, after an interlude of nearly three hundred years during which there was very little philosophy of an original or interesting nature. This philosophical hiatus was due in no small part to the fact that during the fourteenth, fifteenth, and sixteenth centuries the best minds were engaged in recovering the classical tradition, inventing vernacular literatures, reforming the church, experimenting with the new science, discovering the New World, and developing the economic and political instruments for the new secular states. These developments shattered the foundations of the old medieval order and set upon the scene a confusing array of conflicting intellectual and moral authorities. Gone forever was the monopolizing authority of the Roman church, and in its place stood revitalized pagan traditions, a spectrum of new churches, a cacophony of sovereign nations, and ambitious new methods of scientific discovery. Not since the thirteenth century had there been such a climate for stimulation of philosophical wonder and reflection. The challenge for modern philosophy was partly to work out a rationale for departure from the old medieval order, but more than that, the modern philosophers found their challenge in laying the intellectual foundations for the strange new world of pluralism in which they found themselves. Indeed, the period of modern philosophy might well be called the golden age of foundationalism. The principal concern of the modern philosophers was to find cognitive moorings in these disoriented times—to fix upon the indubitable axioms of thought and reality about which there could be no fear of being deceived.

Rationalism

René Descartes was directly influenced by the revival of skepticism in the late Renaissance, and in particular by the writings of Montaigne and Pierre Charron. But Descartes was also a strong advocate of the new science and regarded the extreme skeptical position as a threat to its philosophical foundations. He therefore set out to defeat skepticism in order to establish the scientific enterprise on firm principles. To a degree, Descartes accepted the conclusions of the skeptics: certainly human beings were vulnerable to being deceived. It took only a moment's reflection upon the nature of hearsay and the testimony of the senses to discover that much of what we casually claim to know is open to serious doubt. As he declares, "There is no novelty to me in the reflection that, from my earliest years, I have accepted many false opinions as true, and that what I have concluded from such badly assured premises could not but be highly doubtful and uncertain."[92] But Descartes was equally certain that humans could know some things—many things, in fact—that were beyond doubt. His challenge was to discover a method and a line of reasoning that could demonstrate the intellectual bedrock of human knowledge. He set out to discover one or two indubitable truths that might provide the foundations for further knowledge claims, one or two axioms that were invulnerable to deception. If he could do this, then the skeptics would be defeated and the foundations of science would be secure.

It occurred to Descartes that he might ultimately defeat the skeptics by adopting their own method of doubt and pressing it to the point of failure. He would doubt everything; he would assume that in all his beliefs he had been victimized by some malevolent deceiver:

> I will therefore suppose that, not a true God, who is very good and who is the supreme source of truth, but a certain evil spirit, not less clever and deceitful than powerful, has bent all his efforts to deceiving me. I will suppose that the sky, the air, the earth, colors, shapes, sounds, and all other objective things that we see are nothing but illusions and dreams that he has used to trick my credulity. I will consider myself as having no hands, no eyes, no flesh, no blood, no any senses, yet falsely believing that I have all these things. I will remain resolutely attached to this hypothesis; and if I cannot attain the knowledge of any truth by this

method, at any rate it is in my power to suspend my judgment. That is why I shall take great care not to accept any falsity among my beliefs and shall prepare my mind so well for all the ruses of this great deceiver that, however powerful and artful he may be, he will never be able to mislead me in anything.[93]

In the process of applying this method of universal doubt, Descartes found one item that was invulnerable to the deceits of his imaginary demon: that he, Descartes, was engaged in doubt, that he existed as a thinking thing who entertained various clear and distinct ideas. From these clear and distinct ideas Descartes generated proofs for the existence of a perfect God, and since a perfect God cannot deceive, he concluded that all ideas having the quality of clarity and distinctness are true: "For every clear and distinct conception is without doubt something real and positive, and thus cannot derive its origin from nothingness, but must have God for its author—God, I say, who being supremely perfect cannot be the cause of any error—and consequently we must conclude that such a conception or a judgment is true."[94] Descartes is here making a claim for the divine origin of human reason. Thus, whenever our thinking about the world bears the marks of clear and distinct ideas, we cannot be deceived. These clear and distinct ideas of human reason, therefore, provide an indubitable foundation for knowledge.

At this point we can make a general observation about the distinctive character of modern rationalism: It attempts to construct a philosophy on the model of mathematics. Just as a mathematical system deduces conclusions from a set of self-evident axioms, so rationalism aspired to deduce truths about reality from a set of God-given innate ideas. The plausibility of this deductive strategy was enhanced by the rather obvious success of the new science. Galileo had convinced his age that nature conformed to the language of mathematics. But if it is true that nature conforms to reason, then one might suppose, as the rationalists did, that it would be sufficient to explore nature by way of exploring the clear and distinct ideas of reason. Indeed, this was the only sure method to avoid being deceived by the intrusion of subjective factors such as sense reports, hearsay evidence, and emotional predispositions. The rationalists were confident that they had hedged against deception by assimilating philosophy to the deductive methods of mathematics, including the reduction of physics to quantifiable formulation and the reduction of the causal nexus to logical implication. The whole enterprise of philosophy and science could henceforth be conceived as a branch of mathematics and logic, the elements of which were *a priori* properties of a rational faculty created by an honest God.

The rationalist premise was extended by both Benedict Spinoza and Gottfried Wilhelm von Leibniz. In Spinoza's major work, *Ethics Demonstrated According to the Geometrical Order*, the mathematical ideal of philosophy becomes palpable. Spinoza even adopts the form of a mathematical system in his presentation, moving deductively from definitions to axioms and then from propositions to proofs and corollaries. Like Descartes, Spinoza was convinced of the adequation of thought to reality, but not merely, as Descartes supposed, because God created both nature and the mind according to the same rational principles. For Spinoza the connection was much less coincidental. Reason and nature correspond because they represent parallel attributes of the same divine reality. Thus the laws of physics are identical to the laws of logic. It was sufficient, Spinoza thought, to pursue knowledge of the essence of things by confining oneself to the realm of deduction. To do so, in fact, was the only sure way to avoid being deceived. If one were to seek knowledge of reality through induction from particulars, one could never come up with clear and distinct ideas, but could achieve only vague and confused images. But these images must be resisted: "So the thing to note here, above all, is how easily we are deceived when we confuse universals with singulars, and beings of reason and abstractions with real beings."[95]

Leibniz was even more ambitious than Descartes or Spinoza about the prospects for realizing the mathematical ideal of philosophy. He entertained the possibility of developing a formal language that could systematically eliminate obscurity and error from the reasoning process. Leibniz thought it would be possible to articulate a universal formal language, a calculus of reason, that would perfectly represent the structure of human thought, and thus would provide an adequate foundation for knowledge claims. Such a language might do for our philosophical thinking what arithmetical notation and geometry have done for our thinking about numbers and ideal space.

Leibniz believed that the mental life of an individual amounted to a manipulation of concepts—their formation, comparison, analysis, and synthesis. These concepts were generally clear and distinct in the mind. But when concepts are given symbolic representation in language, the clarity and distinctness become lost. The realm of language, Leibniz thought, was not sufficiently isomorphic with the realm of concepts. And yet it is by means of linguistic conventions that we manipulate our concepts. Leibniz was bothered by the vagueness, the irregularity, the ambiguity, the general deficiency of natural languages. Natural languages unnecessarily complicate our thinking and introduce a range of distortions, obscurities, and error. We could avoid such obstacles to the reasoning process, he believed, by formalizing our symbols in a universal artificial language. Such a language would produce an isomorphism of concept and symbol, as in mathematics, and would greatly reduce our vulnerability to deception:

> Now the characters that express all our thoughts will constitute a new language that can be written and spoken; this language will be very difficult to construct, but very easy to learn. It will be quickly accepted by everybody on account of its great utility and its surprising facility, and it will serve wonderfully in communication among various peoples, which will help it get accepted. Those who will write in this language will not make mistakes provided they avoid errors of calculation, barbarisms, solecisms, and other errors of grammar and construction. In addition, this language will possess the wonderful property of silencing ignoramuses.

For people will be unable to speak or write about anything except what they understand, or if they try to do so, one of two things will happen: either the emptiness of what they put forward will be apparent to everybody, or they will learn by writing and speaking. . . . This will happen especially with our language, on account of its exactness. So much so, that there will be no equivocations or amphibolies, and everything which will be said intelligibly in that language will be said with propriety. This language will be the greatest instrument of reason.[96]

This proposed artificial language would greatly clarify the process of thinking, so that all truths expressed in it would bear the mark of formal, analytic validity. But such a language would also be a heuristic device to stimulate and direct the mind toward new discoveries, as frequently happens in mathematics. Leibniz never realized his goal of constructing the perfect formal language of philosophy, though he continued to allude to its possibility throughout his career. This project, though never completed, illustrates the rationalist belief that the problem of deception could be avoided, or at least minimized, by the articulation of formal foundations for knowledge that could be found in the structures and innate contents of the mind.

Empiricism

Both rationalism and empiricism attempt to specify the ultimate foundations for our claims to know something about reality. But they differ in their conception of these foundations. Whereas for rationalism the foundations of knowledge are found in the universal principles of innate reason, for empiricism they are found in the particular elements of acquired experience. It follows, then, that whereas rationalism attributes deception to excessive reliance on unstructured sense reports, empiricism attributes it to excessive reliance upon unrestrained flights of the imagination.

In John Locke we encounter the mind of a physician and anatomist, not, as with Descartes and Leibniz, the mind of a mathematician. Rather than spin truths deductively from a body of indubitable formal axioms, Locke followed the analytical approach in an effort to break down knowledge claims into constitutive experiential primes. According to rationalist principles, sense experience represents little more than the occasion for opening the book of reason, which reveals the substance of innate truths. Locke reverses this doctrine with the empiricist claim that the "book" is empty until written upon by experience received ultimately from the senses. To suppose that there are conceptual provisions innately bestowed on the mind is to open the floodgates to enthusiastic prejudice and delusions of all sorts. Locke therefore opens his famous *Essay Concerning Human Understanding* with an attack on the doctrine of innate ideas. And in place of this doctrine he presents an empiricist theory of knowledge.

Locke insists that all knowledge claims are ultimately traceable to particular experiences. Some of our experiences give us knowledge immediately, such as the experience of pain. When I am in pain I know it intuitively and certainly.

But my experience of pain does not give me immediate knowledge regarding the cause of pain. Knowledge of such causes requires some judgment or interpretation on my part. Thus all knowledge is either *intuitive*, in which case it is beyond all doubt, or *inferential*, in which case it is open to errors of judgment. And since most of our knowledge claims involve inferences, Locke allows for a wide range of vulnerability to deception. He gives us three major conditions under which we are most vulnerable to deception. We may be deceived, he says, when we are overly disposed to accept the authority of others, and when we are given to passionate or wishful thinking, and when we lack sufficient breadth of experience. To safeguard the understanding from these three major sources of deception, Locke offers three remedies. The first is to overcome the narrowness of mind typical of those who are given to accept authority. The second is to preclude the self-deceptive influence of passionate and wishful thinking by cultivating the habit of objectivity. And the third is to make sure that one's premises are well supported by observed matters of fact.[97]

The Enlightenment

The principal interest of rationalists and empiricists alike was to articulate the ultimate foundations for human understanding, and especially for the enterprise of modern science. In time the sharp differences between these philosophical extremes began to give way to a practical consensus that both logic and experience, both mathematics and observation, were essential for the conduct of science. Immanuel Kant worked out a compromise of rationalism and empiricism on the dual principle that "concepts without percepts are empty, percepts without concepts are blind." The mature epistemology of the Enlightenment, then, might be called "rational empiricism" or "empirical rationalism." Whether the ultimate foundations of science lay in the reason or in the senses became less important than the practical opinion that science itself should be the foundation for a new society.

The Enlightenment brought the paradigm of Newtonian science to bear upon ambitious programs of social reform. Newton's achievement was to unify the realms of terrestrial and celestial mechanics, thereby demonstrating that all of nature conforms to a coherent system of natural laws. Nature was essentially a rationally intelligible domain. It was this equation of nature and reason that generated the spirit of the Enlightenment and informed its attempts to reform social institutions. Enlightenment thinkers were convinced that what Newton had done for the comprehension and manipulation of natural forces they could do for the comprehension and amelioration of human affairs. If all of nature conforms to natural laws and if human beings are a part of nature, it should follow that a "physics of human affairs" is possible. If a science of humanity were developed, it would provide the foundation needed for comprehensive reforms. Social progress would be boundless once the laws of human nature were brought to light. Whatever ails the human condition could be expelled by a diligent application of these laws. This frame of mind inspired the unprecedented sense of optimism and confidence in human rational faculties that became characteristic of the Enlightenment:

The only foundation of faith in the natural sciences is the principle, that the general laws, known or unknown, which regulate the phenomena of the universe, are regular and constant; and why should this principle, applicable to the other operations of nature, be less true when applied to the development of the intellectual and moral faculties of man?

. . . [W]e shall find the strongest reasons to believe, from past experience, from observation of the progress which the sciences and civilization have hitherto made, and from the analysis of the march of the human understanding, and the development of its faculties, that nature has fixed no limits to our hopes.[98]

Without the free exercise of reason, however, there could be no hope for human progress. Science without reason was mere conjury and magic; politics without reason was chaos or tyranny; religion without reason was fanaticism and dogmatism; morality without reason was wickedness. The fundamental premise of the Enlightenment was that whatever evils had befallen humanity in the past were evils by default of insufficient reason. For example, Locke: "Wherever law ends, tyranny begins"; Baron d'Holbach: "The less men reason, the more wicked they are"; Voltaire: "[L]ess superstition means less fanaticism; and less fanaticism means fewer calamities." These maxims express the common underlying assumption that reason is an essential hedge against the mind's vulnerability to misdirection, intimidation, confusion, and every other form of deception—and where the mind is deceived, there evil prevails.

The Enlightenment unfolds, then, as a critique of every form of unreason. And the point of entry for this general critique of culture was the domain of religion. Thus Voltaire's famous remark about the Roman church ("Crush the infamous thing") expressed the thrust of the Enlightenment agenda. Enlightenment critics viewed supernatural religion as an instrument of deception wielded by fanatical impostors and a despotic priesthood to confound and intimidate the minds of simple folks. The Enlightenment mind was not opposed to religion *per se*, but only to those forms of religion which based their doctrines and authority on the deceitful claims of superstition and supposed revelations. Following John Locke, it was common to distinguish between natural and supernatural forms of religion. Natural religion was reasonable, mimimalist, moralistic, and constructive, whereas supernatural religion was "the source of all imaginable follies and disorders; it is the mother of fanaticism and civil discord; it is the enemy of mankind."[99] Voltaire saw in religion a paradigm for the equation of unreason with deception. In his influential *Philosophical Dictionary* he chose to discuss religion under the rubric of "fraud."

The Nineteenth Century

The eighteenth century was a conventional age, a century with a coherent paradigm. The nineteenth century, in contrast, seems to have made a virtue of miscellany. It was a period of heavy cross-currents, some continuing unabated from the eighteenth century and others springing up in reaction to it. The Enlightenment infatuation with the Newtonian paradigm may have found many scoffers, but the enterprise of science continued to expand throughout the nineteenth century in both the progress it made and the esteem it won. Nor was there any interest in aborting the democratic urges that were conceived in the Enlightenment. Even the Enlightenment aspirations for developing a science of humanity continued to advance throughout the nineteenth century, culminating in the positivism of Auguste Comte. And the spirit of skepticism, maturing since the Renaissance, remained an important feature of the intellectual milieu of the nineteenth century. Nevertheless, it must be said that in respect to self-understanding the nineteenth century was explicitly opposed to the intellectual premises of the Enlightenment. As every age does, the nineteenth century ignored its similarities to the past by simply assuming them. But historical contrasts always rise to the level of consciousness, as they clearly did in the development of romanticism.

Romanticism is notorious for eluding the efforts of historians to define its chief characteristics. Yet many definitions have been offered. In the narrow sense romanticism represents an aesthetic reaction against the anaesthetic classicism and conventionalism of eighteenth-century art and literature. But in a broader sense we may speak of an intellectual orientation so diffuse that it came to influence every aspect of nineteenth-century culture. As Roland Stromberg observes, "whenever we find a doctrine that everyone knows about but no one can quite define we are in the presence of a major intellectual revolution."[100]

The romantic movement was a complex phenomenon with many subthemes and diverse historical antecedents. Its roots may be found in developments that took place simultaneously in the arts, religion, philosophy, and politics. There was an increasing recognition that Enlightenment art and literature had become rigid and lifeless in its measured conventionalism. Religious circles grew increasingly dissatisfied with the austerity of excessive rationalism. German pietists and their English Methodist counterparts encouraged a religion of the "warmed heart" in contrast to the scholastic orthodoxy of German Protestantism and the naturalism of English deism. Friedrich Schleiermacher gave theological expression to pietism by defining the essential religious life as a matter of feeling rather than understanding. Philosophical legitimation for romanticism was drawn from both Jean-Jacques Rousseau and Kant. Rousseau transposed the foundation of truth from reason to passion and experience. And Kant argued that the supposed objective order of nature is not apprehended by mere passive impressions on the mind but rather is actively constructed by subjective categories. And in the political realm, of course, the French Revolution came as a bloody and violent refutation of optimistic doctrines about human reason and progress.

By the end of the eighteenth century various symptoms of discontent with the rational orthodoxy of the Enlightenment had assembled themselves into a radical cultural critique. The substance of this critique was that the outlook of the Enlightenment was based on a grand illusion about nature and humanity. In its rush to silence enthusiasm and in its delirium over the success of Newtonian mechanics the Enlightenment had produced a monstrous caricature of nature and a grave distortion of human existence. The Enlightenment, in other words, had been deceived by appearances into the belief that the final word on reality was Reason. Romanticism, therefore, set out to disabuse European culture of its errors, and in doing so it generated antitheses to nearly every characteristic of Enlightenment mentality. The romantics juxtaposed intuition to reason, feeling to thinking, the concrete to the abstract, subjectivity to objectivity, process to form, invention to convention, spirit to matter, struggle to repose, the organic to the mechanical, expression to repression, the pastoral to the civil, existence to essence, human will to inanimate force, genius to mediocrity, spontaneity to deliberation, adventure to caution, experiment to precedent, art to science, the passionate to the stoic, the exotic to the familiar, primitive to refined, Dionysian to Apollonian—and the list goes on, driving intellectual historians (and their readers) to the brink of exhaustion.

Arthur Schopenhauer is the most interesting philosophical representative of romanticism because he carried its inherent tendencies to their extreme expression. Schopenhauer, like so many others of the romantic period, took Kant as his point of philosophical departure. Kant had distinguished between the noumenal (the world of things as they really are, in themselves), and the phenomenal (the world as it appears to subjective perceivers). Kant further said that the noumenal was unknown and unknowable; the world could be apprehended only as phenomena, which were, moreover, necessarily conditioned by the subjective forms of understanding. Each of these ideas appears, variously altered, in the work of Schopenhauer. For example, he explicitly accepts Kant's distinction between the noumenal and the phenomenal. And he agrees that the phenomena are conditioned by the forms of subjective understanding. Kant's doctrine that we can know the world by appearances only is expressed by Schopenhauer in terms of the "world as idea." That is, the public world that we perceive and talk about is mediated by our senses so that we never have an object directly to mind, but only a perception or an idea of it. The world, then, is present to us *as idea*.

But here we come to a significant departure from Kant. Kant made no exceptions to the doctrine that the world is known as idea, but Schopenhauer does. Kant said that we never know a thing-in-itself, but Schopenhauer said that there is one thing that *can* be known in-itself, and that is the self, or the body. Thus I can never know a tree-in-itself, for it is always mediated by ideas. But Schopenhauer insists that I can know my-*self*-in-itself, for it is not mediated by ideas but directly present to me in my experience. Schopenhauer allows that we have a curious relationship with our bodies, for they are the only slice of reality that can be known both as phenomena (e.g., when I look at my bleeding foot) and as noumena (e.g., when I feel the pain). In other words, the body may be known either as object or as subject. Schopenhauer then declares that when we experience the subject intuitively, in-itself, we find that its ultimate nature is *will*. Human reality, phenomenally speaking, is known by the idea of body, but noumenally speaking it is will: "The body is given in two entirely different ways. . . . It is given as an idea in intelligent perception, as an object among objects and subject to the laws of objects. And it is also given in quite a different way as that which is immediately known to every one, and is signified by the word *will*."[101]

Here we see the metaphysical principle that informs the title of Schopenhauer's major work, *The World as Will and Idea*. This metaphysical principle expresses a distinction between reality and appearance: The world as will is the real world, whereas the world as idea is the world of mere appearances. Physical objects, our bodies included, are the objective manifestations of will—or rather, our bodies *are* will as mediated by the subjective conventions of space, time, and cause-effect. And the same holds for our thoughts as well. Bodies, thought, reason itself are grounded in will. Everything in reality is grounded in the cosmic will, which Schopenhauer insists is without meaning, origin, or destiny. It is fundamentally blind and irrational. The perception that nature is rational (the Enlightenment view) is illusory. In reality the world is will alone— a driving, struggling force field of urging after nothing in particular. Just to *be* is the purpose. Reality is the will of being raging against annihilation.

Is nature rational? No, it is willful. Are humans rational? Ultimately humans are willful too. Reason is no more than rationalization of the will. So what can be said of the Enlightenment doctrine of unlimited progress toward happiness through the application of reason? This is the ultimate deception. Reason, science, law, the state, religion are all devices we use to gratify the urges of the ego. They actually create and sustain the illusion of the world as idea. And they can offer no more than "palliations and anodynes" in the forms of names, doctrines, and theories to disguise the true pain, suffering, and misery that is nature. Artistic genius can do more than theory to provide relief from the veil of illusion, for art is less rationalized and therefore less deceptive than theory. But it is true philosophy (i.e., the philosophy of the Hindu Upanishads) that has the most to offer. The ultimate goal of philosophy is not to reinforce the deceptions of reason with sophistical arguments but rather to undeceive humanity by derationalizing the will to the point of silence:

> From this we can understand how blessed the life of a man must be whose will is silenced, not merely for a moment, as in the enjoyment of the beautiful, but for ever, indeed altogether extinguished, except as regards the last glimmering spark that retains the body in life, and will be extinguished in death. . . . He now looks back smiling and at rest on the delusions of this world, which once were able to move and agonize his spirit also, but which now stand before him as utterly indifferent to him. . . . Life and its forms now pass before him as a fleeting illusion, as a light morning dream before half-waking eyes, the real world already shining through it so that it can no longer deceive.[102]

IV. THE CONTEMPORARY PERIOD

The contemporary period has been characterized by an expanding crisis of self-understanding. New developments in the natural and social sciences, momentous social, economic, and political events, and an astonishing series of technological revolutions have all carried implications for the ongoing task of comprehending and articulating the contours of the human condition. Novelty has been so accelerated and so open to interpretation that a contemporary consensus about humanity's proper orientation in nature and in history appears far beyond reasonable expectation. Radically new and divergent perspectives on the human prospect have emerged during the twentieth century, and they have stimulated a range of reactionary attempts to reinvigorate the orthodoxies of the past. And yet, despite the remarkable diversity of philosophical, social, scientific, and religious trajectories during the contemporary period, it is still possible to discern a persistent underlying concern about the source and the dangers of deception.

Existentialism

Existentialism is a quasi-literary movement which has its roots in the writings of Feodor Dostoevsky, Søren Kierkegaard, and Friedrich Nietzsche. The movement was given further definition and philosophical rigor by Martin Heidegger and Jean-Paul Sartre, and became a significant element in popular mentality during the decades after World War II. Existentialism has clear affinities to the romantic movement. It rejects the attempt to work out an objective and rational account of all reality, and it specifically rejects the view that human existence can be adequately defined by the abstractions of any philosophical system. Hegel was the principal target for the early existentialists. Hegel was an extreme rationalist who claimed to have discovered the logical secrets obeyed by all of reality. Reality proceeds, he said, by the predetermined and progressive unfolding of a universal dialectic. The essence of a thing (or a person) may be seen in its ultimate dialectical relations. The existentialists allowed for the possibility that nonhuman entities may be adequately described by the abstract categories of a deterministic rationalistic system, but to describe human existence in such terms was to them sheer lunacy. Human beings are unique; their existence cannot be described by some preconceived logical essence. Thus Kierkegaard was prompted to declare that, insofar as humans are concerned, "existence precedes essence." By this he means to emphasize the radical freedom of individual human beings to determine their own essence apart from established systems of thought. The Hegelians of the world mistakenly assume that existing as a human being is like adjusting to a job description—that is, one first masters a description of how things must go and then tries to conform to it. But for Kierkegaard this is to put the theory of existence before the fact of existence: "Life can only be explained after it has been lived."[103] Kierkegaard, like the romantics he so admired, was deeply suspicious of the conventional bourgeois life. Such a life, he thought, had the effect of leveling individuals into a homogeneous crowd of mediocrity and boredom. Life within the crowd has an element of security about it, to be sure, for it enables the individual to escape the anguish of isolation and subjectivity. But the danger of life in a crowd is ultimate, for it precludes the possibility of genuine self-fulfillment. To allow one's self to be objectively defined by conventional standards—the standards of popular religion, say, or bourgeois morality, wealth, fame, power, the aesthetic or hedonistic life, or even the campish rebellion of romantic heroism—is to become a fraction, to be leveled, to become an echo, a nonentity.

Kierkegaard's point is that to fall into step with the crowd is to be deceived, and deception is the greatest of all dangers to the human being. The crowd is, after all, an illusion: "In order that everything should be reduced to the same level it is first of all necessary to produce a phantom, a spirit, a monstrous abstraction, an all-embracing something which is nothing, a mirage—and that phantom is *the public*."[104] To enter the crowd is therefore to enter into a deception, a falsehood: "A crowd in its very concept is the untruth, by reason of the fact that it renders the individual completely unpenitent and irresponsible, or at least weakens his sense of responsibility by reducing it to a fraction."[105] To the extent that individuals are drawn into the crowd by social pressures, they are deceived by the phantom public, and to the extent that they flee into the crowd to avoid the anguish of subjectivity, they are self-deceived by their own sophistries. The difference is negligible, and the central fact of human existence remains: It is human vulnerability to deception that constitutes our greatest threat. For Kierkegaard there is only one way to avoid deception, and that is to find the courage to leave the crowd behind, to journey in solitude toward the truth that can be found only in subjectivity: "It [the leveling process] can therefore only be stopped by the individual's attaining the religious courage which springs from his individual religious isolation."[106]

It may be inaccurate to apply the label "existentialist" to Kierkegaard and Nietzsche, yet it is impossible to imagine the development of existentialism apart from their influence. This is especially true of Nietzsche, for many of the twentieth-century existentialists (e.g., Karl Jaspers, Heidegger, Sartre) take Nietzsche as their point of departure. Nietzsche's work begins with the assumption of nihilism, by which he means a radical rejection of the moral interpretation of the world. A moral interpretation is one that regards the universe as somehow imbued with value, one that views reality as having a meaning and a purpose which can be apprehended in one way or another by human understanding. Nihilism rejects such moralistic interpretations, insisting that the universe just *is*, without purpose, without justification, without objective meaning. Nietzsche affirms the nihilistic view and takes upon himself the role of undermining the received morality of his day (viz. Christianity) toward the end of preparing Western culture for the self-conscious task of constructing its own values anew. The critique of Christianity is fundamental to Nietzsche's work, and fundamental to this critique is the judgment that Christianity is a monstrous lie: "Wherever the theologians' instinct extends, value judgments have been stood on their heads and the concepts of 'true' and 'false' are of necessity reversed: whatever is most harmful to life is called 'true'; whatever elevates it, enhances, affirms, justifies it, and makes it triumphant, is called 'false.' "[107] Nietzsche believed that all values are human constructions, and that no system of values could be objectively and universally validated by either rational or empirical means. But Nietzsche's moral relativism did not dispose him to the view that all value systems had equal merit insofar as human life was concerned. Value systems are relative, sure enough, but relative to the human prospect some value systems are degenerate. Christianity, Nietzsche thought, was the most life-negating and degenerate religion imaginable.

Yet the facts of history might encourage the opposite conclusion: that Christianity, quite apart from its rational and empirical credentials, has enabled many believers to endure life, and thus has demonstrated its life-enhancing utility. But to Nietzsche's way of thinking there is all the difference in the world between enduring life and living it. For the endurance of life a deception is perfectly sufficient, "and it certainly does appear . . . that life depends on appearance; I mean, on error, simulation, deception, self-deception; and life has, as a matter of fact, always shown itself to be on the side of the most unscrupulous *polytropoi*."[108] If one seeks endurance or blessed repose in life, then a lie may be just the thing. In fact, one might take the comfort value of an idea as a measure of its power to deceive. Moreover, to speak of enduring life is already to have decided that life is an evil. But for Nietzsche this is precisely the point of Christianity's moral failure. The point of life, for him, is not simply to endure it passively in a state of blessed assurance but rather to overcome it, to take it fully on its own terms and to make something more of it, to affirm its every dimension and to enlarge it, to transcend it by giving expression to the will to power. To imbibe a holy lie may in fact make life more palatable but it is also to refuse life on its own terms, and to do so is to refuse the reality of life itself. And this "no" to reality is the substance of the Christian deception: "In the Christian world of ideas there is nothing that has the least contact with reality—and it is in the instinctive hatred of reality that we have recognized the only motivating force at the root of Christianity."[109]

Nietzsche, then, rejects the utilitarian conception of truth because the standards of utility nourish deceptive negations of life. For him, a "yes" to life implies a will to truth: "Consequently, 'will to truth' does *not* mean 'I will not let myself be deceived' but—there is no choice—'I will not deceive, not even myself': *and with this we are on the ground of morality*."[110] Nietzsche is here identifying the will to truth with the will to power, his standard for the truly self-conscious moral life.

For both Kierkegaard and Nietzsche, then, the measure of one's moral character, or one's essential humanity, is the extent to which one can avoid deception. This fundamental theme, carried forward by the existentialists of the twentieth century, is given its most forceful expression in Sartre's doctrine of "bad faith."

Sartre, like other existentialists, places great emphasis upon the unique and radical freedom of human beings. Human freedom is the key to existentialism: "What is at the very heart and center of existentialism, is the absolute character of the free commitment, by which every man realizes himself."[111] Apart from radical freedom, there is nothing whatever to say about the nature of humanity. Human nature is defined by human beings in the course of exercising their freedom. What is important for human beings is just how they define themselves by the choices they make. Humans are free to choose; their choices issue forth in particular actions, and by these actions individuals constitute themselves. For Sartre, human beings are not what they eat, nor are they what they inherit plus what they learn; for him human beings *are* what they *choose*. And since individuals create themselves in choices freely taken, they are left with no excuses. The absolute freedom of the individual to define her own being implies absolute responsibility for that being: "We are left alone, without excuse. That is what I mean when I say that man is condemned to be free. Condemned, because he did not create himself, yet is nevertheless at liberty, and from the moment that he is thrown into this world he is responsible for everything he does."[112] Recognition of this human state of absolute freedom and acceptance of absolute responsibility for the consequences of one's choices puts the individual in the condition of "good faith." One acts in good faith when one refuses recourse to such excuses as "I couldn't help it because I was angry" or "I couldn't help it because I was raised that way." If, however, one attempts to avoid the anguish of freedom by taking refuge in excuses or in assigning responsibility for one's actions to some theory of human nature, then one is acting from a condition of "bad faith" or self-deception.

It is on the basis of this doctrine of bad faith that Sartre claims the authority to make moral judgments about the character of an individual. Moral judgments, he says, have no bearing upon moral content, or the values inherent in an act; rather they bear upon the *form* or the existential matrix of an act. Moral values are chosen, and thus existentialism claims no authority to pass judgment on their content. Sartre's atheism leaves the construction of values entirely in the realm of human freedom, so that "everyone can do what he likes, and will be incapable, from such a point of view, of condemning either the point of view or the action of anyone else."[113] Yet existentialism does render moral judgments about the psychological conditions from which acts proceed:

We can judge, nevertheless, for, as I have said, one chooses in view of others, and in view of others one chooses himself. One can judge, first that in certain cases choice is founded upon an error, and in others upon the truth. One can judge a man by saying that he deceives himself. Since we have defined the situation of man as one of free choice, without excuse and without help, any man who takes refuge behind the excuse of his passions, or by inventing some deterministic doctrine, is a self-deceiver. One may object: 'But why should he not choose to deceive himself?' I reply that it is not for me to judge him morally, but I define his self-deception as an error. Here one cannot avoid pronouncing a judgment of truth. The self-deception is evidently a falsehood, because it is a dissimulation of man's complete liberty of commitment. . . . Thus, in the name of that will to freedom which is implied in freedom itself, I can form judgments upon those who seek to hide from themselves the wholly voluntary nature of their existence and its complete freedom. . . . Thus, although the content of morality is variable, a certain form of this morality is universal.[114]

One might conclude, then, that there is no more profound bias in existentialist thought than its bias against the deception and self-deception of individuals. In fact, one might offer the interpretation that by existentialist principles one achieves authentic existence only to the extent that one becomes undeceived.

Analytic Philosophy

Throughout the eighteenth century and well into the nineteenth, the philosophy of empiricism held sway in Britain. As empiricism developed it was augmented by the moral theory of utilitarianism, and together they fashioned the modern British genius: analytical, piecemeal, fact-oriented, friendly to science, precise, and distrustful of general speculation. This fusion of empiricism and utilitarianism created a climate favorable to science and democratic political reforms. But the British mind-set was not without its critics, and as the romantic movement swelled, a popular reaction opened many British intellectuals to the influence of Hegelian idealism. During the latter half of the nineteenth century, therefore, idealism flourished on British soil. It was in reaction to this idealist interlude that the tradition of analytic philosophy found its roots.

The realist reaction was led by G. E. Moore and Bertrand Russell. Moore began his academic career as a classicist, and he was drawn into philosophy by the bewilderment he experienced upon hearing certain propositions put forth by idealist philosophers. When Moore considered, for example, McTaggart's claim that time is unreal, his reaction was to wonder about the sense in which the proposition could be meaningful. He was certain that McTaggart could not mean that breakfast does not come before lunch. But what, then, *did* the proposition purport to say? Clearly, propositions such as "time is unreal" need further analysis to clarify their meaning. Moore inaugurated the analytical tradition with his insistence that a significant part of the philosopher's role was to engage in analysis of propositions in order to prevent the deceptive effects of conceptual obscurity.

Russell's work in logic serves as a paradigm for the larger program of analytical philosophy. In the monumental *Principia Mathematica*, co-authored with Alfred North Whitehead, Russell attempted to show that mathematical concepts could be analyzed by the more primary concepts of logic. Numbers, for example, could be replaced by logical constructions. Russell soon realized that this principle of analysis had larger philosophical applications. Philosophers, he thought, were disposed to make assumptions about all sorts of unnecessary and dubious entities, often with the result that they became hopelessly befuddled. With the aid of logical analysis the number of metaphysical assumptions could be reduced, and thus vulnerability to confusion and self-deception could be minimized. Thus Russell set out to develop a "logically perfect language" that could be used to analyze not only mathematical concepts but also the supposed entities of science and common sense. The philosophy known as logical atomism represents Russell's attempt to work out the details of this analytical program. Just as the vocabulary of numbers might be eliminated in favor of logical constructions, Russell thought, the vocabulary of "things" might be replaced by the more primary vocabulary of sense data. Russell did not deny the existence of things (e.g., tables, chairs), he only asserted that their most primitive meaning could be expressed in terms of sense data. Russell thus sidestepped various metaphysical issues by substituting sense-data talk for object talk. He was convinced that there occurred no loss of meaning in this analytical dodge, and—this is the point of it all—by reducing our metaphysical assumptions about "things" we commensurately reduce our vulnerability to deception.[115]

In 1921 Ludwig Wittgenstein, an erstwhile student and eventual colleague of Russell, published his *Tractatus Logico-Philosophicus*. The historical influence of this work was immense, for it both pronounced the obituary for logical atomism and inspired the birth of logical positivism. Wittgenstein came to see that all attempts to speak philosophically would take one beyond the limits of language. If our scientific language pictures what our senses tell us about facts in the world, then what is pictured by *philosophical* language? Philosophical language, he believed, attempted to say something in a realm where nothing could be meaningfully said. The implication being that metaphysics is an illegitimate and deluded enterprise. Wittgenstein then closed the door on metaphysics with the dogmatic claim that "what we cannot speak about we must pass over in silence." Wittgenstein's view is that the traditional problems of philosophy are merely pseudoproblems, and those who pursue them are deceived in their failure to see that they have trespassed beyond the limits of intelligible discourse. The only way to avoid the deception is to quit doing traditional philosophy. If philosophers want to remain on the scene, let them apply themselves to the task of undeceiving would-be metaphysicians: "The correct method in philosophy would really be the following: to say nothing except what can be said, i.e. propositions of natural science—i.e. something that has nothing to do with philosophy—and then, whenever someone else wanted to say something metaphysical, to demonstrate to him that he had failed to give a meaning to certain signs in his propositions."[116]

Wittgenstein's critique of traditional philosophy was very appealing to a group of scientists, mathematicians, and philosophers in Vienna who had a particular interest in advancing the scientific worldview to the detriment of metaphysics. The Vienna Circle, as they came to be known, began meeting after 1922 to discuss various problems pertinent to the philosophy of science. Early in their proceedings they focused on a reading of the *Tractatus*, which eventually inspired a distinctive school of philosophy called logical positivism.

The positivists set out to show that all of science could be reduced to physics, much as Russell demonstrated that all of mathematics was reducible to logic. The aim was a noble one: the unification of the sciences. And correlate to this goal was the aggressive rejection of all nonscientific knowledge claims, especially those of metaphysics and theology. As frequently happens in such intellectual movements, the positivists spent more effort on their negative program than on the positive one, and earned greater notoriety for it. They developed elaborate schemes and criteria in their attempts to demonstrate the delusory character of metaphysics. The most famous of these ideas is the so-called principle of verification, which was put forward as a criterion to judge the cognitive significance of any proposition. The positivists were fond of classifying the various types of language use. In their scheme *cognitive* statements were used to express genuine knowledge, *emotive* statements were used to express feelings, and *imperative* statements were used to express commands. The positivists were concerned chiefly about the deception that might arise when these various uses became confused. For example, we can easily be deceived into thinking that an emotive expression—say, "Murder is wrong"—has legitimate cognitive meaning. After all, it sounds as if it were making a legitimate claim to know something. The principle of verification was intended as a criterion to determine which statements were cognitively meaningful and which were not. A refined version of the principle rules that a statement is cognitively meaningful if it is in principle open to verification or falsification. The principle can also be stated as a question: For any statement, are there any observations that would be relevant to the determination of its truth or falsehood? If the answer is yes, then the observations must be listed and evaluated. But if the answer is no, then the statement in question is cognitively meaningless.

The positivists were confident that metaphysical and theological statements would fail this test of cognitive significance, and therefore could be dismissed from serious consideration. The rule, in other words, was employed for the purpose of undeceiving those who held metaphysical, ethical, and theological assertions to be expressions of truth. These notions are clearly expressed in Rudolf Carnap's explanation of the Vienna Circle's rejection of metaphysics:

> Thus we find a great deal of similarity between metaphysics and lyrics. But there is one decisive difference between them. Both have no representative function, no theoretical content. A metaphysical statement, however,—as distinguished from a lyrical verse—seems to have such a content, and by this not only is the reader deceived, but the metaphysician himself. He believes that in his metaphysical treatise he has asserted something, and is led by this into argument and polemics against the statements of some other metaphysician. A poet, however, does not assert that the verses of another are wrong or erroneous; he usually contents himself with calling them bad.
>
> The non-theoretical character of metaphysics would not be in itself a defect; all arts have this non-theoretical character without thereby losing their high value for personal as well as for social life. The danger lies in the *deceptive* character of metaphysics; it gives the illusion of knowledge without actually giving any knowledge. This is the reason why we reject it.[117]

Wittgenstein had only tangential relations with the logical positivists. He was living in Austria during the creative years of the movement, and he even met with the Vienna Circle on occasion as they discussed his *Tractatus*. But for all practical purposes he had given up the vocation of philosophy. And then in 1929 he suddenly returned to Cambridge with renewed interest and thereupon set about to transform analytic philosophy yet again.

Much has been written about the elements of continuity and change represented in Wittgenstein's new way of doing philosophy, but in the end it comes down to this: Wittgenstein retained his earlier views about the goal of philosophy but he revised his thinking about the proper methods for achieving it. The early Wittgenstein believed that philosophical problems were on the order of pseudoproblems; that is, they were not genuine problems to be *solved* but rather a set of problematic conditions to be *dissolved*. This outlook on the status of philosophical problems and the therapeutic goal of philosophy is not much changed in the later Wittgenstein. But his conception of the proper method of philosophical therapy underwent considerable revision, and the revision had to do with a new attitude toward the nature of language. It seems appropriate to say that the later Wittgenstein approached the business of philosophical analysis in a less dogmatic spirit and with fewer prejudices about the nature of language than were evinced by earlier logical methods of analysis. Implicit in earlier methods were strict preconceptions about the conditions under which expressions could have meaning. Wittgenstein's own earlier conception of the pictorial function of language is one example. And when one has fixed and narrow ideas about the proper use of language, one is inclined to formulate criteria which can be used to enforce its use within the approved limits. The positivist principle of verification was one such criterion—it ruled out as meaningless any utterances which did not conform to the scientific paradigm of language use.

But as the later Wittgenstein came to realize, scientific uses of language represent only a small slice of the rich and varied range of ways in which language can have legitimate meanings. The mistake of logical atomism and of logical positivism was in the assumption that the set of rules governing the scientific use of language was the *only* one. But, as Wittgenstein insists, there are other sets of rules for others of life's varied objectives. The concept of language games is helpful here. There is in life a whole range of language games, just as there is a range of conventional games. And to insist that all games follow, say, the rules of chess is to impose unrealistic conditions. Nor does it help us to *understand* other games to approach them with the rules of chess at hand. It is no less ridiculous to assume that the language game of science is the only legitimate game, nor is it any less misleading when one's purpose is to understand language.

Wittgenstein's new appreciation for the diversity of language games suggested to him that if one wants to understand language, it is essential to examine linguistic usages in their appropriate contexts. The appropriate context for the analysis of language is in association with the form of life which is facilitated by the language game. "To imagine a language," Wittgenstein says, "means to imagine a form of life."[118] When we examine language in its proper context—that is, in connection with its peculiar form of life—what we observe is the conspicuous absence of philosophical problems. When language is used as it was intended (or as it evolved), philosophical problems do not arise. It is only when words and expressions are misused, or used apart from their proper niche, that philosophical problems begin to bother us. It is the abuse of language that deceives us into philosophical perplexity.

Even though Wittgenstein considered philosophical problems to be pseudo-problems, it was not his intention to trivialize them as petty mistakes: "The problems arising through a misinterpretation of our forms of language have the character of *depth*. They are deep disquietudes; their roots are as deep in us as the forms of our language and their significance is as great as the importance of our language." It is the deeply disquieting character of these problems that gives urgency to the task of philosophical analysis. Philosophical problems have the power to bewitch our intelligence, to deceive us into existential difficulties. And it is the role of philosophy to free us from these difficulties by undeceiving us: "What is your aim in philosophy?—to show the fly out of the fly-bottle."[119] We might say, then, that what remains consistent throughout Wittgenstein's zigzag career is precisely what has remained consistent throughout the entire career of Western philosophy: a conviction that it is the central task of philosophy to contravene deception.

Theories of Mental Health

In the centuries since the Enlightenment we have witnessed a proliferation of psychological theories which attempt to reveal the key to what has variously been called mental health, the well-adjusted personality, the integrated mind, the actualized self, OK-ness, and so on. I will make no attempt here to present a comprehensive survey of these theories, but will merely dip into the sea of contemporary psychology for a small but representative sampling of its three dominant theoretical currents: the Freudian, behaviorist, and humanistic orientations. My purpose is to see whether the concept of deception plays as fundamental a role in psychology as it does in religion and philosophy. If it does, we will have made a further advance on the thesis that the bias against deception is a fundamental feature of the Western mind.

It has been said that every discussion of personality theory must either begin or end with Freud—such was his influence in shaping contemporary psychological thinking about the structures and dynamics of personality. Freud's views on the elements of mental health were assembled in the context of a materialistic and mechanistic worldview. Just as the scientists of his day were inclined to describe nature in terms of mass, force, and the conservation of energy, so Freud tended to describe the dynamics of mental health in terms of their psychological counterparts. His view of psychodynamics compares favorably with models of fluid dynamics, in which the behavior of a system is the outcome of forces being accommodated to and by counterforces throughout the system. Freud defined mental health minimally as the ability to love and to work. But this ability is not innate; it must develop in the individual through the resolution of fundamental conflicts. When these conflicts are insufficiently or inappropriately resolved, psychotherapy is called for.

For Freud, the basic structures of the individual psyche have their origin in what might be called a social contract. Human beings, threatened at every turn by the elemental forces of nature, sought to overcome their helplessness by forming cooperative communities. The creation of civilization, however, was a mixed blessing. While it allowed humans to prevail against the forces of nature, it also created the conditions for individual psychological conflicts. Social norms, the conditions for collective living, required each individual to make sacrifices by producing work and renouncing basic animal instincts. These sacrifices are the *sine qua non* of communal life, but the making of them establishes a fundamental pattern of conflict within each individual. Freud pictures the conflict in terms of tension between the pleasure principle and the reality principle. All individuals are driven by primitive forces to seek pleasure, but they must mitigate this drive in view of the physical and social realities at hand. These elements of conflict are the source of the three principal components of the personality: id, ego, and superego. The id is the mental structure which seeks to gratify instinctual biological forces. It represents the savage, undisciplined, pleasure-seeking energy that is characteristic of all life forms. This is the driving force that must be contained by the reality principle. At the opposite extreme is the superego, which represents the social norms internalized by the individual. These norms are the ideational forms of perfection as they are articulated in the social order and ingested by the individual psyche. The ego, the rational component of the mind, functions to negotiate harmony between the forces of pleasure and reality.

In the development of the individual the ego is strengthened to the extent that it allies itself with the interests of pleasure and reality alike. That is, it seeks to advance the gratification of instincts, on the one hand, but seeks to do so within the limits of social norms, on the other. If the ego is not strong enough to repress or to redirect the unpleasant impulses of the unconscious mind, the individual will inevitably lose touch with reality and enter into a psychotic state ruled by the chaotic pleasure principle. In its own defense, then, the ego employs a range of mechanisms to maintain control over these impulses. In many respects these defense mechanisms are expedient, infantile, and ultimately deceptive attempts to resolve conflict. And whenever repressed impulses remain insufficiently reconciled to reality we may expect to see symptoms of neurosis. The variety of neurotic symptoms is vast, but they have one thing in common: All are illusory substitutes for ungratified subconscious drives. Freud's discussion of religion provides a good view of defense mechanisms at work:

A special importance attaches to the case in which this attempt to procure a certainty of happiness and a protection against suffering through a delusional remoulding of reality is made by a considerable number of people in common. The religions of mankind must be classed among the mass-delusions of this kind. No one, needless to say, who shares a delusion ever recognizes it as such.[120]

But though defense mechanisms and collective delusions may enable the individual to achieve a tolerable level of functioning for the moment, the neurotic condition can hardly be described as optimal mental health. Whenever conflicts remain unresolved, stress-induced psychosis may erupt. The neurotic remains an unstable hostage to illusions and cannot become free until the reality of the unconscious, fearful though it may be, is brought to full awareness to expose illusions for what they really are. And herein lies the aim of psychoanalysis, which is to free the individual for a responsible life of love and work by the process of undeceiving.

The behaviorist tradition in psychology began early in the twentieth century as an attempt to reconstruct psychological inquiry along rigorously empirical lines. The intention was to place psychology on the same methodological foundations as the so-called hard sciences. This methodological transposition exhorted psychologists to conform to the operational point of view, which states that the basic terms of any science must refer to events (or operations) that are publicly observable and testable. Behaviorism was a profoundly revolutionary development within psychology because it appeared to challenge the very subject matter of the discipline. Psychology, on the behaviorist model, would no longer be the study of the mind, or the soul (psyche), but rather the study of observable behavior with reference to environmental contingencies.

The behaviorist thesis called for the elimination of all mentalistic concepts; that is, concepts that refer to internal states which are of necessity not publicly observable. These concepts include mind, consciousness, self-awareness, personality, sensation, thinking, image, wish, will, purpose, fear, love, and the like. Everyday speech is laden with such mentalistic terms, all of which J. B. Watson called "heritages of a savage past," by which he meant vestiges of the ancient dualism of body and soul. Mentalistic concepts may have been serviceable in the ancient past but they are out of place in a scientific age. They are more than out of place, they are obstructive to human understanding and to social progress because they reinforce an inadequate conception of the reality of human behavior.

Behaviorists, then, like the logical positivists, took on a negative program along with a positive one: They would debunk mentalism while they explained the dynamics of human behavior. The trouble with mentalism is that it deceives us into regarding its unobservable referents as genuine causal factors, whereas they are merely illusorily so. If you were to ask someone why she ran away from a dog, for example, you might get the mentalistic reply "Because I was afraid." In this instance the behavior is attributed to *fear*, which by virtue of our dualistic heritage is regarded as a state of mind, which in turn is regarded as an immaterial causal agent. Behaviorism rejects such explanations as vacuous pseudo-explanations, because fear is not a cause but rather an effect of previous and observable environmental contingencies. That is to say, the person behaved fearfully because she learned, in some antecedent context, that dogs are harmful. To attribute the behavior to a fearful mental state is to stop the inquiry short of genuine causes. As B. F. Skinner puts it, "Mentalistic explanations allay curiosity and bring inquiry to a stop. It is so easy to observe feelings and states of mind at a time and in a place which make them seem like causes that we are not inclined to inquire further. Once the environment begins to be studied, however, its significance cannot be denied."[121]

The "realities" of which mentalism speaks are misconstrued as causes. And one who regards them as such is every bit as deceived by appearances as one who attributes the wind to the windmill. Skinner does not say that experiences of fear do not occur, he merely disputes the conclusion that a fearful mental state is anything more than an activity caused in the organism by external and observable events. It is not a causal factor to be taken seriously in any account of behavior. Skinner attributes the error of mentalism to the process of introspection. Introspection is the methodology of mentalism, it is the act of examining our own subjective experience, whereby we are likely to observe feelings of fear, joy, rage, and other emotional responses. The mentalistic fallacy is to associate these feelings with behaviors that immediately follow them. It is the proximity of mental states to behaviors which follow them that deceives us into making a bogus causal connection: "Feelings occur at just the right time to serve as causes of behavior, and they have been cited as such for centuries."[122]

Introspection, therefore, is a source of deception because it gives us false causal explanations in place of true ones. But this is no trivial and harmless illusion. Mentalism is a serious error indeed, for it effectively precludes human progress by locking us into a false perception of our own nature: "Mentalism kept attention away from the external antecedent events which might have explained behavior, by seeming to supply an alternative explanation."[123]

The mentalistic fallacy lends itself to theories of personality which stress freedom and dignity as the final goals of human existence. To these ends individuals are encouraged to strengthen their sense of self, to get in touch with their deepest feelings, to develop their character, to adopt a system of values, or any number of other strategies that make appeals to "the inner self." The emphasis in mentalistic psychotherapies is upon *being* a certain way and not upon *behaving* in a certain way. The mentalistic way to freedom and dignity is to strengthen internal causal agency. But to the behaviorist this appeal to inner resources is both deceptive and ironic. The irony is that the doctrine of freedom and dignity has closed the mentalist mind to the very techniques that can liberate human beings from the problems that threaten to make human life miserable and undignified. For their part, the behaviorists disparage grandiose theories of personal development. They rather focus piecemeal on particular problems, specifying programs of behavior modification to solve them. Real solutions to human problems call for changes in the causal nexus—that is, changes in patterns of reinforcement—not transformations of the inner self. For behaviorists there is no inner self—as Skinner once remarked, "the individual is nothing, the environment is everything."

It will be observed that behaviorism does not have a theory of mental health. Whatever mental health may amount to, behaviorism will find the conditions for it in the social environment. Instead of theories of mental health and personal development behaviorism offers techniques for social progress. But the absolute prerequisite for this revolutionary program is to countervail the deceptive influence of mentalism.

Humanistic psychology has been called "the third force" in psychology, as distinguished from Freudian psychoanalysis and behaviorism. At first glance the distinction may appear rather weak, especially in light of the fact that some humanistic psychologists, notably Abraham Maslow, claim also to be Freudians *and* behaviorists. But while there are significant theoretical overlaps, humanistic psychologists differ so markedly in their regard for the character of the discipline that they cannot be denied their own stall. Some observers may argue that humanistic psychologists tend to be less rigorously scientific than mainstream Freudians and behaviorists, but these psychologists insist that psychology should be more than *merely* scientific. Against the Freudians, humanistic psychologists stress the positive aspects of human existence. Freudian theory was developed to account for pathological conditions; it was not focused on what might be regarded as the ideal goal of personal development. Like medicine, it defined health as the absence of disease. Moreover, Freud was not exactly sanguine about the human condition. For him the world was a hostile place, society was a source of frustration, and the self was something to be "cured." The humanistic tradition takes a rosier view of things. And against the behaviorists, humanistic psychologists stress the uniqueness and dignity of the human being. They focus attention on the *experiencing person* rather than on the behaving organism. Behaviorists were so intent upon enhancing the status of psychology as an empirical science that they tended to dehumanize persons by regarding them as response emitters. Against both of these major orientations the humanistic psychologists insist upon viewing behavior with reference to experience, and experience with reference to the realization of its full human potential.

Humanistic psychology is a broadly heterogeneous grouping of psychological theories, and for this reason no single figure can represent the entire movement. Nevertheless, if anyone can be described as a mainstream humanistic psychologist it is the founder of the movement, Abraham Maslow. Maslow did not accept the behaviorist view that the individual is nothing and the environment is everything. For him an irreducible reality called the "self" or the "person" has causal influence on all but the most uninteresting and negligible human behavior. On this point all of the humanistic psychologists agree. The differences begin to emerge as they describe the manifestation of this undeniable internal human reality. Maslow pictures the self in this way: "We have, each one of us, an essential human nature which is instinctoid, intrinsic, given, 'natural,' i.e. with an appreciable hereditary determinant, and which tends strongly to persist."[124]

We might also regard the self as the center of an impulse toward experience, for it is by the achievement of certain experiences that the process of self-actualization unfolds. The self seeks experiences by which it becomes progressively actualized. Having said that each self has common human characteristics, Maslow sets about to describe the development of human nature in terms of a hierarchy of needs. The self becomes actualized, he says, in the process of achieving the experiences which are delivered by the satisfaction of these common human needs. As the more basic needs are satisfied, the self presses on toward the satisfaction of higher needs. These needs, when fulfilled, represent the "symptoms" of mental health. The healthy person is the self-actualizing person, the one who operates at the highest level of need fulfillment: "[H]ealthy people have sufficiently gratified their basic needs for safety, belongingness, love, respect and self-esteem so that they are motivated primarily by trends to self-actualization."[125] But Maslow estimates the percentage of self-actualizing persons to be very low. Most human beings get stalled somewhere in the process and never get to the point of actualizing their own inner nature. Maslow says that the neurotic person is one who arrests the internal drive to growth by repressing it and controlling it by the use of defense mechanisms. One of the chief characteristics of the neurotic state is that it locks the individual into an unhealthy and deceptive mode of cognition, what Maslow calls "deficiency-cognition," or "D-cognition." Mental illness is associated with an impairment of one's ability to perceive reality: "Neurosis, psychosis, stunting of growth—all are, from this point of view, cognitive diseases as well, contaminating perception, learning, remembering, attending and thinking."[126] D-cognition is typical of the neurotic state. This mode of cognition is defensively motivated; it has a selfish "angle" on the world; it is organized around the ego, which projects itself into percepts; it is highly selective in attention; it is a thoroughly subjective mode of cognition which actively distorts and denies reality. D-cognition represents a state of extended vulnerability to deception and self-deception. It experiences the natural and social worlds as diminished and distorted, not as they are in themselves.

The process of restoration to mental health is, for Maslow, a liberation of the inherent impulse to growth and self-actualization, but it is also a movement from unreality to reality, from delusion to a healthy mode of cognition. The process of growth is a process of undeceiving: "I could describe self-actualization as a development of personality which frees the person . . . from the neurotic (or infantile, or fantasy, or unnecessary, or "unreal") problems of life, so that he is able to face, endure and grapple with the "real" problems of life. . . . That is, it is not an absence of problems but a moving from transitional or unreal problems to real problems."[127]

An adequate treatment of the place of deception and self-deception in contemporary psychology would fill several large volumes. I have made no attempt to survey the vast and diversified fields of clinical and applied psychology, which have been variously influenced by Freudian, behaviorist, and humanistic theories. These and related fields would figure in a full-scale treatment of the role of deception in psychology. This brief glimpse into the literature is intended merely to show that deception figures decisively in the thinking of key representatives of the major streams of psychological thought. These figures, at least, lend significant support to the thesis that deception is considered the fundamental obstacle to mental health.

Theories of Social Progress

Social progress has been variously defined in terms of freedom, prosperity, equality, national power, moral perfection, technological achievement, the acquisition of knowledge, and a host of similar collective goals. However it may be defined, the belief in progress itself is perhaps, as Robert Nisbet has argued, one of the most persistent and salutary beliefs in the history of Western culture.[128] Theories of social progress abound, each with its own views about what it is, what its forces are, whether it is necessary or contingent, and what impediments it faces. My purpose here is to ask whether or not the concept of deception plays a role in contemporary thinking about social progress. And for this purpose it is most promising to look at what some recent thinkers have had to say about the failures of history.

Paradoxical as it may seem, several twentieth-century thinkers came to regard the idea of progress as an obstacle to progress. The dominant view of the eighteenth and nineteenth centuries was that progress—social, political, economic, technological—was inevitable, unstoppable, inherent in the dynamics of history. Momentary setbacks were undeniable and to be expected, but in the long view all matters pertinent to the human condition could be expected to improve. This view came under heavy criticism early in the twentieth century, and especially after World War I. The main thrust of this criticism was not that progress was impossible but that it was contingent, not necessary or inevitable. The rose-colored optimistic view of the Enlightenment came to be regarded as an illusion which deceived people into complacency, under which conditions real progress would be precluded by inaction.

Georges Sorel argued in *The Illusions of Progress* that the idea of progress was a bourgeois fabrication used to legitimate and sustain the status quo. If workers could be convinced that historical circumstances were improving rather than worsening, they would tend not to consider rebellion. They would instead regard themselves as passive participants in the same complex of historical dynamics as their oppressors—fellows, as it were, in the stream of historical events. It was in the interests of the ruling class, therefore, to generate an ideology of progress.

But the ideology of progress, Sorel argued, could not be sustained by the facts of history. History tended rather to support a thesis of growing mediocrity and moral degeneracy. An unrestrained moralist, Sorel believed that the illusion of progress was instrumental in moral decline because its optimism encouraged ill regard for the future. To Sorel the ideology of progress was an enemy of real progress because it forestalled constructive revolutionary change by creating a false sense of solidarity between social classes, and because it promoted moral degeneracy by creating a false sense of confidence in the future. Genuine social and moral progress therefore calls the sociologist to undeceive the people: "It is my opinion that it would be well to submit one of these charlatan dogmas (that is, the idea of progress) to an analysis conducted according to that method which alone is able to guarantee us against all deception; that is, an analysis founded on a historical investigation of the relationships among the classes."[129]

Another critique of the doctrine of progress was articulated by neoorthodoxy, a theological movement which grew out of the widespread disillusionment that followed World War I. The movement began in Europe under the leadership of the Swiss theologian Karl Barth, but it was soon to find advocates in the United States, where Reinhold Niebuhr developed neoorthodoxy into a full-scale critique of the liberal culture inherited from the nineteenth century. The main thrust of Niebuhr's critique was that liberal culture had fallen victim to some serious illusions about human nature, and these illusions obstructed the realization of spiritual and historical fulfillment. As the term "neoorthodoxy" suggests, Niebuhr proclaims traditional doctrines of Christianity as the essential resources for unburdening modern culture of its delusions.

Niebuhr attributes the delusions of modern liberal culture to the condition of sin, which he understands according to the Pauline formula: To sin is "to exchange the truth about God for a lie." As Niebuhr puts it, "By giving life a false centre, the self destroys the real possibilities for itself and others."[130] Liberal culture is dominated at turns by two major errors of self-understanding: naturalism and rationalism. The lies of naturalism and rationalism have deceived modern humanity into a false sense of optimism and self-sufficiency.

The illusion of progress is based on the illusion of essential human goodness, and the illusion of goodness is based on a mistaken self-understanding: "The modern man is, in short, so certain about his essential virtue because he is so mistaken about his stature."[131] The modern mind remains committed to the illusion of progress because in its delusion about human nature it fails to see the setbacks in history for what they really are—that is, manifestations of evil: "The ultimate religious problem of evil does not arise for [liberalism] because it is always waiting for the perfect education or perfect social order which will make man moral."[132] The extent to which the liberal mind is deceived can be seen in the stubbornness with which it continues to affirm the essential goodness of humanity in spite of an abundance of contradictory evidence. So deluded is modern humanity that it both affirms what is clearly false and denies what is clearly true, with the result that it pursues all sorts of inappropriate schemes in the name of progress. But Niebuhr sees no possibility of progress in human affairs until the modern mind is disabused of its confused self-understanding. The critical element is for the human being to recognize its limits as a sinful creature before a sovereign God. But so deep is the mire of deception that the recognition of sin is remote: "[T]he self seems so deeply involved in its own deceptions . . . that it seems capable of neither repentence nor remorse." Yet by virtue of revelation the process of undeceiving may begin: "Only in a religion of revelation, whose God reveals Himself to man from beyond . . . can man discover the root of sin to be within himself. . . . Only within terms of the Christian faith can man not only understand the reality of the evil within himself but escape the error of attributing that evil to any one but himself."[133]

Ever since Locke warned against religious enthusiasm in the seventeenth century there has been a steady supply of advocates for the thesis that social progress is contingent upon stripping the mind of its religious delusions. Influential nineteenth-century expressions of this thesis came from Ludwig Feuerbach and Karl Marx. Feuerbach argued that theology is a mere mask for anthropology; that is, to talk of God is to talk in an infantile, self-alienating, and deluded manner about humanity. Feuerbach saw little hope of progress until humans recognized this illusion for what it was and then took measures to transform religion into politics. Marx continued Feuerbach's thesis in the context of his theory of class struggle. Religion, he said, was an opiate administered to the masses to keep them oblivious of their destitute condition. Not until the masses were undeceived of religious illusions would they find the political will to revolt against their oppressors: "The abolition of religion as the illusory happiness of the people is required for their real happiness. The demand to give up the illusions about its condition is the demand to give up a condition which needs illusions."[134]

It was arguments of this nature that helped to provoke the reactions of Fundamentalism and neoorthodoxy to the premises of liberal culture. But orthodox protests notwithstanding, the view that religion is an illusional impediment to social progress has continued to find advocates among contemporary intellectuals. Recent versions of the argument are perhaps most commonly associated with the loosely defined movement known as secular humanism.

Though most secular humanists object to being labeled "naysayers" rather than "yeasayers," it is nonetheless true that the negative aspects of the movement come through more forcefully than the positive aspects. Secular humanism expresses the view that humanity is essentially but not necessarily good, and if this goodness is to be actualized the human community must be guided by the natural resources of humanity rather than harbor illusions that supernatural beings may intervene to ensure human welfare. Thus Paul Kurtz, one of the authors of *The Humanist Manifesto* of 1973, writes as follows:

> The basic assumption of the new morality is the conviction that the good life is achieved when we realize human potential. This means that we ought to reject all those creeds and dogmas that impede human fulfillment or impose external authoritarian rules upon human beings. The traditional supernaturalistic moral commandments are especially repressive of our human needs. They are immoral insofar as they foster illusions about human destiny and suppress vital inclinations.[135]

Individual humanists have tended to single out particular supernaturalist doctrines for special scrutiny of the manner in which they impede social progress. The doctrine of immortality, for example, receives special notice in *The Humanist Manifesto*, as it does in books by Corliss Lamont. Lamont argues that the ideal of personal immortality is a "brain woven conceit," or an illusion produced by wishful thinking. The belief in immortality, he says, breaks down quickly under scrutiny and can be maintained only by the insidious means of denial and appeal to miracles and special revelation, all of which engender credulous habits of mind: "Hence only by believing in miracles can one give credence to the idea of personal immortality; and whoever believes in miracles can literally believe in any fantasy whatsoever." Lamont suggests that such illusions must be discarded in the interests of a mature perception of reality: "It is high time for us to cast aside the intellectual vagaries of the past, to think and act as mature men ready to cope with reality as it is. . . . And in working through to a sound view of life and destiny, we can take no more important step than to discard the illusion of immortality."[136]

In a similar fashion Walter Stace argues against the essence of the religious vision, which he defines as "the faith that there is a plan and purpose in the world, that the world is a moral order, that in the end all things are for the best."[137] But this vision, he says, is a grand illusion that cannot be sustained under the conditions of a scientific society. In fact, the evidence against this illusion of purpose in the cosmos is already firmly in place, as the record of modern science shows. So the question for Stace is not whether and how the undeceiving can be achieved but whether and how contemporary men and women will manage to lead civilized lives under the conditions of its achievement. The answer to this challenge is intellectual honesty:

> I am sure that the first thing we have to do is to face the truth, however bleak it may be, and then next we have to learn to live with it. Let me say a word about each of these two points. What I am urging as regards the first is complete honesty. Those who wish to resurrect Christian dogmas are not, of course, consciously dishonest. But they do have that kind of unconscious dishonesty which consists in lulling oneself with opiates and dreams. Those who talk of a new religion are merely hoping for a new opiate. Both alike refuse to face the truth that there is, in the universe outside man, no spirituality, no regard for values, no friend in the sky, no help or comfort for man of any sort. To be perfectly honest in the admission of this fact, not to seek new or old illusions, not to indulge in wishful dreams about this matter, this is the first thing we shall have to do. . . . Now about the other point, the necessity of learning to live with the truth. This means learning to live virtuously and happily, or at least contentedly, without illusions.[138]

One of the most compelling questions of modern history was asked by Konrad Adenauer in a policy speech in 1946: "How was this fall of the German people into the abyss possible?" This remains the central question which has attracted and preoccupied thousands of historians in the past half-century. And what is most impressive in the mass of accumulated historical commentary on the period is the unanimity with which the phenomena of deception figure in the answer. Accounts of the German abyss vary, to be sure, but virtually all accounts include the decisive role of deception. Variations are matters of emphasis, some accounts focusing on the universal human vulnerability to deception, others focusing on the particular vulnerability of the German people, and still others on the deceptive powers of the Nazi regime. But in no case, historians agree, can the dynamics of deception be left out of the picture.

George Mosse has argued that it is too simple to attribute to Hitler the sirenic power of a pied piper. The success of national socialism must find its account in the exploitation of something deep within the German spirit. Mosse finds the German vulnerability to Hitler in the development of an irrational "Volk" ideology which grew out of a long-standing German passion for achieving spiritual unity. This spiritual longing, he says, was for something more than mere social solidarity; the German quest for unity had something grandiose and metaphysical about it. Hitler's achievement was to create the impression that the German dream of ultimate destiny was imminent. The Nazi phenomenon, then, can be seen as an example of collective wish fulfillment.

Mosse repeatedly makes the point that if the appeals of national socialism had failed, some other variant of Volkish ideals would have succeeded in its place, so vulnerable were the Germans to any material and political confirmations of their collective illusions. Hitler's achievement was to bring forth the political organization and the public rituals that progressively convinced the Germans that "this is it, this is *finally it*." Deluded by metaphysical aspirations and expectations, the German masses saw in Hitler's program everything they were desperate to see and nothing more. That Hitler's exploitation was masterful in its cunning is not denied, but the critical point is that the Germans were psychologically predisposed by irrational Volkish ideology to respond to his deceits:

> Hitler took this opportunity, toward which all of Volkish history had led, and exploited it. Indeed, he drove it to its logical conclusion, for he gave it a concrete direction. . . . The German revolution was that "idealism of deeds" which Volkish thought had always advocated. To be sure, there were similar ideas in other nations . . . but only in Germany had Volkish thought prepared a specific context for this mysticism which enabled Hitler to dramatize and personalize his revolution.[139]

Mosse's study of ideology stresses the unique vulnerability of the German people to mass deception. Other accounts, while not directly inconsistent with his, have stressed the uniquely deceptive and manipulative character of the Nazi political engineers. In his study of Nazi leadership, for example, Joachim Fest concludes that national socialism lacked any consistent or substantive political principles. Ideology figured in the Nazi regime only as a tool to manipulate the masses and as a mask to conceal the psychopathologies of its leaders. In Fest's view the Nazi party leadership amounted to a pack of psychological misfits who festered in their disdain for humanity and who were driven not by ideas but by the will to power. Such men were ready to use any means at their disposal—rational or irrational, symbolic or terrorist—to bring the German people to the point of surrender. The unique genius of national socialism, Fest insists, was its galvanic propaganda:

Carrying it to an extreme, one might say that National Socialism was propaganda masquerading as ideology, that is to say, a will to power which formed its ideological theorems according to the maximum psychological advantage to be derived at any given moment, and drew its postulates from the moods and impulses of the masses, in the sensing of which it was abnormally gifted. . . . The majority of the ideological elements absorbed into National Socialism were nothing but material, assessed at varying degrees of effectiveness, for a ceaseless pyrotechnical display of propagandist agitation. Flags, Sieg Heils, fanfares, marching columns, banners and domes of searchlights—the whole arsenal of stimulants, developed with inventive ingenuity, for exciting public ecstasy was ultimately intended to bring about the individual's self-annulment, with the aim of rendering first the party adherents and later a whole nation totally amenable to the leaders' claim to power.[140]

Fest's account of Hitler's meteoric rise to power is a story of deception reminiscent of the tale of the Trojan horse; that is, the capture of democratic institutions from within. Hitler managed to conceal his revolutionary assault behind a facade of dubious legality as he systematically undermined the effectiveness of democratic institutions, bringing them to support precisely those totalitarian aims they were designed to prevent. Hitler's aim was total power, and his strategy was always to deceive. He selected top party officials by the standard of their competence to deceive. Thus he attracted the likes of Joseph Goebbels, who once boasted of the Nazis' ability to play on the German psyche "as on a piano." The depth of the Nazis' will to deceive can be seen in a remark Hitler made in one of his midnight monologues to his associates. He spoke of the "quite special secret pleasure of seeing how the people around us fail to realise what is really happening to them."[141]

Fest's perspective on the national socialist phenomenon is by no means a minority view. In fact, most historians and political analysts who have taken on the German question have come to regard Hitler as the consummate deceiver, stalking the German masses, carefully looking for signs of vulnerability, meticulously fabricating caricatures both of himself and of German Jewry, and using whatever symbolic ruses were available to place the nation at his feet. One finally takes the impression that the Nazi deception machine was so expert and thorough in its execution that, regardless of the ideological predisposition of the German people, it could hardly have been withstood.

Robert Jay Lifton's fascinating study of the medical profession under Nazi rule is yet another account that attributes the greatest regression in modern history to deception. His *Nazi Doctors* was motivated in part by a desire to understand how practicioners of a profession dedicated to healing could have become so centrally involved in mass killing. That they *were* centrally involved is revealed in the words of a survivor: "Auschwitz was like a medical operation, the killing program was led by doctors from beginning to end."[142] Lifton does not claim that Nazi doctors actually *ran* the place, but they did preside over most of its critical operations, and their prominence gave to Auschwitz a perverse medical aura.

Lifton argues that the perverse medical aura was not limited to the death camps alone—they were simply the final reflection of an ideology that was ultimately biological and medical at its core. What Lifton means to say is that the Nazi analysis of Germany's problems and its programs for solution were driven by the medical model of diagnosis and therapy. He quotes to this effect from Hitler's *Mein Kampf*: "Anyone who wants to cure this era, which is inwardly sick and rotten, must first of all summon up the courage to make clear the causes of this disease."[143] And according to Nazi "medical" doctrine, the cause of the disease was German Jewry. This diagnosis was continuously reinforced by the thoroughly medical imagery that shaped the Jewish caricature. The Jews were variously called "gangrenous appendix," "racial tuberculosis," "parasites," "bacteria," "bloodsuckers," "germ carriers," "maggots," "cankers of decay," and suchlike. Under the deceptive influence of this biomedical model, mass killing of the Jews eventually came to be regarded as a therapeutic imperative. Predisposed as they were to see the Volk as a metaphysical organism, the Germans were vulnerable to the suggestion that selective killing might be therapeutic in the collective sense.

As the "euthanasia" program progressed there developed what Lifton calls a "bureaucracy of medical deception." Patients were deceived, as were their relatives. Bogus and obscure medical procedures were prescribed (which were presented as necessary but high-risk), death certificates were falsified, cremation was routinized on the pretext of wartime exigency to preclude postmortem exams, and so on. The presence of medical personnel was no more than a camouflage for murder: "It is no exaggeration to say that the primary— perhaps the only—*medical* function of the killing doctors was to determine the most believable falsification of each patient-victim's death certificate."[144]

Lifton's study has a double focus. On the level of ideas, he is concerned to show the deceptive logic by which the illusions of Volkish ideology drew the medical profession into progressive complicity with a delusional program of "public health." But this dynamic, though important, is hardly sufficient to explain how so many physicians, individually sworn to the Hippocratic oath, were able to overcome their moral compunctions. And on this level of personal psychodynamics Lifton proposes a theory of self-deception, or, as he calls it, the process of "doubling." Psychological doubling involves a division of the self into two functioning wholes; that is, the "former self," which might include one's identity as a humane physician, husband, father, and an "Auschwitz self" that is allowed to develop alongside to bear the responsibility for doing evil.

Doubling would appear to be an extreme case of the common experience of "wearing two hats," or filling various roles. Doubling, however, takes this dynamic to the point where only the most tenuous connection remains between the two selves, so that the former self can be deceived about the locus of responsibility for evil acts. The former self avoids anxiety by displacing guilt to the Auschwitz self. Lifton says that the self-deceptive and self-preserving strategy of doubling is most likely to appear under the extreme conditions of moral ambivalence that one might find in a criminal subculture such as the Mafia, a terrorist group, a death squad, or a juvenile gang. Doctors, he says, are especially vulnerable to this form of self-deception:

> Doctors as a group may be more susceptible to doubling than others. . . . Medical doubling . . . usually begins with the student's encounter with the corpse he or she must dissect, often enough on the first day of medical school. One feels it necessary to develop a "medical self," which enables one not only to be relatively inured to death but to function reasonably efficiently in relation to the many-sided demands of the work.[145]

My purpose here has been not to attempt an explanation of Nazi atrocities but only to show that such attempts generally attribute the atrocities to a vulnerability to being deceived. We have seen that accounts may vary considerably in their focus, but the common principle among historians seems to be that if deception had been avoided, the Holocaust would not have occurred. And there is no fallacy in generalizing the principle a step further to claim that historians consider deception to be a dominant factor in disruptions of social progress. Further applications of this thesis might involve an examination of various liberation movements. At the core of the feminist critique of Western culture, for example, is the assertion that the rhetoric of male supremacy has been the rhetoric of deceit. Similar assertions have fueled the black liberation movement, anticommunist movements, and the like. One looks in vain for evidence to oppose the hypothesis that where there are notions of social progress, there also are notions about deception.

This entire chapter has been in the service of a very straightforward thesis: that the intellectual and moral traditions of Western culture have in large measure been shaped by an explicit and consistent fear of the dangers of being deceived. Indeed, we may say that fear of the *effects* of being deceived has been so central to our thinking that we have come to regard deception itself as a danger. I have chosen to develop this thesis at considerable length because it is my impression that the directive influence of this fear of deception has not been fully appreciated. Only when we perceive the depth of the bias against deception in our cultural traditions will we be in a position to appreciate how forcefully recent studies of deception challenge our most deeply held beliefs. The next three chapters aim to make this challenge clear.

∽ 2 ∾

Deception in Evolutionary
Perspective

IN CHAPTER I I attempted to defend a rather immodest claim: that the intellectual and moral traditions of Western culture have been shaped extensively by a bias against deception. Having relinquished any pretense to modesty, I shall now proceed to advance an even larger claim: that the dynamics of deception play a decisive role not merely in cultural history but in the process of biological evolution as well. The latter argument is encouraged by the former under the principle that wherever we find unanimity in cultural values, there we may suspect the influence of deeper, biological principles.[1]

A series of questions begins to unfold under this principle. First, is it possible that human beings have been selected by evolutionary processes to be chary of deception? And further, if our species has been so selected, whence comes the selective pressure for human traits that assist us against being deceived? Does the pressure come exclusively from deceptive members of our own species? But if that is the case, does it then follow that humans have also been selected by nature to be deceivers? And if humans have been selected to be able deceivers, is it not possible or even likely that certain other species may have been selected to the same end? And if nonhuman species can be shown to exhibit deceptive traits, then what is to be made of the common notion that deception is a deliberate act? Is the perpetration of deception always conscious and intentional? Or must we broaden our concept of deception to account for its perpetration by species that are incapable of intentional behavior? Let us admit a quick example here to illustrate the difficulties. No one disputes that the mythological account of the Trojan horse represents an example of intentional deceit. But what are we to make of the African bug that bedecks itself with the bodies of dead ants and thereby penetrates the ant colony undetected to binge at will? Can one honestly dismiss the similarity of behavior on the grounds that to attribute deceit to a mere bug is to commit the fallacy of anthropomorphism?

Such lines of thought invite us to consider whether deception plays an important role among insentient as well as sentient forms of life. The argument of this chapter takes us away from our focus on the cultural bias against *being* deceived to focus on a natural bias favoring traits for *deceiving*. The argument is that at all levels of the organization of life nature provides niches for organisms that possess deceptive traits. Whether or not such niches become populated depends on the fortunes of genetic mutation and recombination, but where deceptive traits do appear, they tend to be favored. A correlative principle also appears to hold: that wherever traits for detecting deceit are produced, they, too, tend to be favored. One begins to take the point, then, that the living world is in some respects not unlike a spiral of espionage— deceivers apply selective pressure for better detectives, who in turn apply pressure for better deceivers, and so on. But before we can make our way through these complexities I need to lay some theoretical foundations.

The Nature of Deception

The topic of deception is of inherent interest to human beings because there is so much of it in our daily lives, because it is so often laden with tantalizing ambiguity, and because it is ever an option for our behavior. But for all our interest in the subject, deception as a general phenomenon has a way of defeating our best attempts at conceptual formulation. It belongs to that irritating class of phenomena that are familiar to us all but that land us in a quagmire of conceptual difficulties when we attempt to define their essential features. I had some inkling of the difficulties even before my curiosity about deception reached the point of becoming a serious research interest. But the further I went, the more discouraged I became about the prospects of achieving a satisfying definition of my topic. I realized the troubles ahead when I asked one of my research assistants to gather up a list of cognate terms for "deception" or "deceive" or "deceived." She came back in a cloud of frustration with a list in excess of five hundred words. Many of the entries were a bit tenuous, but even the purified list contained over two hundred items: baffle, bamboozle, bedazzle, bedevil, befuddle, beguile, belie, bemazed, bemuse, benighted, betray, bewilder, bewitch, bilk, bluff, bogus, breach faith—the list goes on and on. One might expect similar results with such concepts as love, fear, work, and beauty. Any phenomenon that comes into human experience in a wide diversity of forms (as deception does) is likely to generate a rich network of associations, and will thus necessitate a large semantic battery to cover all the subtle nuances. And as a consequence, the phenomenon will resist concise definition.

An additional and central difficulty has to do with the fact that deception is a relational characteristic. That is, deception is a property that qualifies the nature of interactions between organisms. Any adequate definition of deception must, therefore, specify conditions that prevail in those interactions in which deception is said to occur. Relational phenomena give rise to peculiar problems of definition because there are always ambiguous cases in which conditions have been satisfied from one side of the interaction but not from the other. Does the concept of love, for example, apply to people who love their country? Their cars? Or is the concept of love properly reserved only for interactions between two persons who maintain mutual affection? Is unrequited love therefore not love? Similar problems arise with any attempt to define deception. Can one be said to "deceive" a thermostat by inventive means that simulate a drop in temperature? Is one "deceived" when one mistakes a hank of rope for a snake? Does deception take place when one inadvertently misdirects tourists by providing confusing directions? There are problems here.

Deception

Despite the difficulties, I will attempt to define deception in a concise way and will then proceed to qualify the definition on the basis of various considerations. Once a working definition is at hand, I will consider the vulnerability of organisms to deception and enumerate some general strategies that deceivers use to exploit dupes. I will then present examples from various levels in the organization of life forms to support the claim that deception represents an important facet in the process of evolution.

To proceed: *deception occurs when a discrepancy between appearance and reality can be attributed in part to the causal influence of another organism.*

We might begin to qualify this definition by considering the nature of a perceiver. If we are prepared to say that deception involves some sort of error in perception, then it will follow that deception has nothing to do with nonperceivers. And already at this early stage in our inquiry we will encounter some discrepancy of language between psychologists and biologists. Psychologists are the more precise, regarding perception as a field of study that lies midway between the study of sensation (the functioning of sense organs and their receptors) and the study of cognition (reasoning and problem solving). Perception, they say, occurs only when an organism can be said to apprehend complex ordered features of the world around, such as the sizes, shapes, distances, and relative motions of objects.[2] Biologists, for their part, are content with a minimalist definition, regarding a perceiver as any organism that is equipped to process information from the world around. For our purposes the minimalist definition will suffice. To restrict perception to the rather high-level capacities of organisms with central nervous systems seems arbitrary and even potentially misleading, since even the simplest of organisms are capable of such "perceptual acts" as self-recognition, species recognition, and the discernment of certain shapes. We take nothing away from the splendor of perceptual achievements among the higher organisms by attributing primitive perceptual acts to the lower.

Human beings should remind themselves on a fairly regular basis that they are capable of doing nothing of an essential nature that is not done with commensurate skill by single-celled organisms. In their various interactions with the environment all species have developed strategies to find food, to avoid predators, and to reproduce. These are the fundamentals, beyond which any differences between species of plants and animals are mere embellishments of structure and process. Nor can it be said that human beings have any greater knowledge about the world around than do one-celled organisms. This sounds patently absurd, but on one level it is literally true. That is, one-celled organisms are equipped to respond to every *type* of stimulus from the world around that humans are. Information from the external environment can be classified basically in terms of electromagnetic, mechanical, chemical, thermal, and electrical stimuli, and one-celled organisms, no less than human beings, are equipped to respond to all of them. We often think of human beings as the most generalized of species, while simpler organisms are characterized as specialists. But in an important sense—that is, in terms of cell functions—just the reverse is true. A single-celled organism must negotiate all its transactions with the world around by a small number of exquisitely designed mechanisms within its membranes and cytoplasm. The activities of these single-celled organisms are not terribly sophisticated by human standards, but if we could calibrate our own accomplishment/resource ratio to theirs we might find occasion for humility.

How, then, may we best characterize the difference between unicellular and multicellular perceivers? All the important differences between them can be seen as the result of specialization and integration of individual cell functions. When an organism has millions of cells to work with, a division of labor among integrated cells becomes a feasible and beneficial strategy. As far as their capabilities as perceivers are concerned, we might say that the difference between algae and humans is comparable to the difference between a general store and a shopping mall. Humans may respond to a wider range of stimuli (greater inventory) and with far greater discrimination (varied selection of goods), but only because the luxury of multicellularity makes specialization possible. Consider, for example, the case of responsiveness to electromagnetic radiation. In one-celled organisms, such as many algae, the detection of light is managed by a small portion of the cell's surface where perhaps a thousand photosensitive molecules, called pigments, are clustered. As the cell scans its environment for needed resources, it positions itself to aim the photosensitive portion of its surface toward the source of light, whereupon the pigments absorb a particular wavelength and transduce its electromagnetic energy into useful biological forms. In humans, by contrast, light detection is managed not by a small cluster of molecules but by whole hierarchies of cells that are specialized and subspecialized in various ways. Light detection still relies ultimately upon pigments, but in humans various kinds of pigments are arranged in clusters on various kinds of cells. And in addition to having differentially specialized pigments, the human eye has legions more of them. Whereas a single-celled perceiver may have as many as a thousand photosensitive molecules, the human perceiver will have on the order of ten billion of them.

But this is only part of the story. The human perceiver also has millions of other cells devoted to the complicated business of coordinating and integrating the process of light detection. The photosensitive part of the eye (the rods and cones of the retina) handles the actual energy transduction, but many ancillary structures (e.g., muscles, cornea, iris, lens) must perform various integrated functions even before light can reach the photoreceptors. And what happens *after* energy transduction is even more complicated. Electrochemical impulses from the retina are consolidated into simpler forms of information as they are passed along the visual pathway to the brain. Messages to the brain are received in the *primary visual area,* where they are further integrated to signify shapes, colors, and motion. These condensed signals are then sent along to the *visual association area,* where they are integrated with information stored from past visual experiences. And then, messages are sent to *gnostic areas* of the brain, where information from various sensory systems—arriving via equally complicated chains of events induced by other forms of stimuli—is further integrated to produce a unified experience.

The differences between unicellular perceivers and human beings are vast and complex. The alga has relatively few molecular receptors that carry out a fairly direct transduction, which is followed by simple responses. The human being has billions of receptors that feed their information into a giant network of communicating cells, whereupon the information is summarized, schematized, stored, retrieved, reintegrated with new information, amplified, suppressed, retrieved again, and so on, in a virtual blizzard of continuous neurochemical activity. But while the differences in perception between algae and humans are staggering, the fundamental similarities are no less impressive. The alga and the human both respond to the same orders or types of stimuli through primary molecular receptors, and the chemical structure of these receptors turns out to be remarkably similar in all living beings. The essential difference, then, is that humans are multicellular and their perceptions derive from the integration of cells that are specifically built for the schematic manipulation of information.

The assertion that differences between perceivers can be reduced to differences in information processing amounts to a large claim for the importance of information. But such a claim need not be muted by qualification. Indeed, it can be amplified into a declaration that information processing is the central characteristic of all life:

> Unlike all other known things on earth animals and plants defend themselves against the universal tendency to fade away, to merge into the surroundings; in short, they remain alive. . . . They are able to do this because they receive from their ancestors a pattern of order, which we identify by saying that it consists of "information," carried by a code. Living things delay the disorganizing effect of the second law of thermodynamics in this way by the use of inherited information to direct their actions so that they achieve the aim of remaining alive. Our thesis will be that the acquisition of knowledge, which we usually think of as subjective, has developed from this process of accumulation and transfer of information that is essential for all living things.[3]

Organisms live by virtue of their capacities to receive, encode, manipulate, and transmit information in an orderly fashion. And it may further be said that any and all statements made about the agency or behavior of an organism are ultimately descriptions of the organism's stock of information. That is to say, anything I do as a causal agent has its source in the information that has been encoded in my body, whether genetically or by learning. Obviously this does not apply to things that happen *to* me. If I fall from the top of a building, for example, the rate of acceleration in the fall is not a function of my incarnate information. Nor can the fall be attributed to me in the case of my being pushed. But if I elected to fall, or if I fell by virtue of clumsiness, the act would be attributable to my agency and therefore to my stock of encoded information. Anything at all that can be attributed to *me* is of necessity attributable to my incarnate information. The same principle applies to the behavior of all organisms. If my dog bites the neighbor's child, she does so only because she was "informed" to do so. If a plant follows a source of light, it does so because of its encoded information. All behavior, everywhere and under all circumstances, is a function of the behaving organism's information state. I am making no claims at the moment about the relative influence attributable to various forms of information. We may distinguish between *inherited* information (genetic), *stored* information (retrievable memory), and *immediate* information (perceptions), and in any act of human behavior all of these forms would be involved in some measure. The only point I am advancing here is that all attributable behavior is wholly contingent upon incarnate information.

Another point to be raised is that all living organisms make an attempt to replicate the world around by their mechanisms for encoding information. Surely I do not intend to say that organisms literally attempt to clone the world or to produce an exact physical duplicate. That would amount to a multiplicity of real worlds, one for each perceiver. But organisms do attempt to codify or simulate elements of the world around.

These principles provide a useful approach to a second feature of our definition of deception—that is, the distinction between appearance and reality. I am suggesting that we may appropriately define appearance as *the sum total of information encoded by a living organism.* What is intended here is the suggestion that incarnate information may be construed as a set of propositions about the world around. The sum total of an organism's information (i.e., its information stock) *just is* the way the world appears to that organism—it is that particular organism's attempt to replicate the world around. The implication is that even genetic information may be construed as a set of propositions about the world. This sounds a bit odd. DNA amounts to ordered sequences of nucleotides containing chemical instructions for producing proteins, and ultimately for building up cells. So how does this amount to a set of propositions about the world? Well, in roughly the same way that your method for selecting lottery numbers constitutes a proposal about the lottery. When you apply your method for selecting lottery numbers, you are wagering a proposal that the lottery is *such that* your method will generate numbers that will be adequated to the winning numbers. DNA is not dissimilar in effect. The DNA of an organism wagers a set of instructions on the proposition that the product of its designs (i.e., a certain self-regulating processor of information) will be appropriate to the world. So, just as we speak of an organism being well adapted to its environment, we may speak of genetic information being *adequated* to the world around. It is the adequacy of genetic information to the world around that results in the adaptation of an organism to its environment. The DNA of a particular organism says, in effect, that the world is *such that* if its instructions are carried out properly, the consequences for the organism will be reproductive success. In this sense we may say that the genes of an organism represent a set of rudimentary hypotheses about the world which are then tested out in the course of the organism's lifetime.

But there is more to incarnate information than DNA. As I mentioned earlier, every organism is equipped by its heritage to search out and gather in new information. Thus the inherited information transmitted from previous generations by the genetic material is augmented continuously by a supply of newly processed information from various sensory systems. And in those species that have the luxury of memory systems there is the added dimension of building up a rich network of associations throughout a lifetime, all of which provides additional information schemas relevant to adapting to the features of the world around.

And now for reality. If appearance is the sum total of an organism's incarnate information, then reality may be regarded as *the sum total of potential information on offer to any and all perceivers from the world around*. Whatever might conceivably be encoded as information by a perceiver is what is meant here by the real world.

We can now propose that the difference between appearance and reality *just is* the difference between the incarnate information of a perceiver and the potential information on offer to it (or any other perceiver) from the world around. And it should be evident that there will always *be* a difference, if for no other reason than that the world changes constantly. No perceiver could possibly render a complete codification of potential information. The achievement of perfect adequation of incarnate information to the world around would amount to omniscience. And since no stock of information is ever completely adequate to reality, all organisms can be said to exist in a state of relative ignorance or delusion—ignorance when information is lacking, delusion when the information is wrong. I am suggesting that discrepancies between appearance and reality amount to the inadequation of incarnate information to the world around, and that any inadequation may be attributed either to the organism's failure to encode information or to its misconstruction of information. And a final point is simply that any organism's information state may be either enhanced or debased—that is, it can be rendered more or less adequate to reality.

And now we have a working definition at hand: *Deception occurs when a discrepancy between appearance and reality can be attributed in part to the causal influence of another organism. That is, a deceiver is an organism (A) whose agency contributes by design to the ignorance or delusion of another organism (B). Self-deception may be said to occur when A and B are the same organism.*

This definition makes no concessions to the view that deception is in essence an intentional act perpetrated by a conscious individual for nefarious motives. It is among the aims of this book to challenge this popular misunderstanding of deception. We may therefore prepare ourselves for the evidence that lies ahead by setting down a distinction between intentional and nonintentional deceit. The notion of intentional deceit may be reserved for those cases in which deception involves conscious motives. There will be many such cases, to be sure. But most instances of deception do not involve intention at all, and they are not for that reason any the less deceptive. When a young man gathers up his courage to phone a young woman for a date, he is quite deliberately and intentionally engaging in courtship behavior. Yet no one would deny that the unconscious and nonintentional cricket is engaged in the same type of behavior when he emits a courtship song. The intentional factor does not disrupt the continuity in courtship phenomena. Nor, I am asserting, should it do so in the case of deceptive phenomena. Female impersonators among nonsentient insects are no less deceptive than their human counterparts.

The trouble is that the conventional understanding of deception takes intentional human acts as the standard, and under these conditions it is difficult to see how nonhuman phenomena such as camouflage and mimicry can qualify as deceptive. They clearly lack the conscious and premeditative qualities essential to acts of lying and pretending, so presumably they cannot be deceptive. In the present inquiry, however, we ask not whether camouflage and mimicry resemble lying and pretending, but rather how the intentional acts of lying and pretending represent instances of camouflage and mimicry. When the inquiry is thus reversed, the question of intentionality drops completely out of the picture. The conventional view defines deception by the exception rather than by the norm. The distinction between intentional and nonintentional deceit may be useful in activating our moral sensibilities, but it is of no consequence for identifying a given interaction as deceptive. Any attempt to enlarge our understanding of a phenomenon will exact a price in terms of departures from accepted usages. One such departure is to quit thinking of deception as a characteristic exclusive to human interactions.

And while we are on the subject of intentionality, it might be ventured that the conscious life of intentional behavior has nothing going for it that is not essentially present within the laborious mechanics of evolution. Except for speed, that is. William Calvin's fascinating book, *The Cerebral Symphony,* argues that the human brain resembles a highly accelerated version of evolutionary mechanics, that the logic of human thought is formally identical to the logic of evolution.[4] Evolution proceeds on the Darwinian principle of selection upon random variations. But the human brain, Calvin insists, is itself a sort of Darwin machine, producing random variations on incarnate information (i.e., spontaneously spinning out a multitude of scenarios constructed from existing schemas) and then employing short-term and long-term memories to rule out candidates for cognitive survival. Thus our conscious thoughts are the ones that make it through the editorial process and, on occasion, are "gated out" into motor activity. We tend to regard our conscious life as anything but random. Our thoughts and decisions have a determined quality about them which appears to be the very antithesis of chance and randomness—they are clear, distinct, and focused. And so they may be, but Calvin's argument is that the clarity and distinctness of our conscious life have their primitive origins in a cacophony of more or less random synaptic activity in the brain, and it *becomes* focused only as a result of selective interactions within the ecology of the brain's memory systems. Consciousness is entirely a product of cognitive selection, not its directive source. Simpler organisms are less conscious than humans only because they have fewer scenarios competing within their neural environment. Once again, the difference has to do with the multiplicity and integration of cells. The concepts of consciousness and intention, then, appear much less than they are cracked up to be. Most modern intellectuals have long since given up the idea that the elegant structures of simple organisms are "designed" (as if by some intelligent creator), preferring instead to see their order as the blind result of generations upon generations of preferential selection upon chance. But not many are willing to accept the same explanation for the elegance of intelligent behavior. On this matter we appear to be pressed toward another departure. And so I repeat: The distinction between intentional and nonintentional deceit is of consequence only as a moral distinction; it has nothing to say about whether or not a given interaction is deceptive.

The rejection of intentionality as an essential feature of deception does not, however, prevent us from speaking of deceit as purposeful behavior. All living organisms manifest purpose and design in their strategies for survival and reproduction, even though few of them (primarily humans) may be said to act with explicit intentions or self-conscious motives. Consider again our African bug. This bug is clearly acting by design when it covers itself with dead ants for the deceptive purpose of undetected entry into the ant colony. But there is no question here of intentionality. As we shall see, many species have evolved with elegant strategies for influencing the ignorance and delusion of organisms with which they interact, but without the embellishment of consciousness. It may well be that nature's most elaborate mechanism for deception is the self-conscious and foresightful human brain, but this is not by any means the exclusive one, nor is it even a mechanism whose logic is essentially different from the laborious trial-and-error/success process of evolution.

In any identification of a deceptive interaction at least three perceivers are involved. First, there is the dupe, whose vulnerability to deception is exploited. Second, there is the deceiver, exploiting the vulnerability by designs that contribute to the ignorance or the delusion of the dupe. And finally there is the observer who presumes to attribute inadequacy to the dupe and causal agency to the deceiver. It is fairly obvious, but worthy of note, that the observer is making some rather remarkable claims for his or her own information state. That is, if I assert that A has deceived B, I am claiming the adequacy of my own information state over against that of B. I am asserting that B is in a state of ignorance or delusion in relation to my own information state. And with respect to A, I have judged that it has information (whether acquired by the defaults of evolutionary history or by learning) that enables it to exploit deficiencies of the sort I have attributed to B. All of this should warn us that the study of deception will necessarily involve some imaginative and speculative thinking. Our topic is framed by a situation in which the observer is called upon to make judgments about interactions between independent information states. Nothing could be less straightforward.

In this section we have considered the nature of deceptive interactions. We have observed that differences between perceivers derive from differences in cells—that is, the numbers of cells, their specialized functions, and the manner of their integrations. It follows that differences between perceptual systems may be viewed in terms of structural and strategic components for the processing of information. Having said all this, I assert the following: A perceiver is vulnerable to deceit to the extent that its structures and/or strategies for perception are exploitable by other organisms. And further, an organism may become a deceiver by virtue of possessing structures and/or strategies for exploiting the perceptual vulnerabilities of a dupe. In the next section we shall explore factors relevant to the susceptibility of organisms to perceptual errors, regardless of the influence of deceivers. And in the subsequent section we shall make some preliminary and general observations about how such errors may be induced by deceivers.

Perceptual Systems and Their Vulnerability

Perceptual systems are mediating devices that stand between stimuli from the external environment and an organism's response to the stimuli. In the very simplest of organisms the mediating function of a perceptual system amounts to a relatively direct sequence of biochemical reactions. In organisms with primitive nervous systems the mediation becomes more complex, involving neural reflexes. And in organisms with central nervous systems perceptual mediation involves highly complex neural schemas. In subneural organisms perceptual systems can be analyzed in respect to their structural and chemical properties alone. But in neural organisms strategic components are superimposed on the perceptual system by learning. These considerations will shape our discussion of vulnerability around a basic distinction between structural and strategic components of perceptual systems. *When deception occurs, it does so by somehow defeating the designs of structural and/or strategic components of perception.*

No perceptual system is foolproof—a fundamental fact of life that has made the evolution of deception inevitable. The question before us at the moment asks for an identification of the structural and strategic factors that may predispose a perceiver to being duped. The most promising approach to the limitations on perceptual systems is to focus on their selectivity. The selectivity of a perceptual system is a measure of the statistically relevant information necessary for the survival needs of a particular species. In other words, there is selective pressure on organisms to achieve a proficiency in information processing commensurate with their needs for survival and reproduction. Organisms that do not process enough relevant information will too often fail to find food, attract mates, and avoid predators. On the other hand, organisms that process information superfluously will reduce their reproductive fitness by wasting valuable time and resources on trivialities. The result is that various species will develop structures for perception that are specialized to process only a small portion of the potential information in the environment. Thus, for example, the human eye is not equipped to encode the entire spectrum of electromagnetic energy; it can encode only that small slice of it known as the visible spectrum. The rest of the spectrum (more than 98 percent of it) is relatively unimportant for human survival and reproduction. The same is true of auditory structures. The human ear can detect sound vibrations between 20 and 20,000 cycles per second. Beyond these limits are "sounds" that are statistically irrelevant to human interests. The perceptual systems of all species are similarly restricted in their receptive range. If these structural limits were suddenly to expand, the perceiver would find itself unable to cope with the onslaught of irrelevant information. The order we perceive in our world is partly due to the poverty of our experience.

With the evolution of the neuron, new dynamics of perceptual selectivity came into play. The neuron made several innovations possible. The communicating properties of the neuron, for example, enabled the efficient integration of larger organisms having interdependent subsystems—in the same way that a postal system or a telephone network makes it possible to sustain an integrated society on a much larger scale. Larger and more complex organisms would have needs for greater supplies and thus new sources of energy. Exploiting new sources of energy would call for abilities to negotiate life within expanded environmental boundaries, and this development would entail an expansion of the information statistically relevant for survival and reproduction. In short, the more complex an organism, the more information it needs to process from the world around. The neuron was just the thing to make new dimensions of information processing feasible. An organism equipped with a nervous system could manage to integrate signals from thousands, even millions of primary receptors. A simple organism with a single type of photoreceptor could never detect more than "photon here now." But not all photons are equal; they vary in intensity and in chromatic qualities. An organism equipped with millions of photoreceptors (somewhat varied structurally) will receive millions of "photon here now" signals representing a staggering diversity of information about the intensity, hue, and purity of individual stimuli. Neural systems make it possible to organize such a barrage of discrete and varied signals into coherent patterns. A multiplicity of primary receptors, therefore, results in a greatly expanded range of sensitivity to potential information. In the case of human vision, the quantity of raw data has been so greatly expanded that it would appear to defy organization. Various editorial processes evolved simultaneously to keep the actual processing of information at a manageable level and prevent an overload of input. These neural processes give a perceiver the ability to select preferentially which of the raw data will proceed toward the final stages of information processing. In other words, neural networks establish the conditions for a new perceptual strategy: *selective attention*. We are coming to the view that the evolution of the neuron made possible two very remarkable operations: first, a vast expansion of potentially relevant input data, and second, an array of programs for selectively attending to the most immediately relevant among them. This concept of programs for selective attention is of critical importance for the study of deception, so I will digress for the purpose of further clarification.

I have said that deception occurs as a result of "defeating the designs" of structural and/or strategic components of perceptual systems, resulting in an inadequation of appearance to reality. And now I want to suggest that the strategic components of perception can be more fully described by the concept of schemas. It is largely by virtue of schemas that neural organisms encode a stock of information, the totality of which I have called "appearance." The idea of a schema is both simple and complex—simple in its conceptual features, complex in its extensive and intricate manifestations. We may say that in the most fundamental sense that schemas are assemblages of nerve cells that function as strategic units both to encode information and to direct behavior.[5] Given this basic definition, we can proceed to make several observations about the properties and functions of schemas.

First the properties. Schemas may be seen to vary considerably in their complexity. The very simplest schemas can be identified as "feature detectors," meaning that they respond only to highly specific features in the environment. In the human visual system certain cell assemblies are keyed to detect edges or lines, such as a black bar drawn on white paper. Some feature-detecting schemas show a reflex preference (i.e., are more easily activated) for specific orientations, such as vertical, horizontal, or oblique lines. More elaborate feature-detecting schemas have been identified to respond to more complicated patterns in a stimulus, such as length, width, contour, motion, and spatial frequencies. Thus we may speak of low-level schemas which encode for various visual primes. Similar processes for encoding feature primes have been identified in auditory systems.[6] These low-level schemas can be regarded as the rudimentary constituents of all perception and information processing in neural organisms. It is on the basis of these primary constituents that organisms may build up "stacks" of interactive schemas at various levels of complexity. For example, feature-detecting schemas will contribute to the establishment of schemas for shape recognition, event sequence recognition, sound and sound sequence recognition, and the like. The construction of schemas and stacks of schemas eventually results in abilities to recognize and associate objects, faces, their expressions, letters, words, phrases, ideas—name any perceptual or conceptual act at all that can be performed by a neural organism and you will find that it is executed by schemas. Everything from the frog's detection of a dark spot moving across a light sky to the bigot's stereotypes of minority groups will call for the activation of neural schemas.

Another general property of schemas is that they constitute the very substance of both learning and memory. Something is learned by virtue of constructing or modulating a schema, and schemas are the structural frames or units in which memory is stored and retrieved. Whenever we learn a song or remember one, whenever we master a skill or practice it, we are activating schemas. One could say that learning takes place by the construction of schemas, or alternatively, that schemas are constructed by the process of learning. Similarly, one could say that memories are retrieved by the activation of schemas, or that schemas are activated by the process of recollection. But this is only to say that schemas are the substance of both learning and memory.

One of the most interesting and vexing issues surrounding the ontogeny of schemas is the extent to which they are influenced by the factors of heredity and environment. Species differ markedly in their schematic versatility. In simpler organisms the degree of genetic determinism is greater; that is, very little stacking of schemas is going on, which means that these organisms will be limited in the range of their abilities. Thus they are not especially versatile as perceivers, and their behavioral responses tend to be invariant and hard-wired. More complex organisms with an abundance of neural matter have stacks upon stacks of schemas, which allow for broad ranges of perception and vast repertories of behavior. But a significant genetic factor remains at even the highest levels of schema formation, which may account for the variable difficulty individuals experience in learning. A person who is genetically predisposed to left-handedness, for example, may learn to be right-handed, but with considerably more difficulty than someone with a right-handed predisposition.

William Calvin has ventured an interesting hypothesis about the evolution of high-order cognitive abilities, including language use, music, problem solving, planning ahead, and the like. Such abilities, he suggests, may well represent variations on neural assemblages that evolved in connection with the adaptiveness of such behaviors as hammering and throwing. In other words, language, music, and other serial-order abilities may have emerged as spare-time uses of the same neural machinery that was required for accurate throwing.[7] If this is the case, then we may well postulate transferability of function as an important property of schemas. This property helps to explain how some schemas, once in place, provide the conditions for analogous operations. The schema for cat recognition, for example, can be redeployed for metaphorical uses, as when we describe someone as having feline features.

The functional aspects of schemas may be compared with theories. As David Rumelhart says, "It is useful to think of a schema as a kind of informal, private, unarticulated theory about the nature of the events, objects, or situations that we face. The total set of schemata we have available for interpreting our world in a sense constitutes our private theory of the nature of reality."[8] Like theories, schemas possess both powers of explanation and powers of prediction. They enable a perceiver to assimilate discrete data by integrating them into coherent patterns, thus creating the conditions of intelligibility. It is by virtue of schemas that mere data become information. Neural schemas are assembled and modulated from the bottom up. They are "data driven," and in this sense they arise as the consequence, the culmination, of perception. All neural organisms are predisposed to schematize data as they attempt to discern the relevance of features in the environment to their needs. In the absence of interpretive schemas, the presentation of stimuli will place an organism in a state of arousal while it "figures" for the meaning of the stimuli. When the meaning is discovered (new schema constructed) or recognized (existing schema activated), the organism has thereby assimilated the data and will be restored to a state of equilibrium. It is, in fact, the process of schematizing that gives rise to meaning.

Many accounts have been given of the experience of discovery that comes with the achievement of schematizing, but perhaps none so dramatic as that recorded by Helen Keller:

> Someone was drawing water and my teacher placed my hand under the spout. As the cool stream gushed over my hand she spelled into the other the word *water*, first slowly, then rapidly. I stood still, my whole attention fixed upon the motion of her fingers. Suddenly I felt a misty consciousness as of something forgotten—a thrill of returning thought; and somehow the mystery of language was revealed to me. I knew then that W-A-T-E-R meant that wonderful cool something that was flowing over my hand."[9]

I take this to be a subjective account of schema formation. Keller's discovery of the significance of language resulted from the schematic integration of sense data, those from one hand being associated with those from the other. Once the initial pattern of meaning had been formed, Keller had the resources for further elaborations: "That living word awakened my soul, gave it light, hope, joy, set it free! There were barriers still, it is true, but barriers that in time could be swept away. I left the well-house eager to learn. Everything had a name, and each name gave birth to a new thought."[10]

The interpretive or explanatory function of schemas can also be seen in the process of recognition, in which case new data are assimilated into established schemas. Consider the following passage:

> The procedure is actually quite simple. First you arrange things into different groups. Of course, one pile may be sufficient depending on how much there is to do. If you have to go somewhere else due to lack of facilities, that is the next step, otherwise you are pretty well set. It is important not to overdo things. That is, it is better to do too few things at once than too many. In the short run this may not seem important but complications can easily arise. A mistake can be expensive as well. At first the whole procedure will seem complicated. Soon, however, it will become just another facet of life. It is difficult to foresee any end to the necessity of this task in the immediate future, but then one can never tell. After the procedure is completed, one arranges the materials into different groups again. Then they can be put into their appropriate places. Eventually they will be used once more and the whole cycle will then have to be repeated. However, that is part of life."[11]

Most readers will find this passage nearly incomprehensible. The individual sentences are coherent enough, but they fail to hang together. It is only when the reader is told that the passage describes the act of clothes washing that recognition takes place. The passage becomes intelligible when its elements are assimilated by activation of the clothes-washing schema. Perceptual schemas operating at lower levels of intellection function in the same way. A blue jay that has learned to feed on butterflies will have formed a butterfly-recognition schema to confer intelligibility on otherwise meaningless patterns of sense data.

But schemas are not merely the data-driven products of perception. Once established, schemas function to guide the perceptual process by serving as sources of expectation and bases for inferences about unobservable objects and events. In this way they may be said to condition the way in which perceivers orient themselves in the world around. Perception is not simply a passive event; it normally involves a fair degree of active contribution on the part of the perceiver. Schemas provide the basis for the perceiver's participation, and thus we may say that schemas function both as causes and as consequences of perception.

At the very least, schemas contribute to the construction of a perceptual event by conditioning the selective attention of perceivers. Indeed, some investigators have suggested that the function of all learning is to educate a perceiver's attention.[12] The blue jay, having discovered a routine for eating butterflies, will scan its environment for the familiar pattern; it will "read for" the pattern encoded in the schema. Recognition of the pattern will then trigger the appropriate attack response. The blue jay that has suffered a cardiac reaction after eating a toxic monarch butterfly will have encoded a subschema for recognizing and then ignoring the monarch. The blue jay's attention has been educated.

The amount of research conducted in recent decades concerning the influence of schemas on perception is impressive. Much of the research simply bears out what common sense tells us about ourselves. The nursing mother, for example, will be more easily aroused from sleep by an infant's cry than will other members of the household. When you expect a phone call, you are more apt to hear it ring through the din of the shower. When you expect to be touched by something, you will be more sensitive. When you are in need of some item, you will be more likely to see it. When you are absorbed in some activity, you will be less receptive to other happenings around you. When you know the color of something will be relevant, you are more likely to remember it. When you fear something, you will be more wary of signs of its presence. And so on. In each of these cases a schema is at work conditioning the processes of perception. Familiar examples of this sort can be multiplied without end to reinforce the view that schemas influence the selectivity of attention by telling a perceiver both what to look *at* and what to look *for*.

It has been shown that neural organisms develop schemas to govern their selective attention to certain features in the environment. Included within the complex of strategies for selective attention are certain strategies for inattention as well. When organisms are presented with novel stimuli, their sensitivity increases markedly. In other words, sensory systems show a preference for novelty. When something new happens, the organism must respond by evaluating its relevance. If the stimulus defies schematization, or if it is schematized without reinforcement of some kind, then the stimulus will be judged irrelevant to the organism. Given either of these circumstances, the organism will become less sensitized to the stimulus as time passes. This is the process known as habituation. Habituation serves the process of selective attention by filtering out large quantities of inconsequential stimuli from the environment. Therefore, given the construction of schemas to condition positive attention, and given the dynamics of habituation to condition inattention, an organism will be appropriately disposed toward the most relevant features of its world.

But the power of schemas to influence perception often goes well beyond the education of attention. Schemas provide a basis for inferences about what is actually perceived, sometimes in the absence of sensory data or even in spite of contradictory data. That is, schemas can function to provide missing data or to alter the data that are given. Perceptual events are not only directed by schemas, they are often constructed by them.

Many visual configurations can serve to illustrate the power of schemas to construct perception. Consider the ambiguity in figure 2.1. In each case the perceiver must resolve ambiguities in order to achieve a coherent perception. In the first case the viewer is helped by contextual clues to activate the appropriate alphabetical or numerical schema needed to resolve the ambiguity. But in the case of the rabbit/duck and the face/vase figures the ambiguity-resolving schema must be activated entirely by subjective factors.

Perceivers of figure 2.2 will claim to "see" a white triangle superimposed upon a lined triangle and three black squares, even though no actual contours outline the supposed figure. This visual effect is constructed as the perceiver activates the triangle schema to simplify an otherwise complicated array. Seeing what is not there is sometimes simpler than seeing what is there.

Similar constructive effects have been observed in auditory phenomena. Researchers have found that listeners will claim to have heard certain words in recorded messages even though the words were excised and replaced by static or coughing noises. Schemas for the structure and meaning of language enabled these listeners to fabricate the missing data by inference from contextual clues.[13]

FIGURE 2.1

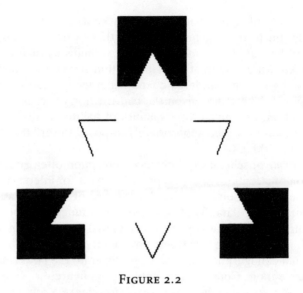

FIGURE 2.2

Even more dramatic examples of the power of schemas to construct the elements of perceptual experience can be cited. In one particularly revealing experiment researchers flashed before subjects various line drawings that were incomplete or distorted, such as images of three-armed people or faces with missing parts. Observers presented with an image of a three-legged dog reported seeing elaborate details, including the number of toes on the missing leg. Even after the experimenter directed the observer's attention to the legs, the observer continued to correct the data by making them conform to the schema of a four-legged dog. In another experiment an observer was shown an image of a woman's face with a large third eye in the middle of the forehead. After the observer's attention was directed several times to the irregularity, he continued to insist that what he had seen on the forehead was a curl, not an extra eye.[14]

Perception, it seems, tells us just as much about the perceiver's encoded schemas as it does about the world around. This is the inference suggested by the Rorschach test. This test consists of a series of amorphous inkblots which are given to subjects for identification. Subjects often give detailed descriptions of the significance of the images, even though they are entirely random patterns. These reports amount to schema-controlled projections. Even more dramatic are experiments involving the autokinetic effect. When a subject is placed in a completely darkened room facing a small stationary point of light, the light will eventually appear to drift about. This illusory effect results from involuntary eye movements. Some researchers have exploited the autokinetic effect as a projective test. Subjects were told that the experiment was a test of their ability to identify the words that would be traced out by the movement of the light. Even though the light never moved, subjects insisted that it had written several words.[15]

We are now in a position to make some general observations about perception to see whether they may advance our understanding of vulnerability to deceit. All living organisms, I have said, are perceivers, each species with its own characteristic systems for perceiving relevant features in the environment. These perceptual systems have both structural and strategic components which are responsible for determining both the selection of potential information that will be processed and the manner in which data will be construed as information. No organism will process more than an infinitesimal fraction of the total amount of potential information on offer in the real world. And yet, given the structures and strategies of perception, organisms will, by and large, do very well in adequating their "appearances" (i.e., their total stock of encoded information) to reality. Those whose appearances are insufficiently adequate to reality will not survive. Still, even when adequation of appearance to reality is optimal it cannot be maintained that any particular view of the real world represents anything like an isomorphism, or an exact replica. Indeed, we would have to say that no perceived assessment of "the way things really are" can ever qualify as more than a contingent caricature of the world—caricatured because the structures and strategies of any perceiver can process only a highly selective fraction of potential information, and contingent because any particular incarnation of this fragmentary information is necessarily conditioned by the peculiar evolutionary and individualized history of the perceiver.

All perceptions, therefore, amount to contingent caricatures of reality, and the precise nature of these contingent caricatures is described by the designs that are embedded in the structures (i.e., receptors, organs) and the strategies (i.e., schemas, habituations) of an individual perceiver. It goes almost without saying that such designs can never be foolproof; that is, they are never infallible. They can be defeated by changes in the environment, they can be defeated by changes in the perceiving organism, they can even be defeated by one another, and all such defeats will result in error, or a further inadequation of appearance to reality.

The systematic study of illusions amounts to a funhouse of examples to illustrate how structures and strategies of perception can be defeated. Those who apply themselves to this field will try to explain illusory effects by specifying which particular features of our perceptual designs may be defeated by particular patterns of stimuli. Some illusions occur as a result of certain structural or mechanical limitations of perceptual systems. Faults of various kinds in the mechanical components of vision, for example, will render the perceiver more susceptible to illusions. If a lesion prevents rightward movement of the eye, any attempt to move the eye in that direction will cause the entire field of vision to appear to have shifted suddenly to the right. You can experience the same effect by closing your left eye and then gingerly tapping at the side of your right eyeball. Various illusions classified as after-image or aftereffect illusions also result from structural factors. When a chilled hand is placed in lukewarm water, the water will feel warmer than it does under normal circumstances. If a perceiver looks at an illuminated colored patch for a period and then shifts attention to a plain white surface, a figure of complementary color will appear as a result of sensory fatigue. A similar fatigue effect can cause illusions of motion. The next time you go to a movie, fix your attention on the center of the screen as the credits roll upwards. When the credits are done you will experience the illusion of downward motion for a period of time. This effect results from momentary fatigue in the cells keyed to upward motion, leaving an imbalance of sensitivity biased in favor of downward motion. A comparable aftereffect is experienced after you carry a heavy load in your arms for some period of time and then pick up a familiar object. The familiar object will appear strangely light in weight. Or press your arms outward against the frame of a doorway for a few moments and then step out of the doorway only to feel your arms elevate themselves, seemingly without effort. Each of these illusory effects is generated by structural properties of perceptual apparatus.

Illusions of time perception also appear to be linked to physiological factors. When body temperature is elevated, time is reckoned to pass more quickly. In one experiment persons with a body temperature of 103° F were asked to count out sixty seconds. They did so in less than forty seconds. Conversely, subjects with slightly lowered body temperature took considerably more than a minute to count out sixty seconds.[16]

Various visual illusions rely for their effect on the process known as lateral inhibition, whereby activity in one nerve cell can decrease the activity in nearby cells. This is the process that makes the area surrounding a bright spot appear darker than it actually is. The same process can affect perception in other ways as well. When two bright spots are presented close together, for example, the excited cells overlap, causing the perceiver to see a single spot rather than two. Also, when two separated spots are shown, the inhibitory effect is offset by a concurrent excitatory effect, causing the two spots to appear farther apart than they actually are.[17]

A great variety of illusions occur because the designs of strategic or schematic components of perception are defeated. Certain illusions, for example, take their effect from defeat of the designs of perceptual constancies; that is, schemas that enable a perceiver to judge the constancy of some features of the environment in spite of variations in actual stimuli. Humans as well as many other animals develop constancy schemas for such features as size, shape, position, color, and brightness. If I hold up my thumb at arm's length and gradually draw it closer to my face, I do not perceive the thumb to be getting larger, even though its retinal image increases by several times. If I walk across the room and view my desk from a different perspective, I do not judge the shape of the desk to have changed, even though the geometrical image on the retina clearly has changed. I will judge a lump of coal in full sunlight to be darker than bedsheets in dim light, despite the fact that the amount of light reflected by the coal may be considerably greater. Likewise, if a cloud passes overhead while I am washing my car, I do not conclude that my car, now shaded, has changed to a deeper shade of red. Such examples tell us that compensating perceptual strategies are at work, enabling perceivers to behold stability in the world around in spite of gross variations in the actual sensory data. Detailed accounts of these strategic processes become very complex and cannot detain us here, but basically the story is that each of the so-called constancies involves an integration of various schemas for monitoring subjective sensory changes and for construing their data as information in relation to unchanging objective realities. Without the operation of such schemas we might judge the man pictured in figure 2.3 to be the same size as the boy.

The point to be pursued here is that these strategies are not foolproof. Under certain conditions the constancy schemas may be activated to produce illusory effects. Consider the following examples. In figure 2.4 the circle on the right appears larger than the one on the left. In figure 2.5 the two parallel lines appear to be curved. In figure 2.6 the top pattern appears to be larger than the other. In figure 2.7 line XY appears to be two parallel lines. In figure 2.8 the gray patch on the right appears to be darker than the one on the left. In figure 2.9 the line on the right appears to be longer than that on the left. Each of these patterns induces a systematic error in perception (i.e., an illusion) by inappropriately activating constancy schemas which overpower alternative constructions of data. It is interesting to note that these strategic processes take place in spite of conscious attempts to preclude them.

I have suggested that illusions can occur when the designs of structures or strategies of perception are defeated. In fact, most illusions rely for their effect on some combination of both structural and strategic factors. In a detailed analysis of the Poggendorf illusion, Stanley Coren and his colleagues estimated that half of the illusory effect results from structural factors, while the remaining half result from strategic factors.[18] Finally, consider figures 2.10

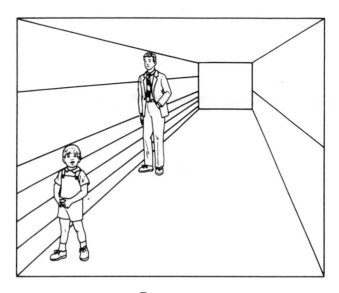

FIGURE 2.3

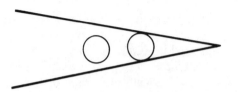

FIGURE 2.4. *Ponzo illusion*

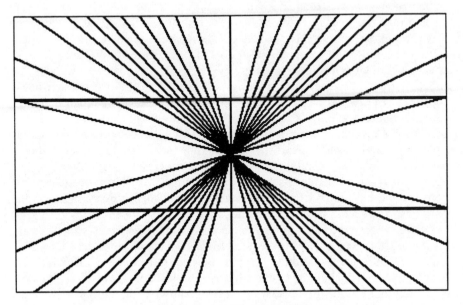

FIGURE 2.5. *Hering illusion*

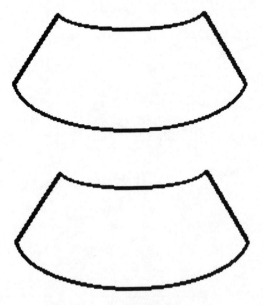

FIGURE 2.6. *Jastrow illusion*

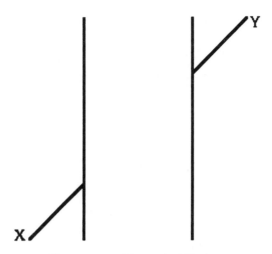

FIGURE 2.7. *Poggendorf illusion*

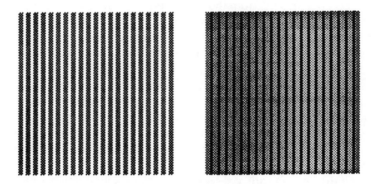

FIGURE 2.8

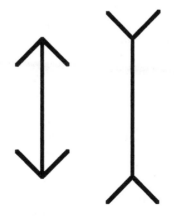

FIGURE 2.9. *Mueller-Lyer illusion*

FIGURE 2.10

and 2.11, showing how simple patterns can defeat both structural and strategic designs of the human visual system. As you view figure 2.10, close your left eye while you fix the attention of the right eye squarely on the X. Now adjust the page so that the O disappears from view. The O disappears when its image is cast upon that segment of the retina where the optic nerve departs for the brain. This is the so-called blind spot, where there is no array of photoreceptors. Failure to see the O results from the structural design of the eye. But at the *same time* (try it again) you will "see" a continuous line where in fact there is none. This effect results from the activation of a visual schema which fills in the missing data by inference from data given in the rest of the pattern. Hence we observe a simultaneous defeat of both structural and strategic designs, resulting in our seeing what is *not* there and not seeing what *is* there. The combined effect of structural and strategic factors in illusion can be illustrated again by two variations on the Mueller-Lyer pattern. As I mentioned earlier, this illusion takes its effect from the inappropriate activation of strategies for constancy perception. The effect can be magnified by a blurring of the retinal images, as in the case of a perceiver with slightly impaired vision (figure 2.11). The enhancement of distortion by the blurring of retinal images is a structural factor, resulting from the process of lateral inhibition.

I opened this section with a concern about the vulnerability of organisms to deception. I close with the suggestion that perceivers are vulnerable to deception by the same logic as that just illustrated—that is, the logic of design defeating design. *Deception occurs when the designs embedded in the morphology and/or behavior of one organism can defeat the designs embedded in the perceptual structures and/or strategies of another organism.* The study of deception is an attempt to explain which particular designs of the deceiver are responsible for defeating which particular designs of the dupe.

Strategies of Deception

It should be clear that various structures and strategies for perception would be favored in the process of natural selection. If the survival of an organism depends on its abilities to process information from the environment, then any improvements in those abilities would tend to be favored. If a fortuitous genetic mutation results in more acute sight or hearing, for example, then the organism bearing the improved trait will be better able to acquire resources and avoid danger. The trait will be *adaptive* and therefore will tend to be preserved in future generations. But of course the most significant elements in the environment are often other organisms, some of which represent resources (food, mates) and others of which are predators. And since all organ-

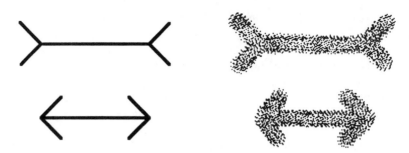

FIGURE 2.11

organisms are perceivers, it follows that the perceptual abilities of other organisms are something worth adapting to. This observation suggests that many traits by which an organism might defeat the perceptual abilities of a statistically significant other are likely to be beneficial. This principle will be seen to hold true for both offensive and defensive purposes. A predator that can defeat the perceptual abilities of its prey will be at a significant advantage. Likewise, any organism that is preyed upon will benefit from traits for defeating the perceptual abilities of predators. Whenever two organisms interact it should be possible to describe the interface between the perceptual structures/ strategies of one and the morphology/behavior complex of the other. It is in the context of these interfaces that selective factors for the evolution of deception will operate.

The next part of this chapter focuses on particular examples of deception at various levels in the organization of life, and in the course of this survey we will be looking for selective factors in the form of designs for defeating perception. What remains for the present is to articulate the categories for a typology of deceptive strategies which will shape our survey of examples. We may do so by identifying three general headings under which a deceptive interaction may be analyzed: the *deceiver's objective* (offense or defense), the *type of defeat* (evasion or perversion), and the *means of defeat* (morphology or behavior).

There is no surprise in the assertion that organisms deploy various offensive and defensive strategies in their struggle to survive. Offensive strategies are those by which organisms seek to procure resources, such as food and mates, from the environment. Defensive strategies are those by which organisms seek to resist threats posed by various elements in the environment. Several general traits are refined by various species to achieve offensive and defensive objectives. They include speed, strength, agility, armor and armaments (e.g., shells, teeth, claws), toxicity, and sometimes even sheer disgustingness. Deception is another strategy—a very common one—that finds both offensive and defensive applications. It is not the case that all species are deceitful (nor are they all swift), but far more deception is going on in the natural world than is commonly supposed. Generally speaking, strategies of deceit represent a good investment because the energy costs to the organism are typically low and far exceeded by the benefits. This is no doubt a significant factor in the prevalence of deception.

I have said that deception amounts to a defeat of one organism's perceptual designs by another organism. We may now recognize two main types of such defeats: evasion and perversion. An organism may evade the perceptual systems of another by taking measures to avoid being detected by predator or prey. Thus evasive techniques may be used either offensively or defensively. Evasive deception has the same curious logic of causation that is characteristic of preventive medicine. It sounds just a bit odd to say that the absence of illness is caused by a healthful diet and regular exercise. In the same way, it appears odd to say that the evasive deceiver has *caused* ignorance in a dupe by remaining silent and motionless, or by blending visually into the background. This is a negative form of causation, a form which allows me to take credit for saving the president's life by virtue of not taking up a gun and shooting him. But the difference is that the evasive deceiver does take positive measures to achieve negative results. The ignorance of a dupe may be said to be a consequence of a state of affairs which takes place partly because the deceiver has made an investment toward it. In some cases, certainly, the "investment" may be open to question, but this is only to say that the study of deception will involve some measure of speculation. But in a sufficient number of cases there will be little doubt that the ignorance of a dupe may be attributed in part to a deceiver.

The other main type of perceptual defeat I will call perversion, which amounts to stimulation of an inappropriate perceptual event in the dupe. Perversive techniques may serve either offensive or defensive objectives. Here the deceiver takes certain measures to cause delusion in the dupe. In many cases perversive techniques are responsible for the activation of schemas which are inadequate to the reality at hand.

Finally, we may say that a deceiver has two principal means to defeat the perceptual system of a dupe; they are morphological means and behavioral means. These represent the only two possibilities by which an organism may present itself to a perceiver. Morphological means include size, shape, coloration, smell, and all such characteristics of structure and form. Behavioral means have to do with process, or what an organism does. Both morphological means and behavioral means will be seen to have offensive and defensive applications, and may be involved in either evasive or perversive defeats. As a general rule, we may expect higher organisms to rely more heavily on behavior, while lower ones will rely more on morphology. And in many cases it takes a combination of morphology and behavior to defeat a perceiver. The coloration of a moth may be an effective evasive technique, for example, but only if the moth lands on the proper surface and remains motionless. And in some cases we will observe behaviorally induced morphological characteristics, as when a spider crab decorates its carapace with various objects. As a summary of the preceeding discussion, I offer the diagram of deceptive strategies shown in figure 2.12.

	Means	
	Morphology	Behavior
Evasive strategies	Offensive	Offensive
	Defensive	Defensive
Perversive strategies	Offensive	Offensive
	Defensive	Defensive

FIGURE 2.12

We now have before us a typological apparatus that will be helpful when we analyze particular deceptive interactions. From the side of the deceiver an act of deception will be aimed at offense or defense, the strategy will be evasive or perversive, and the means will be morphological or behavioral. But before we proceed to the survey it may be worth noting how our typology departs from the conventional categories of camouflage and mimicry. I have said that deception is essentially an interactive phenomenon, and as such it requires categories of description that focus directly on the dynamics of interactions between deceivers and dupes. The concepts of camouflage and mimicry, however, emphasize relations between deceivers and something *other than* their dupes. Camouflage speaks of the resemblance of organisms to background, while mimicry speaks of resemblance of mimics to models. These resemblances are essential to an understanding of the way some forms of deception work. But if we are not careful we may be misled into thinking (as many people have thought) that the designs of the deceiver are directly adapted to the background or to the model. In fact this is rarely the case. Deceivers are adapted to dupes, and any resemblance between a mimic and a model is purely circumstantial—that is, indirectly mediated by the dupe. The important adaptations are those between the dupe and the background (or model) on the one hand and between the deceiver and the dupe on the the other. These *separate relations* make it possible for the dupe to mistake one set of circumstances for another, but there is normally no direct correlation between the two circumstances. I am not suggesting that the concepts of camouflage and mimicry are not useful—indeed, I will have occasion to use them—but they are insufficient in themselves to describe what goes on in a deceptive interaction. For a complete account of deception these concepts must be supplemented by our typology for direct interactions between deceivers and dupes.

DECEPTION IN NATURE

The following survey makes no attempt to catalogue all the known examples of deception in the natural world. So extensive are the phenomena of deception that such an undertaking would be hopeless. It is my purpose only to show that deception occurs frequently throughout the living world, from the simplest forms of life to the most complex; and that it does so with sufficient variation of purpose, type, and means to support the claim that deception is one of the fundamental dynamics of the evolutionary process.

Molecular Deception

Most of what is known about deception in the microscopic world comes from the field of immunology. Here we will consider some deceptions perpetrated by human pathogens (viruses, bacteria, protozoa) to defeat the detection system collectively known as the human immune system.[19] The immune system is designed to detect and kill pathogens. In order to do so it must first recognize subtle biochemical differences between self and nonself substances, and then it must mobilize defenses against the nonself substances in such a way that self cells are not killed by "friendly fire" (which is precisely what happens in autoimmune diseases). One of the body's earliest lines of defense is the complement system, a set of blood proteins that target invader cells for destruction. To avoid inadvertent activation of the complement system, the self cells of mammals are surrounded by sialic acid. Several bacterial pathogens (e.g., *E. coli*-K1) have evolved to coat their surfaces with polymers of sialic acid, and in so doing they evade detection by the complement system. This is a form of offensive evasive morphology which defeats the detection system, allowing the bacteria to colonize the intestinal tracts of newborn babies.

Some viruses, such as polio and influenza, have evolved with complicated surface structures that serve to evade the defenses of the immune system. The polio virus, for example, hides the chemical binding site by which it is enabled to bind to¯(and thus infect) the nerve cells of the host. Polio is recognized as antigenic and the body responds to it by producing antibodies, but the viral binding site is inaccessible to antibodies while remaining accessible to nerve cell receptors. The body is aware of an invader and even dispatches the guards, but the crucial molecular targets on the virus are obscured by its structure—like an assassin's pistol, the lethal binding sites are concealed in molecular pockets waiting for the opportune moment. A similar strategy has been hypothesized for the HIV virus. These viruses represent defensive evasive morphology.

The foregoing examples fit the conventional category of camouflage. Other examples of microscopic deception have been classified as molecular mimicry. Molecular mimicry is a concept that has gained considerable currency since 1964, when the term was first coined by R. T. Damian.[20] The term deliberately emphasizes a continuity of mimetic phenomena between the microscopic world and forms of mimicry long recognized among insects, birds, and other animals. The most common form of mimicry in host-pathogen interactions enables the pathogen to enter a host cell by the same route as a useful molecule, in a process similar to defeating a locked entry system with a bogus plastic card. The outer membranes of cells are coated with surface proteins which routinely bind to useful molecules (e.g., hormones, serum proteins) and eventually drag them into the cell. Some viruses mimic the ligands of these useful substances and bind to the proteins, whereupon they are invited into the cell. Examples include the rabies virus (binds to acetylcholine receptor), the vaccinia virus (binds to epidermal growth factor receptor), and the Epstein-Barr virus (binds to C3 complement receptor). Several intracellular parasites also bind to cell surface components by mimicking the ligands of useful molecules. All of these examples represent offensive perversive morphology, for they defeat the designs of cells by stimulating an inappropriate response.

Several protozoan parasites deceive their host immune systems by employing a "bait and switch" strategy to serve both offensive and defensive ends. The African trypanosome, which causes a form of sleeping sickness, provides a good example of this strategy. When this organism enters the human bloodstream it displays a surface glycoprotein which triggers a host immune response. By the time the bloodstream becomes populated with antibodies to fight infection, the trypanosome has changed its chemical armament to display a new variant of glycoprotein. The first line of defense has thus been rendered inappropriate, and the immune system now musters up a new battalion of antibodies. But by this time the trypanosome has activated a third variant of glycoprotein, calling for yet another immunological response, and so on. It turns out that the invading trypanosome carries genes for no fewer than one thousand antigenic variants—an impressive armamentarium by any military standard. Several bacteria achieve the same result of antigenic variation, not by carrying a battery of genes for different surface proteins, but by carrying a single gene that is prone to mutation. The mechanism is different but the strategy of frequent switches is the same, resulting in potential chronic infection. Each of these invaders defeats the immune system by perversive morphology.

Plant Deception

We are normally unaccustomed to thinking of plants as deceptive creatures, but in fact a surprising number of plant species have developed ingenious ruses to defeat the designs of other organisms, and thus to serve their needs for survival and reproduction. Plants, like molecular deceivers, do not go in for deception by behavioral means, but many of them are equipped for both evasion and perversion by morphological means that serve both offensive and defensive purposes.

Any plant that achieves enhanced reproductive success as a result of designs for avoiding detection exemplifies offensive evasive morphology. Wolfgang Wickler reports that several erstwhile weeds have entered into the ranks of cultivated plants by such means.[21] The gold-of-pleasure plant once grew wild in fields of flax, and since its seeds were undetectable to the designs of the winnowing machine (a surrogate extension of the human detection system), it entered by stealth into the cultivation program of the flax plant. A similar process is responsible for the cultivation of rye, a weed grass which got its start by virtue of seeds that were indistinguishable from wheat seeds. Under the pressures of domestic selection the rye grass evolved from a perennial to become an annual. Camouflaged among the wheat seeds, the rye grass was transported by cultural means to harsher climates, where its hardier character-istics resulted in its domination in cultivated fields, until it became the pre-ferred crop in some regions. The same was true of oats, also originally a wild grass. Wild oat seeds were inconspicuous among barley seeds, and so were transported along with the barley to poor climates where the true cereals perished, leaving the oat plant with the status of a viable crop.

Many plants exhibit offensive perversive morphology. Some plants use deceptive means to attract food and others use them to solicit help in reproduc-tion. The redoubtable Venus flytrap, for example, displays a bogus flower to attract insects, whereupon it traps them for dinner. Sundews have hairy leaves saturated with sticky glue that glistens like beads of nectar. This pretense defeats the designs of insects that are attracted by the prospect of nourish-ment. When they land on the sundew leaves they become mired in the glue and are eventually digested by the plant.

Many other plants use perversive means to achieve reproductive ends. The voodoo plant, for example, dupes flies and dung beetles by resembling excre-ment in both appearance and odor. The base of the voodoo plant has the appearance of drying feces, and the plant emits a foul odor not unlike that of a diaper pail. Insects are attracted by these morphological features to find food and egg-laying sites, but to no avail. All they get for their trouble is an opportunity to pollinate a deceiver. Dung and carrion mimicry for pollination purposes is a common phenomenon in the plant world. Such deception is practiced by the cuckoo-pint flower, the amorphophallus, the wild ginger, the stinkhorn, and many others. Some nonflowering plants (e.g., various mosses and fungi) have developed bogus flowers and odors to sucker insects into the job of dispersing seeds. Dummy fruit and pseudoprey are also common mor-phological decoys to attract the services of naive bats, birds, and insects.

If the designs of insects to seek food can be perverted by deceptive plants, then as much may be expected of the lure of sex. And indeed, it turns out that many plants have exploited the sexual designs of insects to achieve pollina-tion. Orchids (of which more than fifteen thousand species are known) are especially adept at specific ruses, as might be concluded from the names "fly orchid," "spider orchid," "bee orchid." These orchids use the full gamut of morphological wiles (structure, coloration, odor) to seduce their dupes into the act of pseudocopulation, resulting in pollination for the plant and, one might surmise, frustration for the dupe. Many orchids have become specifi-cally adapted to a particular species of bee or wasp. The flower of the bee orchid, for example, looks sufficiently like a female long-horned bee to en-courage the male to come in for closer inspection; and the flower smells enough like the female to induce the male to attempt a mounting. Further, the flower feels enough like the female to activate the male's schema for copulation. In the process, pollen sacs are attached to the bee's head, whereupon he departs for a rendezvous with another orchid, only to complete the pollination. Variations on this theme are quite common.

Many plants have evolved evasive and perversive characteristics for defensive purposes as well. Evasive morphology is common among plants in arid regions where browsing herbivores are found. These plants, usually succulents, defeat the designs of grazers by appearing to be dead. Several species of cactus have long spines which are indistinguishable from dead grasses. In parts of Africa numerous edible plants thrive among dead shrubs from which they cannot be distinguished because of their gray and withered appearance. Also common in arid regions are plants that closely resemble stones and pebbles. The African rock plant, for example, evades the notice of herbivores because its shape and color make it look just like a small cluster of rocks. And several plants both in Africa and in parts of North America grow close to the ground and accumulate a protective coat of dust on their sticky leaves, making them indistinguishable from the soil. Others send their stems just beneath the surface of the soil, with the occasional leaf exposed to gather nutrients. These deceivers cash in on the habituation of grazing animals to ignore unpromising features of the environment.

Perversive morphology is also common among plants for defensive purposes. Some, such as parasitic mistletoes, mimic the appearance of their distasteful hosts, thereby defeating the designs of herbivores that have acquired schemas for avoiding them. The same process protects a number of edible mushrooms. The passionflower does a particularly impressive job of defense by perversive morphology. The leaves of the passionflower are the preferred sites for heliconius butterflies to lay their eggs. Once the larvae hatch, they feed on the leaves. In self-defense, some species of the passionflower have evolved to produce swollen yellow sacs at the tips of their leaves, perfect fakes of the heliconius eggs. Since the female butterflies are programmed to avoid laying eggs on overpopulated sites, they are frequently duped into passing over these plants to search for more favorable sites. This deceptive defeat has been verified by researchers who clipped the decoy eggs off the plants and then observed the predicted increase of egg deposits.

Insect Deception

The realm of insects and spiders has more species variation than any other part of the living world, suggesting that here we may expect to find an abundant variety of forms of deception—as indeed we do. In the insect world we begin to encounter behavioral means of deception, which call us to bear in mind that behavior is not always clearly distinguishable from morphology. Very often morphological and behavioral traits must work together to defeat the designs of a dupe. And these traits often serve both offensive and defensive purposes at the same time. This is especially true in cases of evasive morphology, in which an organism may simultaneously evade the perceptual designs of predator and prey alike. Another general observation worthy of note is that many insect species use a variety of deceptive techniques, and the variation may depend on several factors, including the development of the life cycle (as with moths and butterflies) as well as the complexity of the environment.

Crab spiders and flower mantids are excellent examples of offensive evasive morphology. Some species of the crab spider vary considerably to match the colors of various flowering plants. The spider hides among the petals of the flower and waits for nectar-feeding insects to approach. Even the legs of the spider are colored to blend in with the spiny petals of dandelion or thistle flowers. Unnoticed, the spider strikes at the head of the insect and sucks fluid from the body. Sometimes the carcass of the prey, usually a butterfly, serves as a lure to attract additional unsuspecting victims. Flower mantids, too, use both coloration and body structure to defeat the perceptual designs of their prey. These mantids position themselves on a flower, which they resemble in color and form, to wait for nectar feeders. The wings and legs of the insect are often shaped or curled to give a petallike appearance. Some mantids so closely resemble the real thing that one wonders if its appearance alone, quite apart from the protective flower, might be sufficient to lure prey. If so, the mantid would represent an example of perversive morphology. In fact, though most mantids require the help of plants to remain inconspicuous, many species *have* dispensed with the protective cover of real flowers to go it alone, suggesting that the evolution of insects may transform a wallflower into the belle of the ball. The African devil's flower, a relative of flower mantids, manages to defeat the designs of insects by sheer pretense. This insect is frequently fifteen centimeters long, much too large to hide among the flowers. But it doesn't need to; its shape and coloration are compelling enough. The devil's flower typically hangs from a tree branch and spreads out its ornamental shield, which even has decoy flyspecks to attract these gregarious feeders. As flies and butterflies are tempted to make a close inspection, the devil's flower snatches them with its pincers.

The spider web signals a form of offensive evasive behavior. Spiders construct delicate snares which are virtually invisible to many insects, and then they frequently hide themselves while they wait for victims. But even more dramatic examples of evasive behavior for offensive ends are offered by the African bug *Acanthaspis petax* and the lacewing fly. *Acanthaspis petax* preys upon ants by disguising itself. The bug first captures a few itinerant ants and glues their corpses to its back, whereupon it strolls undetected into the ant colony for a feast. When ants are not available, the bug improvises by decorating itself with fragments of soil and small pebbles. The larvae of the lacewing fly use the same trick to prey upon the woolly alder aphid. These aphids are protected by ants, who husband the aphids for their abundant supplies of honeydew. The lacewing larvae are able to defeat the formidable defenses of the guardian ants by covering their bodies with the "wool" of the aphids. If the disguise is removed by a human investigator, the larvae are immediately attacked by the ants.

Offensive perversive behavior is common in the insect world. The females of some species of fireflies have developed deceptive strategies to exploit the sexual communication systems of other species. Firefly courtship is initiated by the male, who sends out coded flashes. The receptive female then replies with a species-specific signal. After mating with a member of her own species, a female will frequently emit the reply signals characteristic of other species. When a duped male arrives for a mating, she eats him. Examples of intraspecific deception are also common. Courtship behavior among the hanging fly typically involves a gift of food from male to female. While the female eats the nuptial gift, the male copulates with her. Some males of the species dupe conspecific males by mimicking female courtship behavior. When the gift-bearing male arrives, the impersonator snatches his prize away and eats it.

There are literally thousands of examples of defensive deception throughout the insect world. Some insects exploit their capacity to detect ultraviolet radiation to evade the perceptual apparatus of predators while remaining visible to conspecifics. Some insects have transparent wings to minimize detection. And the majority of insects have some measure of protective coloration. All of these strategies help to defeat the perceptual designs of insectivores, which abound throughout the animal kingdom. Some forms of defensive deception are truly spectacular. Consider the tiger swallowtail. The life cycle of the tiger swallowtail butterfly amounts to a clinic in deceit. When the young larvae emerge from their eggs, they represent an example of defensive perversive morphology. The swallowtail larvae are among the many shit mimics of the insect world. They are quite conspicuous, but their resemblance to bird droppings will inappropriately activate the avoidance schema of any self-respecting bird scanning for food. When the larvae molt to the caterpillar stage, additional defensive ruses come into play. The caterpillar is green to evade detection by predators as it crawls around feeding on leaves. But if a predator does take notice, the caterpillar has yet another deceptive ploy— markings on its head give it the uncanny appearance of a snake. The attention of predatory birds has been educated to avoid snakes, so if a bird gets close enough to find itself face to face with the swallowtail caterpillar, it may very well dodge away, defeated by perversive morphology. In its next stage the swallowtail pupa is protected again by evasive morphology. The pupa is attached to a tree or shrub and has the appearance of a twig or a shag of bark. And when the butterfly finally emerges, it has further deceits in store. Markings on the posterior portions of the mature butterfly's wings may be mistaken by scanning predators for the butterfly's head. If the deception works, the swallowtail may survive an attack with nothing more than a slightly damaged wing. But there is more. A certain percentage of the delectable tiger swallowtails mimic the colorings of the distasteful pipe-vine swallowtail. Birds that have acquired schemas for recognizing the pipe-vine will inappropriately avoid the tiger. A total of six deceits practiced by a single species of butterfly!

Various other species combine evasive and perversive strategies to defeat the designs of their predators. The *Pterostoma palpina* moth evades notice by looking exactly like a weathered chip of wood. When the moth is disturbed, it falls over and remains completely motionless. The wood-chip ruse holds up even under close scrutiny. The moth coordinates its evasive morphology with perversive behavior. The peacock butterfly doubles up on deceptive morphology. The outer surface of the butterfly's wings are shaped and colored so that when they are closed the butterfly is indistinguishable from a leaf. When the butterfuly is disturbed, however, the wings open suddenly to reveal large menacing eye spots. The first strategy is evasive and keeps predators in a state of ignorance; the second is perversive, resulting in a state of delusion.

False heads and eye spots are very common morphs among moths and butterflies. Some species of lantern bugs in Asia and South America have elaborate false head structures. The Brazilian lantern bug has an enlarged and hollow false head protruding in front of its real head. This false head is stunningly similar to the head of an alligator, right down to the eye spots, the prominent nostrils, and the teeth. Birds educated to the dangers of alligators are put off by this bug. The Southeast Asian lantern bug has a conspicuous false head positioned at the rear end of its body. The real head is well concealed. When this bug is threatened, it leaps backward, reinforcing the effect. The nice thing about this perversive false head is that it is completely dispensable, so even if a predator attacks it, the insect has a good chance of escape.

Insect cocoons are especially vulnerable to predators because they are necessarily stationary, but many species have developed remarkably clever evasive and perversive strategies for their defense. Parasitic wasp larvae often devour butterfly pupae and then spin their own smaller cocoons on the surface of the emptied host cocoon. This phenomenon provides a useful premise for butterflies to defend their cocoons against raids by predatory birds. Many birds will bypass cocoons with appended structures because they have learned that such cocoons are normally empty. Some butterflies are able to defeat the schemas of these birds by attaching dummy wasp cocoons to their own. This practice represents behaviorally induced perversive morphology. A particularly impressive instance of perversive morphology is found among certain species of Oriental and African butterflies. The cocoons of these species are defended against predatory birds by the threatening visage of a bird-eating monkey emblazoned on the surface. Birds that approach these cocoons for a closer look are schematized to change their minds. The counterfeit face is so effective that some human researchers have been able to identify particular species of monkey from their "photographs."[22]

Equally impressive are the collective deceptive strategies practiced by several insect species. Some butterfly species cluster in groups to resemble flowers, doing so with such aplomb that they have even on occasion defeated the designs of botanists![23] The same effect is frequently achieved by insects in their larval stage. Some larval plant hoppers, for example, look like feathery blossoms when they are assembled along a vertical branch. The caterpillars of the peacock butterfly achieve a somewhat different collective ruse. These insects feed en masse on nettle plants, and when they are disturbed they begin to gyrate in unison, putting off predators by giving the impression of a somewhat larger who-knows-what? Some caterpillars have the practice of crowding together to achieve the cumulative effect of bird droppings. These collective deceits are instances of defensive perversive behavior.

My own favorite example of perversive behavior among insects involves certain species of night-flying moths that manage to defeat the perceptual designs of bats by scrambling the bats' sonar systems. A bat detects its prey by a mechanism known as echolocation—high-pitched signals which return echo patterns to the bat's supersensitive ears. Some moths pervert this elegant detection system by emitting their own signals, an effective fuzz-busting strategy that confuses the bat.

Aquatic Deception

Various aquatic species can be cited to demonstrate the use of both evasive and perversive strategies of deceit. Aquatic animals, like insects, very often combine morphological and behavioral traits to defeat their dupes. The Atlantic sea devil is a good example of a fish that combines evasive and perversive morphology for offensive purposes. The sea devil is covered with cutaneous fringes that waft about in the water current to give it the appearance of seaweed. In addition, the sea devil burrows into the sand and there awaits its prey. Even though it is a large fish, it is virtually undetectable. The sea devil has only one conspicuous feature, a tiny dummy worm dangling and floating just outside its mouth. When prey are attracted by the color and motion of the lure, the sea devil snarfs them in whole. Some deep-sea species elaborate the strategy by illuminating the lure.

An especially well-developed perversive morph is found in several species of the North American lampsilis clam. This clam has an ancillary structure growing on the surface of its shell to resemble a tiny fish, replete with fins, flexible tail, and appropriately placed eye spots. Water motion makes the fake fish appear to be swimming clumsily, as would a slightly injured minnow. Larger fish are attracted to the lure on the promise of an easy catch, and when one draws close enough, the clam sprays it with nearly 300,000 tiny larvae, many of which then parasitize the gills of the fish.

Mimics of cleaner fish are deceivers by perversive morphology. Cleaner fish enter into a symbiotic relationship with fish of another species. The cleaners scour the bodies of their clients for excess organic debris—bacteria, parasites, damaged tissue, and other unwanted matter. The arrangement is mutually beneficial, an exchange of goods for services—the client is freed from unnecessary and harmful substances and the cleaner enjoys a free meal as well as a measure of protection. Cleaner mimics, of which more than fifty marine species are known, exploit the symbiotic relation of cleaner and client by resembling the cleaner in appearance. This resemblance allows the mimic to bask in the protected niche of the cleaner without doing any of the work. Instead of providing cleaner services, the mimic steals bites of flesh from the trusting client. The mimic typically strikes the client from a blind side, whereupon the client turns upon the attacker but is prevented from counterattack by an inappropriate activation of its cleaner-recognition schema.

Wickler has recorded several observations of offensive evasive behavior in the saber-toothed blenny.[24] This predator attacks its prey by ambush from a blind, steals a bite of flesh, and then retreats quickly. Wickler's observations reveal the unusual resourcefulness of this deceiver. In the initial stages of observation the blenny ambushed its victims from a fixed blind. But the victims soon learned to be wary of the blind and maintained continuous surveillance of the predator. The blenny then found a way to defeat the educated attention of its prey by scheduling its attacks during feeding sessions when the victims were distracted by showers of food. The most impressive evasion of all was the blenny's use of the clown fish as a moving blind. The predator would swim close alongside the clown fish (which was unbothered by the blenny for some reason) and then suddenly attack its prey from behind the mobile cover.

Reproductive strategies of the bluegill sunfish alternate between evasive and perversive offensive behaviors. Most bluegill males reach reproductive age at seven years, but a minority (about 20 percent) are sexually precocious, reaching sexual maturity in two years. The sexually precocious males are similar in size and markings to the female of the species, and thus are unable to compete successfully with other males for breeding sites. These males (called "sneaks") therefore follow deceptive strategies in order to reproduce. In the conventional breeding pattern a male will stake out a breeding site and await a female mate. After the usual courtship routine the male and female will position themselves to shower their gametes into the nest, where fertilization occurs. The male then protects the nest until the eggs hatch. The shower of gametes provides the opportune moment for the smaller male to sneak onto the scene from ambush to release his own sperm into the mix, ensuring that a certain percentage of the progeny will be his. When these sneaky males become large enough to be detected by the territorial males, they shift to the alternate strategy of female impersonation. The sneak that employs this strategy lingers on the surface until the courtship begins, then descends slowly in imitation of the female's behavior, releasing his gametes at the proper moment. The parental male then stays with the nest while the sneak is free to look for another opportunity to deceive.

Deceptive means for defensive ends are common in the aquatic world. The evasive morphology of countershading, for example, is almost universal among species of fish. A dark back and a countershaded light belly minimize detection both from above and from below. In a few species the countershading pattern is reversed, but they normally swim upside down! An interesting variation on the principle of countershading has been worked out by deep-sea fish that evade detection by obliterating their shadows. This effect is achieved by light-producing organs, called photophores, aligned along the belly of the fish. The amount of light absorbed by the upper part of the fish is measured and then precisely reproduced by the photophores. The light emitted by the photophores has the same intensity and spectral composition as that striking the back of the fish. The effect makes the fish virtually transparent.[25] The *Hippolyte* prawn achieves a transparent effect by actually *being* transparent. At night the pigments of this animal contract, giving it a bluish transparency. During the day the prawn is able to vary its color within minutes to match its surroundings, even producing patterns of spots and stripes. Many other aquatic species of fish, prawns, rays, crabs, and octopuses are able to change their pigmentation in impressive displays of evasive morphology. In addition to changing its color, the octopus releases a cloud of inky substance to pervert the visual schemas of predators with worrisome shapes while it flees in safety. In one species of deep-sea octopus the distracting cloud is a luminous, ghostly apparition. The *Sepiola* squid demonstrates a similar form of distraction. When a predator approaches, the squid emits a dense cloud of ink to match the color and contours of its own body, whereupon it changes color and darts away, leaving the predator to investigate a mere shadow of the squid's former self.

Defensive evasive behaviors are found in many species of crabs and snails that make a practice of disguising their bodies with debris. Several species of decorator crabs attach a variety of materials to their backs, some by using a sticky substance and others by using specially adapted spikes or legs. The sponge crab, for example, first cuts out a piece of sponge to fit its own measurements and then covers itself with the sponge, holding it in place with a pair of legs. These crabs have even been observed to improvise with wet paper.

The most interesting examples of perversive behavior among marine species are found in groups of organisms that cooperate to defeat the perceptual designs of predators. Many small fish, for example, have the practice of swimming in close formation, giving the appearance of very large creatures. But by far the most intriguing is a band of sea worms that aggregate to sculpt the body of a sea anemone. This artificial structure manages to activate inappropriate perceptual schemas in small fish. Small fish, which usually relish worms, avoid this sculpture because they are wary of the stinging tentacles of the anemone.[26]

Amphibian and Reptilian Deception

The use of evasive morphology is especially common among amphibians and reptiles. Most species of frogs, toads, turtles, lizards, and snakes are countershaded or have special coloration to make them inconspicuous. Many species, such as the Asian horned frog, combine structure and color to achieve their effect. The horned frog has a flattened body with sharp edges and flanges at the side, rather like a flattened paper carton. The eyes are concealed and the body surface is greenish-brown with a waxy sheen. It looks exactly like a leaf. Many amphibians and reptiles are capable of rapid color changes to conform to their surroundings. Such evasive morphs may serve both offensive and defensive ends.

The alligator snapping turtle uses a combination of evasive and perversive morphology to catch prey. The turtle lies buried in the river bottom with its thick dark shell half overgrown with algae. Like the angler fish, it is completely inconspicuous, except for one feature—a bright-pink dummy worm attached to its tongue. The snapper manipulates the worm to defeat the schemas of passing fish, who quite literally pop in for dinner.

Evasive behavior in the service of offensive ends is also common among amphibians and reptiles. The stealth of snakes stalking prey is a familiar example. Evasive behavior for offensive purposes can also be found in the mating practices of satellite bullfrogs. Male frogs compete with one another for preferred breeding sites. The typical pattern is for large dominant bull-frogs to establish a site and then call for mates. Smaller satellite male frogs furtively station themselves near the calling bulls and attempt to intercept responding females. Not only do these satellite males avoid the physical bur-dens of territorial combat and exhaustive croaking, but they also avoid an-nouncing their location to predators.[27]

Offensive perversive behavior is common among amphibians and reptiles. Predatory snakes, for example, often wriggle their tails in an alluring fashion to attract the attention of prey. Frogs, too, have been observed to wriggle one of their toes to achieve the same effect. More elaborate of perversive behavior is found in the reproductive strategy of the American tiger salamander. The male salamander engages in a time-consuming courtship, then leads his mate along a straight line. He then deposits a sperm packet, which the female inserts into her cloaca. Male cheats defeat the designs of the mating couple by joining the courtship procession at the opportune moment. The cheat imper-sonates female behavior to allay the fears of the male. When the original male deposits his sperm packet, the cheater superimposes his own, which is then taken up by the female.[28] Males of other salamander species use a variation on this theme to reduce competition for mates. Deceptive males engage in homo-sexual courtship with other males, inducing them to waste their costly sperm packets in the absence of any females. This ruse effectively eliminates the dupe from the real action.

Defensive perversive morphology is also common in amphibians and rep-tiles. Some frogs, for example, have huge menacing eye spots on their poste-riors which they use to "moon" predators. A sudden display of eye spots often activates inappropriate recognition schemas in predators, stimulating them to deactivate their attack. A similar effect is achieved by some lizards that have the ability to make themselves appear several times larger than they actually are. The frilled lizard, for example, has a huge collar which is normally folded back against the body. When threatened, the lizard unfolds the collar—the head now appears to be attached to a very large body—and bares its teeth. The bearded lizard achieves a similar intimidating effect by changing its color from olive-brown to a bright yellow-orange and puffing up its head to double its normal size. Threatening displays of this sort are mere bluff, but they very often defeat the designs of predators by making them think twice about attacking.

Another perversive trait commonly found in lizards is the detachable tail. Many lizards have long, brightly colored tails which easily detach from the body when the reptile is disturbed by a predator. These tails then wriggle about vigorously, leaving the predator in considerable doubt as to which structure is the real lizard. If the ruse succeeds, the lizard gets away safely to grow another tail, while the predator is left with a mere morsel.

Mimicry is yet another deceit that can pervert the designs of predators.

Some snakes, such as the coral, are highly poisonous and are thus wisely ignored by most predators. The coral snake is conspicuously colored with red, yellow, and black bands to warn off possible predators. This warning coloration provides a protective niche for a number of species of harmless snakes that have similar coloration. These coral mimics defeat the designs of predators by activating an inappropriate recognition schema.

Some snakes use behavioral means to pervert the perception of their predators. When threatened by a predator, many snakes hide their heads and move their tails in a headlike fashion, thus diverting attention to the wrong target. If the snake happens to be venomous, a predator may well be duped into an early death. The harmless hognose snake uses a succession of wiles to defeat the designs of predators. When disturbed, the hognose first attempts to threaten its predator by inflating the front end of its body and assuming an aggressive posture, making loud hissing and puffing noises. If this bluff fails to put off the predator, the hognose then tries another ruse—it goes into apparent convulsions and then pretends to be dead, lying completely motionless, belly up, with its mouth gaping wide open. Playing dead may appear to be a foolish strategy, but in fact many predators are programmed to avoid eating prey they have not killed themselves. Several species of tree snakes use the same trick; when disturbed they fall to the ground and lie there stiff and motionless, resembling a slender branch.

Avian Deception

Several factors conspire to reduce the need for birds to develop evasive morphological traits. Exceptional eyesight and the mobility of flight give many birds abilities for surprise attack and quick escape. Moreover, many birds live on fruit, and most spend a considerable portion of their lives in trees, well out of harm's way. Thus many birds can afford to be conspicuous. Still, many birds defeat the perceptual systems of predators and prey by means of evasive morphology. We might expect to find a higher frequency of evasive morphology among birds whose mobility is limited, and this turns out to be the case. In many bird species it is the female that incubates eggs and tends the young, so that she is confined to the nest for extended periods of time. Under these circumstances the female is far more vulnerable to predators than the male. In these species the female is normally less conspicuously colored, while the bright colors of the male function as signals for courtship displays and territorial defense. This sexual dimorphism is seen in the northern cardinal and the American wood warblers. In some species, such as the red-necked phalarope, the gender roles are reversed, and in these cases the males are drab while the females are larger and brightly colored. Many ground-nesting birds, such as pheasants and prairie chickens, are colored to evade the notice of predators. The great potoo, a tree dweller in tropical regions where monkeys are common, is a marbled brown and perches in such a way as to resemble a broken branch. Many nonmigratory birds (e.g., the ptarmigan and several species of grouse) change colors with the seasons, speckled in summer and snow white in winter. And most species of birds are countershaded to minimize detection both from above and from below. Another common evasive morph in birds is the protective coloration of eggs, which is especially frequent among ground-nesting birds. Their eggs often resemble pebbles to evade the notice of nest robbers. Many birds, then, use strategies of evasive morphology to keep predators and prey in a state of ignorance.

Many use offensive perversive strategies, too. Especially interesting is the combination of perversive morphology and behavior found in cuckoos and widow birds, as well as several species of ducks, finches, and blackbirds. These birds lay their eggs in the nests of other species of birds, thus duping them into foster parenthood. Cuckoo eggs have actually been found in the nests of 180 species. The cuckoo has the remarkable ability to adjust the morphology of her eggs to match those of the host. In some instances the female cuckoo is too large to enter into the nest of her dupe, so she lays her egg on the ground and then transports it to the nest in her beak. When the young cuckoo hatches, it attempts to force other chicks or remaining eggs out of the nest. The brood parasitism of widow birds is more specific than the cuckoo, each widow bird species being adapted to a particular species of finch. Like the cuckoo, the widow bird lays a single egg in each nest, sometimes destroying one of the host's eggs in the bargain, although she never disturbs eggs laid in the nest by other widow birds. The poor finch lacks such powers of discrimination and incubates all the eggs. Finches do, however, have the ability to recognize their young by the pattern of their gape, a pattern that is mimicked exactly by the widow bird chicks.[29]

The range of offensive perversive behaviors among birds is impressive. The white-winged shrike-tanager and the bluish-slate antshrike, both Amazon species, have been observed to make deceptive use of warning signals to distract other birds.[30] Both of these species act as sentinels to warn other birds of the proximity of hawks. The warning signal stimulates these birds to flee to safety. Both species have been observed on occasion to use the warning call falsely, to distract the competition in multibird tumbles to catch arthropods. Thrushes have been known to use the "cry wolf" ruse as well. Ravens, too, are capable of perversive behavior—they sometimes make phony submissive gestures to hated rivals until the rival draws near, whereupon the raven makes an abusive attack. The zone-tailed hawk uses an especially clever trick to prey upon small animals. The hawk glides in the company of vultures, which small animals ignore because they are not a threat. The hawk exploits the educated attention of these animals by using the group of vultures as a blind until it spots an unsuspecting prey, and then suddenly dives out of the group to make a catch.

An interesting example of defensive perversive morphology has been attributed to juvenile American avocets. Avocets first take flight at about five weeks of age, but unlike most birds of their type, the young flightless avocets develop adultlike plumage after their second week. Tex Sordahl hypothesizes that this unusual development of mature plumage represents a case of "adult automimicry"; in effect, the immature avocet lies about its age.[31] The avocet is an open-country species, and predators that target these birds must select their prey at considerable distances. Early development of adult plumage can defeat the perceptual designs of distant predators, who may easily mistake a vulnerable flightless juvenile for a volant adult.

The bittern gives us a fine example of defensive evasive behavior. When this heronlike bird is threatened, it assumes a rigid posture and stretches its beak toward the sky to resemble the surrounding reeds. The long-tailed titmouse, as well as many other species, disguises its nest by covering it with lichens, an example of behaviorally induced morphology.

Instances of perversive behavior for defensive purposes are not far to seek. Bluffing, for example, is a common defensive strategy. When threatened, many birds fluff their feathers to give the appearance of being much larger than they actually are. Predators may reconsider an attack if they are suddenly faced by a very large bird. Wild turkeys and peacocks also bluff when they are threatened. They display their large fantails and quiver about noisily, appearing far more fearsome than they really are. It is hard to say exactly what schemas are activated in predators by such displays, but they are often quite effectively off-putting. Titmice and chickadees attempt to activate a snake-recognition schema in their predators. If these birds are disturbed in the nest, they open the beak and emit a loud hissing noise, rocking the head from side to side as a snake would do.

Defensive perversive behavior has been studied in detail among avocets and stilts.[32] These shorebirds have been observed to use a variety of deceptive strategies to protect their nests from predators. Sometimes the birds bluff a predator by dive-bombing. Sometimes they move about on the ground, crouching and running and making false incubation displays, gradually leading the predator away from the nest site. Frequently these birds feign injury, flapping about in apparent helplessness and making nasal calls typical of distressed birds. As this display continues, the bird moves farther and farther from the nest, leading its dupe onward in the expectation of an easy kill. At the appropriate moment the bird suddenly "recovers" and flies away, but by this time the intruder is unable to reconstruct the location of the nest.

Mammalian Deception

We have observed that in the microscopic world and among plants, deception is exclusively morphological. In insects, aquatic animals, amphibians, reptiles, and birds we observed a mixture, and often combinations, of morphological and behavioral means of deception. When we turn to mammals, we observe that relatively more instances of deception are behavioral, as we might well predict on the basis of the strong influence of learning on mammalian adaptation. All the same, morphological deceit is to be found among mammals too, usually in the form of protective coloration. The polar bear is a good example of evasive morphology. This snow-white giant has no natural predators, so its camouflage in the arctic environment can be identified as offensive. The opposite is true of the showshoe hare, which evades its predators' notice by changing its color, from white in winter to brown in summer. The tree-dwelling two-toed sloth offers another example of evasive morphology. Unlike tree-dwelling monkeys, this slow-moving mammal cannot depend upon speed and agility to avoid its predators. Instead, it is colored green to remain inconspicuous within its leafy environment. The green coloration results from the growth of algae on the long hairs of the sloth. Most mammals are countershaded with lighter underparts, which reflect light groundward to minimize the appearance of a shadow. Juvenile deer are equipped with white spots to resemble the sun-speckled forest floor where they often rest while their parents feed nearby. The vertical stripes of the tiger, too, may help this large predator to evade the notice of prey as it moves quietly through tall grasses.

The hamadryas baboon represents an interesting example of defensive perversive morphology. The female develops bright-red genital swelling during oestrus, which functions as a sexual releaser signal for dominant males. Many low-ranking male hamadryas baboons have dummy oestrus swellings, which they display to dominant males to inhibit aggression. Another example of defensive perversive morphology is seen in the facial markings of another baboon, the mandrill. The mandrill has a long red nose between bright-blue cheeks, a pattern that closely resembles the pattern of genital display in many species of baboons. Genital display is a common threatening gesture among male baboons, and it is likely that the mandrill face activates the display-recognition schema sufficiently to produce cautious behavior. Also, many mammals (e.g., dogs, cats, monkeys, woodchucks) have the ability to make themselves appear much larger than they actually are by bristling their coats. These are all examples of defensive perversive morphology.

Of the many examples of morphological deceit among mammals, the most common and interesting deceptive tactics involve behavioral means. Foxes have been observed to make false use of the distress cry, diverting the attention of their own young away from food so they can eat it themselves.[33] This ruse qualifies as offensive perversive behavior. There are many anecdotal accounts of domestic pets who have managed to pervert the designs of their keepers by behavioral means. Some dogs, for example, have learned to feign injury by limping, thus eliciting affection from their keepers. In one account a dog was able to lure its keeper from an easy chair by going to the door and behaving as if it needed to go out for a walk. When the keeper responded, the dog then stole the comfortable chair for itself. But not all the evidence of deceptive behavior in dogs is based on anecdotal accounts. Systematic observation of playful relations between dogs and humans have shown that dogs often use false enticements in play situations, presumably based on the dog's ability to assess and thus defeat the designs of the play partner.[34]

Defensive perversive behavior is also common among mammals. Elephants, for example, have been observed to pretend to certain actions in order to thwart the aggression of other elephants.[35] Elephants also make bluff attacks on humans, as do other mammalian species. Other examples of perversive behavior include feigning injury (observed in foxes, coyotes, weasels, dogs, cats), and feigning death (commonly observed in the opossum and several species of foxes).

The most extensive research on deceptive behavior in nonhuman mammals has focused on monkeys and apes. Much of the deceptive social behavior in these animals suggests that they are on occasion capable of planned or intentional deceit. That is, in many cases they not only possess the designs to defeat a perceiver but also appear to be consciously aware of these designs, and may even invent them by insights into the schemas of their dupes.

A clear example of offensive evasive behavior is seen in the practice of low-ranking male chimpanzees of using one hand to conceal an erect penis from the view of a dominant male while leaving it exposed to a nearby female with whom he is trying to initiate sexual contact. The ability of chimps to conceal their emotional reactions to certain events presents us with many examples of evasive behavior. An offensive use of this type of evasion is reported by Frans de Waal.[36] He once observed a chimp passing through a site where some fruit had been hidden in the sand. The chimp appeared to be completely oblivious of the fruit, concealing his delight at the discovery from other chimps nearby. So nonchalant was he that the researchers were convinced that the fruit had escaped his notice. But long afterward, when the other chimps had fallen asleep, he went directly to the site to dig up the fruit and eat it. Emotional concealment has also been observed in monkeys to serve defensive purposes. Subordinate rhesus monkeys sometimes pretend not to notice (and thus do not comply with) threatening displays by dominant males. By concealing its emotional reaction the subordinate manages to dupe the dominant into thinking that the display has not been noticed, thereby thwarting the punishment for noncompliance to be expected in such situations. This strategy resembles that of the child who pretends not to hear a parent's command. If the evasion is successful, the child may avoid both compliance and punishment.

Perversive behavior is common among monkeys and apes. Defensive perversion has been observed in chimps that feign injury by limping conspicuously in the presence of dominant males, thus preventing aggression. Moments later the limp mysteriously disappears, only to reappear when the dominant returns. Monkeys and apes are also capable of perverting the perceptual designs of dupes by feigning certain attitudes. Richard Byrne and Andrew Whiten tell of a young baboon who was about to be punished by a group of adults. Instead of fleeing or submitting, the young baboon stood up on his hind legs and stared intently at the horizon as if he detected some distant threat to the entire group. The pursuers, distracted by this feigned interest, stopped short and stared into the distance as well. The pursuit was not resumed.[37] Frans de Waal relates a touching example of pairs of chimps that feigned interest in an insignificant object for the purpose of achieving reconciliation after a conflict. Chimps who have been in conflict are reluctant to make the first move to restore amicable relations. In these situations the adversaries typically sit opposite each other, avoiding eye contact and clearly waiting each other out. On several occasions de Waal observed that feigned interest served to facilitate reconciliation. One of the adversaries would pretend to take an interest in some trivial object and begin hooting enthusiastically to attract several other chimps, including the adversary. All the other chimps would lose interest in the object immediately, leaving the two adversaries by themselves to examine it together, both pretending to preoccupation. Within minutes the tension would pass and the adversaries would begin to groom each other. By such feints reconciliation was achieved without any loss of face.[38]

Monkeys and apes have proved themselves to be resourceful deceivers within the limits of their natural systems of communication. And we now have good reason to believe that they become even more resourceful once they have acquired the rudiments of an artificial language. Several successful attempts have been made to teach chimpanzees, gorillas, and orangutans a set of symbols, with hand gestures, computer lexigrams, or tokens used as the material means of communication. Whether these apes use symbols as meaningful linguistic conventions or merely as conditioned manipulative devices is a matter of dispute. An especially interesting study involved a male orangutan, Chantek, who had learned an adapted form of American Sign Language. Chantek learned more than one hundred signs, which he used in various combinations. When he was two years old he made his first attempt to use language deceptively. When he was four years old Chantek's caregivers monitored and recorded his deceptive behavior for a period of seven months. During this period he attempted an average of three deceits per week. Ninety-eight percent of the observed deceits involved the use of language.[39]

The observations revealed that Chantek was able to use linguistic means for both offensive and defensive purposes in a variety of situations. Sometimes he would give misleading signs in order to gain access to food or forbidden objects, or to be let out of his room, or to gain advantage in play. He often made the sign "dirty," for example, indicating a need to use the toilet, but when he was taken to the toilet he ignored it to play with the faucets, soap, and other items. He also used signs falsely in order to lure caregivers into play situations. He frequently signed "hug," and when the caregiver came to hug him he would tickle or play-bite or run away. In a tug-of-war game he signed "get down," and when the caregiver got down Chantek yanked the rope away and ran off. On one occasion Chantek was asked to return a pencil eraser he was playing with. Instead of returning it he hid it away and signed that he had eaten it. Moments later he was found playing with it behind his potty. Once he put a visitor's watch into his mouth and then tried to divert the caregiver's attention by signing "listen." Chantek also used deceptive signs for defensive purposes. He often signed "dirty" to avoid being returned to his room or to get out of a training session. After misbehavior of some sort he would sign "Chantek good" in an attempt to avoid reprimands.

Studies of this type among symbol-using apes tend to confirm the larger evolutionary hypothesis that strategies of deception will develop whenever new means are made available, either by genetic mutation or by learning.

Summary and Prospectus

In this chapter I have tried to articulate certain basic features of a general theory of deception and have applied these features to a survey of deceptive phenomena at various levels in the organization of life. Deceptive traits were defined as morphological and behavioral designs, selected in many species for their utility in defeating the perceptual systems of other organisms. This approach led to a typology of deception reflecting the deceiver's objectives (offensive/defensive), the type of defeat (evasive/perversive), and the means of deception (morphology/behavior). In simple life forms and in plants we observed that deceptive traits are exclusively morphological. In insects, aquatic animals, amphibians, reptiles, and birds we found both morphological and behavioral deception. Mammals, by contrast, achieve deception mostly by behavioral means.

The point of all this was to advance the view that the dynamics of deceptive interactions can be important factors in the process of evolution. When deceptive traits appear in nature, they tend to be favored. These traits then become significant elements in the process of natural selection; that is, the presence of deceivers bears upon the fitness of their dupes. In general, deceivers tend to select against the most vulnerable perceivers, leaving the more able among them to reproduce. And able perceivers select against ineffective deceivers, leaving the most evasive and perversive to reproduce. Thus we find something analogous to an arms race in the living world, as talented perceivers and talented deceivers are favored alike. In other words, traits for deceiving and for not being deceived are both adaptive. In rare instances, usually involving symbiotic relations, it may be observed that a dupe takes some small advantage from being deceived, and here it may be supposed that vulnerability to deception is somewhat adaptive. But this supposition has no conclusive evidence in its favor. A better view is that organisms inherit their perceptual systems whole, and certain vulnerabilities inevitably come into the bargain along with the prowesses. Examples from the world of illusion illustrate this point nicely—the perceptual powers of the "constancies" are paid for by vulnerability to certain illusions. In such cases, major perceptual advantages may necessarily entail certain minor disadvantages. It may be unfortunate for the blue jay that it cannot distinguish the monarch from its mimic, but this is a small price to pay for a perceptual system capable of recognizing and avoiding the toxic monarch. In general we may say that vulnerabilities to deception are preserved as quirks characteristic of a perceptual system which is selected for its total survival value. When the disadvantages of vulnerability to deception begin to outweigh the advantages of the system as a whole, then we observe a loss of fitness, perhaps to the point of extinction.

It should come as no surprise when I assert that of all living species on earth human beings are the most resourceful both as perceivers and as deceivers. Humans have evolved largely by virtue of their remarkable abilities to process large amounts of relevant information from the world around and by virtue of their unsurpassed cunning in defeating the perceptual designs of other organisms. Indeed, in humans, as in many other animals to a lesser degree, perceptual prowess becomes a significant resource for the invention of deceptive behavior. The role of deception in human adaptive strategies has been so important that we may suspect it to be essential to our survival. The remainder of this book focuses on the role of deception among humans, so it will suffice for the moment to make a few preparatory remarks.

I begin with the observation that human beings are capable of perpetrating deceptive acts in all eight categories of our typology, though it must be noted that most instances of morphological deceit—the evasive duck blind and the perversive duck decoy, for example—are behaviorally induced.

Another important observation about human deceit is that a clear majority of our deceptive interactions are intraspecific. This was perhaps less true in our deep evolutionary past than it has been since the rise of civilization, but certainly in the domain of recorded history it cannot be doubted that most human interactions, deceptive or not, are with other humans. And from this observation another follows: Most interactions between humans involve the use of systems for symbolic communication—that is, language. Thus we may suppose that most human deceits are probably achieved by linguistic means. We have already observed that the acquisition of language symbols among apes meant an added resource for deception. Language is found to have utility for deceptive purposes from both collective and individual perspectives. Language may not be directly useful in efforts to deceive fish and game, but one can easily imagine debates within hunting parties concerning how best to catch a fish. And we can easily imagine the same with respect to warrior bands planning battle strategies. We may assume, then, that the construction of deceptive strategies was among the earliest, most extensive, and most beneficial applications of language. If this is the case, then we can see how the process of learning a language might amount to initiation into a deceptive frame of mind. It is reasonable to assume that primitive language became refined partly in the context of planning deception. Thus we can imagine that talk about the "other" in these planning sessions would normally mean talk about some dupe (e.g., fish, game, adversaries). Linguistic refinements worked out in these settings would tend to reflect the deceptive purposes at hand. That is, to the extent that a language became refined for the purpose of inventing deceptive designs, schemas for deception would become part of its very substance. Thus children learning the conventions of the language would have their consciousness organized in some measure by the logic of deceit.

It is too much to expect that this logic would not enter into intraspecific interactions whenever they involved some measure of competition. In all human interactions, then, it may be assumed that the option of deceit will appear routinely in the cogitations that ultimately lead to the selection of a behavior. To the extent that the practice of disinformation is judged to be destabilizing, a society will develop mechanisms for detecting it along with sanctions for preventing it. The centrality of cultural admonitions against being deceived, reviewed in chapter 1, tends to reinforce this interpretation. This is not to say that language evolved exclusively in the service of deceptive ends, but it is to suggest that deception was an important factor in the evolution of language, and that for this reason language competence serves to amplify the possibilities, or even the proclivities, for intraspecific deception.

We may come to regard the domain of linguistic interactions, then, as a microcosm of the larger evolutionary dialectic referred to earlier as an arms race between deceivers and detectors.

"Nothing in biology makes sense except in the light of evolution." So said Theodosius Dobzhansky in 1973.[40] We might update this dictum by expanding it to include the entire range of human behavior. We might now say that nothing in the various realms of language, literature, art, music, politics, industry, philosophy, theology, or any other human endeavor is intelligible except in the light of evolution. Implicit in this evolutionary view is the insight that all biological adaptations (among which I include the full range of cultural innovations) stand ultimately in the service of survival and reproduction. But it should be added that we can further clarify this ultimate goal in the case of human behavior by specifying two penultimate goals. That is, humans pursue the ultimate goal of survival by the process of achieving the intermediate goals of personal wholeness and social coherence. By "personal wholeness" I mean a sense of individual well-being, integrity, equilibrium, homeostasis, mental health, self-fulfillment, and the like. And by "social coherence" I mean an acceptable level of collective order and stability, a sense of security, solidarity, predictability, and communion of purpose. Without the achievement of these two goals there is little prospect of human survival. Efforts to show the bearing of particular human actions upon the ultimate goal of survival will always appear speculative and farfetched. But when behavior is construed in the service of these intermediate goals it becomes more intelligible. I believe every instance of human behavior can be seen either to bear directly upon the achievement of personal wholeness or social coherence, or to express frustration at failure to achieve them.

It is obvious that these two intermediate goals are extensively interdependent. No one can be expected to achieve a sense of personal wholeness or self-fulfillment within a context of social chaos. Nor can it be expected that an adequate social order can be constructed by a group of psychologically and emotionally dysfunctional individuals. Personal wholeness and social coherence are, in a sense, mutually prerequisite. But at the same time it should be recognized that these two goals are somewhat mutually exclusive. The achievement of personal wholeness may very well be obstructed by the conventions that define social order; and in some cases the patterns of social order may be disrupted by attempts to achieve self-fulfillment. The simultaneous realization of these penultimate goals will be very difficult to achieve, and will require a continuous process of negotiation and compromise.

Because of the intricate and somewhat paradoxical relationships between the goals of personal wholeness and social coherence, it is essential that they become integrated in the intellectual and moral fabric of a culture. The integration of these goals is achieved in the construction of a cultural myth, which will be the focus of attention later in this book. Meanwhile, the next two chapters focus independently on the dynamics of achieving personal wholeness and social coherence, and it is in relation to these proximate goals that we are able to gain some perspective on the role of deception in human affairs.

❧ 3 ❧

Deception and Personal
Wholeness

I have said that all human behavior can be construed in relation to a search
for two goals, personal wholeness and social coherence, or as an expression
of frustration at failure to attain them. This chapter explores the role of
deception in the achievement of personal wholeness. The subject matter
threatens to be complex and elusive, but at least the questions before us are
simple and straightforward: What is a person? What constitutes personal
wholeness? What is the role of deception in the achievement of personal
wholeness?

THE NATURE OF SELF

Much of common sense and philosophy has conspired to reinforce in us the
belief that nothing is more immediate in awareness or so well known as the
self. As David Hume observed, "There are some philosophers, who imagine
we are every moment intimately conscious of what we call our *self*; that we
feel its existence and its continuance in existence; and are certain, beyond the
evidence of a demonstration, both of its perfect identity and simplicity."[1]
Hume almost certainly had the likes of Descartes in mind as he wrote this
passage. For Descartes the reality of the self was indubitable, for even one's
efforts to doubt the existence of the self have the curious result of confirming
its reality. After all, what is the instrument of universal doubt if not the self?
For Descartes, then, the self, or mind or soul, could be taken as an axiomatic
reality, a fundamental metaphysical category. Descartes described the self as
"thinking substance," some kind of nonmaterial entity to which thinking,
feeling, and willing could be attributed. The self was not physical, but it could
interact with the physical body by experiencing its sensations and by willing its
movements.

But Hume had his doubts about the indubitable self: "For my part, when I
enter most intimately into what I call *myself*, I always stumble on some
particular perception or other, of heat or cold, light or shade, love or hatred,
pain or pleasure. I never catch *myself* at any time without a perception, and
never can observe anything but the perception."[2]

The development of modern psychology has followed the Humean approach. This is not to say that psychologists reject the reality of the self, as

does the Buddhist "no self" doctrine, but it is to say that they reject, as did Hume, the language of metaphysical substance when they consider the self. But if the self is not an independent metaphysical entity, what sort of reality is it? William James, the father of modern psychology, set the agenda for theoretical speculation about the self by suggesting that the self is simultaneously both a process and a structure. During the past century the field of psychology known as personality theory or self theory has become strewn with various attempts to articulate the precise dynamics and structural components of the self. This field is the most speculative domain within the discipline of psychology, and it remains in a state of constant flux as it responds to research in other domains, especially cognitive, clinical, developmental, and social psychology. Many psychologists depreciate the value of personality theory because it lacks the support of rigorous empirical foundations. However this may be, it is not likely that psychology will soon be without a sizable cadre of self theorists. The nature of the self may be elusive, but it is nevertheless irresistible to many curious investigators who intuitively regard the self as the essential feature of human existence.

I take the view that *a person is a set of motivational processes that are integrated into a functional unity*. The topic of motivation is highly complex and could easily take us far afield. Still, enough may be ventured here to bring minimal justification to the claim that the self is appropriately defined in terms of motives. The topic of motivation is complex precisely because it is inextricably bound up with the fundamental operation of the life process. If we inquire about the ultimate nature of motivation, we are asking about the driving force, the power, the verve that impels living beings toward purposeful actions designed to maintain the essential processes of life. To find our bearings in these waters we may turn to two eminent biologists:

> A closer approximation to what really happens in organic nature would be to describe it as follows: life is an eminently active enterprise aimed at acquiring both a fund of energy and a stock of knowledge, the possession of one being instrumental to the acquisition of the other. The immense effectiveness of these two feedback cycles, coupled in multiplying interaction, is the precondition, indeed the explanation, for the fact that life has the power to assert itself against the superior strength of the pitiless inorganic world.[3]

> Living systems . . . continue because they obtain materials and energy from their surroundings, enabling them to do the work of rearranging their parts so as to prevent them from falling into disorder. They are able to do this because they receive from their ancestors a pattern of order, which we identify by saying that it consists of 'information,' carried by a code. . . .[4]

> The order of [living things] is maintained by the continual expenditure of energy in elaborate ways that counteract tendencies to degradation and disorder. . . . Enormous amounts of information are involved in the

control of living organisms. As evolution has proceeded creatures depending on more and more information have appeared.[5]

When an organism ceases to maintain appropriate states of informed
energy it begins to merge with its environment—that is, it dies. We may say
that every living organism is impelled to interact with its environment in
ways that prevent it from becoming disorganized and absorbed by agents in
the environment. To be alive, then, is to be motivated to respond to environmental stimuli in certain ways, namely, those ways that are distinctive to
your species. Distinct species are known by differences in their organization
of information, and the details of these differences (i.e., the resulting differences in structures and processes) make up the subject matter of the life
sciences. The study of motivation is therefore a basic and central component
of the life sciences—it focuses on the behavioral determinants of particular
life forms. And these determinants will vary considerably precisely because
genetic information can be modulated in so many ways. It should be possible
to identify the distinctive motivational processes that determine the behavior
of every species. The motivation of simple creatures might be described
sufficiently by the biochemical properties of individual cellular reflexes. A
bacterium, we might say, is motivated to swim toward a particular chemo-
attractant by virtue of its genetically informed biochemical state. In complex
species it is necessary to recognize that biological substrates can be organized into composite systems which function as units—that is, assemblages
of cells working together to arouse the entire organism and to engage it in a
general course of purposive activity. When we speak of a motivational process, therefore, we are speaking of states of informed energy (simple or
complex, hard-wired or learned) that have the power to initiate the purposive behavior of the whole organism. In simple organisms these informed
states will amount to straightforward biochemistry, and in complex organisms they will amount to the very unstraightforward biochemistry (but biochemistry nevertheless) that we know as hopes, fears, beliefs, desires, and
the like. Motivational processes are homeostatic systems—that is, once they
are activated by a stimulus, the organism will remain in a state of arousal
until either the stimulus passes or the motivated response is carried out,
whereupon the organism returns to a state of relative equilibrium, or
homeostasis.

When I say that a person is a set of motivational processes, I mean that the
informed energy complex of the human species is organized in such a way that
there is a plurality of homeostatic systems having the potential to arouse the
entire organism and to engage it in a general course of purposive action. And
when I say that these processes are integrated into a functional unity, I mean
that the whole person is a synergy of these systems. To anticipate the following
discussion I will say that the self is constituted by three distinct yet interactive
motivational systems: curiosity, pleasure/pain, and self-esteem. We may further say that there is a logic by which these motivating processes become
integrated. That is, the self develops, comes together, *forms* itself out of

certain biological and social conditions. It is to this developmental process that we must attend if we wish to say something about the nature of the self.

The self is, in a primary sense, a human body. Without a living body there can be no self, no person. Despite the wishes and the dogmas of religious tradition, it no longer makes sense to speak of disembodied personal spirits. No function of the self—no thinking, feeling, willing, doing—can take place in the absence of a human body. But while a living body is a necessary condition for personhood, it is not a sufficient condition. That is, one can answer to the anatomical description of *Homo sapiens* without being a person; consider an individual who is brain-dead. Before we can speak meaningfully of a person, a fair amount of cogitation must be going on, by which I mean sensation, perception, learning, memory, anticipation, and the like. It is by virtue of these fundamental biological preconditions that we acquire the first two of the motivational systems that constitute the self, the *curiosity motivator* and the *hedonic motivator*.

Aristotle observed that "all men by nature desire to know." He might well have generalized the principle to include all species of life. Knowing is a form of information processing, and the impulse to seek out and respond to information is characteristic of life in all forms.[6] This impulse, which we call curiosity in humans, is present as a motivating mechanism from the first moments of life, and it continues to motivate the individual straight through to death. A person whose curiosity is aroused will engage in exploratory behavior—not exclusive of the reflective exploration of memory—and remain in a deficit motivational state until the cognitive system manages to assimilate the new information by means of recognition or schema formation. The impulse toward the processing of novel information may be suppressed for complex reasons that will be clarified later on, and it may be channeled in various ways by the results of previously processed information, but it remains a fundamental fact of human existence that where there is life there is curiosity. Aristotle had it right.

But another voice in the ancient philosophical tradition, represented by the hedonistic schools, contends that the primary motivator of human behavior is a desire to experience pleasure and to avoid pain. There is little doubt about the power of this pleasure principle to initiate behavior. Researchers have even provided physiological support to the hedonic view by identifying pleasure centers in the brain. Stimulation of the lateral hypothalamus is known to produce several forms of goal-directed behavior, such as eating, drinking, and sexual behavior. Rats with electrodes implanted in the pleasure centers will repeatedly press a bar to stimulate these centers, often to the neglect of food and water. Conversely, rats will carefully avoid behaviors that stimulate the raphe nuclei region of the brain.[7] Results such as these have convinced many investigators that the motivation to seek pleasure and avoid pain is primary. Learning theorists concur, citing pleasurable and painful experiences as the essential operators in establishing patterns of learned behavior. The hedonists, it appears, had it right.

Both of these ancient philosophical voices have their advocates within the contemporary psychological community. Psychoanalytic theory and many learning theories support the hedonic view that behavior is governed by feelings and emotions, and that the cognitive dimensions of life are derivative, or secondary. Others take the opposing view, that the cognitive system is primary and the affective domain is secondary.[8] It is worth noting, however, that the present state of neural science does not allow this ancient debate to be settled decisively. If anything, neurophysiology supports the view that there is a great deal of interaction at the neural level between distinct motivational processes. This interaction would support the hypothesis that human beings are motivated simultaneously and independently by curiosity and by the hedonic principle. Seymour Epstein expresses this hypothesis concisely:

> If one were to construct a robot that could learn from experience, protect itself from harm, seek what it needs to maintain itself, and avoid what could harm it, it would be useful to include at least two systems: a cognitive system that registered, stored, and assimilated experience into an organized conceptual system and an affective system that provided feelings that motivated the robot to seek certain kinds of experiences and avoid others. There would be a need in the affective system for signals, such as pain, to register biological injury and motivate avoidance behavior, and pleasure to indicate what is desirable and motivate approach behavior. Given the two systems, which correspond to cognition and affection, all kinds of complex developments could then take place, including the development of complex motives that are no longer dependent on direct sensory stimulation. Both systems are necessary for adaptation.[9]

There is justification for the view that the behavior of children in roughly the first two years of life is shaped by the interaction of two motivational processes, the cognitive and the affective. The first orients the child's attention to the environment outside the skin, while the second is attuned to experiences within the body. And further, it is suggested that the interaction of these two systems is important for the continued development of each, and that such development prepares the way for more complex motivational processes to appear at a later stage.

The best way to describe an infant's orientation to life is to say that it is completely without ulterior motives. That is, the infant has no projects beyond the moment; its consciousness is shaped and consumed only by what is at hand, either inside or outside the skin. The infant relishes pleasurable experiences for their own sake, and reacts reflexively when it is in a state of excitement. And if the pleasure/pain needle is stable, the infant works at attending to the world outside. If the infant could speak its mind, it would give us simple affective reports and straightforward cognitive queries. At any given moment we might hear, "What's this, then?"; "How does it feel?"; "Ow, not good"; "How does this taste?"; "Umm, nice"; "Say, here's something new"; "What's that noise?"; "Not this again"; "Ah, yes," and the like.

The infant is busy forming schemas that will enable it to recognize important external objects and processes, and as these schemas develop, the infant evaluates their experiential properties. It is likely that the increasing repertoire of schemas will influence the differentiation of affective states. The day-old infant manifests only two states of affect, excitation and repose. But within weeks the affective repertoire is varied. By three months of age the excited state has differentiated to include distress and delight. By six months the infant begins to show signs of fear, disgust, and anger. By the end of the first year the state of delight has differentiated to include elation and affection. Near the end of the second year jealousy and joy have become identifiable affective states.[10] It is also likely that an increased repertoire of affective states will influence cognitive development by educating the attention of the child. When certain objects acquire positive associations, the child will begin to scan for them and will be more attentive to the conditions under which they appear. As the child develops, it weaves an intricate web of associations between the cognitive and affective systems. The cognitive system helps give shape and texture to the affective order and the affective system educates the attention of the cognitive system. In this interactive process the child's consciousness is becoming more highly organized, enabling it increasingly to take on projects beyond the moment.

There is an unfortunate paucity of empirical research on the parallel development of these two systems, and this situation is unlikely to improve much because of the extraordinary difficulty of designing critical experiments involving inarticulate subjects. Consequently, this topic of intense interest will remain in the realm of theoretical speculation for the foreseeable future. One thing we do know, however, is that social stimulation is important for the development of both systems. Children deprived of occasions for social interaction will be intellectually and emotionally disadvantaged. The development of personality is critically linked to opportunities to observe other persons. The infant must acquire schemas for many objects and processes in the world around, but by far the most relevant "objects" are other persons. In addition to being more relevant, other persons are by far the most complicated entities in the infant's environment—they manifest to the child the most extraordinary diversity of phenomena, and they figure into so many causal sequences. The curiosity of the child is keyed to attend to novelty, and persons provide an abundance of it. Schemas for most objects are relatively simple to formulate, but schemas for complicated realities, such as persons, require a great deal of study. The child is therefore motivated by both the cognitive system and the affective system to be more attentive to persons than to other objects— cognitively because persons are sources of great novelty and emotionally because they are the greatest source of pleasure. From the age of six months the child becomes increasingly more interactive socially, and all the while it is struggling to figure out what kind of thing a person is. The process of organizing the child's consciousness is now dominated by the dynamics of social interaction.

The child has difficulty in schematizing the reality of persons because so much can be attributed to them. When the child pinches the nose of its teddy bear it receives no response, but when it pinches its parent's nose any of several responses may be forthcoming. The teddy bear never initiates interactions, but persons do so regularly and with astonishing variation. The teddy bear's face always presents the same expression, but the expressions of persons are variable. The teddy bear never makes a sound, but persons make sounds without ceasing. In the first months of life visual and tactile stimulation are the primary modes by which a child gathers information about the world. But toward the second year audition comes to the fore. The child now learns to imitate some of the sounds it hears from adults, and in doing so it also learns that the behavior of adults is especially responsive to sounds—indeed, the behavior of adults can be *manipulated* by sounds. The acquisition of language is important for the development of a sense of self. In the first two years of life the child has only the most rudimentary sense of itself. It does not perceive itself as a person because it lacks the resources for self-perception. The child must first formulate a coherent schema for persons, and only then can it begin to apply this schema reflexively. The acquisition of language is essential to this process.[11]

Certain cognitive schemas must be developed before language can be used meaningfully. Object permanence and object recognition, for example, must already be achieved before a child can manage to associate names with objects. But once the cognitive preconditions of language acquisition are in place, a process of labeling begins to accelerate and continues for several years as the child builds up a vocabulary. In the early stages of language acquisition, linguistic categories are mapped onto nonlinguistic schemas. But as language competence progresses, children begin to formulate and refine cognitive schemas on the basis of linguistic categories. That is, there comes a point at which the categories of the received language begin to organize the child's thinking. This is especially the case in regard to verbs and adjectives. Labeling objects is a relatively simple operation in comparison with the attribution of activities and qualities to objects. In many instances, especially those that involve difficult concepts, the child acquires linguistic categories first and assembles the cognitive content later.

This later phase of cognitive conformity to linguistic categories is influential in the child's refinement of its person schema. Before the child becomes competent in the use of language it has only a vague appreciation for the differences between objects and persons—a person is, basically, a very complicated object. But as the child gets to the point of making more sophisticated attributions (around the age of two) it discovers that the language treats persons much differently from things. The child's schema for a person, then, becomes more refined as it conforms to linguistic conventions regarding the attributes of persons. There is some evidence that the competent use of verbs plays an important role in this process.[12] The child's use of personal pronouns ("I," "me," "my") appears at the same time as the competent use of verbs. A child's schema for person becomes refined as it learns to interpret active behavior—that is, as it learns to attribute agency to other human beings. When a child perceives persons to be agents, or actors, then it begins to see that those characteristics and qualities it has learned to attribute to other persons are also possibilities for itself.

As I noted earlier, once a child has a refined schema for persons, it then applies this schema reflexively, and the result is the perception of self as actor. This new measure of self-understanding also amounts to a fresh orientation in the social world, and with it comes an attentiveness to social roles. It is instructive to notice how the play of a child undergoes transformation once it begins to develop a sense of self as agent. All of a sudden the child's play involves a distinctive narrative quality. Instead of simply manipulating objects and labeling them, the child will now compose little dramatic scenes in which objects are assigned social roles. In the third year of life children appear to see nearly everything in terms of narrative possibilities. They will then reinforce their perception of patterned interactions by dramatic reenactment during playtime. This is a sign of role assimilation. The important point to be stressed here is that as the child assimilates social roles, it also internalizes the standards of performance that are implicit in those roles. As these standards are internalized, the child will apply them reflexively in a process of self-monitoring. And from the practice of self-monitoring emerges a self-concept.

The idea of self-concept has been central to the discipline of psychology from its inception, and in recent decades it has figured in the vocabulary of common parlance. By "self-concept" I mean the general schema about oneself, including thoughts as well as feelings and attitudes, that a person constructs out of social experience. A self-concept may be said to have several components corresponding to categories of self-attribution. Morris Rosenberg lists three major components of the self-concept: social identity attributes, dispositional (or character) attributes, and physical attributes.[13] Interestingly, these are the categories of "other" attributions as well, underscoring the idea that we come to hold a self-concept by virtue of seeing ourselves as we see others—that is, as actors in a social arena. These three types of attributes offer an extraordinarily broad range of variables that may be used to describe a person.

In the course of social interactions we routinely construct images of persons by making a series of attributions. In this process we come to "know" them. John, we say, is tall, lean, hawk-nosed, Scandinavian, Protestant, rich, lousy at tennis, not too bright, politically conservative, selfish, stubborn, and the like. Variables such as these are also applied reflexively in the process of self-monitoring. Individuals form images of themselves in several categories of social performance, and in this way they come to know themselves. John may regard himself as average in appearance, hardworking, lousy at tennis, intelligent, generous, and so on. John's attitudes toward himself in terms of particular performance attributes can be expected to contribute to his global self-concept. That is, individuals will continuously consolidate evidence taken from discrete self-images to construct a global self-schema, or self-concept. A person's self-concept—that is, the bottom line so far as self-esteem is concerned—may be either positive or negative. And the relation between discrete self-estimations (e.g., as a tennis player) and global self-esteem (i.e., as a person) is impossible to generalize. A person may be a complete loser in every particular performance category but may nevertheless have a positive self-concept. Another person may be successful at everything she tries but lacking in self-esteem because she thinks she might have done better. But these are extreme cases. Most individuals will find a mixture of positive and negative performances in their self-monitoring, and these estimates will have a fairly direct influence on how they think and feel about themselves in terms of global self-esteem.

Now we are coming to our point. Standards of performance inherent in social roles are applied reflexively in the process of self-monitoring, resulting in a series of discrete self-images and a global self-concept. Once the child begins the inevitable process of self-monitoring, *a new motivational process* slips into place—the process of self-maintenance. As soon as a sense of self emerges, the individual will be motivated to achieve a positive self-concept. The *self-esteem motive* now becomes a powerful organizer of an individual's experience and activity. In general, it will influence the individual's processing of information in all respects, including the education of attention, perception, memory, concept formation, and all manner of judgments. The self-esteem motive will arouse a person to seek out situations and to undertake projects that have a potential for enhanced self-esteem, and simultaneously it will predispose one to avoid situations and to eschew projects that might result in lowered self-esteem. The self-esteem motivator is a derivative motivational process. That is, it is a high-order social information processing system constructed from complex interactions between the cognitive and affective systems. As such, the self-esteem motivator will have both cognitive and affective features, and ultimately may be aroused by changes that affect these systems. Yet there is good reason to assert the integrity of self-esteem as a distinct organizing system within the information/energy complex. This assertion rests on the observation that deficits in self-esteem cannot be repaired by the satisfiers associated with curiosity and hedonic deficit states. A deficit of self-esteem may be consistent with cognitive and hedonic homeostasis, and a positive self-concept may be consistent with cognitive and hedonic deficits. For these reasons I say that the self-esteem motivator is an emergent homeostatic system with its own unique arousal conditions and its own set of satisfiers that cannot be subsumed by the principles governing curiosity and pleasure/pain factors. Curiosity is a deficit state that drives toward the achievement of intelligibility. The hedonic deficit drives toward the experience of pleasure and/or the cessation of pain. But the self-esteem motivator asks for something more—the arousal toward self-esteem can be repaired only by the attribution of self-worth and/or release from self-condemnation.

A child who has acquired the cognitive and linguistic resources to formulate a self-concept will be perpetually engaged in the activity of self-monitoring, a process of scanning for information relevant to the maintenance of a state of self-esteem and avoidance of self-esteem deficits. The operative resources for this process are socially instigated standards which apply to nearly every aspect of life—social and economic status, race, religion, moral behavior, attitudes, habits, tastes, personal appearance, abilities, dispositions, and so on. Standards governing these factors will be the apparatus for attributions of self-worth, and the organization of this social information within the information/energy complex provides the core of the self-esteem motivator. In a pluralistic society these standards will vary considerably from subculture to subculture, but it may be assumed that every functional individual has been sufficiently socialized to internalize a set of these standards. Where there are no value commitments there is no self. In the process of self-monitoring individuals will gather evidence that enables them to render attributions of self-worth. When the evidence contradicts internalized standards of worth, implicit attributions of self-condemnation will result in a deficit state, arousing the individual to make reparations. Self-esteem deficits may be repaired in one of two ways: either by taking measures to construct conditions for positive self-worth attributions or by taking measures to deconstruct the conditions for negative self-worth attributions. Many of these constructive and deconstructive strategies involve deception and/or self-deception, as we shall see in due course. Many self theorists believe that the self-esteem motive is dominant. Howard Kaplan, for example, says that "the self-esteem motive is universally and characteristically . . . a dominant motive in the individual's motivational system."[14] Gordon Allport concurs: "If we are to hold to the theory of multiple drives at all, we must at least admit that the ego drive . . . takes precedence over all other drives."[15] Such claims for the centrality of the self-esteem motive are supported by a large number of empirical studies.[16]

There are many constructive ways to approach the question of what a person is, and I would not like to be heard to say that a motivational account of the self is the only or final answer to the question. I have focused on the motivational aspects of human existence because to me it seems that motives are what we know when we claim to know someone or when we find someone's behavior to be intelligible. I have tried to identify the principal motivational processes that enforce three general categories of behavior that are essential to human survival. The first, the curiosity motivator, is satisfied by the experience of intelligibility, the evolutionary prize for which is an appropriate adequation of appearance to reality. The second, the hedonic motivator, is satisfied by the experience of pleasure or cessation of pain, the evolutionary prize for which is the acquisition of vital resources and the avoidance of fatal injury. The third, the self-esteem motivator, is satisfied by the experience of self-worth, the evolutionary prize for which is the assurance of affiliation with a social group. I have said that a person is a human body which organizes information in such ways that its behavior will be determined by the interaction of these three distinct motivational systems. These three motivators are generic systems in the sense that each relies upon the functions of subsystems. And they are global homeostatic systems in the sense that each has the power to arouse the entire organism to engage in a general course of purposeful activity toward satisfaction. The operations and interactions of these motivational systems and subsystems have everything to do with the prospect of achieving personal wholeness.

PERSONAL WHOLENESS

Both the joy and the pathos of human existence have a common source in the fact that we are a multidynamic complex of information and energy. It is the interplay of these systems and subsystems that gives human life the potential to be richly satisfying. But this same interplay, when it is sabotaged by misfortune or mismanagement, may lead us into the most intolerable depths of despair. The challenge of personal wholeness is not met once and for all time. It is rather a chronic and persistent challenge, calling for negotiated responses at virtually any moment throughout the course of a lifetime.

I believe the general principles that apply to personal wholeness can be stated without difficulty. Personal wholeness is achieved to the extent that an individual is successful in satisfying the needs instigated by robust motivational systems. This sounds palpably simple and linear. When there is a motivational deficit, seek repair. So if you are perplexed by some stimulus, look more closely, try some experiments, and eventually it will make sense or become irrelevant. If you are hungry, cold, or horny, then have a snack, seek shelter, or find a mate. And if you feel ashamed or incompetent, seek the means for reconciliation or recognition. Even if the dynamics of human motivation *were* as linear as beads on a string, great difficulties would remain. Perplexity does not guarantee intelligibility, hunger does not guarantee nourishment, and shame does not guarantee self-esteem. There are complicated strategies to be worked out in the face of motivational challenges, as the complexities of science, technology, and politics show us. But of course the dynamics of human motivation are *not* linear; we do not have the luxury of entertaining one challenge at a time. As it happens, humans are pressed by demands from all three motivators simultaneously. Being human is like playing three games of chess concurrently, with the additional interactive complication that a move in any one game will have several unspecifiable consequences for the other two. The result is that the achievement of personal wholeness is hindered by intrapsychic conflict. Intrapsychic conflict is both inevitable and intolerable, and must be extinguished by the deployment of strategies for conflict resolution. Failure to resolve intrapsychic conflict will eventually erode the functional unity of the person, leading to pathological and maladaptive behaviors.

"Intrapsychic conflict" is merely a fancy way of saying that individuals have lots of information moving through their neural systems, and that this abundance of informed energy very often impels them to act simultaneously in ways that are mutually exclusive. In other words, intrapsychic conflict involves incompatible motivational states. One need not be anything so complex as a human being to experience conflicting signals for behavior. Place a rat deprived of both food and water into a Skinner box, offering food on one pathway and water on another. The rat is motivationally aroused to approach both, but cannot do so simultaneously. It must choose between competing impulses, one originating in the subsystem for thirst and the other in the subsystem for hunger. In such situations rats experience what we call intrapsychic conflict. But rats do make their way to decisions in these cases, and their doing so tells us that they have strategies operating to resolve conflict. We may suppose that many strategies are available to rats as to humans for resolving such difficulties, some of which have been biased by evolutionary history while others have been influenced by learning. But dilemmas of the sort we have created in the Skinner box are relatively trivial. In the world outside the Skinner box the rat will have to contend with additional factors that give rise to intrapsychic conflicts. To the choice between food and water we must factor in avoidance motives arising from sensory signals indicating the proximity of predators. And to these motives we might add the possibility of sexual incentives and the incitement to exploratory behavior resulting from elements of novelty in the environment.

But still, complicated as a rat's life in the wild may become, its problems are trivial in comparison with the burdens placed on humans. The informed energy states of rats predispose them to conflicts arising within and between the hedonic and curiosity motivators. But matters are made infinitely more troublesome for humans by the additional motive for maintaining self-esteem. Consider a simple event—say, being offered a choice between apple pie and cherry pie for dessert—that may seem comparable to the Skinner box dilemma. For humans such occasions have potential for being anything but trivial. The moment the option is presented, a flow of neural information begins. My memory tells me that I have had both apple pie and cherry pie in the past, and that both options are likely to bring a pleasurable experience. We can imagine exceptional circumstances under which the conflict might be resolved by arbitrary choice: "Oh, I don't care, make it apple." But for humans living in the wild (i.e., in social contexts), circumstances are rarely so simple. Suppose I have eaten too much during the main course and now the prospect of a rich dessert represents discomfort. This circumstance will predispose me to avoid both options. But then I realize that my host has spent considerable effort in preparing the meal, and my refusal may be taken in a bad light. Now my pain-avoidance motive (hedonic motivator) is in tension with my desire to perform well in the role of guest (self-esteem motivator). Or suppose I find myself tempted to ask for both apple and cherry. The hedonic temptation to ask for both will be in conflict with information telling me that such requests may be met with opprobrium. Now I have to decide whether I can maintain my self-esteem though I know the other guests are disapproving of me. Or suppose I have concerns about the effect of pie on my body image (self-esteem motivator). This concern weighs against my hedonic attraction to the pie, and may be further complicated by the self-esteem implications of refusing my host. Or suppose I accept the pie only to discover that it makes me nauseous. Now I have to consider the implications of leaving it half-eaten. And so on.

It is a simple matter to assemble a long list of similar conflict situations. They are, it seems clear, the substance of our daily lives. And we are badly mistaken if we suppose that such conflicts may be avoided except by the most radical impoverishment of human life. In fact, it is doubtful that prevention of intrapsychic conflict could be achieved without severe impairment to the nervous system itself, to the point where one would be reduced to something less than a person. To be a person is to have the kind of neural activity that involves intrapsychic conflict.

Given the motivational principles outlined above, it should be possible to analyze intrapsychic conflicts according to six basic types. As we proceed through this typology, however, it should be kept in mind that human motivational systems do not operate in isolation from one another. Nor should it be assumed that interactions between these systems are always or usually characterized by conflict. We are focused on the possibilities for intrapsychic conflict because these are the sources of challenges to personal wholeness.

*   *   *

1. *Cognitive/cognitive conflicts.*   An individual will be aroused by the curiosity motivator whenever novel stimuli sufficient to induce schematizing behavior appear. When I am awakened at night by a sudden noise outside my bedroom, I am aroused by curiosity to know what it was. And I will remain in a deficit state until the stimuli are assimilated into some sort of neural order, either by recognition or by formulation of an original and satisfying hypothesis. But the curiosity motivator is not activated exclusively in direct response to external stimuli. I may just as well awaken suddenly with a query about how the brain functions. Curiosity can be aroused either by the external stimuli of sensation or by the internal stimuli of reflection. The point is that something has changed in my information/energy makeup to provoke purposeful activity of the sort that seeks to understand something. My curiosity about the noise outside my bedroom is not likely to be assuaged by my eating a biscuit or looking in the mirror. Curiosity is motivation toward intelligibility. Under certain conditions it may happen that the search for intelligibility will be blocked by conflicting information. Suppose I am faced with one of the paradoxical drawings of M. C. Escher and attempt to make a coherent perception. The drawing may present me with visual stimuli which appear to contradict my understanding of gravity. Visual clues which I am accustomed to trust will enforce a particular interpretation, but my memory, which I also trust, prevents it. I am left in a state of psychic conflict which amplifies my deficit state and calls for more sophisticated mental strategies to resolve the conflict. Cognitive/cognitive conflicts of this sort are quite common. They arise regularly in science and in everyday life whenever new information challenges established information, forcing us to resolve conflict between alternative paradigms for comprehension.

2. *Hedonic/hedonic conflicts.*   A large class of changes may occur in the body of an organism to activate the hedonic motive. Changes in metabolism, hormone levels, body temperature, and various additional factors can place an individual in a deficit affective state that seeks repair by means of goal-directed behavior. If I am deprived of water for a considerable length of time, I will become hedonically motivated to seek means to quench my thirst; if I am standing outdoors in the rain, I may take a chill and be motivated to seek

repair in shelter; if I encounter an ice cream commercial on TV I may momentarily find myself staring into the freezer; and so on. A considerable amount of our wakeful time each day is spent on purposeful activities aimed at repairing deficit states arising from changes in affective subsystems. And quite frequently we find that we are coincidentally aroused to act in mutually exclusive ways, torn between two goals like the rat in the Skinner box. A child may be torn between the pain of chill and the pleasure of playing in the snow, a hunter may be torn between hunger and the fear of danger, an exhausted tourist may be torn between a museum and a hotel bedroom, a philanderer may be caught between sex and safety. When such conflicts of hedonic interest occur, the individual must make a choice or endure the stress of unresolved conflict.

3. *Hedonic/cognitive conflicts.* Countless situations arise in the course of a lifetime involving hedonic/cognitive or cognitive/hedonic conflicts. These situations arise when one is aroused either by curiosity or by pleasure/pain factors to act in a certain way, only to have the activity countermanded by signals from the other motivational system. The classic example of this sort of intrapsychic conflict is the smoker whose hedonic arousal to seek nicotine conflicts with the cognitive realization that smoking is harmful. Or consider the explorer whose curiosity is in tension with a fear of great danger. In such situations the cognitive and affective systems are in conflict, calling for strategies to negotiate resolution.

4. *Self-esteem/cognitive conflicts.* The emergence of the self-esteem motivator greatly magnifies the potential for intrapsychic conflict. Indeed, it is difficult to imagine a situation that could not be construed, whether justifiably or not, to involve some sort of positive or negative attributions of self-worth. Quite often we experience conflict between our needs for intelligibility and our needs for self-esteem. Consider the first-year college student whose curiosity is aroused by the topic of evolution, only to find resistance from the self-esteem motivator. Curiosity arouses him to understand the principles and perhaps even to achieve a more intelligible view of human origins. But satisfaction of this impulse may well create an occasion for self-condemnation. If the student has acquired a commitment to the authority of the biblical account of creation, then his curiosity about evolution may imply that he is a person of insufficient faith. Now the impulse of curiosity is countermanded by the self-esteem arousal to live up to a religious standard. Or consider the parents who discover drug paraphernalia in their child's bedroom. Their cognitive processes lead them to the conclusion that he has been using drugs, but this information is resisted by their self-esteem need to believe otherwise.

5. *Self-esteem/hedonic conflicts.* Any individual who has internalized the socially instigated values of fairness, unselfishness, courage, or respect for others is vulnerable to self-esteem/hedonic conflicts, for almost daily occasions arise when such standards for attributing self-worth are in tension with the hedonic motive. Consider the child who is expected to wait his turn on the playground, or the one who is expected to share her candy with her siblings. Or consider the sexually aroused individual whose hedonic impulses are opposed by an aroused concern for social reputation. Or consider the many

cases in which the self-esteem motivator calls for a courageous act while the hedonic motivator calls for a repair to safety. Intrapsychic conflicts of this sort are both routine and unavoidable in human life.

6. *Self-esteem/self-esteem conflicts.* Without a doubt the most interesting and vexing cases of intrapsychic conflict are those involving mutually exclusive impulses to maintain self-esteem. We often find ourselves faced with situations in which our self-esteem is contingent upon a plurality of commitments to socially induced standards of self-worth. In these situations an act conferring evidence for self-worth attribution may of necessity entail evidence for self-condemnation as well. Consider the woman whose self-esteem is contingent upon performing well in her roles as both mother and professional. Or consider the dilemma of abortion, when either option calls a woman to violate her commitment to a standard against which her self-esteem is measured. Or consider the politician whose self-esteem motives encourage voting both for and against a bill that protects the environment at the cost of eliminating jobs. Situations like these can be multiplied without end.

* * *

The point I am stressing with this typology of intrapsychic conflicts is that human beings are organized in such a way that serious conflicts within and between motivational processes are inevitable. This fact alone, however, is no cause for lament, for it is clear enough that to eliminate the potential for intrapsychic conflict (i.e., to preclude the influence of one or more of the motivational processes) would be to undermine the conditions for becoming a person. But at the same time it must be seen that intrapsychic conflict is no less intolerable than it is inevitable. If conflicts within and between motivational processes are not resolved, the individual will come under great stress and will be vulnerable to a wide range of psychological disorders that may include some forms of acute disorganization and severe depression as well as a variety of anxiety-related disorders.

The picture we are now getting is that the whole person must be whole in the sense of completeness or complexity, but also in the sense of unity or integrity. The whole person is at the borders of excessive complexity in her curiosity, her passion, and her commitments. She is driven to understand the world around, she is driven to feel alive, and she is driven to fulfill worthy ideals. Her needs for intelligibility, pleasure, and self-worth are robust and complex. But the whole person is also measured, in control, coherent. She has perspective on her experience, is aware of limitations, knows her priorities, is able to act with unity of purpose. "Whole" means both full and one—the complexity of mental life is its content, while the harmonization of this complexity is its form. Chaos, it seems, is the precondition for cosmos. Human life is impoverished to the extent that we make ourselves completely invulnerable to intrapsychic conflict. The whole point about intrapsychic conflict is not to prevent it but to resolve it.

The ultimate question is: How does the brain go about resolving intrapsychic conflict? Neuroscientists are reluctant to identify an executive office within the brain, but were they inclined to do so, the prefrontal cortex would be the best candidate: "The human prefrontal cortex attends, integrates, formulates, executes, monitors, modifies and judges all nervous system activities."[17] This region of the brain is characterized by a profusion of interconnections both with sensory association areas and with the limbic system. And these neural connections include both afferent and efferent pathways; in other words, the prefrontal cortex is well connected to receive input from and send output to various critical cognitive, emotive, and motor centers. In terms of information processing this region of the brain operates at the highest level of integration, receiving preintegrated transmissions from sensory association areas, which it further integrates with information from other areas. But the prefrontal cortex is also that area of the brain which is responsible for obstructing behaviors designed and initiated by lower parts of the brain. If someone tells you to stand up and you then consider standing up but actually do not, it is the prefrontal cortex that has suppressed the act. It is this combination of integrative and inhibitory functions orchestrated in the prefrontal cortex that enables us to develop and assess ordered strategies in various aspects of our daily lives. If our lives reflect an appropriate balance of initiative and restraint, then we have the prefrontal cortex to thank. It is precisely this balance that patients who have suffered damage to the prefrontal cortex cannot manage to negotiate. Imagine yourself to be in the process of moving your household. The movers have arrived and boxes are standing everywhere waiting to be unpacked. There are rooms to organize and arrangements to be made for utilities and phone and postal services. So much to do. Situations like this are sheer torture for prefrontal-impaired patients—they want everything to be done at once, with the result that they become hopelessly scattered. They lack the ability to construct an agenda of sequential tasks, to anticipate results, to assign priorities, and then to attend to more important matters while momentarily suppressing the demands of the rest. Without the integrating function of the prefrontal cortex an individual remains stimulus-bound and unable to perform complex perceptual and conceptual tasks, including tasks of self-assessment. And without the inhibitory functions one is unable to suppress selectively among competing impulses in order to focus attention on tasks within a purposeful sequential strategy. Consequently, loss of prefrontal cortical functions results in a diffusion of experience and a loss of will. Patients with disorders in this part of the brain lack unity of purpose and are vulnerable to uncontrolled emotions and bouts of depression.

I am suggesting that among the many tasks of the prefrontal cortex is the execution of what I am now calling the *harmonic function*. The integrative and inhibitory activities of the prefrontal cortex enable us to achieve a state of functional unity against the odds generated by a plurality of competing impulses. Our entire lives are constructed, moment by moment, through our efforts to harmonize the demands put upon us by our relentless needs for intelligibility, pleasure, and self-esteem. Personality is the final outcome of compromises negotiated among these conflicting psychodynamic processes. The harmonic function operates to establish order both within and among

motivational processes by facilitating interactions among them and by developing compromise strategies when they are in conflict. It operates within the
cognitive system to resolve ambiguities in perception and discrepancies of
memory. It operates within the affective system to resolve emotional ambivalence. It operates within the self-esteem system to monitor and manage information relevant to the maintenance of a stable self-concept. And the harmonic function operates among each of these motivators to resolve inevitable
conflicts arising within a multidynamic system of information processing. The
air traffic control booth is not an inappropriate analogue for the prefrontal
cortex. The harmonic function is a strategizer that emerges with the increasing
complexity of an individual's mental life, and it becomes a decisive influence
in shaping a unique personality.

Becoming a person is not a simple matter. We begin with an inherited
information/energy complex that equips us with a constellation of basic
designs—potentials, limitations, biases, aversions, temperament—which have
been organized by evolutionary history. But the organization is unfinished; it is
like a kit that must be further organized within the flow of socialization, environmental challenges, experimental strategies for coping with them, and the reinforcement consequences of these strategies. In this process of developmental
organization a unique personality will emerge by the strategizing influence of
the harmonic function on the behavioral designs of competing motivational
processes. In consequence of these dynamics, distinctive intellectual, emotional, and moral characteristics bundle themselves into a more or less whole
person.

Deception and Self-Esteem

I have defined deception as the disadequation of appearance to reality that
results when the designs of a deceiver defeat the perceptual designs of a dupe.
And I have defined personal wholeness as a state of being that is achieved
when a person is able to satisfy harmoniously the needs instigated by robust
motivational systems. Now I ask whether deceptive strategies may have a
bearing on the achievement of personal wholeness. In general, it appears
obvious that this would be the case, although we shall see that the story is not
always an uncomplicated one.

The Dynamics of Self-Deception

I have said that individuals deploy strategies for the achievement of personal wholeness, and that some of these strategies involve deception and/or
self-deception. We are nearly at the point where we can begin to explore
these strategies. First, however, it will be necessary to say a bit more about
the nature of self-deception, for it is a phenomenon that some investigators
have declared to be an impossibility. The principal arguments against the
concept of self-deception come from philosophers of psychology and from
evolutionary theorists. Both forms of challenge to the concept deserve to

be taken seriously, although I believe they can be answered without much difficulty.

Philosophical skeptics about self-deception focus on the paradoxical nature of this supposed phenomenon.[18] Their charge is that the literal concept of self-deception is no less incoherent than the bogus concept of a square circle. Just as there can be no square circles, so there can be no self-deception. One might be tempted to believe in square circles upon viewing closed figures composed of arcs. But there are proper names for these things, such as "closed spline curves;" square circles they are not. Similarly, if by self-deception one means only certain attempts at denial or rationalization, then why not use these terms and desist from incoherent locutions? To be in a state of self-deception, critics claim, one must simultaneously believe and disbelieve something to be the case, a cognitive achievement that is assumed to be impossible. Even to attempt a literal deception of oneself is patently absurd; as T. S. Champlin puts it: "It is as if you were running in a race. A sign-post stands at a fork in the road to indicate the route. You stop and twist the sign-post round, hoping thereby to deceive those following into running in the wrong direction. But how could *you* twist the sign-post round and thereby deceive *yourself* into running in the wrong direction?"[19]

Critics of the square-circle concept will offer definitions of both "square" and "circle" to demonstrate the incoherence of the composite concept. In a similar way, philosophical critics of self-deception appear to make assumptions about the nature of deception and the nature of the self that preclude the intelligibility of the concept. In the first place, it is assumed that deception must always involve an intentional act. And second, it is assumed that the self is both simple and centralized, a rational entity that is incapable of encoding contradictory information and making preferential retrievals. It must be agreed that if these two assumptions are granted, then acts of self-deception appear to be both paradoxical and unsustainable. But there are no compelling reasons to grant either of these assumptions. First of all, it is by no means clear that deception (even self-deception) must of necessity involve intentionality. In chapter 2 I noted that all that is required for deception to occur is for some morphological or behavioral design to defeat some perceptual design, such that an organism becomes impaired in its adequation of appearance to reality. Nothing here implies that these designs must be intentional in the conscious or deliberate sense, even though they may be motivated. And nothing implies that these opposing designs must have their origins in different organisms. What *is* implied is that a self-deceiving organism must be capable of entering into an informed state that effectively precludes the normal corrective operation of a contradicting information state. And such cognitive acts are not in the least mysterious or paradoxical for humans unless one assumes, further, that the mind is the sort of thing to which one is justified in applying the principle that two objects cannot occupy the same space at the same time. But of course the mind is clearly not such an entity. Even the lowly computer is capable of storing contradictory information and then reading it out preferentially. It may be impossible to store contradictory rules at the same site, or to read them out at the same time, but it does not follow that it takes two separate computers to manage contradictory information.

Self-deception is really not such a paradoxical phenomenon when one considers a person to be a set of distinct yet interacting motivational processes. If the role of the harmonic function is to devise strategies of behavior by manipulating and inhibiting information in relation to these potentially conflicting motivators, then it may be expected that many of these strategies will amount to designs for defeating alternative designs within the information structures of the individual. I am suggesting that self-deception is a process that may be perpetrated by an individual upon herself or himself for the purpose of achieving intrapsychic harmony. An individual may process information in ways that either evade or pervert some of its own designs, thus reducing the individual's adequation of appearance to reality.

The evolutionary argument against self-deception fixes on a different sort of paradox. It is less concerned with the logical coherence of the concept than with the causal difficulties implied by the evolution of a maladaptive trait. Principles of evolution lead us to expect that an organism's ability to deceive itself would be selected against in the evolutionary process. This expectation is conditioned by the view that an adequation of appearance to reality will always play to the advantage of an organism, while inadequations would be evolutionarily self-destructive, and would eventually be selected out.

This evolutionary reasoning against traits for self-deception has been answered in a very clever argument put forward by Robert Trivers.[20] Trivers asks us to picture an arms race between traits for deceiving others and traits for the detection of deceit. Traits for deceiving others would be selected for their obvious survival value. But so too would traits for the recognition that deceit is in progress. That is, I may avoid the harmful consequences of a lie attempted against me if detectable indications in the voice, eye movements, and body language of the liar tip me off. But if the liar could bring himself to *believe* his own lie, then his body language would reflect the confidence of a truthteller and I might be defeated. What the liar requires is the ability to store contradictory information in the brain and to read out the false while keeping the true suppressed in the unconscious. Thus, Trivers concludes, this trait for self-deception could very plausibly have evolved as an indirect strategy for deceiving others.

Despite the cleverness of Trivers' argument, it leaves open several questions. First of all, we are left wondering about those individuals who are capable of storing and preferentially retrieving contradictory information (i.e., self-deceivers) but who incidentally happen to be very bad liars. The argument implies that all self-deceivers would make fine liars, which does not seem to be the case. Moreover, it happens that many gifted liars do not go through anything so complicated as convincing themselves of their falsehoods. They appear to conceal their telltale stress indicators by some means other than self-deception. All that is really necessary to inhibit stress indicators is the confidence that one will not be caught out. But finding confidence of this sort is not necessarily contingent upon an act of self-deception. Finally, one need not invoke the deception-of-others advantage in order to make an evolutionary case for traits of self-deception. It is sufficient to say that a partial loss of one's adequation to reality is a small price to pay for strategies that enable one to integrate a multidynamic system of information management. It happens all the time in evolution that significant adaptive gains will involve a modicum of loss. In the following two sections we shall see how a loss of adequation to reality—one's own in the case of self-deception, that of others in the case of other-deception—can bear upon the achievement of personal wholeness. And then in the final section we shall see that there are some dangerous limits to this bearing. But first, a transitional digression on method and on the importance of language.

A person is a set of interactive motivational processes that are more or less integrated into a functional unity. This tells us that when persons are involved, we cannot expect to find simple motives. By this I mean that a person cannot be in a state of simple hedonic arousal without creating implications for the self-esteem motivator. Nor can one expect to be in a state of curiosity that is completely free of the attention-educating influence of the self-esteem motivator. To be a person, I said, was to live under the conditions of intrapsychic conflict. But to be a person is also to live under the sovereignty of the self-esteem motivator. The matter of achieving personal wholeness, therefore, is distilled into a quest for maintaining a positive state of self-esteem. The question that carries the remainder of this chapter is whether strategies of deceit and self-deception have any bearing on this quest.

My method will be to fill out a modified version of the deception typology used in chapter 2. I shall complicate this modified typology somewhat by adding the dynamics of self-deception, but I will also simplify it by limiting its application to the behavioral strategies of a single species. The modified typology is shown by the schema in figure 3.1. Earlier I suggested that arousal

	Constructive ends	Deconstructive ends
Evasive means	Other–deception	Other–deception
	Self–deception	Self–deception
Perversive means	Other–deception	Other–deception
	Self–deception	Self–deception

FIGURE 3.1

of the self-esteem motivator might be repaired by either of two means—by measures to construct the conditions for positive self-worth attributions or by measures to deconstruct the conditions for negative self-worth attributions. These measures may well involve evasive or perversive strategies for deceiving the self or others.

When we consider these strategies it will be clear that most of them entail the manipulation of symbols. Ludwig von Bertalanffy once wrote that "except for the immediate satisfaction of biological needs, man lives in a world not of things but of symbols."[21] This is but a slight exaggeration. Most human interactions with the world around involve other human beings, and nearly all of these interactions involve some form of symbolic communication, usually language. The human capacity for language is undoubtedly our most unique and powerful adaptive trait. It enables us to benefit from the experience of others, thus streamlining the process of learning. And the invention of writing enables us to store information outside the body's information systems, thus greatly increasing the amount of information that is accessible to humans. But whatever the advantages brought forth by the evolution of language, not the least of them were to be enjoyed by deceivers. Any means for communicating information could be exploited as means for communicating disinformation as well. The designs for using language may well enhance our adequation to reality, but these designs are not invulnerable to defeat. Languages are stocked with various nouns, verbs, and modifiers that allow us to describe what types of things behave in what kinds of ways and with what sorts of effects. Our designs in selecting, omitting, arranging, and sending these variables will make an enormous difference in the informed states of receivers. Every act of communication, whether verbal or nonverbal, will bring the sender's designs to bear upon a receiver's adequation of appearance to reality. If I use the term "terrorists" rather than "freedom fighters" to refer to a political faction, I may be attempting to influence your vote in the next election to my advantage, or perhaps I want you to hire me and my word choice is an attempt to establish a base of political compatibility, or perhaps I am attempting to put you off your plan to hit me up for a political contribution, or perhaps I use the term to reassure myself of the rectitude of my country's official position, or whatever. The point is that our language provides us with a rich diversity of symbols that can be used to bring our designs to bear upon the informed states of receivers. And some of these designs may deceive.

Constructing Positive Self-Esteem

Every social order must develop a system of values together with the means for their dissemination and enforcement. In tribal societies the elders represent the final moral authority. In theocratic societies moral authority resides in the religious elite. In a totalitarian secular state moral authority is the province of a despot or a central planning committee. In a capitalist democracy moral values in time gravitate toward market values. But regardless of the form of social organization, every minimally coherent society has a set of shared values that are in one way or another imposed on the young and enforced by measures of social control. In nondemocratic societies there tends to be a uniform conception of human nature, and the range of social standards for behavior is commensurately narrow. In tribal societies and chiefdoms, for example, strength, courage, and personal loyalty are prominent factors in the attribution of social worth. In medieval Christendom the standard of religious piety was considered the ultimate measure of worth. Democratic societies tend toward a pluralism of ideas about human nature, with a resulting proliferation of standards for valuing personal and behavioral traits. Socially valued characteristics imply that individual performance may be judged against standards ranging from good to bad, depending on whether they are considered beneficial or destructive to the group. Examples include:

Good	Bad	Good	Bad
pacific	violent	happy	unhappy
honest	deceitful	tolerant	intolerant
courageous	cowardly	fair	partisan
industrious	lazy	loyal	disloyal
competent	incompetent	funny	humorless
wealthy	poor	serious	flippant
powerful	impotent	respectful	disrespectful
autonomous	dependent	friendly	hostile
wise/smart	foolish/stupid	forgiving	resentful
judicious	credulous	reliable/	unpredictable/
educated	uneducated	consistent	erratic
mannered	rustic	patient	impetuous
attractive	ugly	creative	unimaginative
caring	indifferent	generous	miserly
healthy	sickly	patriotic	treasonous
strong	weak	humble	conceited

No attempt was made to be scientific in the construction of this list. It includes redundancies, it confuses levels of generality, and it omits several important items. The point is, however, that this is the sort of list that could be generated in a few moments by an average adolescent for her own social ecology (as this very list was). Members of a society are aware at a fairly early age of the standards by which they are being judged. And these standards are the ones by which individuals come to judge their own worth in the process of self-monitoring. As I said, it is by virtue of such standards that one's consciousness becomes organized.

The constructive task for a person whose consciousness has been shaped by socially instigated values may be expressed in this question: *Under what conditions and by what means may I come to be judged well against these standards of performance?* And as it turns out, there are only two possibilities—that is, I may actually *perform* well, or I may only *appear* to perform well. Either condition will be sufficient for the attribution of worth. When one is aroused to seek attributions of self-worth, then, one may take measures either to perform well or to create the appearance of performing well. We will focus on the second of these options for constructing the conditions for self-worth attributions, although it should be stressed that most of our lives represent combinations of the two.

I propose that there are four general types of deceit by which one may create the conditions for positive attributions of worth:

In a *constructive/evasive other-deception* the deceiver devises a strategy to leave the dupe in a state of ignorance on some matter, such that the result is enhanced social esteem for the deceiver.

In a *constructive/perversive other-deception* the deceiver devises a strategy to put the dupe in a state of false belief on some matter, such that the result is enhanced social esteem for the deceiver.

In a *constructive/evasive self-deception* the self-deceiver devises a strategy to inhibit certain information from reaching consciousness with the result that self-esteem is enhanced.

In a *constructive/perversive self-deception* the self-deceiver devises a strategy to fabricate or distort certain conscious information with the result that self-esteem is enhanced.

Constructive/evasive other-deception

Frank Abagnale walked into a bank one day and placed a veneer of generic deposit slips upon several stacks throughout the bank lobby. These were deposit slips he had taken from the very same stacks the day before. They differed now from the others in one small detail—Abagnale had used press-on numerals to add his own account number to the computer-sensitive code numbers in the lower left corner of the deposit slips. Four days later he returned to the bank and withdrew more than $40,000 from his account.[22]

A young woman is approached by an attractive man at a cocktail party. He notices an unusual ring on her finger and inquires about it. The ring, she explains, was awarded to championship team members at the national collegiate swimming tournament the year before. "I must confess," she says, "it was an exciting and rewarding year"—and she quickly adds, "And you? Did you play sports in college?" What she doesn't bother to elaborate upon was her position on the team. She was the towel stewardess.

Here we are given two examples of constructive/evasive other-deception—one exotic and criminal, the other commonplace and harmless, but both capitalizing on the same logic of evasion to produce the conditions for enhanced self-esteem for the deceiver. Frank Abagnale knew that the attention of bank tellers was educated to ignore code numbers on deposit slips and to feed them directly into the computer. The generic deposit slips (i.e., the ones without readable account numbers) would be processed manually once they had been rejected by the computer. The doctored deposit slips evaded the tellers' detective designs and the computer's detective designs, with the result that the generic deposits were automatically siphoned off into Abagnale's account.

But how did Abagnale's evasive ruse construct the conditions for self-esteem? In two ways. In the first place, Frank Abagnale took great pleasure in pulling off a successful bilking operation. Defeating the designs of others was to him a sort of game, and winning the game provided him with occasions for self-congratulation. And second, the deceit made a substantial contribution to Abagnale's wealth, which he recognized to be a means of self-esteem. Wealth means many things in our society. It means freedom from want and it means freedom to do. But not least, wealth is a generator of self-enhancing signals in social interactions. The plain fact is that many people respond positively to those with financial resources. Their adulation is expressed in the fixation and dilation of the pupils, in the tone and volume of the voice, in hand movements, in smiles and facial gestures, in body orientation. These nonverbal cues (together with the verbal ones) function as reinforcers and enhancers of self-esteem.[23] It is remarkable the lengths to which people will go to elicit these simple yet powerful gestures of approval from others. They are the interpersonal equivalents of applause, honors, awards, prizes, promotions, and monuments. They are the stuff of ego enhancement that the young towel girl could not bring herself to relinquish by making a confession. So she evaded the possibility of subsequent revealing inquiries by making an inquiry of her own. His ignorance, her bliss. By leaving her dupe in a state of ignorance, she was able to bask in the glow of his adulation. In both of these cases, then, the deceivers were motivated to devise evasive strategies that would result in conditions for enhancing their self-esteem.

The psychological payoff inherent in social esteem is evident. When a person performs well on a social value standard and receives signs of adulation, the self is enhanced. But what is not so obvious is the relevance of social reinforcers that are elicited illicitly, by acts of deception. Wouldn't the deceivers *know* that social esteem was based on false pretenses? And wouldn't this knowledge neutralize the self-esteem benefits? Indeed, might it not *diminish* one's self-esteem by producing a sense of guilt? The answer to each of these questions is possibly yes, but not necessarily so. We are very selective in what we allow into our consciousness. Moments of social reinforcement—the widened eyes, the warm smiles, the attentive gaze—are often so intoxicating that one doesn't even think about the false pretenses. And if feelings of guilt descend upon one later on? Well, then other strategies may come into play to deal with them.

In many situations it is possible to combine a measure of genuine performance with a dose of evasion to create conditions for attributions of self-worth. The vanity-press author provides a good example of this combined strategy. A published book does represent a genuine performance against a value standard, though perhaps not one of sufficient quality or interest to merit recognition by a reputable publisher. The vanity-press strategy offers the possibility of eliciting social rewards on the evasive gamble that most people are not equipped to tell the difference between a vanity press and a reputable one. To the extent that the gamble succeeds, the author has traded on the ignorance of his audience to enjoy the self-esteem benefits of their adulation. Another example of a combined strategy is seen in a person who is engaged in a profession or activity for motives that differ from the presumed motives, and who takes measures to conceal the true motives for self-esteem purposes. Individuals who choose helping professions, such as nursing, are presumed to do so out of humanitarian concerns. The social esteem that accrues to these professionals is premised largely on respect for their self-sacrificing commitment to others. The young woman who enters the nursing profession solely to enhance her opportunities to marry a doctor may actually hate the work but enjoy the adulation that comes with the role. In such a case her self-esteem payoff is contingent upon keeping her audience ignorant of her true feelings.

Irving Goffman's discussion of "mystification" gives us further examples of constructive/evasive other-deception. Goffman says that "restrictions placed upon contact, the maintenance of social distance, provide a way in which awe can be generated and sustained in the audience."[24] This strategy is especially effective for public figures such as politicians, media personalities, teachers, ministers, and athletes. The idea is that a modicum of recognition, when it is attended by evasive social behavior (aloofness, secrecy), will tend to magnify the reputation of the actor. Left to its own devices, the primed imagination of the audience will idealize the performer to the point where the persona bears little relation to the real person. Monarchs often capitalize on this evasive logic by allowing mere fleeting glimpses by the audience. The designs of the imagination take it from there to produce a discrepancy between appearance and reality. Cary Grant and Greta Garbo were fine actors, for sure, but hardly deserving of the celestial mystique surrounding them as a result of their aloofness. The same dynamic, to state the obvious, is at work on college campuses everywhere, to the self-esteem advantage of football players and sorority celebs.

Constructive/perversive other-deception

In April 1978 Elias A. K. Alsabti stole a completed grant application and several drafts of scientific papers from a research lab at Jefferson Medical College in Philadelphia, where he had been working as an assistant. Within months he had parlayed the stolen materials into articles published under his name in American, European, and Japanese journals. By the end of 1980 this twenty-five-year-old Iraqi expatriate had published sixty pirated articles, gained membership in eleven scientific societies, pretended to both M.D. and Ph.D. degrees, and held research positions in a number of prestigious medical labs around the county.[25]

In a get-acquainted session at summer camp a twelve-year-old boy announces that he lives in a sixteen-room house with his doctor father, artist mother, and Porsche-driving black-belt brother. Their summer vacation on

Martha's Vineyard, he explains, has been delayed by a remodeling project, and he can't wait for its completion so he can get out on his sailboat again.

A pair of prodigal fabricators, perhaps, but different in degrees only from the rest of us.

The practice of controlling the content of our appearance before an audience has been labeled by Irving Goffman "impression management": "Thus, when an individual appears in the presence of others, there will usually be some reason for him to mobilize his activity so that it will convey an impression to others which it is in his interests to convey."[26] In many instances we will best serve our designs by presenting ourselves as we really are, and in these cases we will take care to be clear and open and unambiguous in our performances. That is, we will often take measures to help our audience get the best possible adequation of their appearance to our reality. When we do so we are being honest. But in perhaps many more instances we will best repair our arousal to self-esteem ends by perverting the perceptual designs of our audience into perceiving us other than we really are. As La Rochefoucauld writes in his *Maximes*, "To succeed in the world, we do everything we can to appear successful."

Whole industries are given over to helping us deceive others in the social arena. There is a cosmetics industry to make us look younger and less blemished than is really the case; and there is a fashion industry to make us appear taller, shorter, shapelier, and basically comelier than we really are. In the workplace we strive to appear more competent than we really are to the management, and to our co-workers we want to appear less solicitous of the management than we really are. To our teachers we want to appear smarter than we really are. At church we try to look more pious than we really are, and we admonish our children to behave better than they normally do. Young men will try to appear more resourceful to their girlfriends than they really are, and young women sometimes appear more vulnerable or less skilled than is the case. We buy status symbols to appear wealthier than we really are, and when the charities come around we want to look sorrier than we really are. We sometimes admit to limitations to look more humble than we feel, or we smile widely to say we are happier or less fearful than we really are.

It is less cynical than realistic to say that when we have an audience we spend a good deal of our energy "mobilizing our activity" so that we will appear other than we really are. That is, we design our behavior—choose our words, shape our face, position our body—in ways that will pervert the perceptual designs of our audience so that their responses can be counted on to reinforce our self-esteem. And there is no compelling reason to label these attempts to manage our impressions Machiavellian—after all, to appear other than we really are is in most cases consistent with living up to socially instigated standards of performance.

Successful impression management, whether deceptive or not, calls for an accurate assessment of the designs of the audience. Actors in a social arena, then, will mobilize their activities in the first instance to get a reading on how the audience really is. What will the situation bear? What does the audience know? What are the attitudes, the motivational states, the habits, interests, fears, hopes, commitments? How vulnerable is the audience to confusion or distraction? How attentive? How credulous or skeptical? Thus we are cognitively aroused in each social interaction and sensitive to whatever relevant information it may yield about the audience's designs.

Every social interaction is likely to be a complicated and fluid mixture of deception and honest exchanges, with the proportions changing as situational features bear upon past experiences and motivational factors. Measuring the prevalence of deception will be very hard to do, and it is clear that more research should be undertaken in this area. One such project was attempted by Ronny Turner, Charles Edgley, and Glen Olmstead, who recorded and analyzed 130 dyadic conversations to measure the frequency of deceptive strategies. They asked participants in these conversations to consider each unit of verbal conversation and to indicate whether the units were honest, and if not, what they would have said if they had been honest. They found that of the 870 units of verbal communication contained in these conversations, *more than 60 percent* involved some form of deceit (i.e., lies, exaggerations, half-truths, secrecy, or diversionary tactics). And of these deceits, nearly one-third represented "individual endeavors to negotiate a positive validation of [the speaker's] announced identity."[27]

Now we are brought face to face with another evolutionary paradox. If strategies of other-deception are as common as this research suggests (which I think they are), then we are hard-pressed to give a social-evolutionary account of this fact. From an evolutionary perspective we would expect other-deceptive strategies to be uncommon, on the principle that, as Trivers expresses it, "deception is a parasitism of the pre-existing system for communicating correct information." In other words, deceptive strategies may be expected to work only when they are relatively rare. Trivers theorizes that the arms race between deceptive and detective strategies is frequency-dependent; that is, "as deception increases in frequency, it intensifies selection for detection, and as detection spreads, it intensifies selection on deceit."[28] The overall thrust of this arms race works to keep deception at a minimum, creating a general presumption on behalf of veracity. The real things will always outnumber the mimics. This principle can be expected to govern interpersonal relations as well as interspecific relations, thus creating a presumption of honesty in symbolic interactions. It should also be noticed that this presumption of honesty is a precondition for the efficiency of symbolic interaction. As Georg Simmel observes, "In a richer and larger cultural life, . . . existence rests on a thousand premises which the single individual cannot trace and verify to their roots at all, but must be taken on faith. Our modern life is based to a much larger extent than is usually realized upon the faith in the honesty of the other."[29] Without the presumption of honesty and the slackening of defenses implicit in trust, human interactions would become very inefficient. We enjoy an efficient monetary system, for example, only because people have confidence in the currency. An economy that becomes saturated with counterfeit currency will soon fail or revert to barter. It is far easier to spot a bogus fish than a bogus buck. The same principle bears upon the efficiency of language. Our verbal interactions flow as smoothly as they do because there is a presumption of truthtelling. If this presumption were shattered by a saturation of lies, then our defenses would stiffen and in our suspicion we would be reduced to communicating with each other through the grossly inefficient medium of legalese.

These considerations will tend to reassure us that deception in human interactions is a relatively rare event after all. As long as we are getting by without speaking legalese, the position of extreme cynicism remains unfounded. Yet our assurance should not take us to the point of naiveté. Despite the presumption of veracity, interactions between human beings are absolutely rife with deception. If there is no contradiction here, then there must be an undisclosed distinction, which of course there is. The frequency-dependency argument rests on the assumption that the state of being deceived is universally harmful. But this is not the case. In very many cases deceptive interactions bring no harmful effects upon the dupe at all, and when the effects of being duped are harmless, we should not expect any elaboration of defenses against the deceivers. I am suggesting that it makes sense to distinguish between malignant and benign deceits. This will prove to be a very tricky distinction, for as everyone knows, a benign deceit may very well become malignant, and as Sir Walter Scott warns, "Oh, what a tangled web we weave, when first we practise to deceive!" My only point is that an abundance of *benign* deception will not necessarily be inconsistent with sustaining the presumption of truth.

Here, then, is the problem: I want to assert, on the one hand, that strategies of other-deception are very common in social interactions, but I also want to claim that a presumption of truth is an important part of a perceiver's designs in normal interactive situations. I believe the tension between these assertions can be resolved in the following way. Human beings are in fact well equipped with sophisticated defenses against interpersonal deception, but these defenses are designs that will be left in reserve until one has good reason to suppose that one might be harmed.[30] But when there is no suggestion of harm, then the defensive designs will default to designs for a presumption of honesty. When a perceiver's presumption of honesty is evident to an actor, then the actor may lie with the confidence of a truthteller (i.e., without showing nonverbal stress indicators). These conditions are right for a wide range of relatively harmless deceits to flourish. When defenses remain slack, conventions will remain efficient and interactions will remain fluid. And in these circumstances individuals will have sufficient opportunities to garner by harmless deceits the sorts of experiences that are conducive to self-esteem. Without these dynamics allowing for petty deceits there would be very much less personal wholeness in the world than there is. We may therefore agree with Turner and his colleagues that "not only are forms of deception frequently employed, they are necessary, even mandatory discursive elements."[31]

Constructive/evasive self-deception

In our discussion of other-deceptions we considered how individuals achieve self-esteem in part by imposing upon others to sacrifice a modicum of adequation of appearance to reality. And now we consider how individuals manage to negotiate away some of their own adequation for the purpose of achieving personal wholeness.

If our towel stewardess had been completely honest with her young admirer, she would have offered him the information that she was not really a champion swimmer. The signals inherent in his responses told her that he had reached a false conclusion, and to disabuse a conversation partner in such circumstances is normally expected. Her evasion was deceptive. But there is also good reason to suspect that persons in her situation will often be dishonest with *themselves,* to the end that self-esteem is enhanced. Thus we hypothesize that constructive/evasive strategies of self-deception are common. In a constructive/evasive self-deception a person tends to ignore information that may preclude opportunities for self-worth attributions. The case for this form of deception is strengthened by recent research on the selectivity of attention and memory. What is involved in our attending to one thing rather than another, or in remembering this rather than that? Of course, many factors are involved in these choices, but it is becoming increasingly clear that a bias toward enhanced self-esteem is operative in the selectivity of conscious experience.

In a very influential paper, Anthony Greenwald describes three strong biases that affect a person's processing of information: a bias that sees the self as the focus of knowledge, a bias against cognitive change (i.e., schema modification), and a bias of "beneffectance."[32] This third bias is a tendency to perceive oneself as deserving credit for desired outcomes even when the attribution of credit seems to be unwarranted by the evidence. C. R. Snyder discusses essentially the same process in slightly different terms. He suggests that persons are biased to link themselves to valued results, and to unlink themselves from devalued results, and that one's perceptions of these linkages are often deluded. He says, "In this process, in fact, there is growing evidence that the person biases feedback such that there is more perceived linkage to positive acts than the data would actually suggest."[33] These theories predict that persons will be biased toward evading information that may neutralize attributions of self-worth. Thus persons who perform well on an examination will be biased to ignore any evidence suggesting that the exam was not an adequate measure of ability. This evasion resolves psychic conflict between the self-esteem motive to attribute self-worth and the cognitive motive to acknowledge some feature of the world around. Also, when the record of successful and unsuccessful past performances in some domain of activity is balanced, the successful ones will be better remembered.[34] When the historical achievements of a distinguished family are being celebrated, the adopted children in the family may well lose track of their artificial linkage to these achievements.

Strategies of constructive/evasive self-deception have appeared frequently in the history of science. In this setting the strategy is to ignore data that do not fit theoretical expectations in favor of those that do fit. It happens often enough that much is to be gained by positive outcomes in scientific work. The lure of tenure, publication of one's research, a grant, possibly a Nobel prize—such incentives are often sufficient to bear out Neitzsche's aphorism "The world is interpreted by our wants." The famous N ray episode provides a good illustration of collective self-deception of the evasive type. In 1903, just eight years after the German physicist Wilhelm Roentgen discovered X rays, a French researcher, René Blondlot, claimed to have discovered yet a new form of radiation which he called N rays. Within the next few years the pursuit of N rays became a minor discipline among French scientists, sustained by the promise of emerging from the shadow of German science. Hundreds of papers appeared, claiming to have detected N rays emanating from gases, magnetic fields, chemicals, and even the human nervous system.[35] The interesting fact is that these French scientists continued to conduct this research even years after the American physicist R. W. Wood had shown N rays to be a fiction. The French scientists simply ignored Wood's exposé for reasons of national self-esteem. Mary Jo Nye postulates that the N ray "discovery" brought a momentary flash of attention and prestige to the French scientific community—a moment of glory that they were not prepared to relinquish, so they preserved it by ignoring countervailing evidence.[36]

It should be emphasized that a person may achieve selective ignorance either by suppressing certain contrary information or by displacing it with attention to legitimate positive information. Thus the towel stewardess, for example, may effectively displace her tenuous linkage to the achievements of the championship team by selectively remembering those out-of-pool situations (e.g., locker rooms, hotels, buses, banquets) in which her status was indistinguishable from that of the swimmers. In this way she preserves a constructive self-enhancing effect by a strategy of self-induced evasion of compromising information.

Before we dismiss our towel stewardess from our discussion, let us use her to make some general points about our categories. I am proposing eight categories to analyze the various forms of deception practiced by human beings, four constructive and four deconstructive. But it may be objected that these eight categories were generated by logical extension from a definition, and not constructed to conform to the demands of a wide range of data. In other words, these appear to be formal categories as opposed to empirically generated categories. Thus serious questions of method arise. Are we in danger of misrepresenting phenomena by insisting that they conform to *a priori* categories? Might it rather be that real cases will tend to overlap these formal categories to reveal redundancies among them? The towel stewardess, for example, has already appeared in two categories. Does this mean that she has engaged in two distinct deceptive acts? What if she shows up again? Three, then? Does this not complicate matters beyond necessity?

I am inclined to defend these categories by insisting that the original definition, from which they derive, does have empirical justification, as I hope I demonstrated in chapter 2. The modified categories of this chapter will not be as testable, given the inaccessible nature of human thought processes. But this does not mean that the categories do not, in fact, represent eight distinct types of mental strategy. If some cases appear to overlap, we may take them to be cases in which strategies are combined in complex ways. A single verbal response, for example, may often have the effect of both evading and perverting a perceiver's designs. This should come as no surprise when we consider the immense schematic complexity of our minds. If puns and double-entendre can achieve simultaneous effects on different schemas, then it should be possible simultaneously to pervert and evade various of a dupe's designs in the same way. In fact, many diversionary tactics may operate in this way. So we may assume an occasional coincidence of different forms of deception, but these exceptions present no obvious difficulties for our categories. It may also happen that certain forms of deception will have the consequence of committing the deceiver to sequential combinations of strategies. Thus the towel stewardess might be seen to complement her initial act of evasive other-deception with a subsequent act of evasive self-deception. It may go as follows. The young admirer inquires about the ring and she sees an opportunity to enhance her self-esteem by evading further inquiry. Once she has done so, thoughts of her real status on the team begin to neutralize the self-esteem effect, so she evades them with displacive thoughts about team interactions on the bus trips (thus she resolves intrapsychic conflict and sustains the self-esteem effect by a subsequent act of self-deception). But now let us suppose that the admirer persists further to ask about her particular role on the team. At this point intrapsychic conflict will intensify, perhaps to the point where she begins to emit telltale signs of stress. To continue the charade she must now employ a more desperate form of evasion or construct a blatant perversive lie. Perhaps she will go into a fit of coughing or catch the eye of a passing friend, or perhaps she will say, "My event was freestyle." In any case she will have engaged in yet a third form of deception. The coughing fit represents a *deconstructive* evasion, for now the purpose is less to prolong the self-esteem effect than to avoid the condemnation that comes with being perceived as a pretender. But if she takes the perversive option, then she may suffer pangs of guilt for having told a blatant lie. And this may produce the sort of intrapsychic conflict that could lead her to devise yet a further strategy of deconstructive self-deception. Oh, what a tangled web . . .

Constructive/perversive self-deception

I am on a luxurious cruise ship in the Atlantic Ocean, headed for Bermuda. It is late afternoon, and the sun is beginning to set in a soft sky of pale peach, rose pink, and baby blue. The sun is a glowing orange ball whose warmth is sinking into my bronzed skin. I have a gorgeous, refined man standing by my side as we share this wonder of nature together. He pulls me close to him, and soon we are lost in a deep passionate kiss.

The absolutely gorgeous man has a fantastic body (six feet two inches, 200 pounds), black hair, and sparkling blue eyes. This man is sensitive, mature, wealthy, and tan, but best of all, he is modest. He is perfection.

As for me, I have a slender, shapely figure on which I put the most classic clothes. I never go out of style, and I always have the perfect outfit for the occasion. I am a multifaceted woman. I am also consistently beautiful from the time I wake up to the time I go to bed. My makeup always looks fresh and my energy is boundless. I am a wonderful lover for my wonderful lover, and I understand his every gesture and mood, but I am a career woman, always aware of local and world events. What more can I say? I, too, am perfect.

My lover and I are on our way to Bermuda for a perpetual vacation. Once we arrive, the weather is always perfect, the beach always has pure blue water and glistening white sand (no rocks or shells to step on), and we never run out of money.[37]

The reality of this woman's life included broken relationships, a small apartment shared with her sister, a difficult job, no vacation opportunities, and a sense that "life is boring, pressured, and stagnant."

This woman is fabricating information in consciousness for the sheer delight of a momentary self-esteem high. If one has too few opportunities to feel good about one's real life, then one always has the option of a fantasy life in which things turn out right for a change. We are encouraged by our self-esteem motivator to become a certain kind of ideal person, with various traits, skills, and achievements. But the realities of everyday life always fall short of the ideal. On those occasions when we manage to come through with a small triumph we experience the exhilaration that comes with self-worth attributions. But there are too few of these occasions for most of us. The need for self-worth attributions always seems to exceed the legitimate conditions for making them. Thus, most of the time there is a discrepancy in our lives between the ideal and the real, between the ideal values and the perceived facts. This discrepancy is sufficient to arouse us to various strategies for closing the gap. As I said earlier, we may close the gap by taking measures to become more like the ideal, or we may take measures merely to appear so to ourselves and/or others. In our fantasy lives we take the strategy of self-deception to extremes by fabricating in consciousness alternative realities in which we appear to ourselves as we wish to be. In such moments of fancy as that described above, the demands of the cognitive motivator are completely negotiated away and the ideal self is perceived. We resolve the intrapsychic conflict between cognitive demands and self-esteem demands by momentarily relaxing the cognitive demands. There results an extreme disadequation of appearance to reality which brings with it a golden opportunity for abundant attributions of self-worth.

In our moments of fancy we become heroes, we win the lottery, we get promotions, we hobnob with celebrities, we dazzle audiences with our talents, we earn the admiration of the entire world. As John Caughey says, "a key element in these fantasies is social recognition, acclaim, and adulation. . . . American fantasizers win an enormous number of Olympic gold medals, Pulitzer Prizes, Emmy Awards, gold records, and Academy Awards." Caughey suggests that fantasizing is extremely common in all cultures, amounting to a normal and perhaps necessary element in the achievement of personal wholeness.[38]

Fantasies need not be elaborate productions that take us off on cruise ships. Sometimes they are fleeting interludes that we allow ourselves while we drive to work or fix supper. While riding in an elevator I may think of the perfect quip that I might have inserted into dinner conversation the night before—so I compose an imaginary scene in which I play my verbal trump card with a flourish, to the amazement of all. And as I do so I receive a token of the self-satisfaction that would have been mine the night before. And the residual effect of my elevator episode upon my global self-concept may just rival that of the real thing. The biochemical aspects of fantasy have been little explored, but it would not be surprising if they turned out to involve attenuated versions of the neural splendors of actually winning a Nobel prize.

The same dynamics involved in fantasizing are at work when we read fiction or attend the theater, with the difference that here we follow the compositions of the artists. Again we momentarily sacrifice our adequation to reality for the sake of appearing to ourselves as being more than we really are. As Norman Holland says,

> In effect, the literary work dreams a dream for us. It embodies and evokes in us a central fantasy; then it manages and controls that fantasy by devices that, were they in a mind, we would call defenses, but, being on a page, we call "form." And the having of the fantasy and feeling it managed give us pleasure. We bring, then, to works of art two expectations that permit a "willing suspension of disbelief": we do not expect to act on the external world; we expect pleasure. Even if the work makes us feel guilt or anxiety, we expect it to manage those feelings so as to transform them into satisfying experiences.[39]

Whether we manage our fantasies by our own compositions or by submitting to those of the artist, the effect is the same: reality is momentarily negotiated away and the self-esteem deficit is repaired. Without periodic and momentary engagements in such perversions of our own designs there is little prospect of maintaining personal wholeness. Arnold Ludwig concurs:

> Fantasy, then, often represents a convenient way for man to temporarily lie to himself in order to make life more palatable. Although he may not fully believe in the actual reality of the products of his fantasy, he can invest enough belief in them to offer himself some degree of satisfaction. If man were to remain chronically frustrated in the satisfaction of his hopes, ambitions and desires, without having access to the solace of fantasy and the temporary solutions and attenuated pleasures it provides, it would become difficult to sustain hope and optimism toward the future.[40]

In addition to the periodic and momentary grand delusions of our fantasy lives, we also engage in systematic and petty perversions of our perceptual designs. That is, our interpretations of everyday events are routinely biased by our self-esteem motive in such a way that we can scarcely perceive anything in a realistic way. As Shelley Taylor suggests, normal people perpetually harbor a myriad of "positive illusions": "That is, rather than being firmly in touch with reality, the normal human mind distorts incoming information in a positive direction. In particular, people think of themselves, their future, and their ability to have an impact on what goes on around them in a more positive manner than reality can sustain."[41]

A quaint example of the unrealistically positive nature of self-assessment is revealed in a survey showing that 90 percent of automobile drivers considered themselves to be better-than-average drivers. Taylor's view is that such overly positive interpretations are generalized in the healthy person's orientation in the world. In most categories of performance John Doe will think more generously of himself than of his friends, and his friends will think less generously of him than he will.[42] These positive illusions about oneself show up in the process of constructing a life history. We have already seen that a person is likely to suppress from consciousness information that may neutralize self-worth attributions, and now we see that one is likely to overstate the evidence favoring self-worth attributions. When persons look back at their past performances, they tend to remember them in a positively distorted way. The record of my college career may indicate that I was a mediocre student, but in reconstructing that career in memory I may conclude that I was a promising young scholar. In other words, as personal historians most people tend to be unabashed revisionists. Experiments have shown that subjects tend to attribute their present views and attitudes to their former selves, even though the record contradicts these attributions.[43] We often distort the relevance of the past to allow present attributions of self-worth. The former high school athlete who has achieved nothing noteworthy since graduation will revel in stories about the past on the illusory premise that his triumphs in high school continue to have self-esteem currency thirty years later.

It is also typical of persons to exaggerate their responsibility for positive outcomes. When individuals are asked to estimate their contribution to cooperative projects, the sum of estimates usually exceeds the realistic 100 percent. On a 1,000-mile trip a husband and wife may each claim credit for 700 miles of driving. In an experiment involving scored performance on a skilled task, subjects were told they had a partner working with them in the blind (whereas in reality they were working alone). These subjects claimed credit for the high scores while attributing low scores to their "partner."[44] But not only do we exaggerate our share of credit for performances, we sometimes assume a measure of credit where none is due. In C. R. Snyder's terms, we fabricate linkages to positive circumstances. Consider, for example, the person who boasts of coming from the same town as a celebrity or attending the same school as a senator, as if these facts had some legitimate bearing on one's self-worth. Or consider the way lottery winners describe their strategies for selecting winning numbers in a game of chance. The perceived linkage in these situations reveals self-induced positive illusions. Psychologists have explored the "illusion of control" among gamblers to show that they typically deceive themselves into thinking that chance outcomes may be influenced by a particular pattern of behavior. Crap shooters, for example, will throw the dice softly when they want low numbers and hard when they want high numbers. They will also wait for silence in order to concentrate, on the illusion that effort will influence the way the dice fall. The practice of petitionary prayer is another rather obvious example of the illusion of control. Such illusions of being in control of chance events are common in everyday life.[45]

* * *

Throughout this portion of the chapter I have been trying to show that human beings are easily aroused to enhance their sense of self-worth, and that once they have aroused it, they will seek homeostasis by constructing the conditions under which self-worth attributions can be made. It is my claim that we very often construct these conditions by deceptive means, sometimes by leaving others in a state of ignorance, sometimes by manipulating others into a state of false belief, sometimes by inducing our own ignorance by suppressing information from consciousness, and sometimes by fabricating or distorting our own sense of reality. In all of these instances I have stressed an underlying theme: that personal wholeness is commonly, and perhaps necessarily, contingent upon "taking away" (*de* + *capere*) from some perceiver a measure of adequation to reality. But so far have I told only half the story. We must now consider those circumstances under which the achievement of personal wholeness calls one to deconstruct the conditions that might otherwise result in attributions of negative self-worth.

Deconstructing Threats to Self

Some observers of human nature will dismiss the distinction between constructive and deconstructive measures for maintaining a sense of self-worth with the argument that self-enhancement and self-acquittal amount to the same thing, that what we have is a single psychodynamic process. This argument takes a good deal of its force from the observation that the continuum of social values from good to bad is, after all, a *continuum*. Nevertheless, I will defend this distinction (and thus eight categories of deception rather than four) on the grounds that circumstances for giving praise differ significantly from those for placing blame. And similarly, the psychological stresses endured by a glory seeker will be seen to differ significantly from those of a defendant. As long as we accept the viability of distinctions between taking credit and escaping blame and between adulation and accusation, the distinction will be sufficiently justified. In this section, therefore, I will seek to balance La Rochefoucauld's observation that "to succeed in the world, we do everything we can to appear successful" with Camus's observation that "each of us insists on being innocent at all costs, even if he has to accuse the whole human race and heaven itself."

In fact, we shall find that our story will be slightly more complicated than this, for more is at stake in the deconstructive task than innocence alone. I have said that there are two general conditions for becoming a person: biological conditions and social conditions. In our consideration of the constructive task of self-maintenance we were able to focus primarily upon the arousal of human beings to establish conditions for an enhanced sense of self-worth. And these were social conditions. The establishment of biological conditions requisite to personhood was simply assumed. So the constructive task was to arrange matters socially and psychologically so as to be judged well against social standards of value. At first sight it might appear that the deconstructive task would be a simple reversal of the process, so that the task might be to arrange things socially and psychologically in such a way as to avoid or diminish negative judgments of self-worth. This will be a major aspect of the deconstructive task, but not the whole of it. For on the downside of self-maintenance we encounter threats not only to the social conditions but also to the biological conditions. We must therefore envision the deconstructive task of human existence in slightly more general terms than the constructive task. Here we address human arousal to avoid or diminish both social and biological threats to self-maintenance. Having said this, we may express the deconstructive task of human existence in terms of the following question: *By what means might I become invulnerable to the conditions of self annihilation?* The conditions of self annihilation will include those conditions under which one's self-worth is threatened, but they will also include those conditions under which one's safety and life are threatened.

How, then, *does* one become invulnerable to the social and biological conditions of self annihilation? Unfortunately, one doesn't, really—at least, not in any final sense. Eventually the self, this wonderfully organized complex of informed energy, will reach a point where its overall rate of chemical composition will be overtaken by the overall rate of chemical decomposition, in which case one is dead, or about to be. The biological conditions of self annihilation, then, are inevitable, and the degree of one's invulnerability to these conditions will be limited. Nor is it possible to become invulnerable to social threats against one's sense of self-worth. Quite apart from the fact that "no one is perfect," certain properties of any social order make it impossible for anyone to escape social condemnation completely. For one thing, there are so many standards of value that no individual can avoid the occasional "damned if you do, damned if you don't" predicament. Moreover, many social standards involve the valuation of traits over which individuals have no control. Beyond this, social values are constantly in flux, making it inevitable that everyone will be on someone's list of villains.

So then, invulnerability to social and biological threats against one's self-maintenance appears to be out of the question—everybody fails, everybody dies. But despite these unpleasantries, we remain motivated to achieve a state of invulnerability, to preserve the integrity of the self against all threats. When threats to the self arise, the self becomes aroused to deconstruct them. Dylan Thomas captures the motive well: "Do not go gentle into that good night . . . ; rage, rage against the dying of the light." So we do what we can. There are some measures we can take in our raging to avoid or diminish particular threats to the self, and some of them will involve strategies of deception.

I propose that there are four general types of deception by which one may deconstruct the conditions of threat to the self:

In a *deconstructive/evasive other-deception* the deceiver devises a strategy to leave the dupe in a state of ignorance on some matter, such that threats of self annihilation are avoided or diminished.

In a *deconstructive/perversive other-deception* the deceiver devises a strategy to put the dupe in a state of false belief on some matter, such that threats of self annihilation are avoided or diminished.

In a *deconstructive/evasive self-deception* the self-deceiver devises a strategy to inhibit certain information from reaching consciousness with the result that threats of self annihilation are precluded or diminished.

In a *deconstructive/perversive self-deception* the self-deceiver devises a strategy to fabricate or distort certain conscious information with the result that threats of self annihilation are precluded or diminished.

Deconstructive/evasive other-deception

If the persons with whom you interact each day suddenly had the power to read your unexpressed thoughts, would they continue to think as well of you as they do now? If a commencement speaker asked all the victims of date rape in the graduating class to stand up, how many would do so? Why are abortion clinics inconspicuous? Why do bank robbers wear masks?

We all have our secrets. It is a safe bet that each of us conceals certain information about our thoughts and past behaviors that, should they become known, would seriously compromise our social esteem. So we take measures to keep our audiences ignorant about certain things, and by these measures we protect the self from potential harm. Consider the overweight person shopping for clothes to wear to a class reunion—the primary objective is to find something to disguise a lumpy body. Or the teenager who applies blemish-concealing paste. Or the ex-con who avoids mention of his record in a job interview. Or the college professor whose verbose technical response to a question is designed to conceal his ignorance. Or anyone at all who changes the subject in a potentially threatening conversation. Examples of this form of deception in everyday life go on without end.

In many situations we use evasion constructively, to invite adulation from the other or to heighten our sense of power over the other. In these ways evasive strategies enhance positive self-esteem. In deconstructive evasions, however, the strategy is to disempower one's audiences by depriving them of incriminating information that might reduce the actor's invulnerability. But there is a deeper sense in which evasive other-deceptions contribute to personal wholeness, and that is by deconstructing invasions of one's privacy. The maintenance of personal privacy is an essential element in the achievement of one's sense of self. Personal identity is achieved in part by the establishment of territorial boundaries, certain regions of a person's activity that are considered off limits to others.[46] The definition and management of the elements of privacy are culturally dependent, but no culture is without conventions that protect the integrity of the private self. A notable exception to the institutionalization of privacy proves the rule. Erving Goffman has shown how inmates of "total institutions" (e.g., mental hospitals, prisons, training camps, nursing homes) are subject to annihilation of self. When a person enters a total institution, "he begins a series of abasements, degradations, humiliations, and profanations of self. His self is systematically, if often unintentionally, mortified."[47] The loss of privacy is a central element in this process of mortifying the self.

To maintain a sense of self, then, it is necessary to maintain personal privacy, and one does so by deconstructing the audience's access to personal information. In some cases the sensitive information is incriminating, as we have seen, but it need not be. There is nothing incriminating, for example, about essential body functions such as urinating and defecating. Yet in most cultures these activities are typically conducted in private. Information concerning these private functions—the sounds of doing them, our individual techniques, whether we experience difficulty—this information is held in secrecy. And if others intrude on this information, we take it as an assault upon the self, not because the information is incriminating but because it is part of the boundary apparatus that defines the self. I suspect that most people would be just as loath to be observed on the toilet as to be observed stealing something. What a dilemma to be forced into such a choice—in either case the self is rendered unacceptably vulnerable to annihilation. A correspondent in Japan relates an amusing variation on this dilemma. Japanese women, it seems, are especially secretive about the sounds of their urination—to be heard urinating is to be compromised, a very tricky problem given the close quarters of Japanese dwellings. So the convention has emerged that Japanese women typically run the water faucet or flush the toilet to conceal the telltale sounds of pissing, an evasive strategy that is commonly used by Americans as well. But this strategy fell upon hard times when the water shortage in Japan made flushing the toilet after urinating a socially irresponsible practice. The resulting dilemma: To flush or not to flush? If the woman decides not to flush, she has left her audience with undeconstructed access to her privacy. But if she decides to flush, she becomes vulnerable to scorn for having wasted water. Damned if she does, damned if she doesn't. This dilemma has produced a further technique for evasive behavior: One can now purchase in Japan taped recordings of a toilet flushing, to be played by those who wish to save both face and water.

Deconstructive/perversive other-deception

Each day in classrooms everywhere teachers are fed lines approximating the following to explain why the day's homework assignment cannot be handed in:

1. My little sister ate it.

2. My dog or cat did his duty on it.
3. We ran out of toilet paper.
4. Our furnace broke down and we had to burn it to keep from freezing to death.
5. I had to use it to fill a hole in my shoe.
6. I gave it to a friend and his house burned down.
7. My mother threw it away by mistake.
8. I got hungry and there was no food to eat.
9. I did it, I swear, but I left it next to my poor sick mother whom I was helping and caring for all night.
10. Because I didn't feel like it![48]

In deconstructive/perversive other-deception the general strategy is to avoid or diminish threats to the self by perverting the designs of a perceiver. We find this strategy most commonly deployed in the fabrication of excuses. The word "excuse" derives from *ex* + *causa*, suggesting that excuses are designed to remove the perception of the actor as a cause of some negative outcome. In other words, excuses are designs for deconstructing responsibility. There are three general tactics by which a perversive deconstruction of responsibility may go forward. In each of these tactics the excuser provides information that is intended to remove or reduce condemnation of the self. The first type of excuse attempts to convince the audience that the actor is not responsible for the negative outcome. The second type grants responsibility for the act but attempts to mitigate the perception of its badness. The third type grants both responsibility and badness but offers information to weaken the condemnation. In each case the "target" for the excuse is the accuser's perception of linkage between the actor and a bad performance. It is the appearance of this linkage that the excuser attempts to alter, thus perverting the adequation of the accuser's appearance to reality. (I hasten to add that many excuses are not fabricated, in which case the accuser may have genuinely misperceived the linkage. And in other cases the excuser genuinely believes in the excuse but is self-deceived. The former cases do not concern us, and the latter will be discussed later).

The first type of excuse has been labeled the "I didn't do it" defense.[49] This defense is a form of denial and will be adjusted to the particular circumstances of the case. If the accuser did not see the alleged act at firsthand, then the deceiver may make up an alibi to claim that she couldn't have done it because she was out of town. If the accuser's information is hearsay, then the excuser may cast doubt on the reliability of the witnesses—they must have been mistaken, or they had the wrong assumptions, or perhaps they have ulterior motives. If the actor was seen directly by the accuser, then there may be a window for the "innocent bystander" defense, or the "circumstantial evidence" defense, or the "accidental discharge" defense. In each of these scenarios the accused is trying to deconstruct the linkage between herself and the alleged bad performance. If the denial tactic succeeds, it is normally decisive, and may even earn an apology from the accuser. It is therefore the ultimate defense. But it is also the most direct and obvious way to deconstruct responsibility, and under the stress of condemnation the actor may not be able to think of anything else. Several studies have shown that when subjects are aroused by threats, their cognitive processes simplify considerably, thus reducing the complexity of factors that might otherwise be involved in decision making.[50] It is sometimes amazing to see the lengths to which some deniers are driven in their desperation. A colleague relays the case of a young woman who showed up in a university health center both pregnant and claiming to be a virgin. She was so persistent in her denial that the physician making an abortion referral finally consented to entering "virginal introitus" on the health record.

When denials of responsibility are too farfetched, an excuser may supply information to alter the perceiver's judgment of the outcome. This is the "It's really not so bad" defense. Here again, the circumstances will guide the deceiver. We see this tactic in the kid who breaks a lamp and then says the lamp was old and needed replacing anyway; or the kid who spills milk and then explains that this sort of thing happens at his friend's house all the time; or the youth who wrecks the family car and appeals to his father to see the bright side: "Look, now we don't have to go to Grandma's this weekend." Another option for reducing the badness of an act is to attack the appropriateness of the rule against it. Thus a deer poacher, for example, may rail against the wisdom of seasonal regulations on deer hunting.

The third type of excuse encompasses a broad class of possibilities for deception. When the linkage to an act is undeniable and the badness of the outcome is unambiguous, then the deceiver may draw from a range of "Yes, but . . ." defenses to mitigate the intensity of scorn. The most common of these defenses are professions of ignorance and good intentions. If an accuser can be made to believe that the actor had good intentions and/or bad information, she may well scale back the intensity of blame. There are also the tactics that serve to diffuse responsibility, such as, "Okay, I punched him, but *he* started it," or "Golly, Dad, *everybody* was doing it." Another possibility is to divert the accuser's attention to the virtuous record of the actor, thus suggesting that the bad act is an exception, a quirk that is partly attributable to the uniqueness of the situation. If this device succeeds, then the actor may be perceived as a victim of circumstances. And, of course, if all of these attempts to alter perceptions of the bad performance fail, the guilty party may feign profound contrition and throw himself on the mercy of the court. Most individuals have a threshold of compassion, and the able deceiver will find ways to exploit these emotional designs. This strategy deconstructs the threat to self by making prolonged scorn or harsh punishment appear superfluous; the lesson has already been learned.

We often make excuses as a compensatory act, to deconstruct our responsibility for bad performances in the past. But we just as often make excuses in an anticipatory mode, to preempt our linkage to bad performances in the future. The practice of malingering is a good example. The child may pretend illness to avoid going to school because he anticipates some unpleasantness ahead, perhaps an exam or a playground bully. To avoid threatening situations such as these is to render the self invulnerable to their inherent dangers. Avoidance behavior is analogous to the denial found in compensatory excuses. If we succeed at avoiding threatening situations, we have the ultimate defense against the possibility of linkage to bad performances. But if avoidance tactics fail (e.g., "I don't feel well," "I already have plans," "My parents won't let me"), then subsequent excuses may be used either to condition the evaluation of impending performances or to diffuse responsibility for them. The compensatory tactic of reducing the badness of a performance has its anticipatory analogue in the attempt to lower the audience's expectations. Thus the employee who is assigned a special project may say, "I haven't any experience with this sort of thing" or "This really isn't the best time, but I'll give it a shot." If the audience's expectations can be lowered, then so are the chances of a negative evaluation of performance. And finally, one may take measures to offload responsibility in advance of an unpredictable performance. The malingering child who is forced off to school may shout back, "Just remember, if I fail the math test it'll be your fault." Or the employee may say, "I think this is more in Jones's area, but I guess it's your decision." Or how about this beauty: "Honey, whatever you do, don't let me drink too much tonight."

However much we are drawn to the argument that fabricating excuses is morally reprehensible or ill advised as an established pattern of behavior, the fact remains that excuses provide persons with viable short-term defenses against threats of self annihilation. As it happens, social circumstances often come down to a contest between an actor's loss of self and an audience's loss of reality. And when an individual is under immediate threat of losing the self, the wiser long-term policy of steadfast truthtelling may not be very attractive, or even feasible. As J. L. Austin observes, "The average excuse, in a poor situation, gets us only out of the fire into the frying pan—but still, of course, any frying pan in a fire."[51] A world in which everyone faces up to responsibilities and bears the social consequences gracefully is a world greatly to be desired. But such ideals must be seen against the realities people face in their attempts to cope with failure. And these realities tell us that in many instances the threat of linkage to a bad performance is harder to bear than the self-condemnation of knowing that one has deceived. And if self-condemnation becomes too heavy a cross to bear, then it too can be deconstructed.

Deconstructive/evasive self-deception

The aim of deconstructive self-deceptions is generally to become invulnerable to internal conditions that constitute threats of self annihilation. Such conditions are legion; they include anxiety about death, anxiety about one's general competence to perform well against social standards, anxiety resulting from self-condemnation for particular bad performances in the past or for some presently contemplated act, and so on. In a sense, and to varying degrees, the deconstruction of these internal conditions will amount to a deconstruction of the self. There are various possibilities for deconstructing the self. If the self is a set of integrated motivational processes, then its deconstruction will involve some intervention with respect to these processes. That is, one may alter the self-esteem motivator in some way, or the hedonic motivator, or the curiosity motivator, with the result that internal conditions threatening the self are precluded or diminished. Some—by no means all—of these interventions will involve self-deception. The most radical deconstructive measure of all is, of course, suicide. The taking of one's own life is not always a strategy for deconstructing threatening internal conditions, but it often is. And when suicide serves the end of eliminating threats of self annihilation it can be seen as the ultimate paradoxical act of desperation. Many alternative measures for deconstructing the self might be discussed, but the ones that concern us are those that involve self-imposed disadequations of appearance to reality.

A useful way to approach these deconstructive tactics is to view them in the context of an individual's basic assumptions about reality. Many philosophers and psychologists have commented on the importance of an individual's basic notions about both the world around and the world within, the schemas that define for us how things are. The constellation of these fundamental schemas constitutes what C. M. Parkes has labeled one's "assumptive world." An assumptive world is "the individual's view of reality as he believes it to be, i.e., a strongly held set of assumptions about the world and the self which is confidently maintained and used as a means of recognizing, planning and acting."[52] This concept of an assumptive world appears under various other labels as well, such as Seymour Epstein's "theory of reality":

> Everyone unwittingly develops a personal theory of reality that includes a self-theory and a world-theory. A personal theory of reality does not exist in conscious awareness, but is a preconscious conceptual system that automatically structures a person's experience and directs his or her behavior. It is not developed for its own sake, but is a conceptual tool for solving life's fundamental problems, which include maintaining a favorable pleasure–pain balance, maintaining a favorable level of self-esteem, and assimilating the data of reality. . . .[53]

Together with a person's emotional dispositions, this idea of assumptive worlds corresponds to what I have been calling "appearances." An important general point to be made about our assumptive worlds is that they are generally resistant to change. Our assumptions about self and world became established and confirmed through years of experience, and they tend to serve us pretty well in our daily lives, so it takes some doing to get us to change them. This is especially the case as the schemas become more abstract and generalized, or as they become more definitive for one's sense of self-worth. Minor postulates in our assumptive worlds are readily modified under the force of countervailing evidence, but the global assumptions—that is, the most general or the most cherished—tend to hang on for dear life; and with good reason, for giving them up requires extensive repair to one's assumptive world. In other words, new information that challenges global schemas will ask for nothing less than new ways to organize information. Thus we see that such information will be unwelcome and will create intrapsychic conflict and anxiety. When faced with threatening information inherent in some negative life experience, individuals will often resolve the intrapsychic conflict by devising strategies of evasive self-deception. One such strategy is the defence mechanism known in psychoanalytic literature as denial:

> Given the very fundamental nature of the threatened assumptions, and given people's very basic tendency to persevere in the maintenance of their theories, the coping task facing the victim of trauma is overwhelming. Victims must revise and rebuild a new assumptive world that is different from the one they have taken for granted all of their lives, without allowing the entire conceptual system to "crash" in the interim. This task is enormous, and yet most victims complete it successfully. Their successful resolution is largely attributable to the often underestimated process of denial.[54]

Denial amounts to a refusal to assimilate the reality presented by a perceptual experience, and as such it represents an attempt to defeat one's own perceptual designs by evasion. When our perceptions present us with unwelcome information, we have the option of sacrificing part of our assumptive world or saving its appearances by sacrificing some measure of our apprehension of reality. The more threatening the information, the more likely one is to deny its reality. These dynamics have been extensively documented among victims of traumatic events, such as serious illness, violent crimes, accidents, and bereavement. Elisabeth Kübler-Ross reports that almost all patients with terminal illnesses practice denial in some form during the initial phase of their ordeal.[55] The news that one has been diagnosed with a serious illness is immediately threatening, and most people will attempt to make themselves invulnerable to the threat by some form of denial; it is the first line of defense. A surprising percentage of terminal patients report no memory of being told the unwelcome information for several hours after the event. Many patients verbalize their denial with something like "No, not me, it can't be true." And some will insist that medical records or test results have been mishandled by hospital staff, or that the physician is incompetent. Denial is often practiced among individuals who only suspect the presence of a threatening disease. A man who has noticed blood in his stools, for example, may go to great lengths to avoid looking in the toilet bowl.[56] Victims of bereavement are also likely to practice denial as an immediate defense mechanism. The sudden death of a loved one is a traumatic assault upon one's assumptive world, a world that will resist information of the loved one's death.

The protean character of denial is shown by a catalogue of its forms compiled by Mandi Horowitz:

- *Avoided associations*, short-circuiting expected, obvious connections to the event that would follow from the implications of what is said or thought.

- *Numbness*, the sense of not having feelings; appropriate emotions that go unfelt.

- *Flattened response*, a constriction of expectable emotional reactions.

- *Dimming of attention*, vagueness or avoidance of focusing clearly on information, including thoughts, feelings, and physical sensations.

- *Daze*, defocused attention that clouds alertness and avoids the significance of events.

- *Constricted thought*, the failure to explore likely avenues of meaning other than the obvious one at hand; an abbreviated range of flexibility.

- *Memory failure*, an inability to recall events or their details; a selective amnesia for telling facts.

- *Disavowal*, saying or thinking that obvious meanings are not so.[57]

Each of these forms is a self-imposed sacrifice of one's adequation to reality for the sake of temporarily reducing the anxiety of unwanted information. Denial is any form of evasive strategy that precludes or diminishes the impact of discomforting information by refusal to assimilate the information. The parent who avoids going into a child's room after catching a glimpse of pornographic magazines is practicing denial, as is the student who receives a poor grade and goes to the instructor insisting that some error has occurred in the recording process. Strategies of denial are normally temporary defenses that are used to resolve conditions of intense intrapsychic conflict. These stopgap measures are usually displaced in time by more sophisticated coping strategies that allow the eventual assimilation of negative information. Occasionally, however, the trauma of negative information is so severe that individuals are unable to relax their defenses, leaving them in a relatively permanent state of denial. This appears to be the case among many victims of posttraumatic stress disorders, as well as those who suffer from psychosomatic sensory deprivation. A particularly poignant example of the latter is found among Cambodian refugees living in the United States. Among the nearly 85,000 Cambodians living in Los Angeles County are more than 150 female victims of psychosomatic blindness. These women were forced to witness unimaginably brutal slayings at the hands of the Khmer Rouge, in many cases seeing their entire families butchered before their eyes.[58] The physical apparatus of eyesight in these women is perfectly normal, and when they are tested there is evidence of neural activity in the primary visual area of the brain. Presumably, then, their visual experience is inhibited at the higher, integrative centers of information processing. When reality is sufficiently unbearable, the organism is equipped to block it out by various evasive strategies, some of which are extreme and irreversible.

Closely related to the concept of denial is the classic defense mechanism of repression, the conceptual cornerstone of Freud's psychoanalytic theory. Repression and denial are sometimes confused in the popular literature of psychoanalysis. While they are similar in many respects, repression must be understood as applying to the exclusion from consciousness of internal meanings, feelings, desires, and memories, whereas denial is oriented to the external field of perceptions. In both cases the individual can be said to sacrifice a measure of reality for the sake of resolving intrapsychic conflict. The individual who engages in denial sacrifices adequation to external realities, and the individual who engages in repression sacrifices an awareness of internal realities that might, if brought to consciousness, threaten to annihilate the functional unity of the self. Repression has been described as "a feedback mechanism that includes the components of anxiety cue and automatic shut-off, which are followed by a reduction of anxiety."[59] That is, as unacceptable thoughts emerge toward consciousness, they elicit "signal anxiety," which triggers the inhibitory response. Consider the individual who becomes sexually aroused in a setting where sexual advances would be scorned. In such a case the impending conflict between the hedonic motivator and the self-esteem motivator will be detected in the preconscious processing of information so that the hedonic urges may be repressed in favor of maintaining self-esteem. Or suppose a person strolling through a department store is overcome by a desire to steal some object. The person is vulnerable to the anxiety of conflict between a desire to steal and a desire to remain honest. In most situations like this, the desire to steal is repressed before anxiety reaches a discomforting level of intensity. But suppose she is unable to repress the desire and comes away from the store a thief. Under these circumstances she may experience guilt for several days afterward. The fact that she has stolen is incompatible with the image she has of herself as an honest person, and the discrepancy between the reality of thievery and the ideal of honesty produces anxiety. Several options for anxiety reduction, such as returning the object to the store or finding a graceful way to pay for it, remain open to the person at this point. But in many such cases the most bearable option will be to dispose of the object somehow and to repress the episode from memory. This tactic amounts to a defeat of one's own designs for recollecting real events. The discomforting discrepancy between the reality of the event and one's ideal of the self is exchanged for a more tolerable discrepancy between appearance and reality.

I have been using the term "repression" to refer to the psychological process of excluding internal thoughts, desires, and memories from consciousness. This generalized usage may be in violation of classical psychoanalytic theory, in which the term is reserved for information that not merely is displaced from consciousness but is somehow *unavailable* to consciousness. It may thus be more consistent with traditional usage to speak of "suppression" when a thought or memory is displaced from consciousness but can still be recalled by normal retrieval mechanisms, and to reserve "repression" for thoughts and memories that are inaccessible even by these mechanisms. Thus a person may be said to suppress the urge to steal, but having stolen she may ultimately repress the memory of it. The traditional distinction between suppression and repression is an agreeable one, but it does nothing to impair the central point being advanced here—namely, that persons can and often do evade their own designs by inhibiting (whether momentarily or more permanently) certain threatening information from conscious levels of experience. And in doing so they sacrifice a measure of adequation to reality for the sake of personal wholeness. For our purposes, then, suppression and repression may be included together with denial as common examples of evasive self-deception.

Denial and suppression/repression are the most common evasive tactics for deconstructing the conditions for self-condemnation, though there may be several others. One that comes directly to mind is the use of alcohol or other depressant drugs as agents of self-deception. Depressants have the property of reducing one's awareness both of the world around and of the world within, thus functioning to desensitize the person to threats to the self. Various tactics of distraction, such as preoccupation with one's work or escape into books or movies, may also have the effect of keeping unwelcome thoughts out of mind. To the extent that these activities are pursued for their distractive value, I include them as instruments of evasive self-deception.

Deconstructive/perversive Self-deception

In the preceding discussion of denial the point was made that each of us maintains an assumptive world, and that we are motivated to preserve its features despite the occasional challenge from reality. Now I shall return to these assumptive worlds with the claim that they are normally laced with illusions to begin with. We have already seen that normal human beings harbor positive illusions about themselves and their world, and that these illusions help to construct the conditions for attributions of self-worth. But it is also the case that normal persons harbor "antinegative" illusions which help to deconstruct the conditions of self annihilation. Many studies have shown that persons who have not been victims of serious negative life events (e.g., crime, illness, divorce) have overly optimistic beliefs about their invulnerability to these events. Psychologists refer to these beliefs as "illusions of invulnerability."[60] Individuals consistently underestimate the frequency of negative events for their own population group, and they further underestimate their own personal vulnerability in relation to that of others, even when they know that their estimates are well below statistical probabilities. Such underestimations have been documented with respect to cancer, heart disease, pneumonia, alcoholism, divorce, automobile accidents, and various types of crime. Moreover, nonvictims believe that even if they were to be struck by disaster, they would cope with difficulties more effectively and recover more quickly than others.[61]

Various underlying mechanisms have been suggested to account for these phenomena. One account holds that illusions of invulnerability are sustained by the assumption of a universal moral order wherein victims somehow deserve the misfortune that befalls them. And since most people think well of themselves as moral agents, it follows that they consider themselves less likely than others to become victims.[62] Another account suggests that illusions of invulnerability are sustained by "downward comparisons." That is, individuals tend to compose imaginary high-risk stereotypes to represent the "kind of person" to whom negative life events happen, and then exclude themselves from the stereotype, leaving the illusion of low personal risk.[63] Whatever the underlying mechanisms may be, it is clear enough that illusions of invulnerability represent perversive strategies to distort information for the sake of diminishing threats to the self.

If the assumptive worlds of most people contain both illusions of control and illusions of invulnerability, then it is to be expected that these worlds stand a good chance of being challenged eventually as negative life events occur. And the illusory character of assumptive worlds is very likely to exacerbate the anxiety and trauma resulting from these underexpected events, thereby predisposing the unprepared victim to deploy additional coping mechanisms such as the evasive measures already discussed or a wide range of perversive self-deceits. Such coping mechanisms offer the threatened individual various opportunities to reestablish the illusion of invulnerability by deconstructing threats to the self.

In his guidebook to practical wisdom the Stoic philosopher Epictetus wrote, "What disturbs men's minds is not events but their judgments on events." Herein lies the logic of deconstructive/perversive self-deception. When individuals sense the signal anxiety of intrapsychic conflict, they may deconstruct the self-annihilating effects of unwelcome information by adjusting the way they think about it. Thus what enters into consciousness may be rendered less threatening. And when such adjustments represent distortions or fabrications of reality, we may say they are self-deceptive.

I have already commented on the constructive benefits of fantasy, but it is clear that fantasies often serve our deconstructive needs as well. The fabrication of conscious information can on occasion mitigate the disunifying effects of intrapsychic conflict. Deconstructive fantasy making begins relatively early in childhood and continues in various forms throughout a lifetime. The imaginary playmate of early childhood is an excellent example of this perversive strategy. Approximately 30 percent of children between the ages of three and six years have imaginary playmates. These fantasies appear to be "triggered by negative circumstances, such as feeling lonely through lack of companionship, or feeling upset because of being scolded." Such negative conditions are often effectively neutralized through fantasy, as is shown by some of the recurrent themes involving imaginary playmates. For example, imaginary playmates are often given the blame for the bad performances of the child. Such displacement of blame may significantly reduce the guilt anxiety experienced by a child who has just been reprimanded. In other settings the imaginary playmate may be given permission to engage in activities that have been forbidden to the child, thus giving the child a vicarious and anxiety-free way to fulfill unacceptable wishes. And in some cases the child will solicit permission from the imagined playmate to engage in some forbidden act, thereby resolving intrapsychic conflict by deconstructing linkage to the act.[64]

Children typically dismiss their imaginary playmates once they enter school, but the practice of fantasy making continues, normally in the form of daydreaming. John Caughey reports that the daydreams of normal adults are filled with imaginative vignettes, many of which are composed to repair the damage of "slights, humiliations, mistakes and embarrassments." He cites the example of an urban barmaid who endures a barrage of demeaning interactions in the course of an evening's work, and who has formed the habit of quietly rehashing the negative experiences of the evening in order to reframe them in a manner that is less threatening to her self-esteem. When we daydream we are very often "creating and imaginatively living through a modified version of the past" in order to "repair the identity damage inflicted by the actual past." A person who has been called on the carpet at work is likely to compose a daydream on his way home in which he features himself as telling off his boss in no uncertain terms. Imaginary conversations are also common after the breakup of romantic relationships and marriages. In such fantasies there is often an attempt to rewrite critical scenes from the past so that the breakup can be attributed to unavoidable external circumstances. Victims of bereavement may use imaginative conversations as a way of bringing the deceased back to life. Such conversations typically go well beyond simple recollections to involve the deceased in the current affairs of the daydreamer.[65] It is not uncommon for distortions and fabrications of past events to become important elements in a person's version of the actual past. In other words, fiction is often remembered as fact. The interpretation offered here is that such fantasies are imaginative constructions that very often serve deconstructive ends—we reduce vulnerability of the self by sacrificing a measure of adequation to reality.

It must be said that much of what goes on in the religious lives of individuals qualifies as deconstructive fantasy. This point has been advanced by many observers of religious phenomena, most notably by Karl Marx, who viewed religious belief as an opiate for the oppressed masses, and by Freud, who saw religion as an exercise in illusory wish fulfillment. There can be little doubt that the scripts of religious drama are widely used as coping strategies to deconstruct threats to the self. Communion with divine reality is believed to put one in a state of grace; that is, a state of complete invulnerability to all threats of an ultimate nature. If one is anxious about death, one finds a promise of immortality in the deconstructive words of St. Paul: "O death, where is thy sting?" And if one is anxious with guilt over some wrongdoing, one finds a standing offer of divine forgiveness that empties all the blame brought by mere mortals. And if one has a feeling that life is out of control, one can "take it to the Lord in prayer." Even the most devout religionists will agree to the deconstructive powers of religious scripts. And they will even agree that the anxiety of negative life events will motivate individuals to seek the solace offered in the assumptive world of religious scripts. But what they will not agree to, certainly, is the charge that these scripts represent perversive designs that manage to reduce threats of self annihilation by defeating the adequation of one's appearance to reality. This is an issue of immense subtlety and complexity, and I cannot discuss it thoroughly here. Briefly, though, it may be said that on the surface of things traditional beliefs about God are so obviously egocentric as to have all the transparency of infantile beliefs about an imaginary playmate. The only thing that speaks against the palpable falsehood of these beliefs is that they carry with them the awesome authority of socially defined reality. And this observation raises the very interesting dilemma of deciding who is furthest removed from reality: the atheist who rejects the socially defined realities of mainstream culture or the traditional religionist who fantasizes conversations with God and expects some form of subjective immortality. It is surely a grave mark against the promise of a culture whose most common options are as unattractive as these.

Fantasy making deconstructs threats to the self by fabricating alternative realities, but in many circumstances it may be more feasible to provide a biased interpretation of the realities at hand. We may do so by resorting to coping strategies that fall into the general category of "optimal framing." Coping strategies in this category range all the way from the use of euphemisms to sophisticated rationalizations, but the underlying process is always the same; that is, the individual resolves intrapsychic conflict by inhibiting an adequate interpretation of events or performances in favor of activating alternative schematic frameworks that are less adequate to reality but are also less threatening to the self. Anyone who has struggled to maintain a diet or to quit smoking knows perfectly well how the dynamics of this self-deceptive process work. When one is hedonically aroused by hunger or by a nicotine deficit, one's thinking processes change dramatically, often to the detriment of one's better judgment. Consider the man who has been placed on a diet by his physician. He has been given a detailed scientific account of the health risks associated with eating certain kinds of foods. He freely admits that eating these foods would be foolish, and he commits himself to avoid them. Yet when the man is hungry and the forbidden foods are at hand, he may very well find himself possessed of an alternative wisdom. The intrapsychic conflict between the hedonic invitation to eat and the cognitive warning to abstain may now be resolved by perversive means. The man may convince himself, for example, that a dish of ice cream would be a just reward for his abstinence during the past week. Or he may make way for the hedonic motive by "reminding" himself that most of these scientific studies are tentative at best—who knows, next week a study may appear with findings on the health benefits of ice cream. Or he may assemble some anecdotal evidence that his physician is overly cautious. So he eats. And having eaten, he now faces the problem of intrapsychic conflict between the cognitive fact and the self-condemnation of the eating, which he may resolve by further self-deception. His guilt may not be intense enough to activate denial, but several perversive options may come to mind—"It wasn't really a full portion"; "It wasn't as bad as having a bacon cheeseburger"; "Who doesn't break their diet once in a while?"; even "What the hell; nobody lives forever, so why not enjoy myself while I'm here?" These are all attempts to convince himself that the act was not such a bad thing after all. But even when the offender admits the badness, he can deconstruct the conditions of self-condemnation by making himself out to be a victim. Thus he may blame the hostess ("She *knew* I was on a diet. How could she . . ."), or he may frame the episode as unique ("This is the one flavor I can't resist"), or he may deflect responsibility to society as a whole ("If it weren't for the lousy eating habits of this country . . .").

Humor is another framing strategy that may be used to deconstruct the conditions of self annihilation. Humor serves many important human functions, to be sure, and it cannot be said that it is *just* a coping mechanism, any more than it can be said that religion is just a coping mechanism. Nevertheless, humor and religion are *at least* coping mechanisms. In a way, these two are not unlike our automobiles—it cannot be said of automobiles that they are "nothing but" devices to get us to the supermarket, but get us there they certainly do. Likewise, humor and religion have diverse functions to perform in human life, but not the least of them is to help us cope with reality by perversive self-deception. The particular point here is that humor is often used to create the illusion of invulnerability to anxiety-producing circumstances.

If humor actually does function as a coping mechanism, we should expect to find a correlation between the amount of anxiety produced by a situation and the potential for humor in that situation. This correlation has been demonstrated experimentally. A. Shurcliff subjected three groups to situations that generated three levels of anxiety, and then asked the groups to evaluate their situations for humor potential. The result was that high-anxiety situations were rated as high in humor potential.[66] But what reason have we to suppose that the use of humor in situations of anxiety has anything to do with self-deception? To see that it does we must first see the connection between humor and the sense of mastery over a situation. Jean Piaget has observed that smiling and laughter are typical reactions to mastery of a situation. When children succeed at a task, they usually smile or laugh. And when a child observes younger children struggling at tasks which once vexed him, the typical reaction is laughter. Moreover, the child will laugh when he masters a situation that only recently got the best of him. As Avner Ziv observes, "The sense of mastery is accompanied in the child by satisfaction, which is expressed by smiles and laughter." The connection of this phenomenon with self-deception is subtle, but nonetheless persuasive: If I am made anxious by a situation that is beyond my control, and if I manage to give it a humorous frame, then I can produce laughter; and having produced laughter, I gain the illusory sense of mastery over the situation. That is, in defeat I may claim victory, and having *claimed* victory, I may *feel* victorious. Ziv proposes that this is the central function of black humor and self-disparaging humor.[67] One can reduce anxiety about one's vulnerability to death by making jokes about death. Thus the virtue of Woody Allen's famous line: "I'm not afraid of death, I just don't want to be there when it happens." Or consider the robust tradition of black humor among morticians, for whom exposure to the anxiety of death is an occupational hazard. In hospitals and foxholes and death camps humor thrives, as if to say, "O death, where is thy sting?" To the extent that we are able to laugh about death, we have deconstructed its threat of self annihilation. The same can be said of many and various personal limitations—if we are able to laugh at our own shortcomings, we render ourselves less vulnerable to the anxiety they might otherwise induce. This tactic in no way removes them, but it empowers us with an illusory sense of mastery over them. Part of the splendor of humor is that it appears to work its self-deceptive wonders even when its content is not directly related to the source of anxiety. A good ethnic joke or sexual humor may be just the thing to relieve a patient who awaits surgery. Even the generic tittering of nervous laughter may be enough on occasion to create faint illusions of invulnerability. Laughter itself is the thing. And the same is true of the illusion of control that accompanies prayer. When anxiety strikes, then, suit yourself: dial-a-joke or dial-a-prayer.

It would be impossible in a book of this scope to discuss fully the diversity of self-deceptive strategies devised by humans in service to the goal of personal wholeness. I have tried to address some of the more common strategies in order to elucidate the typology set forth earlier in the chapter. I have not discussed most of the standard defense mechanisms featured in psychoanalytic literature, though it has long been recognized that these mechanisms reflect the dynamics of self-deception. As Heinz Hartman wrote in 1939, "Indeed, a great part of psychoanlysis can be described as a theory of self-deception."[68] To this day there appears to be widespread agreement about the self-deceptive character of ego defense mechanisms, but when it comes to the task of identifying and describing particular mechanisms, there is much to disagree about. Freud himself described only nine defenses, and his daughter, Anna Freud, saw fit to add several more. Later figures added to and subtracted from the list, and made first-order and second-order distinctions within the list. The most extensive list to appear includes twenty-four first-order and fifteen second-order defenses.[69] One of the more encouraging recent developments in psychoanalytic theory has been the cross-fertilization with evolutionary theory. The emergent field of evolutionary psychology has produced new insights about the self-deceptive nature of defense mechanisms, as well as insights about their adaptive significance.[70]

Before we depart from the subject of deconstructive strategies, two phenomena deserve mention, even though their status as self-deceiving strategies is not clear: relativism and mysticism. Relativizing is a strategy that deconstructs the conditions of self-condemnation by undermining the authority of standards of performance. If a particular value or standard can be shown to derive its authority from a certain set of circumstances (e.g., historical, social, psychological), then that value or standard takes on the appearance of limited, relative, or arbitrary authority. Relative values are seen as dependent, subjective, optional. And if one's performance against an optional standard is poor, one can easily dismiss the judgment by refusing to submit to the standard. The self is thereby rendered invulnerable to condemnation by a standard whose authority has been emptied by relativizing. Thus the child who does poorly at basketball may defend herself by dismissing the sport as unimportant or irrelevant: "It's okay for some people, but I think it's stupid." In many such cases relativizing will be seen as an instance of self-deceptive rationalization. It is self-deceptive because it is a motivated disadequation of the person's conscious belief from the submerged reality. That is, there is reason to believe that her acceptance of basketball as a relevant measure of self-worth is still operative, though suppressed in favor of a defensive perversion. In cases in which no commitment to a relativized value has been defeated, however, we may not say that self-deception has occurred. In fact, the relativizer in such cases may claim that just the reverse has occurred. That is, she may insist that being good at basketball is not necessarily relevant to self-worth, and that debunking the authority of its standards amounts to disabusing the self of a delusion. Excellence at basketball is relevant to the self-worth only of those who accept the relevance of it, and such acceptance is completely optional. In an absolute sense, then, hating basketball and doing very poorly at it is perfectly consistent with self-worth. We may say that those who are motivated to express this view by the anxiety of a poor performance at basketball are self-deceiving, but those who express it without such motivation are not.

The extreme relativist claims that no values or standards can be said to have absolute authority as measures of self-worth. That is, no universal values are written anywhere into the nature of things, such that they are relevant to the self-worth of everyone. And the relativist goes one step further to say that anyone who believes in universal values is in a state of disadequation to reality, for reality as a whole is indifferent to *all* values. This may in fact be true. That is, extreme relativism may well be the most adequate and defensible philosophical position on offer. But the relativist must be careful not to claim too much, lest the claims produce an illusion in spite of themselves. To say that there are no values inherent in the nature of things is one sort of claim, but to go from there to the doctrine that the self (any self) is ultimately invulnerable to *all* values is to create an illusion of invulnerability. It may be true that no particular self is vulnerable to the condemnation of this or that (or any) absolute value, but it is also true that every particular self is vulnerable to *some* values. The relativist may legitimately deconstruct *any value whatsoever*, but she may not divest herself of all values and remain a person. Perhaps there are no absolute values inherent in reality as a whole, but where there is a self *there are* inherent values absolutely, and where there are inherent values there is vulnerability to self-condemnation.

These matters lead us to consider a final strategy for deconstructing the conditions of self annihilation: mysticism. There are of course many forms of mysticism, and this is no place to review them all. What interests me here is that form of mysticism which leads the individual to an experience of "absolute oneness" with the whole of reality, wherein it is given that the manifold reality of normal everyday experience is nothing but an illusion. Variations on this form of mysticism have appeared in several religious traditions, especially Hinduism, Buddhism, and Taoism. Reports of mystical experience vary, but two characteristics are so commonly described that we may take them as definitive: absolute unity or wholeness and transcendence of the self-world dichotomy. Any account of the mystical experience must reckon with these two features. The most exciting scientific work on the subject of mystical experiences is being conducted by Eugene d'Aquili at the University of Pennsylvania. D'Aquili has proposed a neuropsychological model for analyzing mystical experience. According to this model, mystical experiences result when the techniques of meditation induce a "total deafferentation of both the left and right posterior-superior parietal lobules." This means that neural input to the posterior-superior parietal lobules (PSPL) is cut off, so that these structures of the brain now fire either randomly or according to their own internal logic. And from this logic arises mystical experience:

> Since the PSPL does not contain any memory banks its total deafferenta-tion cannot result in unusual or unmodulated visions, sounds, or tactile sensations. Rather its total deafferentation can only result in an absolute subjective sensation of pure space. But space has no meaning except as a matrix in which to relate objects. We propose therefore that pure space arising from total deafferentation of the right PSPL is subjectively experienced as absolute unity or wholeness. At the same instant that the right PSPL is totally deafferented. . . . the left PSPL is likewise totally deafferented . . . The left PSPL is intimately involved with the mainte-nance of the Self-Other or the Self-World dichotomy. We propose that the total deafferentation of the left PSPL results in the obliteration of the Self-Other dichotomy at precisely the same moment that the deaffer-entation of the right PSPL generates a sense of absolute transcendent wholeness. . . . Thus the subject attains a state of rapturous transcen-dence and absolute wholeness which carries such over-whelming power and strength with it that the subject has the sense of experiencing abso-lute reality. Indeed, so ineffable is that state that even the memory of it carries a sense of greater reality than the reality of our everyday world.[71]

The point I wish to stress here is that this form of mystical experience represents a preemptive strike against the possibility of threats to the self. What the mystic appears to achieve is nothing less than a deconstruction of the self itself. His experience convinces him that both the phenomenal self and the external world are derivative, nonessential, and illusory. And when there is no real self there can be no question of self annihilation, or rather, when the illusion of self has been annihilated by a deeper experience there can be no question of vulnerability. When there is no target for the slings and arrows of outrageous fortune, they have no powers of self annihilation. In a sense, the mystical experience achieves a deconstruction of the conditions of self annihilation that is almost as radical as suicide. But not quite. The illusory self returns to the world of illusion, but now with the unflappable assurance that threats of self annihilation amount to precisely nothing.

That this form of mysticism represents a deconstructive strategy there can be no doubt. But who can say whether it amounts to self-deception? The mystic appears to have preempted this interpretation as well. If one were inclined to assign mysticism to one of the categories of our typology, it would surely come in under evasive self-deception, for it evades the realities that constitute threats to the self. But whatever we choose to say about it, one thing remains clear: The mystic will be unperturbed.

The Limits of Deception

The point of this chapter has been to show that some loss of adequation to reality (that of another or one's own) is very often conducive to the achievement of personal wholeness. But now we must consider the limits of this principle, for limits there certainly are, both moral and psychological. The moral question is still a bit premature, and I will dodge it for the moment, pausing here only to justify doing so. It is my impression that the ultimate goal of humanity is to survive, and that the penultimate goals of personal wholeness and social coherence are the conditions by which humans secure the promise of survival. All questions of morality, therefore, acquire their meaning with respect to these conditions. At the risk of oversimplifying the character of the moral life, I offer the diagram in figure 3.2. We may represent moral judgment upon any act or rule by placing a dot within the circle, expressing the values of the act or rule in relation to advancing the goals of personal wholeness and social coherence. It will be seen that "selfish" and "good" acts advance the goal of personal wholeness, while "altruistic" and "good" acts advance the goal of social coherence. The moral question regarding deception and self-deception asks about the circumstances under which such acts might be judged "good." But until we have made our way through the discussion of social coherence in chapter 4 we will be ill equipped to address these issues. Thus the moral question will have to wait.

For the remainder of this chapter we will focus, briefly, on the psychological limits of deception. To assess these limits is a very difficult assignment because these limits vary significantly with respect to individual and situational factors. We might first ask about the limits on strategies of other-deception. There are many situations in which deceiving others may bring significant benefits to an individual without harming the dupe. But acts that deceive others are always

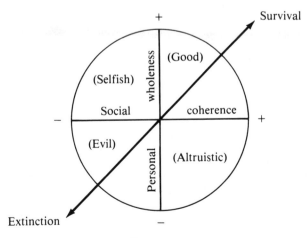

FIGURE 3.2

risky because they may backfire in ways that have damaging effects on personal wholeness. An individual who attempts to deceive too often or too blatantly may earn the reputation of being a liar. With such a reputation he may be subjected to expressions of social scorn, and if he is judged unworthy of trust he may be denied self-affirming occasions for intimacy. Also, in some cases, acts of deceiving others will set in motion a series of cover-up operations (e.g., subsequent deceits, suppression, rationalizations) that may be emotionally costly to the individual and preclude various possibilities for self-fulfillment. We may suggest, then, that there are significant risks of diminishing returns in consequence of excessive or blatant attempts to deceive others. Established patterns of other-deception may ultimately be destructive to personal wholeness by virtue of interfering with some essential dynamics of emotional maturation and self-maintenance.

Patterns of deceitful behavior are frequently associated with several psychopathies, such as antisocial, histrionic, narcissistic, borderline, and compulsive personality disorders. In such cases the suggestion that strategies of deceit play a contributing role would be unfounded; these disorders are rather symptomatic of serious structural or functional deficits that render the individual incapable of evaluating and inhibiting self-destructive deceits.[72]

There are also clear limits to the benefits of self-deception. A person harboring illusions of invulnerability may be spared much of the anxiety experienced by the "realist" who perceives health risks accurately, but she may also be less likely to practice preventive health care. A person who maintains an overly generous estimation of her abilities may be more open to new challenges, but she may also waste valuable time and energy persisting at impossible tasks. And such persons may be less inclined to prepare for future performance tasks, such as examinations, court cases, and athletic contests. An individual who engages in denial or repression may succeed in defeating some of the effects of a negative life experience, but may also thereby miss an important opportunity for growth and learning.

For many individuals the excessive use of self-deceptive strategies will increase the likelihood of psychological entrapment in these strategies. Self-deceptive defense mechanisms are probably universal strategies among humans, and for the majority they are generally adaptive, but they lose their adaptive value and become obstacles to personal wholeness if they become an integral part of the structure of a personality. Under normal circumstances a defense mechanism will be deployed as a specific response to a specific anxiety-producing situation. If it is successful, it may be appropriately deployed again under similar circumstances. But in some individuals defensive behaviors which originate as specific responses to specific circumstances tend to become generalized into all-purpose responses to any anxiety-producing stimulus. When this occurs, then the defensive strategy becomes a permanent fixture in a neurotic pattern of behavior. Neurotic conditions can be seen to result from a peculiar form of learning disorder—overlearning, or inappropriate generalization. Consider the analogy to a young boy who learns to pound nails with a hammer. A specific tool is used for a specific task, and its use is reinforced by success. But soon the boy is seen carrying the hammer along with him just in case he finds a nail sticking out somewhere. And finally he overgeneralizes to the point where he carries the hammer along and begins pounding at any old thing that happens to stick out. Neurosis amounts to this sort of entrapment in learned behavior—it is like giving the same answer to every question. The neurophysiological substrates of neurotic conditions are poorly understood, so direct methods of intervention are not feasible, but like many victims of learning disorders the neurotic can be helped by intensive therapy, the point of which is to degeneralize inflexible behavior responses so that the patient can once again devise specific behaviors for specific stimuli.

Extreme forms of delusion and fantasy are associated with psychotic disorders, and in these cases it cannot be maintained that the disadequation to reality is even remotely beneficial. As with neurotics, there is some evidence that in borderline, paranoid, and schizotypal personality disorders coping mechanisms become permanent and maladaptive features of personality structures.[73] But unlike neurotics, the victims of psychotic disorders appear to be prevented by neurochemical and structural deficits from learning their way out of chaos.

The role played by strategies of deceit and self-deception in the achievement of personal wholeness cannot be generalized without qualifications and ambiguities. On the one hand, we find evidence to encourage the view that these strategies are very often efficient and effective means for resolving inevitable intrapsychic conflict. That is, they advance personal wholeness by facilitating the functional integration of a multidynamic information-processing system. But on the other hand, we have good reason to associate these same strategies with dysfunctional and maladaptive behaviors. In general we might assess the role of deceit and self-deception in the following way: Short-term, occasional, and moderate uses of deceptive and self-deceptive strategies are generally conducive to personal wholeness, whereas chronic and blatant uses are generally counterproductive. This assessment is consistent with C. R. Snyder's curvilinear theory of reality negotiation: "I would hypothesize that no or very slight tendencies to engage in reality negotiation are low in adaptiveness, moderate reality negotiation is high in adaptive repercussions, and very high levels of reality negotiations are low in adaptive consequences."[74]

It is common to hear expressions of longing for a world without deception, yet one does well to consider the cost of such a world. We are beings in whom the fortunes of evolution have brought knowing, feeling, and willing to the level of conscious experience. But if, as I have argued, the dynamics making such complexity of mind possible are those also making deception and self-deception inevitable, then the cost is far too great. Under these conditions, the world of our longings should be one in which disadequations to reality are held within optimal limits, that is, limits that are conducive to achieving personal wholeness and social coherence.

 ⟡  4  ⟢ 

Deception and Social Coherence

I HAVE suggested that human survival is contingent upon the achievement of two penultimate goals, personal wholeness and social coherence. In chapter 3 we considered the nature of personality, the conditions for personal wholeness, and the role of deception in the achievement of those conditions. The present chapter will be developed in a parallel fashion. Here we will ask: What is the nature of society? What are the conditions for social coherence? What is the role of deception in the achievement of the conditions for social coherence?

THE NATURE OF SOCIETY

Any contemporary social theory must begin by reconciling evolutionary biology with the fact of sociality. It is an axiom of evolutionary biology that organisms are programmed in such ways as to maximize their own reproductive interests. But if self-interest is a given, then one might suppose that even a modicum of social order would be an unlikely possibility. If individuals are essentially self-serving, then one might expect that interactions between them would be so thoroughly fraught with conflicts of interest that a sustainable social order would be out of the question. But of course examples of social order are everywhere to be found and cannot be denied. This being the case, most social theories have been premised on the doctrine that individuals are not universally self-serving, that they are capable of genuine altruism, and that this capacity accounts for the possibility of sociality. But if one accepts the biological axiom of universal self-interest then the central task of social theory is to show by what means a plurality of individuals who are independently self-serving are able to achieve sociality. In other words, social theory must begin by asking: What are the means of social cooperation? The most general answer to this question is that the means of cooperation are any means that contribute to establishing an overlap or confluence of interests among individuals. If such means can be identified, then it will be possible to account for sociality without the biologically dubious assumption of genuine altruism. I will argue that the key to sociality is to achieve a high degree of confluence of interests among individuals, such that when an individual acts in her own interests, she thereby incidentally advances the interests of others, or conversely, when she acts in the interests of others, she incidentally serves her own interests. I am suggesting that when such conditions of overlapping self-interest prevail, sociality is possible, but when they do not prevail, sociality is precluded. Richard Alexander expressed the idea well when he said that "conflicts and confluences of interests are the warp and woof of the fabric of society."[1] And from this insight we may derive a definition of society. *A society is an organized group of individuals having the means of cooperation sufficient to establish a confluence of interests among its members.* We may give substance to this definition by first discussing the means of cooperation, then the domains or categories of confluent human interests, and finally the types of human social organization.

Means of Cooperation

Most animal species are social to some extent. That is, in most species it is possible to identify ordered patterns of interaction between individual members of a group. Any species that reproduces by sexual means or invests time and energy in caring for its young has at least a minimum of sociality. It takes only a moment's reflection to see how sociality might have adaptive advantages over solitary living. Individuals who were capable of entering into cooperative projects would find valuable assistance in rearing their young, in defense against predators, in finding prey or in taking prey too large for a solitary hunter, and in defending resources against conspecific competitors. Such advantages can be seen to establish selective conditions favoring many patterns of social existence. Yet, while the advantages of sociality are rather obvious, the means for achieving it have been very elusive. These means are of two types, genetic and cultural.

Genetic means

For more than a century Darwin's theory of evolution by natural selection suffered from an inability to account for the apparent phenomena of altruistic behavior. According to Darwinian theory, traits that work to the advantage of individual survival and reproduction will tend to be preserved, while any traits that work against these selfish ends will tend to disappear through natural selection. Thus behavioral traits that are harmful or costly to the actor while being helpful to some other individual—that is, altruistic traits—would not be expected to appear. But in fact nature appears to abound in such traits. Insect societies, for example, have large castes of sterile individuals who work tirelessly for the reproductive success of others but never themselves reproduce. And individuals of many species jeopardize their own lives to give a warning signal when a predator is detected. Such warning signals appear to be altruistic because they benefit others while increasing the probability that the whistle-blower will be located and picked off. Traits for self-serving behaviors are no problem for Darwinian principles, but traits for helping others at one's own expense appear to contradict the doctrine of reproductive fitness. And when such traits appear, as they obviously do, they constitute a theoretical paradox.

Or so it seemed to most biologists until 1964, when W. D. Hamilton proposed the theory of *inclusive fitness* to show how the selection of traits for altruistic behavior is consistent with Darwinian principles. This theory is indifferent to the matter of individual reproduction, asking instead what conditions govern the selection of *traits*. It matters less *who* reproduces than what genes get replicated. If the name of the game is to get one's genes replicated, then it must be seen that there are more ways than one to score. One way, of course, is to reproduce. But since your siblings share a certain percentage of your genes, you may also enhance your genetic project by advancing *their* reproductive success. This suggests that reproductive success, or fitness, should be defined more broadly, to include the success of all relatives who share particular genes. In other words, there exists a confluence of reproductive interests among relatives, in proportion to their relatedness. The theory of inclusive fitness brings to light an important principle of evolution, the process known as *kin selection*. David Barash defines kin selection as "the evolutionary process whereby individuals maximize their inclusive fitness through their behavior toward kin."[2] Thus the theories of inclusive fitness and kin selection imply that any heritable behaviors that assist one's own offspring *and/or* the offspring of relatives will tend to persist in proportion to the relatedness. That is, traits for helping relatives will be transmitted by the relatives helped, and in proportion to their relatedness to the helper. It is clear that any sacrifices you make for your own offspring will increase the chances that your genes (and the sacrificing traits they bear) will be represented in the future. This is a direct effect. But traits for sacrificing on behalf of your siblings and their offspring will have a similar effect, though indirect, because they share a certain percentage of your genes. Attentive parents are more likely to produce offspring who will themselves be attentive parents. Conversely, inattentive parenting results in a higher rate of infant mortality, which makes inattentive parenting rare in subsequent generations. Inclusive fitness and kin selection theory say that the same dynamic works indirectly for attentive "uncling" and "aunting" and "cousining."

The theory of inclusive fitness gets mathematically complex in a hurry, but the bottom line for our purposes is just this: Human beings have inherited traits for helping out their own kin, and this predisposition toward helping behavior can be quantified according to genetic relatedness. These inherited traits for helping kin (sharing resources, investing time and energy, risking life and limb for their welfare, etc.) constitute the fundamental means of cooperation that establish a confluence of interests among the members of kinship societies.

But these are not the only genetic means of cooperation. Another mechanism that allows for the genetic encoding of cooperative behavior is known as *reciprocity*. This phenomenon accounts for the evolution of altruistic traits without reference to genetic relatedness. In fact, it has been suggested that reciprocal altruism may even operate between species.[3] Reciprocal altruism is a genetic predisposition to help unrelated individuals when the cost to the benefactor is low and the benefit to the recipient is high. The evolutionary scenario for this trait goes as follows: Suppose I find you trapped on the fourth floor of a burning building and I drop everything and run to the corner to phone the fire squad, with the result that you are saved. Since you are unrelated to me, nothing in the theory of inclusive fitness suggests that I should go to this expense, small though it may be. If there is even a slight chance that our circumstances might someday be reversed, however, and if my saving you has increased your predisposition to return the favor, then there will be a great potential advantage to me in saving you. Thus when these conditions prevail, you and I will have a common interest in getting you saved. In circumstances in which the probability of future interactions is high and interactants are capable of forming recognition schemas for individuals, then a trait predisposing individuals to help others in distress will become genetically fixed and evolutionarily stable.[4]

I have now described two genetically conditioned mechanisms (kin selection and reciprocal altruism) which work in combination to establish confluences of interests between self-serving individuals. Robert Trivers takes the argument a step further by suggesting that the same selective factors that allow for the evolution of altruism would also favor the evolution of a constellation of emotional traits by which the dynamics of altruism might be regulated. One such characteristic is the tendency to develop *affection* for certain individuals and to form friendship bonds with them. Friendship bonds are interpersonal coalitions within which affection and altruism reinforce each other: We tend to be more altruistic toward those we like, and we tend to like those who are altruistic to us. Just as affection operates as a regulator of altruistic behavior, so *disaffection,* or resentment, will serve as a releaser for aggressive behavior whenever an altruist is cheated upon in a reciprocal relation. Such tendencies to take aggressive action function to deter cheating, a phenomenon which always threatens to destabilize interpersonal coalitions. Trivers believes this emotional mechanism is evidence that an inherent sense of fairness has evolved in humans.[5] *Gratitude* and *sympathy* are common emotions that have been rendered more intelligible by the theory of reciprocal altruism. These emotions appear to be linked to an individual's assessment of the costs and benefits embedded in a reciprocal situation. Thus the greater the assessed need of the recipient, the more intense the sympathy and the more likely an altruistic response. Gratitude, too, will tend to vary with an individual's assessment of cost to a benefactor. The higher the cost, the more the gratitude and the greater the likelihood of reciprocation. And finally, a sense of *guilt* helps to regulate reciprocity by motivating individuals to avoid misdeeds and/or to compensate for damages by practicing reparative altruistic behavior. These genetically endowed emotional traits, undergirding the dynamics of reciprocal altruism, predispose humans to form social groups wherein they may satisfy their immediate needs as well as advance their inclusive fitness.

I have been trying to make a point about the genetics of sociality. The phenomenon of kin selection is thought to operate in most sexually reproducing animal species to establish a general disposition toward helping related individuals. The helping behaviors are altruistic in the sense that some sacrifice is made by the actor for the benefit of the receiver, but they are also self-serving behaviors in the sense that they enhance the inclusive fitness of the actor. Rather than call such behaviors either altruistic or selfish, we might just say (with more accuracy) that they represent a confluence of interests between the actor and the receiver. The phenomenon of reciprocity also describes conditions of overlapping self-interests, but in this case genetic relatedness is not necessarily a factor. All that is required for reciprocity is that individuals have a good chance of future interactions and that they be intelligent enough to form recognition schemas. Both of these phenomena are at work in the human species, providing the genetic means of cooperation necessary for basic sociality. It would be misleading to suggest that these genetic means result in specific behaviors. They rather set the stage for a wide range of possibilities that may be exploited within the domain of culture.

Cultural means

Some social theorists have assumed that in the absence of cultural innovations there would be no sociality among humans. This assumption is false. Even if humans were incapable of sharing the fruits of their learning, a measure of social order would remain, perhaps resembling that of chimpanzee societies.[6] The genetic means of cooperation are sufficient for a certain amount of overlapping self-interest. Yet it must be said that cultural means of cooperation enable domains of confluent interests and forms of social organization that far transcend the capabilities of other species. At this point I shall describe the cultural means of cooperation in the most general terms. Subsequent discussions will provide opportunities to explore the principal domains of human interests and the types of social organization that have evolved in the course of human history.

"Culture" may be defined as the shared set of learned behaviors and their artifacts that are characteristic of a particular society. Thus the elements of a culture include language, beliefs, attitudes, values, customs, rituals, games, art, tools, clothing, housing, institutions, and so on. When we ask about the cultural means of cooperation, we are hard pressed to rule out any of these elements. Indeed, one is tempted to say that culture itself is constituted by these extragenetic means of cooperation among the members of a social group.

In order to be more precise about the cultural means of cooperation we would do well to proceed by analogy to the genetic means. Human beings have a dual system for transmitting information, the genetic system and the cultural system. The genetic system transmits information from one individual to another by means of units called genes, and the cultural system operates by the transmission of units of meaning which Richard Dawkins calls *memes:* "Just as genes propagate themselves in the gene pool by leaping from body to body via sperms or eggs, so memes propagate themselves in the meme pool by leaping from brain to brain via a process which, in the broad sense, can be called imitation."[7] A meme may be regarded as a unit of meaning which can be replicated in another brain by the apprehension of symbols in the complex processes of social interaction. Memes include words, phrases, ideas, rules, techniques, and the like. We may say that a meme is any neural schema that can be given symbolic form, thereby becoming socially transmittable. And just as organisms that share a sufficient number of genes may be said to belong to the same species, so individuals may be said to participate in a common culture by virtue of sharing a sufficient number of memes.

In summary, the genetic means of cooperation are those heritable traits that predispose humans to form social groups on the basis of the dynamics of kin selection and reciprocity, together with those heritable traits that enable the invention of culture. The cultural means of cooperation are memes, and in particular they are those memes which establish, reinforce and/or expand a confluence of interests among individuals.

Human Interests and Social Domains

We are still trying to answer the question: What is a society? So far we have determined that a society is achieved by establishing confluences of interest, whether by genetic or cultural means. We can make further gains on our question if we inquire about the various social domains in which overlaps of self-interest may exist. It will be observed that the major components of a society are those that have developed to foster and serve the confluent interests of individuals.

The relationship between individuals and society has long vexed philosophers as well as the more recent theorists of personality and sociality. A recurrent motif in the history of this problem has been the idea that human society can be understood as the individual writ large. That is, the structure of social groups may be seen as a macrocosm of the structure of personality. Thus Plato, for example, envisioned his ideal state to be composed of three distinct social castes, corresponding to the appetitive, spirited, and rational parts of the individual soul. This tradition of microcosmic/macrocosmic thinking about the structural similarities of personality and society has fallen out of favor partly because it appears to involve dubious metaphysical principles. But one need not appeal to metaphysics in order to claim that an understanding of personality provides insight for an analysis of society. All that is required is the practical notion that humans will tend to purpose-build their social systems to advance their principal interests.

Let me then dare to suggest that an adequate psychology will provide essential resources for sociological analysis. On this suggestion we may bring forward the motivational theory of personality and assess its implications for an understanding of social systems. I have claimed that a person is a set of motivational systems (i.e., curiosity, pleasure/pain, self-esteem) that are integrated into a functional unity. At the most comprehensive level of inquiry, then, social analysis should concentrate on describing how a particular society goes about providing and managing the resources relevant to satisfying basic human needs for intelligibility, pleasure, and a sense of self-worth. We may therefore speak in terms of the following correspondence between personal motives and social domains:

Personal motives	Social domains
Cognitive	Knowledge (cosmology)
Hedonic	Resources (economy)
Self-esteem	Values (morality)

I will eventually propose a conception of social coherence that corresponds to the harmonic function observed at the personal level. But for the moment let us examine these very broad features of society.

Knowledge

All humans desire to know; we are motivated toward intelligibility. And when it comes to knowing, two heads are usually better than one. What comes along with two or more heads is the possibility of transcending the privacy of a *perceptual field* and entering into the publicity of a *conceptual world*. As we construct a conceptual world, the range of intelligibility expands far beyond what would be possible for a solitary perceiver. Linguistic conventions give symbolic form to neural schemas, which are then refined in the light of feedback from others within the language group. In the process of these refinements schemas become less idiosyncratic, particulars generalize, abstractions are assembled, and unfathomable mysteries become familiar realities. The members of a group will thus negotiate their way toward a common stock of cognitive paradigms defining the features of cosmology and rationality characteristic of their culture. These cosmological and rational paradigms are the cognitive moorings of a society, providing the fundamental means for intelligibility that will be widely shared among its members. Thus the various activities for generating, refining, and disseminating knowledge constitute a primary domain of confluent human interests.

A society, then, offers to its members numerous memes to inform them about the various sorts of realities there are in the world, what properties may be attributed to things, what kinds of events are possible, how things and events stand in relation to other things and events, which realities are primary and which ones are derivative, and so on. From such concepts an orderly and predictable cosmos emerges to shape the consciousness of individuals and to define the parameters of social discourse. But equal in importance to these cosmological features are the paradigms of rationality that operate within a group. Cultures will develop standards of consistency, criteria for judging the relevance and authenticity of new memes, shared methods for acquiring new information, procedures for resolving disputes about matters of fact, and structures for the transmission and suppression of information.

The cognitive paradigms of a social group provide one measure for determining who is and who is not "in" the group. If an individual does not conform to the prevailing memes of intelligibility, he or she is seen as an outsider. And from the individual's point of view, if the cognitive paradigms of the group fail to satisfy needs for intelligibility, then the conditions will be set for seeking out new memes that may eventually transform the group or possibly lay the cognitive foundations for a new group. But cosmological and rational paradigms also provide one measure for determining the integrity of a social group. If consensus on cognitive paradigms is sufficiently lacking, one may rightly ask whether in fact a group exists at all. Thus it will be seen that any deconstruction of these paradigms will be taken as a threat to the survival of the group.

Resources

If two communicating heads are better than one in the acquisition of knowledge, then two coordinated pairs of hands are better than one in the acquisition of resources. What comes along with two or more pairs of hands is the possibility of strategies for production, predation, and defense that transcend the abilities of solitary workers. This is the hedonic logic underlying the development of social economy. An economy may be defined as the strategies for securing, managing, and distributing the collective wealth of a social group, where wealth is understood to be the external means for achieving pleasure and avoiding pain. Such external means include food sources, materials and sites for shelter, sexual mates, labor, tools, health and safety supplies, and the like. A social group is defined in large measure by its technological and political strategies for securing and managing such means and for making them accessible to its members.

To survive a social group must have sufficient access to natural resources together with appropriate technologies for exploiting them and converting them into consumable items. The natural environs within which a social group is situated will determine the range of options that apply to diet, materials for shelter, clothing, tools, and other aspects of material culture. And the resolution of these options will largely determine the types of technologies, skills, and roles that will develop within the group. In the course of time a society will commit itself to various options, and in consequence will construct a distinctive way of life. An important part of any social economy is the political system negotiated within the group. An economy is the arena of competition and reciprocity within a society, and its political system represents the strategies developed to regulate their dynamics. "Politics" is used here in the broad sense to include patterns of family life, group decision making, conflict resolution, patterns of access to wealth, differential privilege, power, authority, and so on. And "economy" is used in the even broader sense to include politics. We will have another opportunity to look into political systems when we examine social organization.

A society provides its members with an ecological niche together with a constellation of memes defining a way of life within which individuals seek to satisfy their hedonic motives. One is "in" the social group by virtue of sharing these memes and participating in the patterns of reciprocity they determine. Indeed, reciprocal hedonism is the very essence of the economic/political realm of a society. Individuals will be well served by their participation to the extent that their access to the wealth of the group is commensurate with their contributions to its production. And when this is not perceived to be the case—that is, when economic roles are denied or access to wealth is denied—then the conditions will be set for social alienation. Among the several factors that may contribute to these conditions are shortages of resources, inappropriate technology, squandering of wealth, poor management strategies, and unfair mechanisms for the distribution of wealth. The social alienation that results from these conditions constitutes a significant threat to the survival of the group.

In chapter 3 I said that the curiosity motivator and the hedonic motivator were interdependent. The cognitive system gives shape and texture to the affective order and the affective system educates the attention of cognition, with the result that a developing child establishes intricate associations between these systems. A similar interdependence can be seen between the social functions of cosmology and economy. What the members of a social group think and believe about the world around will influence their perception of options for an economic way of life. And the economy of the group will influence the direction and development of its learning. I also suggested that the interactions of the cognitive and hedonic motivators created the conditions for the derivation of a third motivational system: self-esteem. We may now extend the correspondence to suggest that a third major realm of social reality (a moral order) is derived from the interactions of knowledge and economy.

Values

At the beginning of this chapter we saw how the theories of inclusive fitness and reciprocity were able to account for the evolution of altruistic behavior, demonstrating that altruism is not inconsistent with the general presumption of self-interest in human behavior. We saw that both inclusive fitness theory and reciprocity theory involved the operation of some sort of calculus telling the actor when it was and was not in his self-interest to act in the interest of another individual. In the case of inclusive fitness the calculus is one of genetic relatedness. This calculus expresses a confluence of genetic interests, saying in effect that it is in *my* interest to act in *her* interest if she and I are genetically related. The closer the relationship, the more self-interest there is to my altruism. The mechanics of this calculus rely upon abilities for kin recognition. The calculus of self-interest governing reciprocity is a bit different because this phenomenon operates quite apart from genetic relatedness. The calculus of reciprocity says in effect that it is in *my* interest to act in *her* interest if the following conditions hold: the sacrifice to me is low and the benefit to her is high, and there is a good chance of future interactions wherein she may have an opportunity to reciprocate. The mechanics of this calculus rely upon the ability of individuals to form recognition schemas for individuals and episodes, and to associate these schemas with emotional responses such as affection, gratitude, and sympathy.

It will be seen that the altruism of kin selection and the altruism of reciprocity are not true altruism because in each case there is a confluence of interests, and this confluence is quantified by the calculi of self-interest. Instances of true altruism—that is, acts in the interests of others when the self-interest values in terms of these calculi are negative—are not expected to appear except as anomalies. But, in fact, acts of "true" altruism do appear among humans in regular and abundant violation of these calculi of self-interest. Consider the woman who risks her life to deliver a package to a complete stranger whom she is confident she will never see again. This example violates the calculus of kin selection by virtue of genetic unrelatedness to the stranger. And it violates the calculus of reciprocity by virtue of involving high cost to the actor and low benefit to the receiver, and also by virtue of poor chances for future interactions. Or consider the thousands of animal rights activists who expend time and energy and risk imprisonment to act in the interests of individuals to whom they are clearly unrelated and from whom there is no possibility of reciprocation.

Such acts are evidence of a *moral calculus.* These altruists do what they do in the interests of others because they believe their actions are *right,* because they are committed to moral values that are seemingly independent of the self-interest calculi of kin selection and reciprocity. And yet, I will argue, this moral calculus, so essential to human societies, can be shown to derive from the dynamics of kin selection and reciprocity. I believe that any adequate social or moral theory should be able to account for this derivation.

I suggest that the moral calculus *just is* the calculus of self-esteem, and that this new and independent means for determining behavior can be constructed by manipulation of the mechanisms that evolved to regulate reciprocity and kin selection. In many nonhuman societies (whales and apes, for example) the dynamics of kin selection and reciprocity provide a sufficient base of altruism to sustain cooperation. But human societies would not be sustainable without considerably more confluence of interest. The confluence of interest among genetically related individuals is too narrow for all but the tiniest of familial bands. And the confluence of interest expressed by the calculus of reciprocity is too sporadic and unpredictable. But together they provide an excellent base of cooperation that is exploitable by cultural means for increasing the confluence of interest between individuals. A principal means for this expansion of common interests is the self-esteem motivator.

The mechanics of kin selection can be expanded by the influence of various memes that affirm relatedness among all the members of a society. These memes are designed to take the place of kin-recognition strategies. They may include public ceremonies, scarring or tattooing practices, circumcision, ornamentation, and the like. The "children of God" in Judaism is one such meme, as is the Christian affirmation that the baptized are all "brothers and sisters in Christ." Such memes expand confluences of interest by artificially extending kinship. The memes of artificial kinship are important elements in the construction of a person's self-concept. Memes may also exploit the mechanics of reciprocity. When altruistic behavior is reinforced by immediate hedonic rewards (and not necessarily by the recipient), the confluence of interests becomes frequent and predictable rather than sporadic and unpredictable. The deliverywoman's efforts on behalf of her recipient stranger are contingent upon the expectation of a salary. Memes may also be used to stimulate feelings of sympathy, gratitude, and guilt, thereby increasing the likelihood of altruism; and memes may also serve to inhibit revenge. As memes encouraging altruistic acts enter into the calculus of self-esteem, the motivation toward attributions of self-worth takes the place of immediate hedonic rewards. The animal rights activists persist as much for their own self-esteem as they do for the interests of their unsuspecting beneficiaries.

One may say that in this process the genetically conditioned altruistic system has been upgraded or augmented by the addition of learned programs for behavior that have been negotiated by the members of a society. These negotiations result in the construction of a moral order—that is, a collection of values that select for behaviors deemed essential for the survival of the group as a whole. There is no question that each human society relies on the maintenance of hundreds of values that form its distinctive moral order. If these social values fail, then there will be a default back to the calculi of kin selection and chance reciprocity. The strategy of augmenting genetic determinants of behavior with learned programs is generally highly adaptive, though there are no guarantees that the distinctive values of a society will remain adaptive over the long haul. As environmental conditions change (as they frequently do under the impact of adaptive values themselves!), it may be necessary to renegotiate the moral order. At the heart of every human society, therefore, is a fundamental dilemma: Failure to preserve the distinctive moral order is a threat to survival, but so is failure to revise the moral order.

Social integration

I have been arguing that a society is a multidynamic system comprising cosmological, economic, and moral components. The memes which define these interacting components represent the cultural means by which the members of a group seek to satisfy their needs for intelligibility, pleasure, and self-esteem. But just as a person must manage to integrate motivational systems into a functional unity, so a society must integrate its cosmology, economy, and morality. In the case of individual persons, the integrative function is carried out, for the most part, by the prefrontal cortex of the brain. By virtue of this integrative function the individual achieves wholeness. The social counterpart of this integrative function is the myth of a culture. Every distinctive culture has a myth, by which I mean a narrative integration of cosmology, economy, and morality. Indeed, a culture comes into being as a coherent social entity by the activity of mythmaking, by involving elements of its known world, its way of life, and its social norms in a comprehensive narrative of self-understanding. Myth expresses the identity of a cultural tradition, and it is generally in relation to the central metaphors of a myth that the memes of cosmology, economy, and morality will find their ultimate meaning and justification. Once established, then, a myth is perceived to embody the essence of a culture in such a way that it takes on a life of its own, quite independent of the cosmological, economic, and moral components. The myth of a culture is elevated to an executive position as the ultimate legitimator of cultural memes. And it becomes the final standard for who is and who is not "in" the culture. Thus we may say that a cultural tradition exists as a social entity by virtue of having a viable myth. And we may further observe that the myth of a culture imposes its own needs for coherence, which may, paradoxically, interfere with individual needs for personal wholeness. Thus we may speak of the possibility of tension between personal wholeness and social coherence. But these issues anticipate the concerns of a later section of this chapter. For the moment let us review the types of social organization that have developed in the course of human history.

Social Organization

Interactions between the social domains of confluent interests will produce a distinctive cultural tradition, of which several thousand have appeared in the course of human history. But despite the range of cultural diversity, many anthropologists believe that all cultures conform to just a few major types of social organization. The most common classification describes four principal types: *kinship bands, tribal alliances, chiefdoms,* and *states.*[8] This classification scheme assumes a process of evolutionary development from simpler forms of social organization to more complex forms. Complexity is understood to mean greater size and density, but also more diversity of specialized parts within the larger whole. And further, the evolution from a simpler type of social organization to a more complex type appears to depend upon the invention of new means of cooperation to integrate the emergent parts. If a social group thrives, it will grow in size and density and segmentation of parts until it outgrows the means of cooperation that have fostered its success. As this happens the group may eventually undergo social mitosis into smaller groups that have essentially the same organizational structure as the original group. An alternative to subdivision is for the society to develop new means of cooperation that may preserve the unity of the group, although in a pattern of integration that is unknown at the previous stage of development. Different types of social organization may therefore be recognized in these different patterns of integration.

Kinship bands

The very essence of aboriginal societies lay in the ability to modify their size to meet the challenges of locally varying ecologies. It is therefore impossible to give an accurate picture of the composition of these earliest groups. In general terms we may say that kinship bands were assemblies of close relatives, ranging in numbers from perhaps a dozen individuals to somewhat larger groups of twenty to thirty nuclear families. They made a subsistence living by hunting and gathering, moving about according to the cycles of flora and fauna in their ecological range. Typically, kinship bands required large tracts of territory and very low population density in order to make a decent living. Where resources were widely dispersed, population density might not exceed one person per ten square miles, but where resources were locally concentrated, density might be as high as two persons per square mile.[9] In environments of great abundance kinship bands might live in relatively permanent hamlets, but it was more common for bands to establish temporary camps that could be moved efficiently. These groups had no formal government. Whatever leadership functions had to be performed were ad hoc and spontaneous, no doubt falling to whichever adult male was most proximate. Nor was there any specialization of skills. Every member of the band had to be a generalist, and when division of labor was called for, it tended to follow distinctions of sex and age. The economy of kinship bands was egalitarian and reciprocal; that is, members of the group had equal access to resources according to individual needs. There was little or no accumulation of material wealth, for any such accumulations would be a hindrance as the group moved about. If the ecology were favorable, a band would thrive and grow in numbers, in which case it might have to move farther and more frequently in order to acquire sufficient supplies. If they didn't move far enough or often enough, resources would begin to thin out and competition would emerge within the group. Under such conditions it becomes more efficient for the group to subdivide, with part of the group migrating into new territories, thereby reducing both competition and the frequency of relocation.

The means of cooperation within kinship bands were primarily biological. That is, bands required no formal or artificial means to keep the group together. The mechanics of inclusive fitness and reciprocity were sufficient. When competition for resources tested the limits of these biological mechanisms, conditions would be set for either social mitosis or the development of cultural means of cooperation. It was common for bands to form seasonal and ephemeral coalitions with other bands to meet occasional challenges presented by hostile competing groups or to engage in hunting expeditions requiring larger numbers. Such coalitions might also form when surplus supplies allowed one group to subsidize another. Periodic coalitions would also facilitate the exchange of females, ensuring the requisite outbreeding of the species. When conditions changed, however, these coalitions would dissolve as quickly and as effortlessly as they had formed.

Tribal alliances

Coalitions between kinship bands were spontaneous and temporary. They would form in response to some particular crisis and then dissolve once the crisis passed. But eventually permanent associations emerged among bands to create a new form of social organization, the tribal alliance. The process of evolution from kinship bands to tribal alliances probably varied considerably under local circumstances, so an accurate account of the process is out of the question. But for our purposes a composite picture will be adequate. In those areas where competition between bands was most intense there would be major advantages in keeping a larger group intact. A larger group would be better prepared to meet sudden defensive challenges and would also have sufficient productivity to survive occasional shortages of resources. But the maintenance of social solidarity within a larger group would call for strategies of social organization that were not necessary in kinship bands. During peacetime it was likely that feuds would break out between kin groups. It became necessary, therefore, to construct new cultural means of cooperation that might preclude disruptions to the unity of the group. Such a means was the formation of *pan-tribal sodalities*.[10] Pan-tribal sodalities were institutions that were perhaps foreshadowed in some ways by certain ingredients of band society, but now they became more formal and regularized. Tribal sodalities included kinship clans, age-group and sex-group associations, secret societies and various special-interest groups occasioned by such tasks as hunting, warfare, curing, and ceremonial events. These associations would bring together individuals from territorially separated tribal subgroups on a regular basis, thereby integrating these groups into a larger whole. Because these pan-tribal associations transcended several local territories, they had to achieve their identity by artificial means, normally by acquiring a name. Clans, for example, were named lineage groups that cut across several residential bands. Membership in such groups was based not on residential proximity but rather on common ancestry. The institution of such groups required, therefore, the concept of descent, a meme that was unknown to band societies. Along with the concept of descent came group names, special symbols, narrative accounts of origins, ceremonial events, and so on. It was not necessary that pan-tribal clans be strictly genealogical—in some cases they might even trace their common ancestry to nonhuman sources, such as a totemic plant or animal.[11] The important thing was to have coalitions (artificial or otherwise) that could establish confluence of interests by interconnecting segments within the larger, transkin society.

The yoking function of pan-tribal clans was supplemented by other forms of association between residential segments, forging bonds of sodality along various social vectors. Some of these sodalities involved recreational interactions between children of common age groups, and others were simple guilds made up of individuals from different villages who gathered to share information relevant to specialized activities or crafts. A large tribe would have several special-interest sodalities, but whatever the special purpose might be, the underlying function was always to foster and maintain the unity of the complex group. The unity of a tribe might be further strengthened by the social convention of exchanging gifts between individuals of different subgroups—a common social manipulation of the biological mechanics of reciprocity.

Tribal alliances would obviously have less mobility than the much smaller band societies. Thus, as a tribe flourished, its territory would become more densely populated, creating a need for technologies that enabled more intensive exploitation of environmental resources. Thus hunting and gathering gradually yielded to herding and agriculture. New techniques of subsistence would also involve a greater specialization of labor, thus proliferating the number of pan-tribal sodalities. As the interconnections between segments developed, awareness of the transcendent identity of the tribal group increased. The tribe became a new social entity.

But in some ways tribal societies were still very similar to bands. The economy of tribal societies remained egalitarian, and despite increased specialization, everyone was directly involved in subsistence activities. Tribes, like bands, lacked formal and fixed institutions of government. Leadership continued to be ad hoc and charismatic. There was often a village headman who joined in council with the leaders of other villages, but such figures were selected informally and served as firsts among equals.

It is a truism of human sociality that a group is only as stable as its means of cooperation. If the means of cooperation are not commensurate with the complexity of the group, the confluence of interests among its members will be insufficient to keep the society together, and it will begin to dissolve as conflicts of interests increase. Confluence of interests was established in tribal alliances by pan-tribal sodalities. If these coalitions failed for one reason or another, the tribe might quickly revert to a plurality of independent kinship bands. We may assume that patterns of tribal waxing and waning were characteristic of much of human history. As stable tribal alliances became the norm for social organization, then the common pattern became one of flourish and fission. As tribal societies grew in size, density, and complexity, intratribal factions would emerge to begin the process of mitosis.

Chiefdoms

An alternative to the pattern of tribal flourish and fission is represented by a new form of social organization: the chiefdom. Several characteristics differentiate chiefdoms from tribal alliances. As we might expect, chiefdoms are larger, more densely populated, and more complex in the number and specialization of parts. Chiefdoms are also more productive than tribes, and they typically have resources in reserve. Because of their greater size, chiefdoms normally range over a diversity of ecological regions, with some areas more plentiful in resources than others. But the feature that most distinguishes chiefdoms has to do with their political structure. With chiefdoms we find a much more formalized political and economic system, highly centralized in the *office* of the chief. In contrast to bands and tribes, with their ad hoc spontaneity of leadership, the chiefdom has a full-time leader whose position of authority is permanent and hereditary. One of the most important functions of the chief is his intervention in economic affairs for the purpose of redistributing resources, a function that may help to account for the origin of chiefdoms. As a consequence of the increased productivity and ecological diversity of large tribes, some segments of the group tended to fare better than others. And where permanent settlement was a factor, it became common for subgroups to hoard wealth. Thus gross inequities of wealth were likely to develop between subgroups, creating the conditions for intratribal conflict. A centralized system for the redistribution of wealth could mitigate such conflict and manage to keep the group unified. Another important element favoring the centralized authority of a chief was the military factor. Campaigns orchestrated by a competent and decisive commander in chief would be far more successful than the inefficient flailings of uncoordinated troops.

The emergence of centralized chiefly authority, therefore, was a strategy that fostered confluence of interests under the conditions of increasing conflicts of interests, both internal and external. Everyone would now have a stake in the decisions of the chief, and it would be to everyone's advantage to please the chief since he held the power to command all the resources of the society. In a sense, all the resources of the group belonged to the chief, whose role it was to husband them wisely for the public good. The chief held the key to military power, deciding when and how to take the field. He also held the key to economic reserves, deciding what and with whom to trade, and determining who among his subjects would pay tributes and who would receive subsidies. He was also the final arbiter of disputes among members of the group.

In the formative stages of a chiefdom the chief would be widely trusted and revered among members of the group. This was essentially how one got to *be* a chieftain—he ascended to the position of sole and permanent leadership because his competence and judgment were considered exemplary. The chiefdom established a confluence of interests precisely because the chief could be trusted to consider the interests of all alike. As chiefdoms matured, however, the honeymoon would eventually wane and the dynamics of confluent interests could be expected to change under demands upon the chief to maintain his authority. Even the most fair-minded chief would expend credibility with certain factions in the course of making decisions for a complex group. No one can please all of the people all of the time. This being the case, a chief would soon find his authority contested by rivals and would have to take measures to consolidate his power. And doing so called for actions that would compromise principles of fairness. Being a chief was an impossible task—in order to remain in a position in which he could serve the interests of the many he had to capitulate in some ways to the special interests of the few. As a result, chiefdoms came to be characterized by nepotism and social stratification. At the top were those favorites of the chief who could be depended upon to defend his authority. These few received a disproportionate share of resources in return for their allegiance against political rivals. And it was to this privileged class, or clan, that the chief would delegate authority in his absence.

Whether the chieftain were fair or corrupt, the institution of his *office* provided a new means to achieve the cooperation necessary to maintain a confluence of interests among members of the group. Under a benevolent chief individuals could expect rewards commensurate with their contributions, so it remained in their interest to follow his leadership. And under a harsh and beleaguered chief the self-interest of compliance was ensured by fear of reprisals for noncompliance. But in either case—whether the chief ruled by respect or by fear—there was a broad social confluence of interests contingent upon a centralized system of differential power and economic dependence.

States

In a field of kinship bands a well-integrated tribal alliance has a distinct advantage in commanding territory and resources. And in a field of tribal alliances a chiefdom, too, has an advantage. The superior size and central leadership of chiefdoms predict that they may gradually increase in size and density by annexing smaller, more vulnerable neighboring groups. Committed as they are to agrarian life, chiefdoms have to excel militarily in order to defend their territory and their storehouses. And rare is the chieftain who does not succumb to the reasoning that the best defense is a good offense. So chiefdoms are fueled by the logic of growth by conquest. The warrior thus becomes an important social role in chiefdoms.

But chiefdoms are notoriously precarious social organizations. And they are so primarily because of their most characteristic feature, the central figure of the chief. In a chiefdom, it seems, far too much hinges on the fortunes of a single individual. If he dies, what then? Presumably his son or nephew will ascend to power, but there are no guarantees that the successor will be a capable leader. In the event that he isn't, prolonged political struggle may ensue. Countless chiefdoms have collapsed in the course of history because a competent chief has been succeeded by a bungler. But, curiously, chiefdoms are no more stable under conditions of success. If the expansive exploits of a chief are successful, he soon finds himself in command of a leviathan too large and complex for his characteristic style of personal micromanagement. And under these conditions two possible scenarios appear: Either the chiefdom becomes badly managed, in which case widespread discontent and infighting erode the chief's power base, eventually leading to social mitosis, or, alternatively, the chiefdom may develop into a state by inventing new means of cooperation.

Again, several characteristics distinguish states from chiefdoms. States are larger, more densely populated, more ecologically varied, and more diversely specialized than chiefdoms. States also typically have cities, precise territorial boundaries, and standing armies. Furthermore, the social ranking characteristic of chiefdoms has ossified to become a full-blown stratified class system. But the most significant distinguishing marks of a state (that is, in terms of fostering confluences of interests) are civil law, bureaucratic institutions, and a market economy. Each of these means of cooperation may be seen to develop in response to problems generated by corrupt or overgrown chiefdoms. And each of them has the effect of reducing the dependence of the group on the whims and fortunes of a single leader.

As chiefdoms grew larger, limitations of time and distance would make it more difficult for the chief to intervene in civil disputes. This development required the chief to articulate, in formal terms, various standards of comportment that could be applied in his absence. In time, such expressions would constitute the elements of a legal tradition. Legal traditions generally represent a confluence of interests because they define certain limits of order and social predictability to the benefit of all alike. As laws and the consequences for breaking them became more standardized, individuals were also less vulnerable to the injustices of prejudicial treatment. Moreover, an established legal tradition would introduce a new element of social continuity, rendering individuals less vulnerable to changes in leadership. As traditions developed it became more difficult for a new chief to disregard legal precedents, so that now definite expectations and limitations came with the office. A formal legal system contributes to the effect of elevating the role of central leadership above the person of the leader. As this happens the state emerges as a new reality transcending its leadership. And in this same process a displacement of confluent interests occurs—the common interests of group members are now found to overlap in the domain of law rather than in the domain of the chief's pleasure.

Along with a legal system came bureaucracies for legislation, enforcement, and adjudication. But these constitute only part of the bureaucratic activities of state systems. In addition, a state requires offices for population control (censuses, coastal and border patrols), foreign relations, regulation of production and trade, management of resources, dissemination of information, organization of public works, the military, and, of course, taxation. As tiresome and perfunctory as bureaucracies sometimes appear, their work is quite essential to the affairs of state. For most practical purposes these bureaucratic institutions *are* the state, for it is by their machinations that the state both extracts the costs and delivers the benefits associated with citizenship. As such, the bureaucratic institutions of a state are the official clearinghouses for confluent interests.

Karl Polanyi distinguished three major principles governing economic systems: reciprocity, redistribution, and the market principle.[12] Reciprocal economies, typical of bands and tribes, involve the informal exchange of goods and services between equals. Redistributive economies, typical of chiefdoms, involve the collection of all produced goods in central storehouses, from which they are redistributed to members of the group. A market economy is one in which goods and services are exchanged according to their value in a central market. In state systems all three forms of exchange may be present. For example, gift exchanges are reciprocal, and taxation represents a redistributive practice. But in a state system most exchanges take place by means of a market, and further, these exchanges are normally facilitated by a common medium of exchange: i.e., money. In addition to being a medium of exchange, money functions as a common standard for the evaluation of exchangeable goods and services. In other words, money provides a common calculus for determining the worth of exchangeables, and to the extent that one's personal resources are exchangeable, money is an element within a calculus of self-interest. The market, then, is a venue in which the interests of individual producers and consumers are brought together and negotiated by the dynamics of supply and demand. The market, by its nature, is a principal means of cooperation. With each and every market exchange a confluence of interests has been achieved.

Subgroups

We have been focusing on the means of cooperation that characterize broadly defined types of social organization. These distinctive social features are essential to the integration and identity of comprehensive groups such as bands, tribes, chiefdoms, and states. And when these means of cooperation fail, the society as a whole will tend toward disorder by virtue of increased conflicts of interests. Yet it would be misleading to suggest that a social order is exclusively contingent upon its most comprehensive means of cooperation. As societies increase in size, density, and complexity there appear subgroups representing regions of overlapping self-interests, functioning more or less as various minisocieties. Subgroups are particularly likely to form in state systems, where a variety of special-interest sodalities manage to reinforce the integrity of the whole by creating a meshwork of interconnections between individuals. A state could not long exist without a large number of these sodalities. And it is in the context of these less comprehensive social groups that some of our most significant interactions take place.

The most important of these sodalities are what sociologists call *primary groups*. Primary groups are typically very small, highly personalized, intimate, and informal associations. The family, peer groups, and cliques are ready examples of primary groups. In these groups individuals interact as whole persons, not merely as actors in conventional roles. All aspects of one's personality, not just fragments, are engaged in primary group interactions. Communication is deep and extensive, involving the full range of human attitudes and emotions. There are few restrictions on topics, and most of the restraints on expression typical of "polite" society do not apply. Primary groups are those social settings in which persons feel free to let their hair down and be themselves. Such groups are characterized by deep and enduring confluent interests—they are dominated by the pronoun "we." It has been suggested that primary groups are the settings in which the fundamental elements of a self-concept are formed and sustained. That being the case, we may expect that members of primary groups will exercise an inordinate amount of influence over the attitudes and perceptions of one another. Such groups are immensely important because they are a principal link between the individual and the larger society. They are indispensable instruments in the process of socialization. It is in primary groups that one's attitudes, opinions, and feelings regarding the larger society are freely expressed and subsequently refined. And for this reason the fate of a larger social entity is critically dependent upon what goes on behind the closed doors of primary groups. Primary groups that foster attitudes of public devotion and pride bode well for the collective entity. But if primary groups exude rancor and resentment, there results a worrisome loss of shared interests.

The primary group is a universal feature of human social organization; that is, such groups can be found in bands, tribes, and chiefdoms as well as in states. But in more complex societies there is also an abundance of *secondary groups*, in which individuals share overlapping interests that are topical, as distinguished from the generalized personal interests shared in primary groups.

Among such groups are professional organizations, businesses, churches, country clubs, political parties, historical societies, trade unions, parent/teacher associations, equestrian clubs, scouting groups, and the like. Secondary group memberships very often follow divisions of social class, residence, gender, or age, but their most distinguishing feature is that they attempt to coordinate the activities of individuals around a special purpose or shared interest. In doing so, these organizations develop formal structures to define rules, roles, objectives, procedures, and traditions that constitute their identity. The sociology of groups focuses its analysis on these formal structures and the manner in which they function as means of cooperation to establish confluences of interests among members. The analysis of groups also explores the ways in which these groups help to address basic human needs for intelligibility, pleasure, and a sense of self-worth. These inquiries we leave to the sociologists.

In this section I set out to answer the question: What is a society? I have argued that we get nowhere in our efforts to understand social reality if we relinquish the biological axiom that individuals are self-serving. Thus I have maintained that social organization is possible only because an overlap of self-interests is possible. A society is nothing if it isn't ordered, and social order is always the result of coordinating and/or manipulating the self-interests of individuals. I have argued that the means for establishing confluence of interests are both genetic and cultural. We have seen that increases in population size and density result in increases of specialization and complexity, and in greater stress on ecosystems. These developments tend to overload established means of social cooperation, making it necessary for social groups either to subdivide or to develop new means of cooperation.

THE CONDITIONS OF SOCIAL COHERENCE

In a sense, a theory of social coherence is already implicit in the above definition of society. If a society is an organized group of individuals having the means for confluence of interests, then it would appear to follow that a coherent society is one that has achieved substantial confluence of interests. The coherence of a society, then, might be measured by the extent to which its members conform to established means of cooperation. This standard of coherence may be applied to any group that has an identity, whether it be a primary group, a political party, a basketball team, or a comprehensive group such as a chiefdom or a state. A political party, we might say, lacks coherence to the extent that it lacks consensus on its most comprehensive means of cooperation—that is, its program or platform. And a basketball team lacks coherence when its players fail to conform to the playbook or the game plan. In the same way, a comprehensive social group lacks coherence to the extent that it lacks a core of widely shared meanings which serve to integrate and regulate the culture as a whole.

A social system is governed by the same dynamics that apply to systems in general. As Leslie White says, "In order to function effectively and, in the last analysis, to survive, a system must realize a synthesis among its several parts—a working harmony among them—and it must subordinate part to whole."[13] This process is reminiscent of the harmonic function executed by the prefrontal cortex of the human brain. In Chapter 3 I suggested that the integrative and inhibitory activities of the prefrontal cortex enable individuals to achieve a state of functional unity against the odds generated by a plurality of competing motives. It is by virtue of these functions that a distinctive personality becomes formed. I now intend to argue that a distinctive cultural tradition may be seen to emerge by roughly the same means. But in this social process the integrative and regulatory functions are executed not by the brain directly but by one of its products: the myth of a cultural tradition. In other words, a comprehensive social group will lack coherence to the extent that it lacks a viable myth. Without a viable myth a culture will begin to break down into a cacophony of competing special interests. Myth, then, is the ultimate means of cooperation within a comprehensive social group. The task at hand is to clarify this assertion.

The Power of Myth

Myth literally means "story." In common usage the term connotes stories of supernatural beings and events, telling of primordial times and the origins of significant realities (e.g., heavenly bodies, earth, life, humans). Yet there is no compelling reason to suppose that a myth must necessarily involve super-natural elements. For a story to qualify as a myth it is sufficient that it unify and clarify the principal domains of human interest in a narrative of universal scope and significance. Myth always contains elements of *cosmos, pathos,* and *ethos.* The cosmological element (cosmos) appeals to the human need for intelligibility. The aesthetic/economic element (pathos) appeals to the human need for pleasure. And the moral element (ethos) appeals to the human need for a sense of self-worth. When these elements are integrated by narrative symbols and images, we have a story which unifies the full range of human experience. A myth, we say, presents us with a compelling vision of truth, goodness, and beauty. Or, to put it differently, *a myth arouses all three motivational systems simultaneously and then satisfies them in the beholding of an intelligible universe infused with objective values, the serving of which promises the fullness of life.*

Myth is not science, yet much of its vocabulary is drawn from the science of the day to present a vision of the ultimate origins, significance, and destiny of the cosmos. Myth goes beyond the science of its day (without contradicting it) to convey a sense that the world around is ordered, and that its order is intelligible. But an intelligible cosmos is not enough. Myth wants to say further that the cosmos is hospitable to the human project, that humans have a proper niche in the natural order. Thus myth employs images from the historical experience of a culture, from its economic and political life, to clarify and legitimate its way of life within the universal scheme of things. In doing so myth gathers the hedonic hopes and dreams of individuals and dispels their fears that the cosmos is a realm of hostility. But the cosmic order is not indifferent to the actions of humans. Myth therefore asserts moral imperatives in the form of laws and/or virtues that give direction to human lives together with resources for attributions of praise or blame.

The power of myth to compel human imagination lies in its assertion of a unified order of being. It bundles together facts, values, and attitudes in a narrative account of nature, self, and society. It condenses the full range of human interest and experience by the integrative power of a few resonant metaphors. In the Judeo-Christian myth, for example, the metaphor of God as person functions as a root metaphor to integrate the domains of human interest. The creative power of God is the ultimate explanation for the origins of all that exists. God created and ordered the cosmos through the power of his word. Furthermore, this same God made a covenant with humans, wherein he promised to provide for their hedonic needs. And to this end, God issued laws to guide his people on the path of righteousness. In a single narrative flourish the Judeo-Christian myth provides resources to address human needs for intelligibility, pleasure, and a sense of self-worth. This myth has endured several major reinterpretations throughout its long history, but the essential elements have remained unaltered.[14] One of the more substantive modifications involved the Christian rejection of Jewish legalistic morality in favor of a more plastic ethic of virtue. That is, the Christian virtues of faith, hope, and love displaced the moral authority of the Torah.

The Judeo-Christian story represents an anthropomorphic myth; that is, its root metaphor is one of human agency. God, the ultimate source of all existence, is portrayed in terms of idealized human attributes. The anthropomorphic myth has been by far the most common type throughout human history, but it has not been the exclusive type. A well-known nonanthropomorphic myth is the story of divination by astrology. Astrology is the practice of judging the influence of celestial bodies on the collective and individual affairs of humans. It combines cosmos, pathos, and ethos by asserting that certain past cosmic relations (cosmos) determine patterns and combinations of qualities, desires, temperaments, aptitudes, and vulnerabilities (pathos) for all time, such that for any group or individual the outcome of actions undertaken at a particular time and place (ethos) will be affected by the cosmic events of the past. Astrologers attempt to determine what these effects will be by correlating information about the cosmic past with information about the human past. The central idea in astrology is that the universe is a deterministic realm, and that its order is sufficiently intelligible to allow an understanding of all humanly relevant causal factors that impinge upon a particular point in time. When these factors are known, it will be possible for groups or individuals to act in accordance with them for optimal outcomes. The complicated categories of astrology, therefore, make it possible to harmonize facts, attitudes, and values within a single order of objective reality.

Yet another nonanthropomorphic myth is offered by the Marxian view known as dialectical materialism. Dialectical materialism asserts that an inexorable logic of development is embedded in human history, and that this logic is rendered intelligible by historical analysis. Marx called this logic of history "the economic law of motion." His analysis of history reveals that there have been four phases of history preceding the modern period. These were the primitive, slave, feudal, and capitalist epochs. Each of these phases emerged as the intensity of social contradictions inherent in the previous phase reached a critical flash point, whereupon revolution produced a new social order containing the contradictions for its own eventual demise. Dialectical materialism further asserts that history will finally reach a state of perpetual equilibrium once the contradictions inherent within capitalism deliver the revolution to end all revolutions—that is, the socialist revolution that will result in the emergence of a utopian classless society. The central metaphor in this myth is that history is a machine, cranking its way through epochs of class conflict until it reaches a point of perpetual equilibrium. Implicit in this cosmic metaphor is the promise that hedonic interests will be advanced by the morality of a socialist revolution. The full range of human interest is addressed by this comprehensive story: there is an intelligible cosmic process by which certain objective moral values hold the promise of perpetual hedonic bliss.

The relation between myth and culture is complex. As we have seen, myth draws together elements from the cosmology, economy, and morality of a cultural tradition. Thus it may be said that myth is an integrated reflection of these domains. But it is also the case that a cultural tradition is a reflection of its myth. That is, once a myth establishes its currency within a culture, it becomes a significant determinant of the culture.

Cultures develop by accretion. That is, changes take place as new ideas, techniques, and values—new memes—gradually work their way into the machinery of cultural transmission. Novelty, like mutations, may refine or transform or even displace what has gone before. But most cultural innovations, like most mutations, are rejected. In general, a culture will spawn a greater diversity of memes than could ever be preserved by a cultural tradition. Thus we may say that cultural evolution proceeds by the same logic as biological evolution—diversity is acted upon by selective agents in the environment. In the biological realm, environmental factors edit out much of the genetic diversity, leaving only the best-adapted specimens to transmit their genes. Similarly, in the realm of culture, factors in the social ecology expunge much of the memetic diversity. For example, more books are written than published, more songs composed than recorded, more laws proposed than passed, more products invented than marketed, more revisions suggested than implemented, and so on. Cultures become distinctive and coherent social entities by virtue of systematic and consistent decisions in respect to the selection of memes. A culture in which innovative memes were received or rejected at random would be fickle, lacking in character and saturated by ugliness. Such a culture would be unlivable, and its members would find themselves hard pressed to give reasons for defending it. Indeed, such a culture would lack the defenses that are essential for social coherence. Stable cultures, like biological species, are well defended against radical changes. Virtually all biological species have elaborate safeguards against mutations, which keep the rate of evolution relatively slow—a very adaptive thing to do, since most significant environmental changes are gradual. Species without such safeguards go extinct quickly. The same is true of cultural traditions. In most cultures a variety of forces are working to keep change to a minimum, and making sure that received changes are consistent with other elements within the culture. In the absence of such regulating forces a culture would quickly disintegrate.

The single most important regulating force within a social ecology is its myth. In general, the myth of a culture will function as the ultimate judge of whether or not new meanings will be received. If a new meme is commensurate with the myth, then it may well be received, but if it is perceived to contradict the myth, pressure will be strong to select it out of the machinery of cultural transmission. Ideas, techniques, and values that do not fit are pronounced unfit. And those that are deemed fit will have an internal consistency about them for having been scrutinized in accordance with a common standard of meaning. This regulatory function of myth is formalized in the religion of a culture. Religion is essentially the institutionalization of myth. It is the custodian of myth, presiding over its official interpretation, managing its selective applications, and seeing to it that the myth continues to be transmitted in its pure form to the next generation. Religion, then, is a centralized selective agency whose mission is to inject the influence of myth into every domain of human interest—cosmos, pathos, ethos—for it is in these domains that new memes emerge. To a pluralistic and secularized audience this regulatory function of myth has a totalitarian ring of oppression and tyranny about it. Nevertheless, it is precisely this function that enables cultures to achieve and maintain their distinctiveness. Without this function a culture would lose its unity of purpose to an onslaught of diffuse meanings and thus begin its descent into social chaos.

The argument of this chapter has been that societies are possible because of genetic and cultural means of cooperation which establish the conditions for overlaps of self-interests among members of a group. And we have just seen that cultural myths are powerful means of cooperation because they function to integrate the domains of human interest into a comprehensible narrative unity and to safeguard the culture against an influx of meanings that might otherwise disrupt social coherence. If the integrative and regulatory functions of myth are effective, then a confluence of interests will emerge as the conscious lives of individuals are organized by the features of the myth. Thus we see that myth is simultaneously a source of both personal wholeness and social coherence. By integrating the domains of human interest into a narrative unity, myth offers me a paradigm for harmonizing my own needs for intelligibility, pleasure, and self-esteem. My perception of cosmic order, my hopes and fears, my commitments—these are all given to me by the conventions of meaning embodied in the myth. The universal story becomes my own particular story. When I ingest a myth I acquire a comprehensive schema that orients the affairs of my life within the objective scope of nature and history. The particular challenges of intrapsychic conflict will continue to arise, but as I reflect on the myth, they tend to be absorbed into a universal order of things that transcends my subjectivity. As the challenges of everyday life erode my personal integrity, I may restore my soul to wholeness by activating the mythic shema.

But the saving grace of myth goes beyond the realm of personal wholeness. To the extent that a myth is ingested widely by the members of a group, a synergy of parts is established in service to the whole. Differences between individuals are trivialized by the sharing of meanings that transcend their immediate interests. When you and I share a myth, we affirm a common origin, a common nature, and a common destiny. We have the same "take" on things in general, we are committed to the same goals, and our identity within the universal order is indistinguishable. There will continue to be moments when self-interest erupts into conflict between us, but the myth provides public occasions for resolving these differences. When the ongoing competition of social life wears away at confluences of interests, then the collective affirmation of a common story can restore the overlaps at the level of ultimate meanings. By the power of myth I become whole and we become one.

But the power of myth is ambiguous. By integrating and regulating memes, myths enable social groups to achieve coherent identity. By the power of myth an aggregate of individuals becomes a unit, an entity. But as Thomas Hobbes observed, such an entity has a way of becoming a Leviathan, a godlike monster of unimpeachable authority. By means of the regulatory function of myth exclusive claims are made for its integrative vision. Its story becomes the only story, the final story. The imaginative work of integrating cosmos, pathos, and ethos has been done for all time. No further revelations of truth can be expected from any quarter. In other words, an established myth presumes to speak for the entire culture; indeed, unlike any other agency, it *is* the culture. And under these conditions survival of the social order is perceived to be bound up with the survival of the myth. Social coherence is construed as contingent upon universal compliance with the meanings of the myth. Critiques aimed at any particular feature of the myth are therefore commonly taken as subversive attacks upon the social order, to be answered in the name of survival.

We now see the deep ambiguities of a cultural myth. On the one hand, shared meanings about the origins, nature, and destiny of things provide a great service to a social group by bestowing the ultimate means of personal wholeness and social coherence. But on the other hand, myths have an inherent tendency to become reified as immutable fixtures, unable to tolerate fundamental changes. The servant of human needs asserts the rights of master; what once emerged as an imaginative response to human needs begins to demand a response that chokes imagination. The liberating gospel of one age becomes the restrictive dogma of the next. The miracle of myth gradually leads us into the mire of amythia.

Amythia

Nothing, of course, is forever—a truism that applies no less to cultural myths than to biological species. Species go extinct when circumstances in their environment render it impossible for them to pass their genes along to the next generation. And myths, too, lose their viability when they fail to transmit their memes within a cultural tradition. Many circumstances may result in such failures, but in general we may say this: Myths fail to transmit their memes when they no longer compel the imagination of their audience, and they fail to do so when they become implausible, and they become implausible when more satisfying memes appear. And why do new meanings appear? Because human beings are self-transcending creatures, and because they always live in changing environments. The combination of these factors is ultimately deadly for any worldview that claims final authority.

Cultural myths may increase their longevity if they can find ways to circumscribe the curiosity motivator, and some have, in fact, been moderately successful in doing so. But where there is life there is curiosity, and such efforts ultimately fail. New experiences, some of them produced by the effects of cultural myths themselves, will call for new formulations of knowledge. And, inevitably, some of these formulations will not cohere with the meanings legitimated by the myth. As new and illegitimate formulations arise, the custodians of the myth will attempt to regulate them out of the machinery of cultural transmission. When Copernicus and Galileo proposed the heliocentric theory, they faced persecution from the church. Darwin, too, was accused of heresy, and more than a century after his death efforts are still being made to suppress his theory of evolution by natural selection. But these new scientific theories could not be expunged from Western culture for the very reason that they were more intellectually satisfying than the biblical account. And in addition to these particular theories there was emerging a general method of scientific discovery that was intellectually more satisfying than the orthodox paradigm of divine revelation. So the custodians of the Judeo-Christian myth found the task of meme regulation increasingly difficult as curiosity raced forward to establish a whole new set of memes that would themselves claim the authority to judge the legitimacy of meanings. The scientific community would henceforth be the final authority in matters of cosmology. The myth had to relinquish regulatory rights over a large domain of human experience and expression.

Cultural myths may also increase their longevity if they can manage to keep the hedonic motivator aligned with their visions of the good life. But this is difficult to do, since economic realities change constantly and often dramatically. And as these conditions change, the hedonic imagination adjusts to them, redefining the good life in relation to newly perceived possibilities. The result is that new economic conditions are likely to render fixed mythic visions of the good life hedonically irrelevant. This process can be seen in the experience of Western culture. The Christian story was assembled under conditions of economic hardship and political oppression. It was a myth of endurance. Its vision of the good life was to be fulfilled in the next life, replete with celestial feasts and streets of gold. The hedonic pleasures of this material realm were nothing; in fact, they were denounced as sinful. Even after the fall of Rome, the myth of endurance was relevant to the masses of people for whom the

Middle Ages offered little but travail and adversity. But as the fruits of Renaissance learning began to ripen, there was a growing sense that a good life might be achieved in this world. The rise of universities, a market system, political reforms, and the life- and labor-saving advances of technology conspired to excite the belief that this worldly progress was possible. In the postmedieval world a new hedonic sensibility arose to make the delayed gratification of heavenly bliss seem a bit remote. This is not to suggest that the beatific vision has been completely abandoned by modern Christians, but only that it tended to become threatened by the encroachment of new hedonic pursuits. The life of this world became more than merely tolerable, it was becoming downright savory. The new hedonism was legitimated and sustained by new memes for defining the good life, drawn primarily from pagan authors and from secular political leaders. These new authorities compromised the influence of the myth in yet another domain of human interest.

A cultural myth might secure its viability if it could find a way to monopolize the calculus of self-esteem; that is, if it were able to maintain exclusive moral authority in a society. But several factors combine to frustrate attempts to maintain a moral monopoly. For one thing, social groups are rarely so isolated that they can avoid contact with other groups. In fact, a certain amount of contact with outsiders is generally beneficial to a society for the purposes of exogamy (outbreeding) and trade. But such contacts will inevitably result in the introduction of new values, some of which will be in tension with the meanings legitimated by the myth. It is also common that new formulations of knowledge will raise questions against the moral teachings of the myth. Consider, for example, how advances in medicine over the centuries have obviated the view that various diseases are to be approached as moral problems.

But beyond these factors are ambiguities inherent in the moral life itself that will inevitably produce challenges to any central moral authority. It often happens, for example, that acting in good faith and in accordance with well-established moral values will produce decisively poor outcomes, and it also happens that acting against received values will produce beneficial outcomes. Any attributions of praise or blame in such cases will be somewhat arbitrary, and at the very least they will be material for dispute. It is unlikely that even the official custodians of a myth will find themselves in possession of moral consensus in these difficult cases. And then there are the genuine moral dilemmas in which every option entails a bad performance. Every culture affirms a multiplicity of values, and too often it happens that service to one value requires violation of another. The very essence of a moral dilemma is that one's moral traditions appear to endorse conflicting options. It is typical for the more commonly experienced moral dilemmas to be debated among moral authorities in a cultural tradition, but such debates always carry the potential for dividing the house.

Yet another dynamic that undermines efforts to maintain a moral monopoly involves those who are judged poorly by the moral standards of a myth. When an actor is blamed for a certain performance, he may well react by attempting to deconstruct the moral standard. As we have seen, this is a common strategy for avoiding negative attributions of self-worth. And under special circumstances such a strategy may produce a countercultural movement, complete with an alternative morality. This may be a useful way to read the experience of Martin Luther. Under the terms of the medieval system of merits Luther found it impossible to come to the assurance that he was worthy in God's sight. Denied sufficient opportunities for making attributions of self-worth and aroused to neurotic extremes by his self-esteem motivator, Luther pounced upon a theme in the writings of St. Paul as a resource for deconstructing the moral order of the Catholic church. The reformers subsequently made the doctrine of justification by faith (not works) a paradigm for working out an alternative interpretation of the Christian myth.

I have been attempting to describe the various processes by which the regulatory function of a myth can become deregulated in the domain of self-esteem—that is, the processes by which moral memes contrary to the myth will inevitably slip into a cultural tradition to undermine moral hegemony. This has been part of a larger argument suggesting that the task of regulating meanings in a cultural tradition tends to become more difficult as time wears on. In all three domains of human interest new memes inevitably arise to compromise the influence of the myth in the organization of consciousness. And as new memes arise, new sources of authority also appear to claim regulatory rights over certain domains of meaning.

I am proposing here a theory of cultural decline (or perhaps social entropy, or even mythic senescence) to follow upon what has already been said about the conditions of social coherence. I have argued that a society becomes a coherent entity by virtue of establishing a narrative integration of domains of human experience, and by managing the apparatus of cultural transmission in such a way that the meanings circulating within the culture remain consistent with those of the myth. When this management is effectively executed, the myth presents a unified order of reality which organizes the consciousness of individuals and establishes confluences of interests among them. But as new meanings seep into a cultural tradition (as they do, despite the efforts to select them out), the unified vision of the myth tends to get ragged. New cosmological memes render its explanations intellectually unsatisfying; new economic and political memes render its vision of the good life hedonically irrelevant; and new values make its moral imperatives appear arbitrary and relative. And under these conditions the myth loses its power to compel the imagination of individuals. Yet there is no reason to suppose that the new and improved meanings, which emerged independently within different domains, will have the internal coherence possessed by memes issuing from a single imaginative source. After all, specialists in science do not feel compelled to make their work conform to moral standards, nor do policy makers feel compelled to inform themselves about cosmology. New meanings arrive as discrete units and gradually wear away at the integrity and plausibility of the mythic vision, but as they emerge there is no guarantee that they will fall together in a way that presents individuals with a unified order of reality.

All of which means that a society without a viable myth will be ill equipped to service needs for personal wholeness and social coherence. When the myth of a culture has been compromised in its appeal to the imagination, individuals will be left to their own devices to resolve intrapsychic conflicts. There will be no plausible paradigm for integrating their experience at the level of ultimate meaning, and they may become vulnerable to the highly maladaptive view that there *are* no ultimate meanings. And the prospects for achieving social coherence without a viable myth are no more promising. As the myth loses its power to shape the consciousness of individuals, multiple perspectives emerge to undermine broad confluences of interests. The social ecology fragments into a spectrum of competing special-interest groups, each with its own distinctive notions about the good life and moral excellence. Under these conditions it becomes very difficult to develop cooperative projects or to resolve conflicts of interests. When a society loses its unifying myth, it loses its most essential means of cooperation.

In an earlier book I employed the term "amythia" to describe the malady that results from the loss of a widely shared myth.[15] The argument of that book traced the onset of amythia in Western culture back to the beginnings of the modern period, when the Renaissance, the reformation, the rise of modern science, and the emergence of the secular state produced an explosion of new meanings that have rendered traditional understandings of the Christian myth unviable. Whereas throughout the medieval period the church remained the dominant source of authority, in the modern period there has emerged a radically pluralistic culture which is increasingly hindered by personality disorders and conflicts of interests. It is not that Western culture is bereft of meanings—quite the contrary. The amythia of contemporary Western culture is a condition of being overwhelmed by a diversity of meanings. In 1989 I described the amythic condition of contemporary culture as follows:

Contemporary Western culture is characterized by an anarchy of meanings. We have no effective way to select memes out of circulation because any efforts to do so are prohibited by one form or another of entitlement. There is no heresy, just variations of piety; there is no treason, just nuances of loyalty; there is no pornography, just art. Any meaning, *all* meaning, is legitimate. Every charge of unacceptable meaning is counter-charged as a violation of human rights. We are therefore increasingly a deregulated culture. Deregulation is certainly not the way in which our culture fashioned its existence from the chaos of the Dark Ages, and it is hardly the way we will survive. In simpler times, in the age of coherence, nearly every occasion for social interaction somehow reconfirmed common meanings to provide a fabric for shared commitments. But in contemporary culture each occasion for social interaction is brimming with possibilities for conflict between values, and each moral situation becomes a moment for internal conflict of values. The proliferation of authorities together with the reduction of selective activity has created a situation in which value conflicts, both internal and interpersonal, are unavoidable, and such conflicts tend to undermine the possibilities for personal wholeness and social coherence. Insofar as we have internalized a plurality of authorities, and insofar as we affirm a wide range of meanings legitimated by them—and that is what participating in Western culture has come to mean—we have created the conditions for the further disintegration of our culture. The real question facing us is whether or not we can stand the strain of too many meanings.[16]

Cultures *cannot,* I assert, stand the strain of too many meanings; the condition of amythia is an unstable one that can be resolved only by the reestablishment of a widely shared myth. There are generally three strategies that may be followed in the attempt to avert amythia. The strategy of *repristination* attempts to reinstate the faltering myth of a culture in its traditional form. The various fundamentalisms of the world are such attempts to turn back the clock by a militant suppression of meanings that have arisen to challenge those of the myth. But fundamentalism is a misguided venture of desperation that can succeed only by the use of naked power. A second, more enlightened strategy involves a *reinterpretation* of the traditional myth to render it consistent with new and troublesome meanings. In the Western experience this approach has been attempted by various liberal theologies, each one striving to demonstrate that at some deeper level of meaning the old myth is commensurate with contemporary cosmology, economy, and morality. But while liberal attempts to reinterpret the myth may avoid the excesses of fundamentalism, they fail to see that once a myth stands in need of reinterpretation, it is already beyond rescue. Viable myths are themselves the vocabulary for ultimate interpretations of human experience. They are the "better known" in terms of which the "lesser known" may be apprehended. But to interpret a myth in terms of contemporary meanings is to recognize these meanings as the better known and to reduce the myth to the status of the lesser known. Reinterpretation is an interregnum strategy, serving those individuals whose consciousness has been organized by some combination of old, well-integrated meanings and new, unintegrated meanings. Liberal theologies are cultural life-support systems, keeping the myth on the margins of viability while new meanings await the metaphors that will integrate them into a new myth.

The third strategy for averting amythia is *mythopoesis,* the imaginative work of storytelling. Mythmakers attempt to assemble the elements of life's experience into a narrative of comprehensive scope and universal significance. Under the conditions of amythia mythmaking can be expected to flourish, adding even more meanings to the confusion. When the myth of a culture falters in its appeal to the imagination, then psychological and social chaos will follow, but these are precisely the conditions that will stimulate the imagination to race forward in search of new stories. The Christian myth itself was fashioned under the conditions of amythia, and now as it lies heaving under the demythologizing life supports of liberal theology, new voices are clamoring to announce a new age. Many of these new voices will sound strange and bizarre, and most of them are unpromising. But in the din of it all, somewhere, there may be cause for hope.

But our hopes and dreams are not focused, they are not gathered. There is a diffusion, a vague generality to our aspirations. We know that we must somehow get it all together, but there is no clarity. We know that life in the past was not so untethered, and that the future may very well brighten one of these days. But on the moment an oppressive uncertainty has descended. We may be able to articulate our longings for personal wholeness and social coherence, but when it comes to constructing the particular conditions for these goals we are at a loss. "Politics as usual" and "therapy as usual" are notable for their failure to help us. And what is more, we have grown accustomed to the view (though we know better) that politics and therapy are not the same enterprise, seeking the same goal and using the same resources. We have lost the mythic insight that they are interdependent. You and I have only a general sense of our own interests—we both want to achieve a full life. And we even share the sense that our interests might be fashioned into a kind of synergy if we shared a common cosmology, economy, and morality. Our sense is that if we only had the right stuff, the right ideas, the right vision, then we would be fortified with the collective wisdom needed for a confident march toward the future.

The custodians of myth, fundamentalists and liberals alike, think we already *have* the right stuff, the right memes. The only problem is to repristinate or reinterpret them. But they are a diminishing majority. A fast-growing number of sensitive men and women see that however forcefully or cleverly an old story is told, it is still the same story—myth as usual.

No indeed! The circumstances are too severe for that, the dimensions of the problem are too large. Ours is rather a time of *kairos*. *Kairos* is the biblical term for "right time," "*carpe diem* time," "decisive time," "critical time." Ours is not a time for anything as usual. If we seek an analogue to our own moment in history, if we seek the meaning of our amythia, we are well served by imagining what it was like to live in a kinship band where the challenge of history was either to fission or to transcend its existing form of social organization. Or in an overgrown tribal alliance where the option was to flee or to fundamentally reorganize the entire social order. Or in a beleaguered chiefdom where the option was to acquiesce in the organs of a mass society or to perish in the battle against them.

The options of our time, our *kairos,* are like these. And they are like them because we have been brought to the brink by the same dynamics. We have been brought to the limits of our established means of cooperation by population growth and ecological finitude. And as we have seen, when such limits are upon us, confluences of interests give way to conflicts of interests, as the future bleakens. It is both our misfortune and our good fortune that our options are less ambiguous than those of *kairos* moments in the past. The possibility of regressive fission is hardly an option for us. There is nowhere to go. The land is taken. Nor are there any sustainable opportunities for intensifying our exploitation of environmental resources. We have already intensified beyond the limits, with potentially devastating consequences resulting from disrupted ecosystems and reduced biodiversity.

The signs are clear to all who will see. The challenge of our *kairos* is to construct new means of cooperation for a genuinely global community. Local, regional, and even continental reorganization will be insufficient. Our challenge is to call forth a new cosmology, a new economy, a new morality, and a new integrative vision on a global scale. Ours is to create a New Federation of Meaning. I have some ideas about these weighty matters (ergo this book), but before turning to them I must complete the assignment at hand.

DECEPTION AND THE SOCIAL ORDER

The assignment at hand is to explore the role of deception in the achievement of social coherence. Our question is whether or not social coherence can be achieved without a certain amount of strategically induced disadequation of appearance to reality.

It may prevent some misunderstanding if I offer my conclusion at the outset. I take the view that social coherence is achievable only within certain optimal limits of deception. That is, if there is too little or too much of it, then the social order will break down. This view is compatible with common sense, for we all know that the fabric of social relations can be threatened by an overabundance of lies and false promises. But we know just as well that the social order would collapse if everyone were to be perfectly honest all the time.

Surprisingly little research has been conducted on the role of deception in social dynamics. Especially noteworthy is the lack of systematic treatment by anthropologists. Anthropology has served us well in describing the various ways in which different cultures manage the phenomena of wealth, kinship, sexuality, production, education, language, religion, and so on. But I have been unable to find a comprehensive treatment of how cultures differentially manage the phenomena of deception. Deception is universal in human cultures, and each culture must find its own patterns for managing it. Anthropologists would do well to make these patterns the focus of investigation.[17] It goes without saying that this chapter, in particular, might have benefited greatly from such research. But there is much to say nevertheless.

The discussion in chapter 3 was shaped by a typology of deceptive strategies. There is no need to develop a new typology to address the question at hand. We may still assume that deceptive interactions that foster social coherence will conform to the categories of evasion/perversion, construction/deconstruction, and self-deception/other-deception. The question is whether these types of deceptive strategies can be shown to play a constructive role in establishing confluences of interests. There may be several ways to shape this discussion, but the one that makes most sense to me is similar to the approach taken in chapter 2. There we surveyed the phenomena of deception at various levels in the organization of life forms. Here we shall survey the phenomena of deception at various levels of social organization. First we will look at the role of deception in establishing social coherence (i.e., confluence of interests) at the level of *primary groups*. Then we will turn our attention to the coherence of *secondary groups*. And finally we shall look to see whether deception plays a constructive role in establishing coherence at the *comprehensive* level of social organization. At each of these levels social entities are created and maintained by the achievement of confluences of interests. Our question is whether these entities are in some way dependent upon sacrifices of adequation to reality.

Before we proceed with our survey, however, a few general words about association and human interest are in order. Human beings are associative creatures. Each of us, especially in a complex society, enters into a variety of associations. Some of our associations are involuntary, such as those with a family, an ethnic group, a nation, or perhaps a prison. But in most cases our associations are voluntary and motivated. Voluntary associations may be analyzed in terms of the motivational needs they satisfy, whether they be cognitive, hedonic, or related to self-esteem, or some combination of these needs. Voluntary groups have members only because for each member the association has value in relation to one or more of the calculi of self-interest. If the self-interest value of the association declines, then the participation of an individual will become marginal, or the person may even pull out. In some cases the self-interest value may change from one calculus to another, as when a person is hedonically motivated to enter an association but then stays active for self-esteem reasons long after the association ceases to be pleasurable.

The critical factor in all of our associations is the *perception* of self-interest value according to one or more of our motivators. In making this observation we come up against the ancient philosophical problem of apparent versus real value. An alcoholic may perceive his purchase of a bottle of whiskey to be in his self-interest, whereas his physician may argue that his real self-interest is not served by the purchase. Likewise, a woman may remain in a disastrous marriage because her self-interest calculi tell her it is valuable, while her best friend may try to talk her out of it. In this case the woman and her best friend have two different judgments on the value of a decision to stay in the marriage. The married woman judges her continued association to be a good act; that is, one that contributes simultaneously to her own wholeness and to the coherence of her marriage. But her friend considers the act to be detrimental to personal wholeness, even though it contributes to the maintenance of a social entity. These matters are very difficult to sort out, not least because some aspects of the marriage may be unambiguously valuable—perhaps the sexual dimension is terrific, even though the association is damaging to self-esteem. The best friend, of course, will maintain that the woman is deluded in her judgment that the association is worthwhile. If only she were to face up to reality she would see that the marriage is not in her self-interest, and then she might take measures to pull out.

I will not attempt to resolve the problem of apparent versus real value at this stage of the argument. I only want to make the point that our associations are premised on our perceptions of self-interest. And, of course, when perception is the operative factor, the way is open for deception.

Primary Groups

Earlier in this chapter I had occasion to comment on the distinction between primary and secondary groups. I said that primary groups are small, informal, intimate, and engaged of all aspects of an individual's personality. Primary groups are the sorts of associations in which we like to think no self-interested motives are involved—just love, sympathy, gratitude, and care for the well-being of others as ends in themselves, not as means. If we view these emotions as part of an affective constellation that regulates reciprocal altruism, however, then we see mutual self-interests as an essential feature of primary groups. We only need to consider the deep sense of loss experienced by those who suffer the death of a primary group member to gauge this element of self-interest.

A primary group may be seen as a rich or complete association; that is, one in which an individual shares overlapping interests with other group members in all three dimensions of human interest. In the ideal sense, the primary group should offer cognitive, hedonic, and self-esteem benefits to its members. We might say that an association that provides such complete benefits to members is a *functional* primary group. A functional primary group is marked by a strong sense of individual identification with the group. The group will play heavily into a person's self-understanding, such that the self considered in isolation from the group is a diminished self. C. H. Cooley suggested that the psychological effect of a functional primary group is to create "a certain fusion of individualities in a common whole."[18] This sense of group identification, this "we-ness," may be seen as the hallmark of maximum coherence for any group, whether primary, secondary, or comprehensive—the greater the sense of group identification, the more coherent the group.

Several forces at are work, however, to diminish the functionality of a primary group. This is especially the case in a complex society, where a plethora of opportunities are available for self-fulfillment external to one's primary group. When individuals pursue these opportunities with satisfying results, their identification with the primary group is likely to diminish. This phenomenon is known to every parent whose adolescent begins to drift away from the family to become involved with groups of friends. As this happens, the "drifter" begins to form a new perception of the association value of the primary group. Now important dimensions of the drifter's needs are fulfilled outside the primary group, and the perception of overlapping self-interests becomes altered. The primary group is seen as less complete, less multidimensional than it formerly was. And as a correlative to this change in perception, an individual may become less affectionate, sympathetic, and grateful toward other members of the group, and consequently less likely to make unsolicited contributions to their well-being. We may say that a primary group that shows such signs of diminishing identification tends to become *dysfunctional*.

A decline in functionality means a decline in social coherence; that is, the overlap of self-interests among members of the group diminishes. When such a decline is perceived by those who have strong interests in maintaining group coherence, we may expect to see measures designed to strengthen the group by enhancing group identification, directed especially at those who appear to be drifting away. Such measures will vary quite a bit, but their ultimate goal is to alter the drifter's perception of self and/or group in such a way that the group is restored to a central role in self-understanding. The measures may include new group activities, greater solicitation or intimidation directed toward drifters, greater isolation from the larger society, and so forth. These measures amount to new means of cooperation. The point is that one's perception of association value may be altered by actual change in the reality of the group. But, as we know, perceptions may just as effectively be altered by means of deception.

Marriage

If any fate is worse than being confined to a marriage mired in deception, then it must be a marriage devoid of it. The key to achieving social coherence at the level of the connubial bond is not to eradicate deception but rather to use it constructively. As Shakespeare notes:

> When my love swears that she is made of truth,
> I do believe her, though I know she lies,
> That she might think me some untutor'd youth,
> Unlearned in the world's false subtleties.
> Thus vainly thinking that she thinks me young,
> Although she knows my days are past the best,
> Simply I credit her false-speaking tongue:
> On both sides thus is simple truth suppressed.
> But wherefore says she not she is unjust?
> And wherefore say not I that I am old?
> O, love's best habit is in seeming trust,
> And age in love loves not to have years told:
>   Therefore I lie with her and she with me,
>   And in our faults by lies we flatter'd be.
> (Sonnet 138)

Two arguments suggest that the institution of marriage itself owes its origins to strategies of deception. The first argument bears upon the evolutionary origins of the connubial bond in general, and the second argument bears upon the social-psychological conditions that give rise to any particular marital relation. The evolutionary argument first.

Human beings are the only primate species to have evolved concealed ovulation in the female. This is a curious phenomenon because one would expect a reproductive advantage in knowing when the female is in her most fertile period. But the strategy of concealed ovulation obscures this information from detection by male and female alike. The human female body, in other words, has evolved an evasive design to defeat the perceptual designs of the mating pair. What could be the evolutionary wisdom in such a strategy?

Just this: Concealment of optimal fertility bestows a reproductive advantage by expanding the period of females' sexual receptivity—that is, an advantage to those who are receptive throughout the menstrual cycle. If you don't know when ovulation occurs, then your chances of getting pregnant depend on the frequency (not the timing) of copulation. The phenomenon of female orgasm in humans is seen to be an evolved mechanism to enhance this continuous sexual receptivity. And once these mechanisms are in place, they provide a powerful hedonic incentive for males to stay in the presence of a particular mate. In species in which females show "heat," the attentiveness of males is periodic, but the human male's attentiveness is expanded along with the female's receptivity.[19] This strategy provides a confluence of hedonic interest that is conducive to a persistent connubial bond. The evolutionary advantage in this bond is that it keeps males at hand to assist females during the prolonged period of vulnerability occasioned by childbearing. Thus the human predisposition to form a persistent marriage bond can be seen to originate in the evasive strategy of concealed ovulation.

A social-psychological argument also helps to account for the formation of particular marriage bonds. This argument suggests that decisions to marry reveal the human predisposition to harbor positive illusions. It is a curiosity of human nature that young people with an urge to marry are oblivious of admonitions about the risks and hardships of married life. Even those who grow up in dysfunctional families become possessed of the idea that for them it will be different—*their* marriage will succeed. Experienced married couples can only smile at such illusory expectations as those carried to the altar. But what accounts for such persistent positive illusions? Two things, in my view. The first is that cultures generally present their youth with unrealistically positive images of married life. Marriage is garnished with a mystique of human fulfillment; it is a kind of promised land to which young people are encouraged to aspire. The wedding ceremony itself is staged as a spectacle of transcendence in which the young couple is publicly launched on a sea of hopes and dreams. The splendor of these occasions, focused exclusively on the positive, reinforces highly unrealistic expectations. But another dynamic of illusion is operating as well, and this one concerns the positive illusions young people hold regarding both themselves and the person they are about to marry. The betrothed pair hold each other in such esteem—are so beautiful and virtuous and resourceful—that onlookers are driven to nausea. To say that young lovers are excessively biased in their perceptions of each other is an understatement. And if a minor character flaw is to be admitted for the sake of reality—well, it's nothing that won't change once the marriage begins.

Young lovers have an impaired perception of reality. Their expectations about the state of matrimony are wildly unrealistic, their assessments of each other are exceedingly exaggerated (in part because of courtship deceits by the beloved), and their confidence in their ability to influence their spouse carries delusion to near-comic proportions. The institution of marriage, then, both has evolved and continues to thrive (at least in part) by virtue of strategies of deception and self-deception.

The first few months of married life may indeed appear to validate the distorted expectations of a young couple. But then, inevitably, reality makes its way into the scene and the honeymoon ends. The spouse who once appeared to be everything—so intellectually stimulating, so hedonically electrifying, so affirming of worth—now begins to show clay feet. The union that was once so complete now leaves one or two things to be desired. Now the work of married life begins.

The work of married life, like the work of any social group, is to prevent and resolve conflicts of interests and to establish in their place confluences of interests. And the domains of these conflicts and confluences are the same as for other social groups: intellectual, hedonic, and self-esteem. When the political realities of married life begin to generate conflicts of interests, and as the sense of we-ness begins to erode, then the marriage stands in need of new means of cooperation to restore coherence. In the case of marriage some advantages are built into the process. The sharing of a household and various material possessions provides conditions for overlapping self-interests. The appearance of children is an obvious means of reinforcing we-ness. And the shared history of intimacy is also a powerful resource that is readily accessible to lift couples beyond petty conflicts.

But these advantages are not sufficient to maintain coherence in a marriage. A marriage is the most densely concentrated arena of reciprocal altruism there is. When altruism in a marriage begins to lose its intensity, the marriage loses its coherence. And the secret to maintaining a high level of altruism is to find the appropriate means for activating the emotional substrates of altruism; that is, affection, sympathy, gratitude, resentment, and guilt. Without the engagement of these emotions, a marriage will begin to dissolve from deficits of kindness, concessions, compromises, demands, and reparations. What, then, *are* the means for activating the level of emotional involvement required for a coherent marriage? The answers to this question have defined a whole industry of marriage counseling, and I will not attempt to summarize its major theoretical directions. I will instead offer some remarks about how deceptive strategies may be of some value to the coherence of a marriage.

I am put in mind of the "candlelight effect" as it was explained by a psychology professor during my college days. The ambience of candlelit dinners, he explained, sometimes has the effect of making people fall in love. When the light is faint, the pupils of diners' eyes dilate, and when voices are softened, these dilated pupils must attend more closely to the facial expressions of the conversation partner in order to "hear" what is being said. So the material conditions of a candlelit dinner elicit dilated pupils and fixed gazes, both of which signs may be read as expressions of affection. And as we tend to respond affectionately to those who like us, there is a good chance that by dinner's end the real thing may have been generated. The point is just that emotional investments must begin somewhere. And if emotional investments tend to decline in a marriage, they can be brought back by some means. I am suggesting that deceptive interactions between spouses can (in fact do) serve as sources for maintaining or rekindling emotional involvement. Consider the candlelight effect of disingenuous displays: feigning affection for one's in-laws, laughing at familiar jokes, lionizing one's partner for trivial accomplishments, gratefully wearing the disgusting gift tie, the faked orgasm, and so on. Coherent marriages are laced with such petty deceits, often to become conventionalized, as Shakespeare's sonnet attests.

But petty deceits, constructive as they may be, are not sufficient means to sustain the emotional involvement required for a coherent marriage. Something larger, something more epic is needed. Like comprehensive societies, marriages need a mythology, a narrative, offering a level of meaning that transcends all emerging conflicts of interests. In some relationships this level of meaning is provided by the conventions of a religious perspective, but this is not necessarily the case. Phyllis Rose, in her excellent account of five Victorian marriages, has concluded that marriages involve imaginative narrative constructs, and what matters most is that couples share such a narrative, even if it is inadequate to reality: "In unhappy marriages . . . I see two versions of reality rather than two people in conflict. I see a struggle for imaginative dominance going on. Happy marriages seem to me those in which two partners agree on the scenario they are enacting, even if . . . their own idea of their relationship is totally at variance with the facts." The facts, Rose insists, are less important than a shared imaginative view of the facts. A marriage, she says, is "a subjectivist fiction with two points of view deeply in conflict, sometimes fortuitously congruent."[20]

The mythology of a marriage need not be politically correct in order to render a marriage coherent—it only needs to be fortuitously congruent. This amounts to saying, basically, that the newlyweds have it right. Deluded as they may be about the state of matrimony, each other, and themselves, one thing is clear: They are full of imagination and fancy. And with the fulsomeness of their delusion comes the we-ness of a complete confluence of interests.

If the women's movement has had a disruptive effect on many modern marriages, it is only because it has stimulated incongruence of scenarios. Couples who shared (and perhaps thrived within) a common scenario of traditional married life suddenly found themselves confronted by two versions of reality, one traditional and another liberated. The point is not that one version of reality is demonstrably better than the other but rather that one version of reality is better than *two*. The critical challenge of a coherent marriage is to achieve a fusion of imaginations, to perceive the marriage, each other, and oneself in terms that enable a mutual satisfaction of intellectual, hedonic, and self-esteem needs, even if these terms fail to meet the facts. One should, as Phyllis Rose does, speak with trepidation about the "facts" in such matters. It may be a fact that my spouse is my intellectual superior by bounds, and it may be a fact that I am a mediocre lover, but if we conspire to play to each other as a pair of intellectual giants and epic lovers, then the facts be damned. Disadequation to reality is far less damaging to the coherence of a marriage than is a mismatch of imagination.

Family

Many social commentators have expressed concern that the family may be on the verge of extinction in today's fast-paced, future-shocked social ecology. This is very unlikely. One should not construe a growing distinction between marriage and family to be evidence of the demise of the family. A few generations ago marriage and family were synonymous terms. But now there are more childless marriages and more marriageless families than was formerly the case. This growing distinction between marriage and family is neither good nor bad in any *a priori* sense. Some marriages are more coherent without children, and some families are more coherent without marriages. Even though the family may diversify in form, it is not likely to disappear, for it continues to function as an essential means of cooperation. It is difficult to find a sector of the social order that is not well served by the coherence of families. For one thing, the family still functions as the principal social means for the regulation of sexuality, reducing the chaos of open competition for sex partners. Second, the family is still the primary venue for socialization of the young, providing children with the moral training and social skills they will need as they enter into the larger society. To the extent that individuals share an interest in the orderly behavior of other people's children, the coherence of families will remain socially desirable. There is also a broad economic interest in the family, since it is still the elementary particle upon which systems of aggregate economics are predicated. Furthermore, parents will continue to have strong reproductive interests in the coherence of families because they are the basic unit of care for their children. And finally, of course, children have a profound stake in the family because it is the proximate source of satisfaction for all their needs. The interests of the entire society, it appears, overlap on the family.

Nevertheless, despite a broad general interest in the institution of the family, it is increasingly difficult to keep particular families intact, for several reasons. For one thing, social pressure against the dissolution of families has been steadily relaxed. In times past, when broken families were stigmatized, very little was to be done in the event of family conflicts but to hang in there and find some means to resolve them. But in the past generation or two families have not had the benefit of these traditional social pressures, and so conflicts that might have appeared minor, or at least tolerable, fifty years ago are today seen as sure signs of irreconcilable differences. Another factor contributing to the difficulty of maintaining coherence in the contemporary family is that there are many more opportunities for human fulfillment outside the family. So when conflicts arise at home, individuals may pull out of the family as an alternative to genuine conflict resolution. And further, members of contemporary families (children included) have more discretionary time and income at their disposal, which enable them to pursue extrafamilial involvements. As a result of these factors it has become increasingly difficult to maintain a coherent sense of we-ness in contemporary families. This is why so many individuals have come to perceive the family as a convenient place to store their belongings while they seek fulfillment elsewhere.

But even in "easier" times the task of maintaining a coherent family was difficult enough. Families are by their nature vulnerable to deep conflicts of interests—conflicts between parents, between children, and between parents and children. And these conflicts are inherent in the dominant feature of family life itself—that is, the development of children from a state of dependence to a state of autonomy. In the course of this developmental process conflicts of interests will appear all along the way, calling for new means of cooperation to be developed as they arise.

The family is a primary setting for the assemblage of personality, a training ground where the raw materials of genetic endowment are enhanced or inhibited by the kinds of learning experiences that should enable the child to achieve personal wholeness. If this process is to go forward, the family must provide essential cognitive and hedonic nurturing. And, in time, the family must begin to provide moral guidance by imposing a set of standards for the child's behavior. Children are very adept at assimilating a moral order by observation and imitation, but as they become more verbally competent, explicit moral guidance in the form of corrections and directions become important. It is in the process of receiving moral guidance that a child begins to develop a sense of self and self-worth.

The two most important functions of the family are to provide for the needs of children and to impose upon them a moral order. It will be found in the child's immediate self-interest to maximize the former and to minimize the latter. Thus children will generally be motivated to demand satisfaction of their needs while resisting the imposition of behavioral standards which they perceive to be costly in terms of immediate self-interest. Parents, on the other hand, will be motivated to impose behavioral standards because they perceive such an imposition to be in the best interest of the child as well as themselves.

These dynamics account for much of what goes on in the normal course of family life. And they also describe the source of a continuous series of power struggles between parents and children. The power struggle between parents and children is continuous because, after all, as children mature they demand a greater measure of self-determination, which requires that parents must gradually relinquish their authority. It is as if every family is caught up in a liberation movement and must systematically transfer power to the new regime. In such cases it is typical for the old regime to be reluctant and the new regime to be impatient. Children will tend to assume that if they want to do or have something, it is therefore okay. And parents will tend to assume that nothing is okay unless they authorize it. Where these conditions prevail, the power balance between parents and children will have to be renegotiated on a continuous basis.

The coherence of family life depends upon the constructive resolution of these power struggles. That is, they must be resolved in ways that achieve a confluence of the parent's and the child's interests without impairing the development of the child toward autonomy. What this means, basically, is that the child must come to perceive compliance with behavioral standards to be in his self-interest at about the same rate as he comes to perceive himself as a free agent. In other words, self-determination and moral development must proceed in tandem; freedom and responsibility go hand in hand. The execution of this process will vary considerably from one family to another, and even from one child to another. Children differ from one another in temperament, perceptiveness, and rates of development (as do their parents). The process may be further complicated by a plurality of children in the family, which inevitably raises issues of fairness. And the process will also be troubled if unresolved power struggles are going on between parents, or if the parents themselves are products of dysfunctional families. So many variables enter into family dynamics that any offering of general principles must be tenuous. Nevertheless, we may say that if family conflicts are not avoided or constructively resolved, some members of the family will come to perceive a decrease in association value and the family will lose its coherence. Strategies of deception and self-deception may play a significant role in these complicated negotiations.

Let us now turn to some examples that show how deceptive interactions may contribute to the coherence of families. We may begin with some observations about the acquisition of standards for behavior. Children acquire the elements of a moral order when they come to perceive that compliance with a particular rule or standard is in their interests. They often come to such perceptions, in the first instance, when some hedonic reward is associated with compliance, or when some hedonic punishment is associated with non-compliance. Thus parents will frequently offer candies to their children to reinforce compliance with a standard. If the child judges the reward of candy to exceed the cost of compliance, she will be hedonically motivated to comply with the standard in future situations. Along with the candy parents may very well display exaggerated signs of affection or gratitude. Such displays are reinforcing once children begin to acquire a sense of self-worth. In time, parents may withhold the hedonic reinforcer and continue to supply the self-esteem reinforcer when the child complies. As this happens, compliance with the standard is no longer in the child's hedonic interest, though it will be in her self-esteem interest. Once compliance with the standard becomes fixed in the child's self-esteem calculus, the parents may withhold their demonstrations of approval while the child congratulates herself for compliance by the process of self-monitoring. Whereas the child initially perceived compliance with the rule as a strategy for hedonic satisfaction, it is no longer that at all, but something quite different.

This is a variation on the "bait and switch" ruse. The parents' use of candy as a reinforcer is a behavioral design that tricks the child into formulating a causal schema which associates compliant behavior with hedonic rewards. The child's initial compliance was premised on the perception of this cause-effect relation, which eventually turned out to be unreliable. But then it happened that the substituted effect (the parents' enthusiastic approval) was sufficiently satisfying to make compliance worth the cost in terms of self-esteem benefit. But even at this stage the parents are deceiving the child by pretending to more affection and gratitude than they genuinely feel. In this process a confluence of interests has been established between parent and child. The child's compliance with the rule is satisfying to the parents and it also delivers a measure of self-esteem to the child. This perversive strategy is used repeatedly to establish patterns of compliance with social norms. It is fundamental to the acquisition of a moral order.

Another deceit is the old "daddy likes it" routine, frequently used in attempts to get a child to take medicine. A confluence of interests is to be achieved in the child's compliance—parents are motivated by self-esteem to do what is best for the child, and the child has a long-term hedonic interest in restored health. But since the child can't perceive this long-term hedonic interest, the father deceives her into thinking an immediate benefit is at hand. He pretends to take a spoonful of the medicine himself, whereupon he further pretends to enjoy it—"Um, that's good, see how daddy likes it!" And the child complies.

Or consider this familiar perversion. A mother is trying to feed spinach to her child. The spoon goes in the mouth and the spinach comes right back out. She tries again, this time with an enthusiastic (and quite phony) "Num, num," but out it comes again. Before the third try the mother drags the spoon lightly through the apple sauce. Presto! The camouflaged spinach goes down.

Parents very often use petty deceits to encourage altruistic behavior; that is, to shape the emotional responses that will predispose the child to help others. Picture a year-and-a-half-old child interacting with her father. The child experiments with the father's face by pinching his nose and pulling his hair. The father is not injured by these assaults but he pretends injury. He may pretend to cry, saying, "Oh, no, don't hurt daddy, daddy will cry—boo-hoo." The child may study the father's response and then pull his ear. More crying. Now the father says, "Be *nice* to daddy; give daddy a hug." The child gives her father a hug. He beams forth a broad smile of approval and says, "That's a good girl, now daddy feels happy." A similar interaction may involve the child's treatment of a doll. If the child throws her teddy bear to the floor, the father may put on a pained expression of sympathy and come to the teddy's rescue. "Poor Teddy," he may say, "be nice to Teddy," and he picks up the bear and gives it a warm hug. Then he offers it to the child so that she can give it a hug.

The father is play-acting in these scenes. He is not really injured, not really crying, not all that happy with his hug, and not in the least sympathetic with the teddy bear. And yet he goes to great lengths to give a convincing appearance of these responses, all for the sake of conditioning the child's responses to the injury of others. Such little scenarios, enabled by the parents' pretenses, amount to rehearsals for real-life situations. The message in such petty deceits is that the suffering of others is a stimulus for sympathetic response. The pretenses of parents reinforce children's responses so that they will be self-esteem motivated when they encounter the real thing. We saw earlier that human beings possess a genetic predisposition to reciprocal altruism. But this inherited trait is not sufficiently robust to produce the kind of consistent helping behavior required for coherent human societies. Therefore, the inherited trait must be strengthened and directed by learning at a very early stage in a child's emotional development, long before the child is capable of assimilating verbal instructions about the appropriateness of sympathetic responses. Children learn these responses most effectively in real-life situations, but such situations are (fortunately) too few in the normal stream of events to ensure that the requisite learning takes place. So we fabricate them by petty deceits. The positive effect of such role-playing on the development of altruistic behaviors has been demonstrated in experimental settings.[21]

Here follows a sampler of additional deceits that parents commonly use to influence the compliance of their children with behavioral standards.

Several studies have shown that children are more compliant when their immediate sense of self-esteem is positive.[22] Parents often exploit this factor by lavishing empty praises upon a child in advance of some request for the child's compliance.

Children will be more likely to join willingly in helpful tasks if they perceive others engaged in the task to be having fun. This "Tom Sawyer effect" can be exploited by parents who feign enjoyment and invite the child to join in.

Many parents bluff children with empty threats of punishment in order to deter noncompliance.

Parents frequently exaggerate the benefits of a reward for compliance, and sometimes entice children by promising a reward that is kept secret until after compliance.

Parents often induce caution in a child's behavior by presenting highly unrealistic assessments of the dangers involved in some activity.

Parents use (evasive) tactics to distract children's attention from certain objects, activities, or topics.

Parents often distort or conceal information about themselves and their past in order to present a positive example to their children.

When a child does something in a helpful spirit, parents may laud the child's positive contribution, whereas in reality the child may have created extra work for the parent.

When a child misbehaves, the parent may respond with a scornful expression even though the parent may find the behavior genuinely amusing.[23]

The many petty deceits that parents use to defeat the perceptual designs of their children may seem insignificant at first sight, but when one considers the frequency and the pedagogical timeliness of these deceits they appear anything but petty. Readers, I am sure, can produce many additional examples from their own experience to support the claim that minor deceits are instrumental in the compliance of children with behavioral standards. Some strategies may be more effective than others, and some of them will have questionable long-term moral consequences. But I think no one can doubt the pervasiveness of minor deceits in the ongoing project of moral instruction. Indeed, I seriously doubt that any parent can claim to have raised a child without deception.

We have considered several examples of deception in service to the task of imposing a moral order upon children, a task which establishes confluences of interests both within the family and within the larger social ecology. And now we turn to another category of constructive deceits: those which avoid or resolve conflicts of interests within a family. We may include within this category any designs that work to avoid or reduce the distress of particular family members, when distress is not directly related to the incidence of conflict within a family.

The most common deceits for avoiding conflicts within a family involve the evasive strategy of withholding information that has potential for creating conflicts of interests or for causing distress. Under some conditions family members will conceal "sensitive" information indefinitely, and under other conditions the information is withheld temporarily, to be disclosed at a more opportune moment. Parents very often withhold information from their children and from each other in the interest of avoiding conflicts. They routinely discuss what information should be shared with their children, and strategize over the timing and framing of shared information. If parents have decided to move the household to another city, they may keep the decision secret for months and then finally inform the children when they are in especially good spirits. They may even follow the evasion with a perversion by giving the false impression that the move is mandated by external circumstances. And if the parents find themselves beset by second thoughts concerning the effects of the move on the children, they may engage in mutual self-deception by rationalizing the decision. Parents frequently withhold potentially distressing information from each other. A man may conceal the fact that he is up for a promotion in order to spare his wife disappointment in the event that he fails to get it. His wife may spare her husband some embarrassment by concealing the fact that she learned of the denial indirectly. Parents may keep secret the financial status of the family, or even misrepresent financial circumstances in order to spare children worry or disgrace (if the news is bad) or to avoid incessant begging for unnecessary goods (if the news is good). Decisions of this sort are usually based on assessments of mutual self-interest.

Children, too, practice evasion in order to avoid conflict or to preclude distress. A teenager who has dented the family car may withhold the information until she can manipulate her parents into optimal circumstances, whereupon she may even give a misleading account of how the accident occurred. If she feels guilty about misleading her parents, she may convince herself that no good purpose would be served by their knowing the truth. They would only become distressed and would lecture and punish her needlessly, for she has already learned a profound lesson from the experience. Siblings will discuss among themselves whether and how they should disclose sensitive information to their parents. In such conspiracies it is common for children to assess the self-interest implications for their parents as well as themselves. Their decisions very often reflect the optimal confluence of interests.

Parents and children alike often avoid conflict and distress by using distractionary tactics. When my own children were young a sighting of the local ice cream stand would typically result in minor squabbles, so I adopted the practice of driving home by a circuitous route in order to avoid the stimulus. I once announced to my children that I was about to inspect their bedrooms, at which point they very cleverly took turns distracting me until each had an opportunity to slip away and straighten up their mess.

Various acts of self-deception on the part of parents and children may play a significant role in the avoidance of conflict between family members. For example, parents usually hold unrealistically positive views of their children's appearance, abilities, and character. And for their part, children will have grossly biased estimations of their parents. Positive illusions of this sort serve to maintain high levels of affection and respect, which enhance the frequency of cooperative interactions within the family.

Families may be rendered more coherent by virtue of a variety of playful deceits. Erving Goffman includes in this category things like kidding, leg-pulling, practical jokes, and surprise parties.[24] Humorous and harmless put-ons may have the effect of making dupes (parents or children) more tractable, or they may make the ambiance of the family more relaxed and affectionate. Surprise parties are especially effective means for producing confluences of interests. The deceivers may have great fun together in planning the caper, and while the dupe may feel momentarily foolish, upon reflection he will tend to see the incident as an act of generosity to be reciprocated in some way.

Constructive deceits (even the playful ones) often have the potential for backfiring, in which case the intention of producing confluence of interests may in fact generate enmity and conflicts of interests. Deception, in every case, has its inherent risks. And even when deceptive strategies do succeed in avoiding conflict, it is hard to say that the avoidance is unambiguously desirable. Often, of course, it is. But there are occasions when open conflict of interests within a family provides the necessary stimulus to redefine relationships through the discovery of new means of cooperation. Open conflicts might, in fact, reveal deep misunderstandings and misguided assumptions about the real interests of other family members. But it must be said that if there is any constructive value in familial conflicts, it is found in the manner of their resolution. And here, too, deception and self-deception frequently play a role.

Perhaps the most common deceit in the service of reconciliation is the practice of feigned contrition. False contrition may be less desirable than the real thing, but there is no denying the fact that when it is effective the dupe's subjective state will be the same as if the contrition were genuine. And this being the case, one might expect something like the candlelight effect to take hold. If feigned contrition is answered by genuine forgiveness, then it is quite possible that the forgiveness will be answered by genuine gratitude and reciprocation. Once again, emotional investments must begin somewhere. Feigned contrition is commonly attended by false promises of reform. That is, at the moment the promise is made the promiser may not expect to be held to it. But promises are public declarations that have a way of being cited in future interactions, and the promiser who fails to deliver (even on false promises) does so at peril of losing his general credibility. And general credibility is, of course, a great asset to self-interest, an asset that one is motivated to protect. So unless the false promiser can find a way to wheedle his way out of the promise, he may well find himself in compliance in spite of himself.

Feigned interest in some object or activity may provide a pretext for estranged family members to engage in interaction, with the happy result that reconciliation is achieved. We have observed this dynamic of conflict resolution in chimps and it is commonly used by children as well. A related phenomenon is distraction, whereby a conflict may be diffused by the intrusion of a new focus of attention. Sometimes the intrusion may be fabricated by a combatant, as when a mother engaged in conflict with her child suddenly remembers that she must get to the bank before it closes. Or the intrusion may be fabricated by some interested bystander, as when a child feigns illness just as his parents launch into a heated argument. In many such cases the disputes are not resumed.

The most essential and effective resource for resolving family conflicts is a shared vision of the family as an entity of enduring and transcendent value. Such a perception provides family members with a level of meaning that stands above the matter of daily interactions, a level to which they may periodically repair for the purpose of affirming their essential we-ness. Families, like marriages, achieve coherence by constructing a common version of their own collective reality, a mythology that locates the interests of family members within the larger interests of the family. When such a perception prevails, emerging conflicts of interests can be trivialized by the recognition of a more ultimate confluence of interests. The agendas of individual family members are thereby submerged in the affirmation of a greater union.

The manner in which families go about constructing and maintaining their self-understandings varies enormously. Some families embed the shared view of their collective reality within the conventions of some broad historical perspective, such as a religious or ethnic tradition. Others focus on a fairly narrow frame of historical reference, limiting the family narrative to only two or three generations. Others emphasize the experience of living memory, and still others tend to focus exclusively on the future. Some families are explicitly metaphorical in their self-image (e.g., a team, a firm, a flock, a democracy, a crew), while others are not. Some families will emphasize shared recreational ventures, others literary sources, others work activities or community affairs. Some families value frequent socializing with a wide circle of friends, others value occasional interactions with a narrow circle, and still others tend toward social isolation. Some families have homogeneous origins, others not. Some perceptions reflect a context of hardship and social prejudice, others a context of privilege and prosperity. So many variables enter into the shaping of family life that it is quite out of the question to propose that there is a correct way for families to perceive themselves.

The relevant point about family coherence, however, is not how families perceive their collective reality but that they perceive a reality collectively. And every attempt to construct a familial self-understanding worth sharing will be somewhat idealized and inevitably sustained by a collage of deceptions: positive illusions, deconstructed failures, distortions of memory, closeted skeletons, sanctified ancestors, and collective fantasies. Families that claim to be exceptions to this principle only prove the point.

Secondary Groups

In the most primitive of human societies virtually all associations of individuals were in the context of primary groups. But as societies became larger and more complex, networks of interconnected secondary groups began to emerge. In fact, the number and diversity of these secondary associations is our best measure of the complexity of a comprehensive society. Basically, a secondary group can be defined as any enduring voluntary association that falls somewhere between a primary group and a comprehensive group. The nature and goals of these groups are determined by a wide range of factors, such as the form of comprehensive organization found in a society, its ecological niches, its technology, its decision-making processes, its economic system, its values (or lack thereof), and so on. The principal interest of social historians is to provide an account of the conditions that give rise to secondary groups.

These secondary associations are formed and maintained because they represent a measure of overlapping self-interest among the associates. The confluences of interests among secondary-group members are not, however, as deep or extensive as they are among members of primary groups. If they were they would *be* primary groups. Primary groups are those that engage all aspects of one's personality in intimate and enduring relations with other members of the group. In secondary groups it is typical for the association to engage only a fragment of one's personality, a particular role or interest. Most secondary groups can provide a formal statement of purpose, a *raison d'être,* which members will typically cite as the stimulus that motivated them to venture forth into an association outside of the primary group. If I have a passion for Schubert's music, for example, I may advance this interest by joining the Schubert Society, or if I am deeply concerned about the environment, I may join the Sierra Club.

From these observations one might reason that an individual's association with a secondary group will be a simple reflection of the group's appeal to some domain of self-interest, either intellectual, hedonic, or self-esteem. In general this seems to be the case, but it would be misleading to say there is anything simple about such appeals. My association with either the Schubert

Society or the Sierra Club may cut across all three domains of self-interest. I may find Schubert's music to be both intellectually stimulating and hedonically rewarding, and I may also find that my associations with other Schubert enthusiasts are affirming of my self-worth. Likewise, I may find the Sierra Club to be an excellent source of information about the state of the world, as well as a defender of the wilderness areas in which I enjoy hiking. And my membership may impress my friends as well, or give me a sense of doing the right thing. So my involvement in these secondary groups is not necessarily one-dimensional, even though they do not appeal to all aspects of my personality in the way that my spouse or family may attempt to do. And even if my association with a group is one-dimensional, my motivation need not be in line with the expressed purpose of the group. Perhaps I don't give a fig for Schubert's music but I have learned that the Schubert Society throws great parties, or perhaps my interest in the Sierra Club has only to do with the fact that it employs me as a photographer.

So the matter of association with secondary groups can become very complicated. But one thing is sure: When we find an individual associated with a secondary group we may assume a perception of self-interest, even though that interest may not be what it appears.

I have already suggested that the character of secondary groups is related to circumstances in the larger fabric of society. To understand the dynamics of a particular group, therefore, it is necessary to view it with reference to this larger context. If we wish to examine the dynamics of a business organization or a trade union, for example, we must view it in relation to the economic system in which it functions. Or if we wish to examine a political party, we must see it in the context of a political system. Even the Schubert Society and the Sierra Club find their places within the comprehensive scheme. This method of "contextualizing" is especially important when we raise questions about the role of deception in secondary groups. And it is consistent with the method we followed when we examined the role of deception in the achievement of personal wholeness. In that discussion we had to frame our questions in terms of the larger context of psychic organization and intrapsychic conflict. There I tried to show that some strategies of deception and self-deception were psychologically adaptive given the challenges of harmonizing a multidynamic system of information processing. Here I am suggesting something very similar: that the social adaptiveness of deception may be judged in relation to the imperatives of a particular social system. Just as deception was seen to be an important factor in negotiating harmony within a psychic system, it may also be an important factor in negotiating confluences of interests within a social system. In other words, it is quite possible to construct a social system in such a way that deceptive strategies will be encouraged, expected, rational, and adaptive. I believe that every social system has such features, but because social systems differ in important ways, we may expect them to rely upon deception in different ways.

There is no need to make these matters sound more difficult than they really are. It can be viewed as a matter of rules. The rules of baseball, for example, are written in such a way that deceptive strategies have become a major feature of the game. (Baseball fans will recall how the 1991 World Series championship was won on the strength of a faked throw, which momentarily and decisively confused a base runner.) Deception in athletic contests has become so adaptive that teams without tricky plays and great fakes are lined up in the losers' column. The point is that if we are going to appreciate the role of deception in achieving coherence within secondary groups, we will have to view these groups in terms of the rules of play.

Business groups

The earliest secondary groups in human experience were probably the pan-tribal sodalities that began to form as kinship bonds gave way to tribal alliances. These sodalities drew individuals into secondary associations as new cooperative means to acquire the resources necessary for a livelihood. And so it has been ever since. Contemporary industrial societies are vastly complex social ecologies with a great diversity of interconnected secondary groups. If individuals aspire to satisfy their basic needs, they are forced to find some sort of vocational niche within the vast system, whereupon they will discover that the system is organized (more or less) by various rules.

One of the main organizing features of complex nations is the market system, whereby individuals convert their personal resources into currency, which may be used to acquire various desired goods and services. A market system, as I noted earlier, is a terrific means for establishing confluences of interests *if and only if* the system succeeds at providing individuals with the goods and services they want at prices they can afford. But constructing the rules that will enable a market to accomplish this task is no simple matter, and various sets of rules have been proposed by market theorists to get the job done. Some sets of rules are good at providing goods and services but not at setting affordable prices, while other sets of rules are good at keeping prices affordable but fail to generate adequate supplies of desired commodities. A set of market rules may be seen to fail at providing confluences of interests because of the types of behavior it encourages and/or discourages. An economy organized by socialist rules will systematically reduce incentives for greedy and exploitive behaviors by eliminating the profit motive. But on the downside, a socialist economy provides few incentives for efficiency, quality, innovation, and productivity. The result of such rules will be that goods may be affordable enough but poorly supplied, insufficiently diverse, and badly made. In addition, socialist rules encourage apathy, corruption, and the creation of an alternative black-market economy. On the other hand, an economy organized by capitalist rules (i.e., no rules) will provide incentives for efficiency, productivity, and diversity but will encourage the underpayment of workers, the monopolizing of resources, and the overcharging of consumers. The desired goods may be there but the underpaid and overcharged consumers can't afford them. Doctrinaire socialist rules fail to give consumers what they want and unfettered capitalism fails to give them what they can afford. Neither system is capable of generating confluences of interests.

But of course neither of these extreme sets of market rules describes what is actually the case in modern industrialized economies. There are no thoroughly regulated markets and there are no unregulated markets. Contemporary Western market economies have regulations to minimize the exploitation of workers and to ensure a competitive business environment by disallowing monopolies and price-fixing. Privately owned businesses are lured into this environment by the profit motive, where they must compete with other businesses to provide what consumers want at prices they can afford.

And such, in summary form, describes the milieu in which contemporary secondary groups seek to thrive (or at least the profiteering ones, upon which, incidentally, virtually all the others depend). And it is a milieu, I will argue, that has so strongly encouraged deceptive behavior that it has become an inherent feature of the system as a whole.

What are the means by which a secondary group may achieve coherence within such a system? I have defined a coherent group as one in which a confluence of interests is established among associates. With respect to groups competing in a free market system, a confluence of interests must be maintained among the owners, workers, and customers associating with a group. Owners have an interest in the group because it is a source of profit and perhaps pride. Workers' interests have to do with wages and perhaps also a sense of self-esteem. And consumers have an interest in the company to the extent that it remains a source of desired goods (whatever the motive) at affordable prices. If the company fails to make a profit, the owners will not perceive any association value in the group and will close it down. If the compensation is too low or the work too dangerous or unpleasant, the workers will fail to see any association value and will seek employment elsewhere. And if the product is inferior or overpriced, the customers will not buy. It is hard enough to maintain a confluence of interests among these associates in the best of circumstances, but doing so in the face of competition with other groups becomes a very delicate proposition. And doing so without resort to strategies of deception may be next to impossible.

So how is it done? The logic of success in a free market system is very simple and straightforward: Give them what they want at a price they can afford. There are lots of nondeceptive ways to give consumers what they want at affordable prices. One can satisfy the first part of the equation (giving them what they want) either by discovering a need and then coming up with the goods to satisfy it or by stimulating a need for the goods on hand. If a company can invent a desired product that no other company offers, then it will enjoy a virtual monopoly until the competition catches up. The company can sell the product at high prices because consumers can't purchase it elsewhere. Another way to arrive on the scene with a new product is simply to arrive on a new scene. Successful businesses are always hunting for new markets where the early bird gets the whole worm. And yet another way to innovate is to come up with a new marketing device which may tap sectors of the consumer market left untouched by conventional techniques. Another way to give them what they want is to make them want what you've got. There are many nondeceptive ways to generate new interest in an old product. This is what advertising agencies are for.

The second part of the equation (at prices they can afford) can also be satisfied by a variety of nondeceptive strategies. An obvious method for keeping prices competitive is to reduce the profit margin per unit on the gamble that increased volume will make up the difference. New methods of production or increased efficiency in old methods can reduce the cost of production. Incentives for workers may increase productivity enough to justify a reduction in prices. And simple relocation may also result in lower prices by reducing transportation costs, tax liabilities, or labor expenses.

There is a great range of nondeceptive strategies that business groups can use in order to maintain or even enhance a confluence of interests among owners, workers, and customers. But the range of deceptive strategies is much broader and often just as effective. And it is very difficult for business groups to resist turning to deceptive means, especially when they (and their competitors) have already exhausted all the nondeceptive options. Many players in the market game have learned that they can achieve success by *appearing* to give consumers what they want at prices they *think* they can afford.

There are basically two deceptive means for giving the appearance of providing what customers want without actually doing so. One is to evade the consumer's perceptions and the other is to pervert them. Many companies practice evasive strategies by adulterating their products on the chance that customers won't notice. A tavern may water its beer or backfill the bottles of expensive liquor with cheap stuff; restaurants may serve flounder under the pretense of fillet of sole, or shredded halibut in place of crabmeat; a meat market may pump water into meat cuts to increase their weight, or fashion chuck steak in the shape of porterhouse; clothing stores may pass off seconds as first-quality merchandise; a jewelry store may substitute smaller or inferior stones for the size and quality ordered by the customer; a florist may deliver a recycled flower arrangement to a wedding, knowing that attention will be focused elsewhere; a service station may use cheaper brands of oil but charge customers for a more expensive brand; a cab driver may take unsuspecting tourists on a long ride to a nearby destination. Paul Blumberg's book *The Predatory Society* contains a cargo of examples of evasive deceits in the marketplace.[25]

Consumers may also be deceived by a variety of perversive strategies that misrepresent the relevance of a product to their needs. The seller may present false information about the product itself, or present extraneous false information to induce a perceived need for the product. The greatest perpetrators of these deceits are sales personnel and advertising wizards. Sales personnel are notorious trucklers, eager to flatter, fawn, and falsify whenever a sale is in the wind. They are trained to do so by the firms that employ them and rewarded when they succeed. The sales game bears out Leo Durocher's comment that "nice guys finish last." Yet no one works harder at *appearing* to be nice than sales personnel. Joe Girard, the all-time world champion car salesman, made a practice of sending monthly greeting cards to every person who ever bought a car from him. By the end of his career he was sending out more than 13,000 cards per month. And on the face of each card was a simple printed message: "I like you."[26] Month after month, year after year, former customers received a reminder that Joe liked them. So when it came time to buy another car, the insincerely induced dynamics of reciprocity would bring customers back to Joe like homing pigeons. Aware of their professional reputation for deceitfulness, sales personnel have developed clever tricks to create the illusion of honesty. They sometimes, Blumberg points out, "steer customers away from one product by confiding supposedly inside information about that product's deficiencies." Now confident that the salesperson has their best interests at heart, customers are predisposed to believe whatever falsehoods they are told about the alternative product. Blumberg gives an account of a muffler shop where customers are encouraged to linger in the work area and observe as their cars are being repaired. This open and informal policy removes any suspicion of backroom shenanigans, for which auto repair shops are renowned. Once admitted to the shop area, however, the customer is unaware that the mechanic doubles as a salesman, drawing a commission on each sale. While he is under the car the mechanic warns the customer that the "whole line" (the entire exhaust system) needs replacing, even though he knows it doesn't. Replacing the whole line will make the car much safer and will save the customer the expense and inconvenience of coming back for additional repairs. Customers typically buy "the whole line."[27] It may be argued that such deceits do not establish genuine confluence of interests because they extract a cost in terms of the dupe's *real* interests, and were the dupes to discover these deceits they would be the first to complain; as they should. But the victims of business deception seldom make these discoveries, with the result that what normally remains is all that really matters to a consumer: consumer satisfaction.

Modern consumers have many fewer dealings with sales personnel than former generations did. In the age of supermarkets and discount stores we are allowed the dignity of making our own selections. These days the real action in marketing strategy is in media advertising, where we encounter the deception before we even enter the market to make our selections. The genre of advertising, Blumberg assures us, is "dominated by half-truths, puffery, exaggeration, misinformation, distortion, outright lies, and the exploitation of carefully researched human needs, fears and insecurities."[28] One of my own favorite commercials from several years ago promoted a brand of margarine on the claim that its producers used a secret process for extracting the flavor from real butter (nothing else, just the flavor) and transferring it to the margarine. Misleading information of this sort is common in TV ads. Donna Cross says that "the job of the television commercial is to promote 'special' qualities a product doesn't have, and to cloak its defects in a smokescreen." Many television ads are in a sense inherently deceptive. That is, they are dramatized fictions, wherein the personalities are actors pretending to be enthusiastically satisfied with a product. Yet there is enough reality in TV commercials to make them differ in important ways from most fiction. The *products* are real. And the innuendo is unmistakable: The purchase of this product gives you access to the kind of excitement or satisfaction (usually hedonic or self-esteem) depicted in the ad. Some ads, of course, use "real" people whose testimonials are filmed in candid settings. The intention is to induce the belief that this is *not* fiction, this is not mere staging, so it can't be deceptive. But it usually is. In the first place, advertisers prescreen the subjects used in candid testimonials and then make dozens of takes involving only the most promising subjects. What we see on the tube is the one take that suits the advertiser, not the dozens in which consumers showed lack of enthusiasm for the product. And even that one take may involve a setup. In an ad for a dishwashing detergent a California schoolteacher was asked to dip his hands in two dishes of unidentified suds and announce which of them felt most pleasant. The one on the left, by far. And sure enough, it turned out to be the advertiser's product. What the viewers could not see was that the soapy water on the left was nicely warmed, while the bowl of rival suds was ice cold.[29]

A majority of products advertised on TV are products that consumers do not really need in order to lead a full and satisfying life. So the burden of most of the ads we see is to stimulate a perceived need. One of the starkest examples of appearing to give consumers what they need by inducing a need involves the mouthwash industry. Mouthwash ads induce the unwarranted fear that consumers may lose their jobs and friends if they fail to rinse. In spite of debunking reports from the American Dental Association and the National Academy of Sciences, many people believe the false claims of advertisers that mouthwash has a lasting effect on bad breath. The splendor of these ads is that they use deceptive means to get us to buy a deceptive product.

There are several deceptive strategies for providing products at prices consumers can afford. One method is to keep costs low by manipulating workers. A common practice is for companies to use insincere measures to build up the goodwill of employees toward the company, and then to cash in on this goodwill at contract time. Some organizations attempt to fabricate a false sense of family, knowing that workers will produce more and demand less to the extent that they identify with the group. As William H. Whyte observes, an "organization man" is willing to subordinate personal interests to those of the company.[30] The same co-optative process is described in sociologist Robert Merton's concept of *false community*: "In place of a sense of Gemeinschaft—genuine community of values—there intrudes *pseudo-Gemeinschaft*—the feigning of personal concern with the other fellow in order to manipulate the better."[31] It is also common for employers to misrepresent the financial state of the firm to employees who are hopeful of wage increases. Owners may point out that if prices are not kept competitive, sales will decline and layoffs will probably be necessary. Often, of course, the scenario will be accurate, but just as frequently it is a bluff.

More frequent, though, are the many deceits of pricing and packaging which are designed to make consumers think they are getting a favorable price. A common one is the "markup, markdown" gambit used in many department stores. Merchandisers are well aware that many shoppers hold off on some types of purchases until they can find them on sale. So in advance of a sale a store may mark its prices up considerably and then slash the prices for the sale and still make a respectable profit. Another clever tactic is to mark the price of an item down ever so slightly and then to announce, "Only two to a customer at this new low price." The "lowball" is a standard negotiating device used in many car dealerships. A customer may succeed in getting a salesman to agree to a very favorable price on a new car—maybe $400 below the competition. The salesman then begins all the paperwork on the purchase, only to have the sales manager intervene at the last minute with the objection that such a low price represents a substantial loss to the dealership. This tactic is highly successful for a couple of reasons. First, once the paperwork is started, the customer is firmly committed to buying the car. And to reverse such a commitment over a few hundred dollars would be embarrassing. And further, even under the new terms, the customer can find reasons for feeling confident that a favorable deal has been struck.[32] Packaging and labeling can often be deceptive, as most consumers know. If there is any advantage in concealing the product from view, then you can be sure the package will be opaque, and probably larger than necessary. A package label may announce boldly, "25% more," without indicating that the price has been adjusted by the same percentage. Or perhaps it will say, "New ingredients, same low price," without letting on that the new ingredients have actually lowered the production cost.

Business groups are not the only type of secondary group in a complex society. There are many other types—recreation groups, hobby clubs, professional societies, civic groups, service organizations, political coalitions, and many more. We will not take the time to investigate the role of deception in establishing the confluence of interests that gives each of these groups its being. I have focused here on business groups because they are the most numerous and because they tend to involve everyone at one level or another. The argument I have been trying to make here is that secondary groups are formed and maintained as entities of overlapping self-interests within the context of a larger social ecology. In the case of business groups we may speak of their survival and coherence in terms of "holding niche" within an ecosystem, or economic system. And to hold niche within a complex system calls for behavioral designs that are appropriate to the features of the system. Given the private market system of modern Western social economies, various strategies of deception can be shown to be encouraged, rational, and adaptive behaviors. Indeed, they help to advance the goals of the system, which are to give people what they want at prices they can afford.

I want to be very deliberate and clear about the claims I am making here, for I do not wish to be misunderstood. That I *might* be misunderstood is surely possible, for I have focused exclusively on only half of the story. I have tried to show that deception will be inevitable and adaptive within the private market economy. The other half of the story is that strategies to counter deception will also be rational and adaptive. That is, the system encourages a fair

238 / By the Grace of Guile

amount of suspicion, some sophistication among consumers, and some establishment of regulations to keep the risks of deception reasonably high. In other words, the "free" market system has evolved in such a way that it works optimally (i.e., to give people what they want at prices they can afford) when some balance is achieved between freedom to deceive and regulations to counter deception. Thus we find the central players within the system faced off in power struggles to determine the regulation of the system. This face-off occupies a large share of the realm of public discourse. Let me give just one example. In the 1960s counterdeceptive forces coalesced to place a bill before the U.S. Senate designed to put an end to deceptive pricing and packaging in the food industry. In an attempt to preempt public attention and support for the bill, the president of the Grocery Manufacturers of America met with the publishers of sixteen national magazines and suggested to them that there be some serious communication between their advertising departments and their editorial departments.[33] A television network heeded the same "advice" when it canceled a scheduled appearance by the bill's sponsor under pressure from food industry advertisers. Business, as they say, is business.

I hope it is clear that I am neither defending nor attacking the private market system itself. Nor am I advocating the practice of deception in business. I am only saying that the dynamics of deception are a significant part of the system. As Paul Blumberg says, "Deception . . . represents the chronic essence rather than the occasional excess of the system."[34] It is very difficult to assemble reliable statistics on such matters, but if Blumberg's study is representative, then more than 70 percent of American business groups use deceptive strategies, in varying degrees of seriousness, as a matter of routine practice. And this figure does not take into account a systematic survey of advertising practices. We may surmise, then, that virtually every group will at least occasionally use designs to defeat perceptual designs for the sake of the coherence of the group. And if this is the case, then we must conclude that deception has rooted itself deeply within the traditions of capitalism itself. As I tried to say in chapter 2, wherever there is a niche for deceivers (as there clearly is in the free market system), there will be deception. If this is perceived to be a problem, then I suggest it is not one that can be solved short of dismantling the system itself. But what would be the point of dismantling an economic system if not to replace it with some alternative system? And what are the chances that some alternative system could be designed in which deceivers would be denied a niche?

Comprehensive Groups

Comprehensive groups are the largest organized entities of human association. Most comprehensive groups in the contemporary world are nation-states, although a few chiefdoms and tribes remain. It may be argued that the United Nations and various treaty organizations constitute even larger social organizations, but these should rather be seen as cooperative ventures between comprehensive groups. If member states were to relinquish their sovereignty to the United Nations, then *it* would be the largest comprehensive group.

The fundamental question concerning the coherence of comprehensive groups has to do with the means of cooperation by which they maintain their unity. I have already addressed this issue in my discussion of myth, where it was said that a comprehensive group will be coherent to the extent that its members share a myth, or an integrated vision of cosmology, economy, and morality. The myth of a culture provides the ultimate meanings whereby conflicts emerging within a comprehensive group may be resolved. The memes of myth also provide the ultimate legitimation for the political and legal traditions of comprehensive groups, as well as serving to bolster their leaders' claims to power. Chieftains, for example, commonly established their authority by claiming to be descended from or appointed by supernatural (mythic) forces. Even the monarchs of so-called secular states claimed religious sanctions to legitimate their authority. Thus it can be said that the organization and authority structures of comprehensive groups are established on the foundations provided by the meanings embedded in their myth.

On this view, then, it is almost unthinkable that a comprehensive group could remain coherent if its political, economic, and legal traditions were incommensurate with its mythic traditions. In practical terms this means that modern states in which the custodians of secular institutions are not also the custodians of the myth will have the potential for incoherence. In other words, a society will not remain coherent if it is torn between two masters. A house divided will fall. There cannot be a City of God and a City of Man unless, as Augustine saw, one is subservient to the other.

Yet such a division of the house has been roughly the case in Western civilization since the Renaissance. I say "roughly" because the two masters (state and church) have worked out a compromise of authority that has effectively forestalled the breakdown of social coherence. The terms of the compromise are well known. One major feature of the compromise was achieved in the policy of territoriality laid down in the sixteenth century. This policy declared that the territorial boundaries between secular states would also be the boundaries between variants of ecclesiastical authority that had emerged during the reformation. The policy resulted in the establishment of state churches, with which secular rulers were careful to stay on friendly terms. Another major feature of the compromise was for church and state to focus on different objectives of human existence. The church would see itself as the instrument of personal wholeness (individual piety and morality), while the state limited its concerns to social coherence (public policy). In terms of domains of human experience, the church claimed for itself the voice of moral authority, while the state took the final word in the domain of economy. And gradually, of course, the authority of modern science came to preside over the domain of cosmology. Thus since the Renaissance, Western civilization has been characterized by somewhat strained relations between religious, political, and scientific authorities. Social coherence has not been completely lost in the process partly because territory and resources have been sufficiently abundant to enable the resolution of some conflicts through emigration. But just as important has been a robust intellectual tradition which has struggled to maintain a semblance of compatibility between independent voices of authority.

The myth of Western culture (basically, the Judeo-Christian myth) has therefore remained reasonably well intact, with the result that Western states have been reasonably coherent. I have already intimated that this coherence shows signs of breaking down under the conditions of amythia, and more will be said about this in the final chapter. For the moment, however, I have something to say about the reliance of both secular and religious authorities upon strategies of deception in their efforts to achieve social coherence.

The following discussion is shaped by two distinctions—one between outsiders and insiders and the other between the secular and sacred realms. My thesis is that comprehensive groups rely on deceptive strategies in order to achieve and maintain social coherence. In some instances these designs are meant to defeat outsiders, and on other occasions they are aimed at members of the group itself. And I intend to examine this thesis with references to state and church authorities, the two claimants to custody of comprehensive groups in the West.

Deceiving outsiders

The two principle means by which comprehensive groups seek to establish and maintain their coherence vis-à-vis outsiders are war and diplomacy. Both are means of defending or extending a way of life in which members of the group have a shared interest. And neither of these means is effective without the use of deceptive strategies.

In a 1917 speech before the U.S. Senate, Hiram Johnson declared that "the first casualty when war comes is truth." This observation is consistent with the view of the ancient Chinese commander Sun Tzu, that deception is the essence of warfare: "All warfare is based on deception. Therefore, when capable, feign incapacity; when active, inactivity. When near, make it appear that you are far away; when far away, that you are near. Offer the enemy a bait to lure him; feign disorder and strike him."[35] Sun Tzu believed that the supreme goal of warfare was to subdue the enemy without fighting, a principle that is reflected also in Machiavelli's advice that a wise commander never attempts to win by force what can be won by deceit. The annals of military history are filled with evasive and perversive deceits—secret codes, cover planning, camouflage, calculated leaks of misleading information, construction of dummy bases, double agents, disingenuous broadcasts, and so on. There are even cases of phantom forces, as when World War II allies used sonic devices and balloons to mimic the sounds of landing convoys, thus distracting the enemy forces away from Normandy. Even the prestigious *National Geographic* was drawn into the deception game by publishing a special issue about the insignia of the armed services. The issue falsely inflated the size of the U.S. forces by including emblems of many fictitious units.[36] It is a certainty that no war has ever been won in which deception has not played a significant role. Even the celebrated technological blitzkrieg in the Persian Gulf was not without its deceitful moments. According to General Norman Schwarzkopf, allied troops were able to prevail against superior Iraqi ground forces "because of our deception plan and the way it worked."[37] Most comprehensive groups can trace their origins to warfare, and most are forced upon occasion to defend their national interests militarily. And to the extent that the confluent interests of a group are dependent upon the instruments of war—as they inevitably are, it seems—to that precise extent the social coherence of the group is dependent upon strategies of deception.

It is often difficult to distinguish between warfare and diplomacy, and in fact most political and military theorists hold the view that war is essentially an extension of foreign policy. Or, as Sun Tzu might say, diplomacy is warfare without the fighting. One might take the point that deception is as much the essence of diplomacy as it is of war. More than humor is intended in the definition of an ambassador once attributed to Sir Henry Watton (himself an ambassador): "An ambassador is an honest man sent abroad to lie for the good of his country." The literature on deceptive operations in international relations is massive, including accounts of deceptive treaty negotiations, forged documents, propaganda campaigns, espionage, disinformation, impersonations, fabricated identities, front groups, ciphered communications, psychological warfare, secret arms deals, money laundering, bugging and wiretapping, burglary, cover-ups, covert military operations, and much, much more.[38] Many of the more serious deceptions are carried out by members of the growing professional intelligence community. But this should not be taken to suggest that there is anything recent about deception in diplomacy. Even Moses is reported to have dispatched a retinue of spies to assess the prospects of overthrowing the Canaanites (Num. 13–14).

Comprehensive groups have no difficulty in justifying the use of deceptive strategies in their interactions with foreigners. Any group will feel it has an inherent right to know if and when affairs abroad might infringe upon collective interests at home. It is in the name of this right and these interests that the deceits of diplomacy are legitimized. The point has been made frequently, for example, that the democratic way of life depends upon a variety of shady operations. Some such reasoning presumably informed Winston Churchill's famous remark that "the truth is so precious, it must be attended by a bodyguard of lies." But democracy has no monopoly on pretensions to possess the truth. Every form of government in every period of history has exercised its self-defensive right to evade and/or pervert the perceptual designs of its adversaries.

Descriptions of diplomatic deceits tend to be lengthy and involved, so I shall limit myself to a single example with the excuse that popular literature on the subject is easy to find. From 1921 to 1929 the fledgling Soviet intelligence office sustained one of the most elaborate and effective deceits in diplomatic history. It began when a handful of Soviet officials, diplomats, and military leaders made clandestine contact with various influential Russian exiles throughout Europe. These dissident exiles were informed that a starchy anticommunist underground movement back home in Russia was poised to take over the government once the communist experiment failed. The underground movement, which called itself the "Trust," used a credit association in Moscow as a front operation to conceal its activities. The dissident exiles were also told that communism was all but finished in Russia—the economy was failing, a free market was beginning to emerge, there were food shortages, the army was at the brink of mutiny—and that the Bolshevik government was expected to fall within months. The dissident exiles were thrilled by the prospects, and took their exciting news to the Western intelligence agencies which had been supporting them. These agencies were pleased to learn that Soviet communism was in disarray, and for nearly a decade they helped the dissident exiles to maintain links with the Trust. By these links the exiles were provided with secret documents on the Soviet economy and military, which they passed along to the European intelligence community. Soviet secrets routinely passed from the Trust to the dissidents, and then to Western intelligence groups. By the mid-1920s about a dozen intelligence agencies were completely dependent upon the Trust for their information about Russia.[39] The perception of Russia formed in Western nations was that communism was faltering and that a free market economy was beginning to evolve. Of course, the entire situation was a hoax fabricated by Soviet intelligence. There was no Trust, no underground movement, no emergent capitalism, and no expectation that the Bolshevik government would topple. Indeed, the Soviet regime used the Trust links to consolidate its power. Consider the ways in which this elaborate scheme made contributions to the coherence of Soviet society:

Soviet intelligence was able to identify precisely and to monitor closely its most intense adversaries (exiled dissidents), and to lure the most dangerous among them back into Russia, where they were dealt with in the usual manner.

Western nations generously extended trade credits, technology, and diplomatic privilege to the Soviet government, for they believed that it would soon evolve into a noncommunist, pro-Western regime.

The flow of disinformation was a source of considerable revenue to the Soviets, as Western intelligence groups were prepared to pay large sums for any information from the Trust.

European nations were duped into policies of passivity with respect to Soviet communism, for they were persuaded by dissident exiles that active anti-Soviet policies would be counterproductive.

It's not called "intelligence" for nothing.

Let us now shift our focus to consider how deception may advance the efforts of religious authorities to establish and maintain social coherence in a comprehensive group. The primary objective of religious authorities is to unify the group by eliciting conformity with an integrated myth; that is, by bringing individuals to the point where their consciousness is organized by the meanings of the myth. With this objective in mind, we may understand an "outsider" to the myth to be anyone whose consciousness is not sufficiently conformed to its memes. And among these outsiders we may identify two major categories: those who are hostile to the myth and those who are ignorant of or indifferent to it. These categories represent separate but related challenges for the custodians of the myth. The first challenge is to defend the myth against attacks upon the plausibility of its meanings, and the second is to extend the myth by transforming the consciousness of the audience.

A common defense against hostile attacks is to evade them, as several Jewish groups and early Christians attempted to do under the oppressive conditions of Roman occupation. Some religious groups (e.g., the Manichaeans) attempted to evade criticism by keeping certain essential teachings secret from outsiders and novices. The deepest truths were revealed only to those who had spent many years in serious study. But evasion is a poor strategy if one wants to establish conditions for extending the influence of a myth. Thus, in the face of harsh criticism from outsiders, there developed within Christianity a tradition of apologetics, or the practice of defending the myth on the critic's own turf. Justin Martyr was among the first apologists to have answered Roman charges that Christians were guilty of atheism, infanticide, promiscuity, sedition, and a host of additional villainies. Justin wrote a defense of Christianity and sent it to the emperor and several Roman philosophers. In this work he refutes the charges and then goes on to develop the pretentious argument that Christianity is the one true philosophy. In his eagerness to fabricate philosophical credentials for the faith he offers up specious claims, including the notion that Socrates was a Christian, that Plato stole his material from Moses, and that Greek philosophy and poetry were in general little more than blundering attempts to imitate Hebrew prophets.[40] The modern version of this pretense is found in the fundamentalist campaign known as "creation science." Justin tried to make Christianity out to be a philosophy (which it wasn't), and his contemporary counterparts are trying to make the biblical account of creation out to be science (which it isn't). They do so, argues Michael Ruse, by assembling an array of dishonest quotes, denials of evidence, misleading tactics, deliberate omissions, sleights of hand, phony figures, and blatant lies.[41] Justin Martyr and creation scientists should not be viewed as a pack of narcissistic charlatans serving their own exclusive interests. Their deceits are intended to preserve the integrity of the Christian story, which they sincerely believe to be a source of social coherence for their comprehensive group.

If deceptive strategies are of use in defending myths, they are more useful still in extending them. In the Christian tradition there is very early precedent for the use of deceptive means for evangelistic purposes. St. Paul himself makes a remarkable admission of his chameleon-like behavior in winning converts. Like the consummate used-car salesman, Paul pretends to share the concerns of his immediate audience in order to manipulate them into submitting to the gospel:

> I am a free man and own no master; but I have made myself every man's servant, to win over as many as possible. To Jews I become like a Jew, to win Jews. . . . To win Gentiles, who are outside the Law, I make myself like one of them, although I am not in truth outside God's law. . . . To the weak I become weak, to win the weak. Indeed, I have become

everything in turn to men of every sort, so that in one way or another I may save some. All this I do for the sake of the Gospel, to bear my part in proclaiming it. (1 Cor. 9:19–22 [New English Bible])

The author of Matthew's gospel, too, took certain liberties for the sake of evangelistic ends. The gospel writers were no mere collectors and transmitters of tradition. They were imaginative interpreters and authors of tradition as well, bringing their own biases to bear upon the narrative. Matthew's agenda was to present the figure of Jesus as one whose authority surpassed that of traditional Jewish leaders. To make his case, Matthew fabricated episodes to enhance the impression that the life of Jesus fulfilled Old Testament prophecies. In some cases he added to or omitted details from his sources, in other cases he made obscure citations that defy verification, and in other cases he rewrote the narrative for dramatic effect or to idealize the portrait of Jesus— always to exaggerate the claim for Jesus' superior authority.[42] The ultimate purpose of Matthew's rhetoric was to bring coherence to a community that had been divided by conflicts between Jews and Christians.

It is an irony of history that the subject of miracles, one of Christianity's greatest liabilities in the contemporary world, was its greatest asset in the ancient context of its origin and development. The secret of Christianity's phenomenal success as a missionary religion in the late Roman period was the power of its appeal to credulous minds. It was, of course, a credulous age, an age when many minds were organized by deluded expectations of visitations from celestial beings who could command the forces of nature and work wonders too terrible to comprehend. Christian missionaries exploited this credulity, as did virtually every other aspiring group in an age of miracles. If the Christians could produce no accounts of miracles associated with Jesus, then their proclamation would appear empty by comparison. So there were miracle stories, some fabricated by Christians themselves and others adapted to the Jesus myth from external sources. That Christianity spread by exploiting the superstitious and delusional mentality of a prescientific age is not the important issue. That it did so can be deduced from the fact of its success. The more interesting question has to do with why the miracles of the Christian sect were more appealing than those of other groups. It is not because the miracles associated with the Christian community were more dazzling than the others. In fact, they were considerably less so, and the gospels even report Jesus as refusing on occasion to perform miracles.[43] The important difference seems to be that the Christian miracles were embedded in a broader appeal to human interests, and it was this broader appeal that ultimately made the Christian miracles more compelling. There were reports of wonder-workers in the ancient world that outdid any miracles reported by Christian missionaries. But these reports could do little more than excite the curiosity of an audience, as magic shows continue to do even in a scientific age. The Christians, however, appear not to have used miracles merely to astonish. The miracles of Jesus were reported in a way that managed to excite the whole person—intellectual, hedonic, and moral. The miracles of Jesus did excite curiosity, but they also had a didactic purpose that came to bear upon one's destiny (the ultimate hedonic appeal) and upon one's moral righteousness. This broader appeal elicited such depth of commitment among converts that the Christian community could produce the ultimate verification of its miracles—the witness of martyrs.

The ancient world was awash with accounts of miracles, and the typical method for judging their veracity was to consider the degree to which the miracles were believed by other individuals. The Christians believed the miracles of Jesus' life and the miracle of his resurrection to the point where they were prepared to die for their beliefs, as many did. And the fate of the martyrs in turn generated the fabrication of a secondary stratum of miracle stories surrounding the martyrs themselves, which had the effect of validating the martyrs' belief. In other words, there was a cascade of miracle traditions in the expansion of early Christianity. The blood of the martyrs, as Tertullian observed, was the seed of the church. The Christian myth appeared compelling precisely because of the extremes to which its witnesses were compelled. I am not suggesting here that a Christian cult of martyrdom was orchestrated as a grand deceptive scheme. The beliefs of the early Christians were completely sincere, and the willing sacrifices of the martyrs were certainly real. Indeed, in some locations the zeal for martyrdom was such a problem that church leaders, ironically, were moved to disabuse the faithful of their enthusiasm.44 Yet one has to wonder what the peculiar psychology of these willing martyrs was contributing to the mere hearsay evidence for miracles. It is not unreasonable that the expansion of Christianity at the end of the Roman period, and well into the Middle Ages, finds its best account in a contagion of self-deception.

Deceiving insiders

Shortly after Richard Nixon took office as president of the United States he sent a letter to the chairman of the Subcommittee on Information of the House Committee on Government Operations in which he said:

> I want to take this opportunity to assure you and your committee that *this Administration is dedicated to insuring a free flow of information to the Congress and the news media—and thus to the citizens.* You are, I am sure, familiar with the statement I made on this subject during the [1968] campaign. Now that I have the responsibility to implement this pledge, I wish to reaffirm my intent to do so. *I want open government to be a reality in every way possible.*45

Nixon's presidency proves that in this letter he was either insincere or naive. But whichever the case may have been, the same question emerges: Is it ever possible for leaders of comprehensive groups to succeed without employing strategies of deception against members of the group? Machiavelli did not think so: "A prince who wishes to achieve great things must learn to deceive."46 But however apt Machiavellian principles may be to *other* forms of government, there is widespread belief that the practice of deceiving insiders is inconsistent with the social coherence of a democratic state. In a democracy the public decides who will govern, and for the sake of wise choices the public needs accurate information—democracy cannot tolerate the manipulation of public perception by either evasion or perversion. A true democracy, then, asserts itself in opposition to Machiavellian principles of manipulation—at least in theory. But in practice there is no reason to believe that a democracy could survive guileless leadership any more successfully than other forms of government. The truth is that Machiavelli's descriptions of the dynamics of leadership apply even to those systems that abhor his prescriptions. In other words, it seems to be in the nature of leadership itself that effectiveness is contingent on the leader's ability to deceive in some measure those who are led. It may be true, as Lincoln observed, that leaders cannot survive by deceit alone, but it is equally true that if social coherence is to be maintained, then leaders must fool at least some of the people some of the time. I offer this hypothesis without any disrespect for political leadership, and with a fair amount of generosity regarding the motivations of political leaders themselves. They have the impossible task of building and maintaining confluences of interests among diverse groups of diverse individuals. I am only arguing that they cannot succeed without deceit.

The first order of business for any political leader is to ascend to a position of power. Machiavelli believed that it was impossible to do so without the use of either force or fraud or both. Political systems are distinguished by the ways in which their means of cooperation encourage one or the other. Democratic systems for determining leadership encourage deception. The principal task of any aspiring politician in a democratic system is to create the perception among voters that their interests will be better served by the candidate than by the opposition.

There are many honest and truthful ways to elicit positive responses from voters, but it has long been recognized that they are less effective then deceptive means. Exaggeration, distortion, quoting out of context, innuendo, false promises, pandering, scare tactics, and flat-out lies have become the standard fare of political campaigns. If democracy were truly inconsistent with deception, then how does it come to pass, one wonders, that election campaigns are dominated by it? It comes to pass because the political system rewards it. For a year and a half Richard Nixon vigorously but unsuccessfully opposed a bill granting the vote to eighteen-year-olds. But in the 1972 election his campaign ran an ad giving him credit for the legislation. Even more effective are the negative ads that deceptively exploit the fear and greed of voters. In the 1934 California gubernatorial race Republicans rented two thousand billboards which purported to quote Upton Sinclair, the democratic candidate: "If I am elected governor, half the unemployed in the country will hop the first freight to California—Upton Sinclair." Voters assumed that Sinclair himself bought the ads. A 1964 television ad for Lyndon Johnson showed a pretty young girl counting petals on a daisy. As she gets to ten the frame is frozen and a harsh male voice counts backward to zero, whereupon a nuclear blast overtakes the screen. At that point LBJ's voice says, "These are the stakes—to make a world in which all God's children can live or go into the dark. We must either love each other or we must die." The message was that a vote for Barry Goldwater amounted to a vote for death.[47] In 1988 George Bush's campaign ran the infamous Willie Horton ad, the subtext of which was that a vote for Michael Dukakis would release violent black rapists and murderers from jail to prowl the streets of American cities. Voters are generally opposed to such blatantly deceptive and predatory ads, yet they respond to them because the brain processes exaggerated negative information more deeply than accurate positive information.[48]

It would be a mistake to suppose that all political deceits are made to serve the narrow interests of self-aggrandizing politicians. In general, most politicians sincerely regard their own victory as a means to greater confluences of interests for the whole nation. But they also perceive that they cannot bring greater coherence to the nation without first getting themselves elected. And the surest way to do so is to deceive.

But how do leaders of comprehensive groups conduct themselves once they ascend to positions of power? Do they stash away their wiles until the next election, or is it also the case that deceptive strategies are essential to effective leadership? Before addressing this question we must find our way toward an understanding of leadership. In the first place, leadership involves the exercise of *power*. Power in interpersonal relations exists when the will of one person is exercised to determine the behavior of another. But power is not sufficient for leadership—a lone gunman in the town square certainly possesses power but does not thereby qualify as a leader. One becomes a leader when one's power is legitimate or sanctioned, so that compliance with the will of the leader is recognized as an obligation of followers. That is, a leader is invested with *authority,* or legitimate power. Leaders are elevated to positions of authority by the graces and resources of their power bases. Political authority may be defined as authority to act as a causal agent to determine the behavior of members of a comprehensive group. Leadership, then, may be defined as *the exercise of political authority to achieve the intended goals of the leader.* We may further say that the effectiveness of one's leadership is measured by the extent to which desired goals are achieved. James MacGregor Burns summarizes these ideas clearly: "Political leadership is tested by the extent of real and intended change achieved by leaders' interactions with followers through the use of their power bases. Political leadership is broadly intended 'real change.' It is *collectively purposeful causation.*"[49]

The critical idea here is that a leader will be effective only to the extent that the resources of a power base can be organized and mobilized in service to the leader's will. A power base will vary with respect to forms of social and political organization. In a chiefdom or a totalitarian state the power base may simply be an army. In a democracy the power bases are more complex, including party leaders, government officials, special-interest groups, the media, and ultimately a sufficient percentage of voters. So our original question (does effective leadership require deception?) is reduced to this: Is it possible to lead effectively without using deceptive strategies to organize and mobilize a sufficient power base?

F. G. Bailey answers this question with a resounding negative. He believes that the mark of an effective leader is the ability to command the willing service of followers through images that are rhetorically constructed: "Life in society involves power, and power involves persuasion, and persuasion in practical affairs where interests are at stake is not determined by dialectical reasoning, by logic but by its false equivalent, rhetoric. Rhetoric, moreover, is a form of deceit." Bailey argues that effective leadership depends upon trust, but the public trust has less to do with specific moral expectations than with a general and irrational devotion which, he says, is generated by rhetorical appeals:

> Leaders endeavor to create in the mass of their followers that nonspe-
> cific personal and direct form of trust which is akin to love and which
> prevents a close and impartial scrutiny and accounting of their perfor-
> mance, while not being seen openly to do so. The leader claims a per-
> sonal and direct moral relationship by two main rhetorical devices: the
> familial and the numinous.[51]

These devices, the familial and the numinous, correspond to public images cultivated by a leader's rhetoric. The familial style projects a leader
who is a nurturing member of the family, an elder kinsman who shares and
genuinely understands the challenges and frustrations of common people.
Especially important is the establishment of a moral bond between leader
and followers—the familial leader is cast in the mainstream of popular morality. Bailey says that the familial image excites a universal predisposition to
follow, an irrational tendency to trust and forgive the leader, as one might
have confidence in and make allowances for a family member. The numinous image, by contrast, excites devotion not by projecting the ordinary but
by constructing an extraordinary persona. The numinous leader is perceived
to be worthy because of exceptional fortitude, endurance, courage, and
determination—heroic virtues in abundant supply. Especially important to
the numinous style is the projection of a simplified yet grandiose vision of
the future, together with the impression that no other mortal is so uniquely
qualified to realize it. Both of these images seek to captivate a following by
triggering the irrational:

> The leader as numen is in some ways the mirror image of the familiar
> style. The latter emphasizes the everyday and the comprehensible.
> Numen, however, has a larger-than-life quality that belongs to the world
> of the sacred. . . .
>   Both the familial and the numinous styles are aimed at exciting devo-
> tion. Both, also, transcend rationality and reject calculation and account-
> ability. In the former case devotion is of the kind that exists between
> intimate friends and above all between kinfolk, who see and understand
> all about each other and are forgiving and trusting: it is not charisma.
> The numinous style has in addition a dimension of respect. There is no
> familiarity. The devotee does not expect to empathize, to see all and
> understand all, still less to forgive, for there is nothing to be forgiven.[52]

Ronald Reagan was a master at projecting the familial style. Garrison Keillor saw him as "the old masseur," always cultivating the image of kinship: "a genial uncle, the first one you'd want at your wedding to make a toast and charm the in-laws."[53] The numinous style was evident in the Kennedy mystique—transcendently wealthy, daring, heroic, visionary, an extraordinary figure who swept forward like a messiah to lead the country to greatness.

In addition to practicing the deception needed to project the imagery of leadership, leaders will find it in the public interest to withhold information and to circulate disinformation for public consumption. Consider, for example, covert intelligence operations (both foreign and domestic) that are conducted in the name of national security. It is also maintained that national security demands the withholding of certain technological information. Very often sensitive treaty negotiations must be kept from the public, if only to oblige other nations where secrecy in these matters is the norm. Wartime propaganda aimed at an adversary may entail deceiving the domestic public as well. When a nation is considering sweeping economic policy decisions (such as devaluing currency), forthright disclosure could lead to fiscal panic. There appear to be many situations in which "it seems to even the most intelligent and conscientious statesmen that the price of telling the truth, or not lying, is greater than can be borne."[54] In the course of many decisions to deceive or not to deceive, leaders of comprehensive groups actively shape the social reality which they find it in the collective interest for the collectivity to behold. Such is the very nature of power; and power is the essence of political life.

Therefore, to the extent that the social coherence of comprehensive groups is dependent upon effective leadership—which requires the group to grant its leader latitude to make personal judgments regarding the public interest—to that extent it is also dependent upon deception. As Bailey says, "Deception, at least in the mild form of withholding information, is a social and political necessity."[55]

A public's perception of its leadership is surpassed in importance only by that public's perception of itself. And this is so because what a mass responds to in its leaders is determined in subtle ways by the character of its collective *self*-understanding. And thus we are brought to consider the role of history in the achievement of social coherence. If social coherence depends in part on collective self-understanding, then collective self-understanding depends in part on perceptions of history. As Michael Kammen says, "An entire civilization may depend upon historical consciousness as its most vital mode of self-understanding."[56] The uses of history are manifold. Historical understanding frees us from certain conventions of the past and reaffirms our commitment to others. It guides us into the future by exposing the failures and triumphs of the past. It creates a sense of continuity, and thus solidarity, with a larger frame of reality. It orders that reality. It tells us who we are. As David Hume said, the chief use of history is to "discover the constant and universal principles of human nature." Historical perspective was probably not relevant to the social coherence of kinship bands, but in more complex forms of social organization what is known of the past becomes a powerful and indispensable means of cooperation. It is no exaggeration to say that confluences of interests are cast in the forge of collective memory.

And yet it may further be said that collective memory is constructed by a process of self-deception. We have already seen this to be the case with personal memory, which is influenced by the positive illusions of self-enhancing constructions and deconstructions. We could hardly expect a collective memory to be different. As Arthur Schlesinger, Jr., says, "The purpose of history is essentially therapeutic; to build a sense of self-worth."[57] The historical perspective of a social group will tend to be characterized by selective biases which expunge or deconstruct negative elements while preserving and embellishing (even fabricating) the positive. All perspectives on history are relative to the present—so much so that the past can scarcely ever be more than the present in disguise. And since the present is ever new, with its own climate of opinion and frame of reference, historical perspectives stand in constant need of revision. And when historians revise, they lay themselves open to the charge of manipulating the past to serve the present. Samuel Butler wrote, "It has been said that though God cannot alter the past, historians can; it is perhaps because they can be useful to Him in this respect that He tolerates their existence."[58] Historical understanding is not what it appears to be—that is, the adequation of a contemporary historian to the reality of the past. The historian is always contemporary and the evidences of the past are contemporary as well; they are the few vestiges of the past that have survived into the present. Thus historians must contend with special problems that necessarily compromise their objectivity. For one thing, the data that support historical reconstructions are lousy—always incomplete, often indirect, never replicable. In other words, the sources for a historical perspective are wide open to variations of evaluation and interpretation; so wide open, in fact, that historians themselves do not expect to be taken at face value. Jakob Burckhardt wrote that "in the wide ocean upon which we venture, the possible ways and directions are many and the same studies which have served for this work might easily in other hands not only receive a wholly different treatment but lead also to essentially different conclusions."[59]

Not only are the data lousy; their interpreters are likely to be heavily biased by a range of social and personal factors. Carol and Michael Kammen have considered various reasons why historians may be deluded into manipulating the past. Group chauvinism is perhaps the most common bias resulting in self-deceiving reconstructions of the past.[60] Chauvinism operates on various levels: national, regional, provincial, local, ethnic, and gender. In addition, the past is often manipulated to justify some present policy, as when pro-lottery researchers in New York found historic precedent for lotteries during the colonial period. Religious and ideological biases, too, influence the manner in which historians select, evaluate, and interpret data. Atheists and fundamentalists will come up with radically divergent historical perspectives, as will capitalists and socialists.

The result of all these factors is that perspectives on the past are necessarily specious; that is, they may appear to be plausible adequations to the reality of the past, but in fact they are thoroughly contingent caricatures—caricatures because of limitations on the data, and contingent because of limitations on the interpreters. This does *not* mean, however, that one is forced to agree with Henry Ford that "history is more or less bunk." Bunk is dispensable, historical perspectives are not. To the extent that a comprehensive group lacks historical perspective it lacks a vocabulary for achieving social coherence. Yet to the extent that it has such a vocabulary it is dependent in various ways upon the dynamics of self-deception.

Let us now consider sacred deceits upon members of comprehensive groups. Religious leaders have always understood (and correctly so) that the coherence of a society is dependent upon the broadly shared meanings of an integrative myth. If the shared meanings of a cultural myth lose their hold on the imagination of a social group, the social chaos of amythia will follow. In general, the deceits perpetrated by religious leaders upon their followers have been designed to avert amythia by maintaining the authority of the myth and its institutional infrastructure. These designs may be gathered in two main categories: those to *construct* the conditions for adherence to the myth and those to *deconstruct* the conditions for emergent rival authorities.

The Judeo-Christian tradition has thrived on a particular perception of its leaders; namely, that their authority is identical to the authority of a transcendent deity. God created the universe and is in control of its destiny. Therefore, authority of any sort whatsoever is ultimately derived from and must defer to the authority of God. God's authoritative word is made known to the world through various instruments of his choosing—that is, religious authorities. These religious authorities have been variously construed to be the Law, the prophets, the monarch, the Jewish priesthood, God's incarnate self (Jesus), his disciples, the priesthood they founded, and the sacred writings. Each of these agencies ostensibly exists in the natural world, but each claims the credentials to speak on behalf of the transcendent deity. And the strength of these claims has been maintained in part by the dynamics of deception and self-deception.

Much religious authority has been premised on biblical stories which appear to certify the status of certain figures as instruments of God's choosing. Moses, for example, is portrayed as having been chosen by God to bring the divine Law to the nation of Israel, and as a way of enhancing this claim many stories are told about Moses that would appear downright implausible without the supposition that he was an instrument of the deity. By the graces of the Pharaoh's daughter he narrowly escaped an Egyptian campaign to kill off male Hebrew children; God appeared to him in the form of a burning bush; he performed miraculous signs of his authority from God; he brought scourges upon the Egyptians; he led Hebrew slaves through a harrowing escape from bondage. And lots more. These stories about the wonderful deeds of Moses were not told for their entertainment value alone, much less to establish a Mosaic hero cult. They were intended to give credibility to the central claim that resounds over and over again throughout the Moses narratives: *The Lord spoke to Moses.* The stories were intended to excite listeners and to convince them that the Mosaic Law comes directly from God. We now know that many of these stories were the results of fabrication, embellishment, and simple plagiarism. The story of Moses in the bullrushes was told of Sargon the Great nearly twelve centuries before the time of Moses. Stories of gods appearing in fire and sending plagues were also common conventions in Near Eastern folklore, readily available for imitation and adaptation. In other words, the association of these wondrous events with Moses cannot be taken as genuine. Nevertheless, they were intended to be taken at face value; that is to say, they are deceptive. We cannot say whether the first tellers of these legends actually believed them or not, but if they did, they were deluded. As for the laws themselves, they were crafted by Hebrew leaders on the model of existing legal systems, entirely human in origin, yet presented as hand-delivered goods from God. To appreciate the value of these deceits one has only to ask the question that must have occurred at some level of awareness to Israel's religious leaders: What would it take to get these unruly and credulous people to accept a set of rules *without which* they would surely perish as a group? It would have taken exactly the kind of fantastic tales we find recorded in the Old Testament narratives. Those who heard the stories would have been awestruck by the accounts of numinous power, and in their astonishment they would perceive Moses as a figure possessed of divine authority. So the fictions were told as facts, and the group thrived.

The same effect underlies the claims of biblical prophets to be oracles of God. The prophets were undoubtedly convinced that they were genuine conduits of divine authority. It was typical of them to become lost in ecstatic trances wherein they would hear the voice of God. The certifying evidence in the case of prophets included miracles and marvelous forecasts of the future, but especially convincing were accounts of the circumstances under which they were called by God, and the spectacular visions they experienced in the process. Again, such accounts are better explained by the dynamics of self-deception than by history or theology. Nevertheless, the purpose of these visionary accounts was to excite the listener, and in so doing to create the perception that when the prophet prefaced moral and political imperatives with "thus saith the Lord," divine authority was assured.

The use of deceptive strategies to construct the perception of divine authority in the persons of religious leaders was continued in the New Testament period. We have already seen how the miracle stories attached to the person of Jesus together with the deceptive manipulation of Old Testament texts served to bolster the claim that "Jesus is Lord." Claims for the religious authority of Paul, too, have the taste of fabrication about them. Many members of the early Christian community considered Paul's teachings suspect because he was not among the special circle of apostles who had known Jesus directly. Some regarded him as a loose cannon who went about making up his own stylized version of the faith. The topic of credentials always has the effect of turning Paul defensive. Thus he attempts to establish his claim to authority by giving vague accounts of how Jesus appeared to him personally in a special revelation, thereby putting him on an equal footing with the other apostles.

He protests that he is teaching not on his own authority but on that of Christ himself: "I must make it clear to you, my friends, that the gospel you heard me preach is no human invention. I did not take it over from any man; no man taught it me; I received it through a revelation of Jesus Christ" (Gal. 1:11–12). Yet Paul gives us no details of this decisive revelation. What details we have come years later from the hand of Luke whose account of Paul's conversion is conveniently parallel to the commissioning of the prophet Ezekiel.[61]

The point of all this is to suggest that Paul's claim to authority has the appearance of being contrived. He was a peripheral figure in the Christian community, passionate and visionary about the church's mission, yet lacking the credentials that would give him recognition and influence. He needed those credentials. This is a hypothetical account (as all versions of Paul's conversion are), but it has the advantage of being consistent with anthropological accounts of peripheral groups for whom ecstatic religion functions as a strategy to short-circuit the established organization of power.[62] There was a payoff for Paul's "revelation" in terms of social coherence: Paul's authority was eventually recognized within the church, to the extent that his brand of spirituality became a model for conversion, a model that helped save the uncertain mission of early Christianity from extinction.[63]

Religious leaders have sometimes used deceptive strategies to manipulate popular piety, often with the result of enhancing social coherence. Surely this was never more true than it was during the period from late antiquity through the early Middle Ages. The popular piety of the early Middle Ages was dominated by a pervasive sense of evil. No sooner were the Christians freed from the fear of Roman persecution than they were subjected to the extreme hardships of a disintegrating social ecology. As the Roman Empire collapsed, a process of decivilization swept across Europe, wiping out established means of cooperation. Social chaos quickly translated into psychological chaos as individuals lost all sense of ability to control their own lives. An atmosphere of unpredictability, vulnerability, and gloom prevailed. This was no more clearly reflected than in the popular cosmology of late antiquity. Evil lurked everywhere in the cosmos; all the elements of nature were potential instruments of sinister powers that were hostile to humankind. The wind, the lightning, the moon, spiders, pigs, bulls, dogs, even birds—all of nature's forms were as likely as not to be possessed by malevolent agents. Nor was there the assurance of a merciful God. The prevailing image of God was that of a remote and vengeful judge who was prepared to use the instruments of nature to punish the sinful. And "the sinful" included just about everyone. The Lord himself had said that "many are called but few are chosen," and this saying was taken quite literally to mean that the vast majority of men and women were ultimately destined for hell. These were the conditions of desperation. The daily lives of individuals were exposed to overwhelming and unpredictable hostile forces, offset only by the horrible prospect of eternal torment. It was under these fatalistic conditions that Christianity, at the level of popular piety, became a cult of saints.

Completely powerless against the forces of doom, individuals sought to protect themselves by association with the merits of those souls whom they knew to be among the chosen few—that is, the martyred saints. The saints surely had God's favor, for they had fought the battle against evil and had prevailed. The belief spread abroad that the physical remains of saints had intrinsic powers of holiness that could be transferred to those who venerated them in faith. By ritual association with holy relics, then, a believer might gain sufficient strength to resist evil and enter into a state of grace. Burial sites of saints became the nuclei around which public worship was conducted and around which villages grew. The tomb of the saint was declared public property, accessible to all, and a focal point for the whole community. The relics of saints provided the basis for new means of cooperation. So important were relics to medieval piety that they became the defining feature of the Christian faith: "Wherever Christianity went in the early Middle Ages, it brought with it the 'presence' of the saints . . . late-antique Christianity, as it impinged on the outside world, *was* shrines and relics."[64] Most of the relics venerated in the fourth century were the remains of local martyrs who had died in the final wave of Roman persecution. By the early fifth century, however, the demand for relics had gone upmarket as reports circulated about remains from more distinguished saints, such as the head of John the Baptist and the body of St. Stephen. Response to the "discovery" of these relics was so intense that even more spectacular finds followed: the staff of Moses, manna from the wilderness, the bodies of Samuel the prophet, St. Peter, St. Paul, Mary Magdalene, hanks of hair from the Virgin Mary, vials of her milk, blood from the birth of Jesus, pieces of the cross, the crown of thorns, Jesus' milk teeth, his umbilical cord, the foreskin from his circumcision, and so on. The only limitation on discoveries appears to have been the imagination of the discoverer. Inevitably, of course, problems of duplication arose. At least three churches claimed to have the head of John the Baptist, and eventually there were enough fragments of the cross about to build a battleship, and enough of the Virgin's milk to sink it. Questions of authenticity arose, only to be settled by the validation of bishops, reports of related miracles, or some satisfactory "explanation." How did Mary Magdalene's body come to be buried in France? Easy; she went there after Jesus' death to expiate her sins. How could there be so much wood from the cross? Easy; the holy cross (like Jesus' love) does not diminish by subtraction. One could lay to rest any doubts about the authenticity of a relic by fabricating or even provoking a miracle. In the ninth century the bishop of Friesing stopped doubts about a relic of St. Felix by making the clergy of his diocese fast until the relevant validating visions occurred. Moreover, doubts were generally discouraged by stories of misfortunes that befell those who scoffed at relics.[65]

It is difficult to say how much of the hoopla over relics was generated by outright fraud and how much by the phenomena of self-deception. A measure of each, no doubt. But the significance of these deceits for the establishment of Christian culture in Europe is hard to question. Local communities crystallized around their relics, which became sources of public pride as well as personal piety. Interest in the lives of saints provided a base for moral instruction by the clergy. Relics provided stimulation for the building of churches and monuments, resulting in the development of skills and industries. The economic growth and security of many towns could be directly attributed to the remains of their saints. The veneration of relics was the inspiration for pilgrimages, and pilgrimages became sources of social coherence. Victor and Edith Turner surmise that "the crisscrossing of pilgrimage ways formed by these devotions of international repute must have had bonding effects on the entire sociocultural system of Christendom."[66] The cults of the saints played a decisive role in the growth of cities, the development of marketing systems, the building of roads, and the exchange of ideas. To the extent that one ignores the cults of the saints, one ignores the principal social dynamic of Europe's recivilization.

We have seen that religious leaders occasionally use deceptive strategies to construct the perception that their own assertions of human authority carry with them the strength of divine authority. And now we shall consider a final example of how religious leaders have used deception deconstructively to preclude the conditions under which adherents to a religious myth might defect. They do so by deconstructing the authority of human resourcefulness. A fundamental hypocrisy is to be discovered here, in that religious leaders bedeck their own human authority in the guise of divinity while at the same time discrediting the human authority of their followers, not to mention their rivals. Consider the following passage in which Isaiah attempts to deconstruct the religious practices of a rival sect:

> A man plants a cedar tree and the rain makes it grow, so that later on he will have cedars to cut down; or he chooses an ilex or an oak to raise a stout tree for himself in the forest. . . . The one half of it he burns in the fire and on this he roasts meat, so that he may eat his roast and be satisfied; he also warms himself at it and he says, "Good! I can feel the heat, I am growing warm." Then what is left of the wood he makes into a god by carving it into a shape; he bows down to it and prostrates himself and prays to it, saying, "Save me; for thou are my god." Such people neither know nor understand, their eyes made blind to see, their minds too narrow to discern. Such a man will not use his reason, he has neither the wit not the sense to say, "Half of it I have burnt, yes, and used its embers to bake bread; I have roasted meat on them too and eaten it; but the rest of it I turn into this abominable thing and so I am worshipping a log of wood." He feeds on ashes indeed! His own deluded mind has misled him, he cannot recollect himself so far as to say, "Why! This thing in my hand is a sham." (Isa. 44:14–20 [New English Bible])

Here Isaiah is deploying a very rational argument to claim that since the idolators have constructed their gods by their own artifice, these gods have no authority. This practice of rationally deconstructing the authority of other gods represents a strong tradition throughout Judeo-Christian history. During the Roman period Christian theologians used similar arguments to debunk the authority of pagan deities, which they regarded as nothing more than human constructs. Yet whenever this same form of rational argument is aimed at the Judeo-Christian myth, we encounter the protest that the resources of human reason are irrelevant to matters of divine truth. That is, when it comes to rival myths, the powers of reason may be used to deconstruct their plausibility, but when it comes to the Judeo-Christian myth, it is *reason* that must be deconstructed.

The attempt to deconstruct the authority of human resourcefulness is clearly seen in the ways in which various religious leaders have promoted the notion of faith. The concept of faith has functioned to deconstruct human reason by encouraging the systematic self-deception of believers, with the end in view that they will continue to adhere to the myth. And adherence to the myth is, of course, the foundation of social coherence in a comprehensive group. Consider a few prominent examples. Abraham has been considered an exemplar of the religious life because he was a man of great faith. The test of his faith came when God instructed Abraham to sacrifice his son, Isaac. Nothing in the biblical account suggests that Abraham's compliance with this command would be anything but absurd. God had promised to make Abraham's descendants as numerous as the stars through his sole heir, Isaac. And yet this very promise was about to be undone by God's own command. Had this episode been a test in logic, God would have failed. Of course there is an unexpected happy ending, but the whole point of the story is to present Abraham as a virtuous servant because he consented to obey in spite of the absurdity inherent in the command. Another exemplar of the religious life is seen in the figure of Job. Job is initially presented as a good and faithful servant who has been justly rewarded for his righteousness with good health, progeny, and prosperity. But all of a sudden his family dies off, he loses his wealth, and he is stricken with disease. Job is dumbstruck. None of this makes any sense. He questions God about the justice of it all, having understood all along that the righteous would be blessed. But here is evidence of a righteous man suffering misfortune. After much debate with his friends, Job is encountered by God, who explains that God's ways of doing things are not to be questioned by the likes of Job. It was not Job's to reason why, it was his to do or die. The story emphasizes the point that human reason cannot fathom divine justice, and therefore the testimony of reason is to be disparaged.

St. Paul continues the theme in the New Testament. In his first letter to the Corinthians Paul writes,

> This doctrine of the cross is sheer folly to those on their way to ruin, but to us who are on the way to salvation it is the power of God. Scripture says, "I will destroy the wisdom of the wise, and bring to nothing the cleverness of the clever." Where is your wise man now, your man of learning, or your subtle debater—limited, all of them, to this passing age? God has made the wisdom of this world look foolish. As God in his wisdom ordained, the world failed to find him by its wisdom, and he chose to save those who have faith by the folly of the Gospel. Jews call

for miracles, Greeks look for wisdom; but we proclaim Christ—yes, Christ nailed to the cross; and though this is a stumbling-block to Jews and folly to Greeks, yet to those who have heard his call, Jews and Greeks alike, he is the power of God and the wisdom of God. Divine folly is wiser than the wisdom of man, and divine weakness stronger than man's strength. (1 Cor. 1:18–25 [New English Bible])

The point is unmistakable: The central content of Christian teaching defies the expectations shaped by the conventions of worldly wisdom, and by such standards the Christian proclamation appears absurd. But even more absurd is allowing oneself to be hindered by the wisdom of the world. Christians live by faith, not by reason. Tertullian carried the theme forward into the third century. He was upset by the disruptive influence of philosophical thought within the church. The reasoning of philosophers could only draw people away from pure doctrine, and ultimately would destroy the unity of the church. To preserve the coherence of the church reason must be ignored. Tertullian makes the point with characteristic hyperbole: "The Son of Man was crucified; I am not ashamed of it. And the Son of God died; it is by all means to be believed, because it is absurd. And he was buried and rose again; the fact is certain, because it is impossible."[67]

As if to outdo Tertullian's deconstruction of reason, Martin Luther offers this:

Contrariwise we, excluding all works, do go to the very head of this beast which is called Reason, which is the fountain and headspring of all mischiefs. For reason feareth not God, it loveth not God, it trusteth not in God, but proudly contemneth him. It is not moved either with his threatenings or his promises. It is not delighted with his words or works, but it murmureth against him, it is angry with him, judgeth and hateth him: to be short, "it is an enemy to God."[68]

Luther did not stop with reason. He also deconstructed the authority of religious leaders of his day. The only authority for Luther was the Bible. What human resources had to offer was nothing but trouble.

In each of these examples the authority of human resourcefulness is rejected in favor of faith, which is regarded as the chief virtue of the religious life. Faith here means the resolve to adhere to the myth in spite of anything that might be offered by reason or observation. Faith is not merely belief in what is unseen, it is refusal to see whatever might potentially challenge orthodox belief. It is the deliberate evasion of evidence. It is the elevation of credulity to the lofty status of virtue. It is systematic self-deception. And yet it must be said that this practice of faithful self-deception has helped to preserve the coherence of Christian culture by stalling out countless flirtations with doubt. One thinks of Pascal in this regard, and Kierkegaard, Tolstoy, William James, and who knows how many additional thousands, perhaps millions, of reconstructed believers.

The Moral Issue

The argument of this book so far has gone as follows: In chapter 1 I argued that the intellectual and moral traditions of Western culture (both religious and secular) have expressed an explicit and consistent bias against deceiving and being deceived. In chapter 2 I developed a general theory and typology of deception and argued that there has been an evolutionary bias in favor of deceptive traits. There I claimed that deception involves morphological and behavioral designs that defeat perceptual designs, with the result that "defeated" organisms are left or put in a state of disadequation of appearance (subjective state) to reality (objective world). I further argued that the phenomena of deception appear at every level in the organization of life, and that deception plays a fundamental role in the dynamics of evolution. In chapter 3 I argued that a person is a multidynamic set of motivational processes that can achieve optimal functioning (personal wholeness) only by harmonizing the inevitable conflicts between motivational systems. I further argued that, within limits, both deception and self-deception play important roles in this achievement. In this chapter I have argued that a society is an organized group of individuals having sufficient means of cooperation to establish sustainable confluences of interests; and further, that some of these means necessarily draw upon deceptive and self-deceptive strategies. Throughout the arguments of these chapters I have attempted to defer the moral issues raised by the phenomena of deception, focusing instead on descriptive accounts of history, evolution, personality, and sociality. Here, however, the deferment expires.

A colleague of mine has a theory about the allocation of resources involved in setting exams for students. The options are, she explains, (a) to devote the bulk of one's efforts to constructing an exam that can be graded expeditiously, and (b) hastily to construct an exam that requires long and laborious grading. In either case the evaluation of performance is demanding. The challenge of moral evaluation is not dissimilar. One might spend a great deal of effort elaborating the details of a complete and consistent moral system, whereupon moral issues might be resolved summarily, or one might proceed with a few general principles of the moral life, leaving the worry of interpretation and application to particular circumstances. The moral systems of scholastic thought give us examples of the former, while the ethics of utilitarianism exemplifies the latter. Again, in either case, the moral evaluation of behavior will be demanding. The following may be taken as a variation upon the utilitarian approach.

Emerging from the arguments of these chapters is the view that a certain amount of deception of the self and others is essential to the achievement of personal and social well-being, and thus to human survival. And if survival is prerequisite to the good life (as it must be in a naturalist view of humanity), then we must conclude that deception, too, is frequently among the many conditions of human excellence. But this is not the view that has dominated the intellectual and moral traditions of Western culture, which have taught that deception is always inimical to human excellence. There are problems with this dominant view, however, if one takes seriously what is implied by these chapters, which is that *adaptation to the world around is not to be equated with the adequation of appearance to reality*. That is, though truth and adaptivity overlap for the most part, they cannot be considered congruent. Thus we may assert, against the dominant view, that some truths may be maladaptive and some falsehoods may be adaptive, in the way seen in figure 4.1.

It is easy to see how these matters come to bear upon the moral life, for many circumstances will arise in practical affairs in which one will be forced to decide which value, truth or adaptivity, is the more sublime. If one values truth above adaptivity (as many nonnaturalists do), then one will be committed, on occasion, to defending truths and/or rejecting falsehoods to the detriment of personal wholeness and/or social coherence. But if one values adaptivity above truth, then there follows a commitment to abjure harmful truths in favor of adaptive falsehoods.

If one takes an adaptive view—which I associate with naturalist ethics—then the model diagrammed in figure 4.2 may be viewed as relevant to judgment of the moral worth of an act or rule. An act or rule may be judged to have moral worth to the extent that it (*a*) fosters personal wholeness among the majority of those affected by it *and/or* (*b*) fosters the coherence of associations of individuals. This model itself is simple and straightforward (like a hastily written exam), but it is extraordinarily difficult to apply in concrete circumstances. Too many relevant yet incalculable variables would have to be factored into the model to make it practicable for day-to-day moral decision making. In fact, for any given moral circumstance the same model might be used to justify radically different actions. But clearly a standard that is so thoroughly subjective in its applications is hardly an improvement on no standard at all. As a calculus for particular actions, then, the model will be even more cumbersome and indecisive than the utilitarian standard, which calls for a measure of the greatest happiness for the greatest number. The model *is* useful, however, as a guide for judging the moral worth of rules proposed for ingestion into the moral calculus of individuals. But in saying this I appear to have given the entire game over to those who value truth over adaptivity. For they may argue with great cogency that the adaptivity model

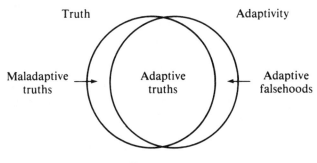

FIGURE 4.1

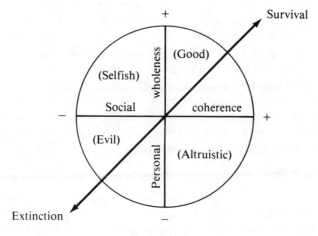

Figure 4.2

itself favors a rule for truthtelling over any alternative. And it does so, they will rightly argue, because in the majority of circumstances adequations of appearance to reality are adaptive. And it is indisputable, I think, that in the majority of cases personal wholeness and social coherence are better served by truth than by ignorance or falsehood. Thus we must agree that the adaptivity standard does favor a rule to bias moral decisions against deception. Nevertheless, it must be granted that the very same reasoning which favors a general rule for truthtelling may be used to justify exceptions to the rule. In other words, if one is faced with a situation in which telling the truth clearly bears against personal wholeness and/or social coherence, then one is justified in violating the rule by the same logic that endorsed the rule to begin with. Still, the burden of proof remains upon the choice to deceive.

Of course a nonnaturalist (a theist, perhaps) may seek to justify the rule for truthtelling on nonnaturalist premises, in which case the rule will not be negotiable even in extraordinary circumstances. In the face of such arguments the naturalist can only point out that the nonnegotiability of the rule can be no stronger than the nonnaturalist position itself—at which point the debate shifts its focus and questions arise as to whether or not the nonnaturalist position can be maintained without decisive feats of self-deception.

So where does this leave us? It leaves us in a position of sharing and defending a general preference for the truth, as best we can know it. And yet we are liberated from the view that truth is an end in itself. It is a means only, and as a means it is ennobled only by the ends it serves; which is to say that truth is a moral option, an option we must be prepared to forswear in favor of noble lies.

↜ 5 ↝

The Saving Grace of
Noble Lies

THE focus of this book is about to change. In the Introduction I indicated that the bulk of my argument would serve as a preface to a noble lie that might give us resources for reenchanting the universe despite the maladaptive truth of nihilism. Having done with the preface, we may now turn to the context and the substance of a noble lie for our troubled age.

AN AGE OF *KULTURKAMPF*

In 1864 Pope Pius IX issued the *Syllabus of Errors*, a document listing eighty propositions which he condemned as unacceptable to faithful Christians. The document amounted to a wholesale rejection of modernity and a stern call to the Roman Catholic laity to hold fast to the conventions of medieval piety. Five years later Pius called the First Vatican Council, which declared his authority over matters of doctrine to be infallible. Bismarck, ruler of the Prussian state, did not take kindly to these papal gestures. He viewed them as intolerable attempts by the church to influence the attitudes of the German citizenry. So Bismarck responded by enacting a wave of legislation intended to subvert the cultural influence of the church. Pius answered the challenge to his authority with anti-Prussian legislation of his own. This conflict between Bismarck and the Roman pontiff continued for nearly two decades, and has since come to be known as the *Kulturkampf* (culture war). At stake in the *Kulturkampf* was the mind of the German population; that is, which set of ideas (memes) would henceforth organize the consciousness of the German people?

Kulturkampf is a chronic condition of ideological struggle within human social groups. It is a characteristic of the species. Wherever human beings craft memes by which to organize themselves, there we will find competition among incompatible meanings. The condition is incurable. Nor is a cure even desirable, for it is the vigorous struggle of ideas that provides resources for adaptive change. A culture without *Kulturkampf* is moribund. This is not to say, however, that ideological struggles are necessarily benign. There are periods when the condition flares up and becomes more noticeable, periods when ordinary, low-level competition rises to the point of pitched battle between identifiable belligerents. Such was the case when Bismarck faced off against Pius IX in the 1870s. And when a *Kulturkampf* becomes intensified there is always the possibility that it cannot be resolved amicably, with the result that ideological warfare may give way to political and military struggles.

It is the judgment of many observers that the condition of contemporary Western culture is one of intensifying *Kulturkampf*. The term itself has crept back into public discourse, appearing in various books, op-ed articles, speeches, and conferences, to signal a growing sense that the Western mind is up for grabs. In this final chapter let us try to find our way to the deepest level of our current intellectual and moral crisis, and then see if we can find a way of thinking it through that may lead us in the direction of adaptive change. We may begin at the surface, by examining a particular and important episode in the contemporary cultural struggle to see who the belligerents are and what they are saying. This strategy, I hope, will enable us to follow the issues to a more fundamental philosophical level where we may begin to see the role of deception in charting a future course of adaptive change.

The Politics of Education

The competition between memes within a culture will take place primarily in those arenas where memes are publicly transmitted; that is, in books, newspapers, magazines, movies, and television, but especially in the schools. Indeed, it was a controversy over the clerical control of education that sent up the first sparks in the *Kulturkampf* of the 1870s. In our present struggle, too, a controversy has erupted over the content and character of the curriculum in American education. And as one might expect, the belligerents in the controversy break down into two camps: the liberals, who seek fundamental change, and the conservatives, who wish to maintain the status quo.

Let us begin by trying to characterize the status quo. Before the twentieth century less than 4 percent of young Americans attended college, and those who did encountered a classical curriculum that was inherited from European traditions. The primary focus of the classical curriculum was on humanistic studies; that is, ancient languages, history, literature, and philosophy. There was very little diversity in the curriculum and virtually no question of elective courses. The nineteenth century had witnessed an explosion of discoveries in the sciences, however, and as these new subjects found their way into the university, the curriculum came under pressure to diversify and specialize. By the turn of the century the exclusiveness of the classical curriculum had been overtaken by a new elective system. Driven by the ideal of progress and financed by influential industrialists, American universities became diverse, specialized, and utilitarian. The cohesiveness of the classical tradition was gone, and for the first two decades of the twentieth century the implications of the new specialization were worked out: faculties departmentalized, major and minor courses of study were defined, graduate and professional schools flourished, and larger numbers of students streamed into the system. By 1920 American universities had been transformed by growth, diversification, specialization, and professionalism into a new type of educational institution, utterly unlike their European forebears. The distinctive character of American life, with its emphasis on the practical, the immediate, and the democratic, had finally triumphed over the soul of the academy, virtually wiping out the humanistic emphasis of the old curriculum.

But soon enough there was a reaction against the excess of freedom and lack of direction in the elective system, a system that many people thought undermined the very concept of a liberally educated person. By 1920 a "general education" movement was emerging, nourished by those who aspired to gain back at least a measure of the classical ideal of learning. The hope of traditional humanists was to balance the pluralism and specialization of the new elective system with the breadth and coherence of learning typical of the old classical curriculum. The model for compromise was provided by a new course developed at Columbia University. In 1918 Columbia, along with a few other universities, designed a course at the request of the U.S. State Department that was intended for American soldiers bound for service in World War I. This "War Issues" course would acquaint soldiers with "the European heritage in whose defense they were soon to risk their lives."[1] In 1919 the Columbia faculty adapted this survey of Western civilization and made it the core of a general education program which was to become a model for colleges and universities across the country. Around such core courses there assembled a canon of standard texts selected from the old classical tradition. In American higher education the period between the wars was one of academic consolidation around a core curriculum with a canon of texts. For a full two generations there persisted a remarkable equilibrium in the American curriculum, celebrating a core and a canon which together represented a fair sampler of the old humanistic tradition, that which Matthew Arnold had praised as "the best that has been thought and written."

To many observers the new core curriculum represented the perfect compromise. Students could still specialize within particular disciplines enabling them to take positions in the increasingly professional workplace, yet there was a sufficient veneer of the humanistic tradition to ensure that American culture would retain an essential continuity with its European heritage. Such a veneer, it was hoped, would nourish intellectual and spiritual resolve against the threats of undemocratic ideologies. The core curriculum was the status quo when the issues of the 1960s started to erupt.

Our age of *Kulturkampf* began to sort itself into opposing camps just as the paint was drying on the compromise curriculum of liberal arts education. The years following World War II were to bring forces of social change to bear upon the universities once again in such a way that the core curriculum would lose ground. The postwar population increase and the availability of financial aid brought an unprecedented number of students onto college campuses. In the 1960s student enrollment nearly doubled. An increase in diversity was apparent, too, as lower-income students, minorities, and women began to break through the barriers of exclusion. The Cold War emphasis on science and technology heightened the need for research programs and engineers.

Advances in medicine created demands for new programs for health professionals. And the proliferation of subdisciplines in science called for fundamental changes in undergraduate education.

Such factors exerted both internal and external pressures, forcing colleges
and universities to rethink the status quo. Government, business, industry,
and students were each placing demands upon universities to make the curriculum more relevant to their needs. And the needs were, once again, for greater
specialization and diversification. The cumulative effect of these demands was
to erode the core curriculum, which appeared to many faculties as a dispensable luxury to be weighed against the utility of expanding scientific and professional programs. And to an increasing number of students the core and canon
of the liberal arts curriculum were even worse than a luxury, they were instruments of social and psychological oppression.

As the campuses became more diverse in ethnic background, gender, and
social class, it was inevitable that questions would arise about lack of diversity in the content of the core curriculum. African-Americans asked why
there was no mention of the role of blacks in American history, and why no
black writers were featured in the canon. Women wondered about the systematic exclusion of the role of women. Similar queries came from Native
Americans and Latinos. Queries translated into requests and then into demands for new courses and new faculty to enable students to explore aspects
of the nondominant culture to which they could personally relate. The academic community responded paternalistically, by adding a few peripheral
courses in the hope that the whining voices would go away. But the voices
did not exactly go away—instead, they developed into a strident and comprehensive critique of the academy and the dominant culture in general. And
the critique was followed up by a determined effort to "liberate" liberal
learning by dismantling the core and canon of the status quo, and by radically transforming the curriculum.

The liberal critique, as it was articulated in the 1970s and 1980s, may be
summarized as follows: The traditional core and canon of the liberal arts curriculum presented a deeply biased, distorted, and chauvinistic version of Western civilization. It was *biased* in its exclusive focus on the cultural contributions
made by white, European males of the privileged class. It was *distorted* because
it told only part of the story, leaving out significant contributions made by
women, non-Anglo ethnic groups, people of color, and those of the middle and
lower classes. And it was *chauvinistic* because it treated the contributions of
white upper-class European males as norms by which the contributions of all
other culture bearers were judged inferior or deviant. Our culture, the liberal
argument says, is far more rich and complex than the Eurocentric, sexist/
heterosexist, racist, and classist version of it that has been ensconced in the
traditional core and canon. A culture is what it is because of the *full range* of its
experience and creations, and because of *all* of the traditions that bear them.
Surely, privileged white European males have made contributions to Western
culture, but they are not the only ones, and their contributions are not inherently more valuable than those of, say, black women of the slave class. These

women had experiences too, and they created meanings, and they transmitted culture. To say they didn't is patently false, and to devalue their experience and their expressions as trivial according to a "higher" standard amounts to an act of hostility against race, class, and sex. To say that American culture would not be what it is without the thoughts and deeds of privileged European males is a truism. But it is just as true that American culture would not be what it is without the thoughts and deeds of African-American, Native American, Asian-American, and Latino-American men and women. American culture is what it is because of the thoughts and deeds of all those Americans who have thought and done. To single out one thread of a complex culture as its definitive heritage is to distort history, and to value that thread above others, either morally or aesthetically, is to assume that moral and aesthetic standards are not culturally determined. And to act on that assumption is an intolerable gesture of political violence.

According to the liberal argument, the traditional core curriculum has been both historically inaccurate and politically hegemonic. The reform program that follows from this argument has called for a radical transformation of the liberal arts curriculum. The transformation does not stop with a token recognition of cultural diversity. Rather, writes Johnnella Butler, "it demands that we do something with these experiences, this diversity, in order ultimately to understand the whole. It demands that we add, delete, decenter, re-vision and reorganize in order to transform our curricula to reflect a kind of unity, a wholeness that is all-inclusive in its content, methodology, and pedagogy."[2] The implications of this decentering program are profound. The historical experience and the cultural achievements of the dominant Euro-American tradition (e.g., in art, music, literature, philosophy, religion, morality) are to be reduced to subcultural status. It is not that the great "classics" of the Western world cannot be studied anymore, just that they should no longer have a privileged place in the curriculum in relation to other elements in this highly pluralistic culture. The definitive character of American culture is not its Euro-American heritage; rather, its definitive character is its astounding diversity of race, gender, class, color, ethnic background, and historical experience. The curriculum for a liberal education should represent all of this diversity; that is, it should be thoroughly inclusive and multicultural. Anything less would be intellectually irresponsible, politically divisive, and pragmatically inappropriate for the pluralistic future. This liberal agenda presents a radically new conception of a liberally educated person, and as the agenda was applied to college and university curricula in the 1970s and 1980s the traditional core and canon of the liberal arts began to erode.

A conservative reaction to such an "irreverent" agenda was inevitable, and by the mid-1980s the curricular *Kulturkampf* was in full swing. The most highly publicized and influential conservative voices have been those of William Bennett and Allan Bloom. The gist of their reaction has been to reassert the ideals of the traditional core and canon as essential to the fabric of a free and moral society. William Bennett's 1984 report to the National Endowment for the Humanities opens with a revealing quote from Walter Lippmann: "Our civilization cannot effectively be maintained where it still flourishes, or be restored where it has been crushed, without the revival of the central, continuous and perennial culture of the Western world." Bennett's fear is that Western culture is in danger of being crushed by the loss of "the best that has been said, thought, written, and otherwise expressed about the human experience."[3] He stresses the point that some things are more important to know than others, and the most important things to know are what certain "great souls" have expressed in the "landmarks of human achievement" that "define the development of the Western mind." Bennett's list of the great souls with which every liberally educated person communes is a sampler from the traditional canon. To replace these landmarks of human thought in the name of diversity is to forsake the essential legacy of Western culture. More than anything else *they are* Western culture. While affirming diversity, Bennett rejects the notion that the traditional core is either ethnocentric or chauvinistic:

> The solution is not a return to an earlier time when the classical curriculum was the only curriculum and college was available to only a privileged few. American higher education today serves far more people and many more purposes than it did a century ago. Its increased accessibility to women, racial and ethnic minorities, recent immigrants, and students of limited means is a positive accomplishment of which our nation is rightly proud. . . . But our eagerness to assert the virtues of pluralism should not allow us to sacrifice the principle that formerly lent substance and continuity to the curriculum, namely, that each college and university should recognize and accept its vital role as conveyor of the accumulated wisdom of our civilization.
>
> We are a part and a product of Western civilization. That our society was founded upon such principles as justice, liberty, government with the consent of the governed, and equality under the law is the result of ideas descended directly from great epochs of Western civilization— Enlightened England and France, Renaissance Florence, and Periclean Athens. These ideas, so revolutionary in their times yet so taken for granted now, are the glue that binds together our pluralistic nation. The fact that we as Americans—whether black or white, Asian or Hispanic, rich or poor—share these beliefs aligns us with other cultures of the Western tradition. It is not ethnocentric or chauvinistic to acknowledge this. No student citizen of our civilization should be denied access to the best that tradition has to offer.[4]

Allan Bloom's best-selling book, *The Closing of the American Mind* (1987), bears none of Bennett's conciliatory rhetoric. It is a caustic and impassioned indictment of the university's role in creating "an intellectual crisis of the greatest magnitude" by relinquishing its responsibility to assert claims for cultural superiority.[5] Bloom's veneration for human culture was profound, bordering on the religious. Culture is the source of human dignity, it is "everything that is uplifting and edifying" about us. As natural beings humans aren't much, but as products and producers of culture humans become capable of selfhood and community. Personal wholeness and social coherence are possible only because of culture. Even though Bloom believed it was difficult to discern exactly what defines a culture, he was careful to distinguish it clearly from nature and from the state. But at the same time he associated it closely with the conventions of art that bind a people into a unity. At the heart of Bloom's critique of liberalism is his insistence upon a radical distinction between culture and society. Beasts can be social, but only humans possess culture. And it is on this very point that we can appreciate Bloom's deep disdain for the open and inclusive nature of liberal society. Liberal society is an enemy of culture, and thus the enemy of humanity. Society, especially liberal society, is cheap—you can have a society on nature's terms. But culture is an expensive endeavor, it is an achievement, the result of high aspiration and hard work. One can belong in liberal society by default, but belonging to a culture requires the sacrifice of remaking oneself. Liberal society is a mere accidental collection, but culture is a distinctive and determined assembly; a society is a cacophony, culture is a chorus. Thus Bloom's revulsion against "low" culture: it is the profane, untamed, unearned expression of human nature, whereas "high" culture is refined: "A culture is a work of art, of which the fine arts are the sublime expression."[6] Bloom did not soften his rhetoric, as Bennett did, to escape the charge of chauvinism. For Bloom, culture is by its very nature chauvinistic. Indeed, cultures come to *be* only by the hard process of exclusion. For Bloom, the very idea of multiculturalism was oxymoronic. True culture does not tolerate liberal society's easiness with particularity and difference, it aspires to universality and the conquest of differences.

The capitulation of Western culture to the slough of liberal culture was to be seen most dramatically in the American university. In a prolonged state of self-doubt American faculties caved in under the demands of radical individualism in the 1970s, leaving nothing but a supermarket of mediocrity in place of the core and canon of the humanizing tradition. And with the demise of the Great Books there arose the specter of illiteracy and barbarism. The barbarians of our age are the academics who have relieved the university of its costly duty to civilize young people by reshaping them, together with the misshaped youths themselves who have been dispossessed of their legacy. Bloom, like Bennett, had not given up all hope of restoring this legacy. Despite the scourges of liberal society, the embers of culture remain: "The books in their objective beauty are still there, and we must help protect and cultivate the delicate tendrils reaching out toward them through the unfriendly soil of students' souls."[7]

Conservatives accuse liberals of politicizing the curriculum; liberals say the curriculum has always been, essentially is, political. Liberals charge that the curriculum is racist; conservatives point to the reverence W. E. B. Du Bois and Martin Luther King had for the classics. Conservatives claim that the liberal agenda waters down the curriculum; liberals say there is no substance without diversity. Liberals deride the chauvinism of highbrow culture; conservatives point to the empirical test of time. Conservatives berate liberals for having disrespect for the past; liberals have disrespect for the conservative berating of the present. Conservatives complain that the liberal agenda will undermine democracy; liberals say their agenda is the embodiment of democracy. For the most part, it has been an engaging and lively debate, and there are no clear signs that it will soon end. After all, the stakes are about as high as they can get, for what could be of more consequence to a culture than the memes that are selected for transmission to its next generation?

The philosophical dimensions of the debate become clear as we discover what it is each camp most fears about the implications of the opposing agenda. The conservatives have defended the traditional core and canon as the best of human guides through a thicket of perennial questions and on toward the clearing of truth. The classics have struggled with all the key questions of human existence, and they have made some indisputable gains. Indeed, the traditional canon is a repository of truth. But the liberal agenda's endorsement of radical cultural pluralism is in effect an endorsement of relativism, the view that truth is a variable of time and circumstance, that it is no more than an enhanced version of opinion, something to be made up and not discovered or revealed. But if truth is mere opinion, then moral virtue is mere convention, or worse, political power. Such, say the conservatives, is the road to barbarism. The liberal agenda affirms pluralism, which implies relativism, which descends into the vulgarities of nihilism, wherein the exclusive virtues are force and guile. The specter of nihilism is the ultimate fear of the conservatives, as M. H. Abrams makes clear:

> A specter is haunting this discussion of the philosophy of the curriculum—the specter of nihilism. We humanists are forever embarrassed at the uncertainty of our conclusions, whereas the logicians and the mathematicians can define precisely the validity of their inferences. We can never, alas, determine absolutely the truth or falsity of any proposition about history, nor of any interpretation of literature, nor of any evaluation of art. Therefore [it is implied] anything goes![8]

The ultimate fear in the liberal camp is tyranny and oppression. The relativity of truth, goodness, and beauty is a fact of life, to be denied at great peril. A single, privileged vision of truth or value is always someone's limited version of it. To impose a final version of truth and value is ultimately to create victims. And the only way to prevent that is to legitimize a plurality of truths. Truth is always politicized—to have an absolute truth is to have an absolute political order, and *that* is tyranny, to be maintained only by intimidation, deceit, and naked power: "After all," writes Benjamin Barber, "it was the tyranny of 'Truth' politicized that justified the divine right of kings, the Inquisition, the Reign of Terror, and such modern orthodoxies as totalitarianism."[9]

I have found it impossible to align with either side in this contemporary debate, for the simple reason that I find the negative arguments on both sides compelling and the positive agendas on both sides repulsive. This is the hapless condition of an undecided voter in a two-party system, wishing a third candidate would appear to combine the strengths and avoid the weaknesses of the choices on offer. I believe there is a third viable option in the wings that might be brought forward after we examine the negative arguments of both sides at closer range and at the level of their philosophical principles.

The Philosophy of Culture

I have focused at some length on the contemporary crisis within higher education because I take it to be emblematic of a much deeper philosophical crisis having to do with the foundations of human culture. In our discussion of the politics of education (i.e., the battle over the content and character of the curriculum) we have been well served by the labels "liberal" and "conservative." These labels may be somewhat misleading in a general discussion of philosophy of culture, so I will trade them in for a new set of labels to describe what I regard to be two important and basic perspectives on the nature of culture. One position argues against the theoretical plausibility of all claims to validate any universal vocabulary or myth or worldview proposed as a unifying foundation for culture. The other position argues against the practical possibility of achieving any tolerable form of human existence apart from such a foundational myth or vocabulary. It should be clear that whatever labels we attach to these positions will lack the symmetry connoted by "liberal" and "conservative" at the level of debates over the curriculum. Both positions offer negative arguments, but they are asymmetrical in the sense that the first is theoretical and the second is practical.

Now the labels. To characterize the first position I will use the term "postmodernism," an all-purpose label describing a general intellectual orientation that has emerged in Western culture over the past two centuries. "Postmodernism" has been applied vaguely to developments in art and literature, but the term finds its most precise meaning with reference to philosophy since the Enlightenment. I will use the term "adaptivism" (ugly, I agree) to characterize the second position. Postmodernism bears negatively upon the theoretical plausibility of universal mythmaking, while adaptivism bears negatively upon the practical implications of amythia. My purpose is to put both of these negative arguments in a positive light; that is, I find both of them agreeable.

Postmodernism

In the negative sense, postmodernist philosophy can be described as a thorough rejection of the entire Western philosophical program extending from the pre-Socratic philosophers of ancient Greece right through the philosophers of the Enlightenment. In essence, postmodernist philosophers view this long tradition as being dominated by the quest for ultimate foundations. From the beginning of the Western tradition philosophers were impressed by a sense that permanence and order were intelligible behind the apparent changes known to experience. To describe the conditions of this intelligibility was to achieve the ultimate human adequation to reality. In the history of this foundational tradition there have been two general orientations, metaphysical realism and epistemological realism. The metaphysical orientation attempted to formulate the foundations of intelligibility by describing the ultimate features of reality outside the experiencing subject. That is, order and regularity are to be found in human experience because there are permanence and order "out there" in the real world. One thus becomes adequated to reality by conforming the instrument of intelligibility (the mind) to the object of intelligibility (the world out there). The knowing subject conforms to the known object by formulating the ultimate categories of external reality. Various metaphysical categories of substance, process, and form were proposed to describe the ultimate foundations for intelligibility. Some pre-Socratic philosophers described the ultimate foundations as an eternal material substance. Others proposed a rational cosmic process, and still others proposed the existence of absolute forms. Plato's metaphysical system postulated an eternal realm of rational forms that were approximated in the realm of sensible objects. As the intellect discerned these forms, the knower became adequated to the known. Aristotle combined the categories of matter, process, and form in his concept of substance, conceived as matter in the process of progressive formation. St. Thomas attached Artistotle's metaphysical scheme to the Christian proclamation by declaring that the ultimate goal of the Aristotelian process was the perfection of nature by grace. Postmedieval philosophers were preoccupied with reinterpreting the ancient doctrine of substance to make it compatible with the findings of the new science. In all of these attempts we find a consistent function for philosophic discourse: to come up with a final and universal vocabulary that is adequate to the ultimate conditions of constancy in the extramental world out there.

David Hume delivered a decisive blow to this program of metaphysical realism by demonstrating that there are no grounds in reason or in sense experience to compel one's adherence to any metaphysical formulations about the world out there. We are never able to get out there to see whether our formulations about the world are adequate or not. The whole idea that one can escape experience in order to validate one's inferences from experience to reality was, Hume thought, misguided. We are imprisoned in a realm of experience, even though what happens "in here" may tempt us to infer certain things to be the case out there—there *must be* some permanent substance, or some enduring forms, or some cosmic process, or some intelligent deity out there. But despite the strength of our temptations to formulate inferences, nothing can change the fact that they are just that—mere inferences. And nothing can change the fact that we have no means by which to certify their adequacy, unless, of course, one is prepared to accept the authority of additional inferences. But where do we get ourselves by creating hierarchies of uncertifiable certifiers? Certainly we do not get beyond the inferences themselves to some sort of transcendent foundations. So Hume concluded that there were no certain grounds under any proposed philosophical formulations about the way things really are. Indeed, we cannot even know that an extra-experiential world exists out there, let alone have the assurance that our inferences about its essence are adequate. Hume acknowledged that some profound psychological needs may be driving our inferences from experience to reality, but this state of affairs only forces the admission that our formulations say more about the knower than about the known.

Hume appeared to have undermined the entire program of the foundational tradition, leaving no recourse for deciding whether any particular formulation about the world out there was more or less adequate than any other formulation. In the wake of Hume's devastating critique of metaphysics, Immanuel Kant attempted to restore the integrity of the foundational tradition. He was stunned by Hume's conclusion that no vocabulary for adequating appearance to reality could be known to be better or worse than any other vocabulary. This conclusion, he saw, would have the effect of relativizing the authority of the scientific enterprise. So he set about to achieve a "Copernican revolution" by which he proposed to reorient the foundational tradition on epistemological grounds.

Kant was disturbed, and rightly so, by the relativizing influence of Hume's skepticism. If we have no direct access to what is out there, then we have no means for claiming our knowledge or values to be objective or universal; thus universal knowledge claims have no foundation. But Kant couldn't give up his deep conviction that universal claims were possible. What, then, was their foundation? His answer was that the mind, the apparatus of knowing, gave us the ultimate conditions for intelligibility. Objective and universal knowledge does not result from the conformity of the mind to the true categories of an external reality (as all previous philosophy held); it results rather from the process by which reality becomes conformed to the ultimate categories of the mind. Adequation of appearance to reality is achieved by our rational manipulation of raw sense data to fit the terms of the intellect. Kant was not worried about Hume's suggestion that knowledge claims reveal something about the knower. In fact, he makes it the centerpiece of his new foundational philosophy. The foundation of knowledge claims was not the extramental reality out there but rather the mental reality in here. What gives grounding to objective and absolute knowledge is just that we all share the same uniformly constructed instrument of knowing; that is, we all have the same built-in categories of sensation and understanding. Differences between alternative formulations of knowledge are not, therefore, unresolvable subjective differences, as would be the case under Hume's relativism. Conflicting accounts of experience may be resolved by proper use of the instrument of reason.

Hume dealt a severe blow to foundationalism by denying the objective adequation of mind to reality. Kant restored foundationalism by asserting the objective adequation of reality to mind. The intellectual developments of the nineteenth and twentieth centuries, however, were to undermine Kant's epistemological foundations just as decisively as Hume had undermined metaphysical foundations. The Kantian instrument of knowing, it turns out, is not so uniformly constructed as Kant supposed it was. That is, the developments of the past two centuries have demonstrated that the reality in here is relative to time and circumstance.

One major development of the nineteenth century supporting this conclusion was the emergence of historicism. Briefly, historicism is the view that meanings are relative to the historical conditions that bring them forth. Thus, for any formulation of truth or value one must suppose that concrete circumstances were conspiring to produce it in the particular manner in which it was produced. If the circumstances had been otherwise, then the formulation might have been vastly different in form and content, or might not have been called forth at all. The forms of understanding and the forms of expression are shaped and reshaped as historical circumstances change, so the reality of mind is not historically constant, as Kant assumed. The emergence of sociology and anthropology since the nineteenth century have made it just as clear that the forms of experience and expression are relative to social, political, and economic circumstances as well. The influences of one's race, class, gender, and political environment have a way of shaping the categories of intelligibility in ways that Kant could not have foreseen. These factors, as well as the time factor, deabsolutize the reality in here. Nor was Kant able to appreciate the extent to which the semantics and syntax of one's language condition what the knowing instrument is equipped to perceive and to think. Recent developments in linguistics have helped us to see both how extensively our thinking is shaped by language and how vastly different language systems can be. Moreover, one of the principal lessons of modern psychology has been that experiences are shaped by experiences. That is, individuals of the same age, sex, race, class and language group may be expected to perceive and to reason in diverse ways that reflect their diverse experiences.

As one begins to assemble the implications of the past two centuries, the epistemological foundations proposed by Kant begin to crumble. Kant believed that humans tend to interpret the meanings of their experiences in common terms because they all share the same absolute categories of interpretation. But this is not completely the case, contemporary psychobiology notwithstanding. Our interpretations vary enormously in accordance with a wide range of particular factors. In other words, the reality in here is highly relative and not the secure foundation for absolute knowledge that Kant supposed.

Postmodernism is a philosophical orientation that rejects the dominant foundational program of the Western tradition. It pronounces metaphysical realism dead with Hume's critique, and it pronounces epistemological realism dead with the emergence of the social sciences. We simply cannot have what foundationalism tried to give us—that is, a final vocabulary for speaking publicly and with assurance about truth and value. There are no absolute truths and no objective values. There may be local truths and values around, but none of them has the endorsement of things as they really are. All vocabularies for speaking of truth and value are contingent. All interpretations of the meaning of things are caricatures; there are no uninterpreted meanings. Foundational philosophy, as a genre, is defunct. God is dead, Zeus is toppled. Contingency reigns. There are no external winching posts for bringing the self into adequation with the world, and there are no internal winching posts for bringing the world into conformity with the self. If it is winching posts we seek, then we haven't taken the past two hundred years seriously. There is no Ur-language, there are no original meanings. All meanings are rooted in contextual soils, nourished by other meanings. There are no certified certifiers, only hierarchies of inference, without end. There is no right or wrong way to behold the world or ourselves. Any beholding can be made to look bad by an alternative beholding. There is no right or wrong way to live; there are only alternative ways. There is no correct reading of a text or a picture or a dance. Whatever meanings a speaker intends necessarily defer to the meanings a listener infers. As for reality itself, it does not speak to us, does not tell us what is true or good or beautiful. The universe is not itself any of these things, it does not interpret. Only we do, variously.

Postmodernism does not disallow the holding of beliefs about the meaning and value of things, it only disallows claims for their orthodoxy. Orthodoxy is the only heresy. Postmodernism is the very antithesis of the idiom of myth as I described it in chapter 4. *It articulates the skeptical doctrine of amythia.* There can be, it says, no final cosmology, no final economy, and no final morality. And above all, there can be no final narrative integration of these domains. The very idea of a metanarrative is anathema. Even to propose categories for describing the ultimate domains of human interest is to give way to the error of foundationalism. And to propose that personal wholeness and social coherence can have a single narrative source is to run straight against the grain of postmodernist philosophy. Richard Rorty, the leading American postmodernist, addresses this issue directly in his influential book *Contingency, Irony, and Solidarity*: "This book tries to show how things look if we drop the demand for a theory which unifies the public and the private, and are content to treat the demands of self-creation and of human solidarity as equally valid, yet forever incommensurable."[10] If the separation of church and state had the effect of divorcing therapy and politics in practice, Rorty wants to ratify the divorce in theory.

This, then, is the postmodern perspective. It amounts to a radical skepticism about any public philosophy or mythology. It rejects all descriptions of the way things really are as contingent pretenders to objective truth. If individuals need myth and philosophy in order to describe themselves, then fine. They are free to pursue personal wholeness by whatever meanings they find suitable. Go ahead, be a Platonist or a Hegelian or a Christian. But such vocabularies describing the way things really are must not enter into the public domain, where they have the audacity to define others. Individuals want to define themselves and they should be free to do so. If we need a vocabulary for social cooperation, then let it be one that abstains from universal definitions and theories. Personal wholeness is one thing, social coherence is another; they are "equally valid, yet forever incommensurable."

What then becomes of philosophy? This is perhaps the most widely discussed question among contemporary philosophers. Jacques Derrida, the French postmodernist, suggests that this question now *defines* philosophy.[11] Postmodernists agree that one of the important functions of philosophy is to deconstruct the influences of foundationalism by exposing its internal contradictions. This task brings philosophers into line with literary critics, because literature and its interpretive traditions have been heavily influenced by foundationalism. The alliance of postmodern philosophy and literary theory has spawned the controversial school known as deconstructionism—a major player, by the way, in the attack on the core curriculum. But beyond the task of cleaning up after the collapse of foundational thought, philosophy might be useful in helping individuals to develop their private resources for achieving personal wholeness. So philosophy still has both of its original operations intact: criticism and construction. But these operations are now separated by the distinction between public and private. Publicly philosophy engages in the critical deconstruction of its foundational heritage, and privately philosophy engages in therapy.

I have said that I find the postmodernist perspective theoretically agreeable, and I do. Descriptions of the way things really are *really are* contingent caricatures, whether these descriptions be theoretical or narrative. There is no final vocabulary for adequating appearance to reality, nor can there be one. All truths and all values are optional. The universe has no meaning, only interpretations do. And no interpretation is privileged by a transcendent point of reference. In fact, I am so persuaded by the postmodern critique of foundationalism that I am compelled to embrace its nihilism in a way that postmodernists are generally reluctant to do. Here, I'll even say it: *Nihilism is true.* Rorty believes that this sort of truth claim is precisely the sort of thing postmodernism rejects. Nietszche was given to such excesses, but Rorty thinks he thereby lapsed into traditional philosophy. Rorty does not say that nihilism is true. His nihilism stops with the suggestion that truth claims are unprofitable and should be dropped.[12] Presumably one is allowed to declare that "nihilism is true" as a private, therapeutic confession, but as a public doctrine it has a way of deconstructing itself. I must say, however, that the nihilist's disavowal of the *truth* of nihilism sounds rather hollow. The nihilist may be saying only that there is no truth in the way we formerly thought about the truth, but how can we be persuaded that the saying of this statement doesn't sit in the brain in precisely the same way that formerly conceived truths sat there? That is, in the neural machinery of the nihilist's brain there must be a schema signifying "nihilism is true," which has the same organizing force over consciousness that a schema signifying "God exists" has for the theist. If this is not the case, then I cannot imagine how the nihilist can manage a coherent deconstruction of all the old absolutes. It must take one to destroy one, as it were. And if this neurological scenario is the case (as I can only suppose it to be), then I fail to see what is gained by timidly disavowing its publicity. If the public program of deconstruction is to have force, then why not give it some? Why not just admit, as I freely do, that nihilism is our best adequation of appearance to reality? There is nothing lost in this admission except the artificial and dubious distinction between public and private vocabularies.

Adaptivism

I have said that nihilism is true, by which I mean it is our most adequate theoretical account of the nature and status of "ultimate" meanings. To say that nihilism is true is to say that all meanings are contingent caricatures of reality, and that no ultimate account of the way things really are can be universally enforced. But now I want to entertain an argument which says that *nihilism is a maladaptive truth,* a truth that is inconsistent with the conditions of personal wholeness and social coherence, and therefore unconducive to human survival. Adaptivism is neither a school nor a movement, but rather a general intellectual perspective that has been emerging along with the growing alliances between biology on the one hand and anthropology, psychology, sociology, economics, and philosophy on the other. It asserts that human beings share the same ultimate purpose in living as all other forms of life; namely, to survive and to reproduce. E. O. Wilson calls this biologically based perspective "the new naturalism," which holds "that no species, ours included, possesses a purpose beyond the imperatives created by its genetic history . . . that we have no particular place to go. The species lacks any goal external to its own biological nature."[13] Adaptivism may be characterized as the perspective that calls for a general reorientation of all intellectual disciplines (the humanities included) in light of the principles underlying the new naturalism. To be more precise, adaptivism is what I call the perspective from which this book is written, the essential elements of which have found their way into the previous three chapters.

This being the case, there is no need to outline the general perspective of adaptivism, so we can go straight to the practical argument it mounts against nihilism. In general terms, the argument is as follows: Adaptivism assumes that human beings are a social species and require relatively stable social groups in order to thrive. In order to maintain requisite coherence and stability, social groups must have a robust moral order. A robust moral order cannot be sustained under the conditions of widespread nihilistic beliefs. Therefore, nihilism is incompatible with the social conditions conducive to human survival. It is maladaptive.

The value of this argument obviously hangs on the notion of a robust moral order. By a robust moral order I mean the social condition in which a core of moral values is widely shared among individuals who regard these values as nonoptional. This definition is clear enough, but it has shifted the weight of the argument to a discussion of the conditions under which individuals come to perceive values as nonoptional. Individuals regard a value as nonoptional when they believe they are obligated to comply with the value, when they believe they do not possess the authority to violate it. When I speak of individuals believing they are not authorized to violate a value I mean something more than the belief that should they violate it they face the possibility of consequences at the hand of some enforcement agency. I mean rather that the value is perceived by the individual as objective, in the same way that plain facts are perceived as objective. In other words, I mean that values perceived as nonoptional have a neurological status in the brain that will exert the same force in organizing behavior as that exerted by the neurology of perceived facts. When I perceive a stone wall in my path, I conclude that it is an obstacle not in my power to remove by an act of will. Its presence and the implications of its presence for my behavior are not at my option to ignore. I cannot say, for example, "The presence of this wall is an inconvenience to me at the moment, so I shall ignore it without consequence." I cannot do so, for I perceive the presence of the wall to be an objective fact. I am subject to its presence, it is not subject to my will. When values are perceived to be objective they function in our brains in the same way as facts do. If I perceive a value to be objective, then I will consider myself subject to it; the implications of its presence for my behavior are not at my option to ignore.

It is precisely this perceived objectivity of values that I regard to be essential to any robust moral order. And, I believe, one comes to perceive values as objective to the extent that one believes them to be in the nature of things as they really are. I perceive a value to be objective when I regard it as integral to a fundamental order, which includes me, that will somehow be damaged if I violate the value. The perceived objectivity of values is what elicits our commitment to them, in the same way that the perceived objectivity of stone walls is what elicits our circumnavigation of them. A robust moral order is one in which individuals are committed to objectively perceived values. But it is precisely this dynamic of commitment that nihilism cannot activate. The nihilist believes that all values are relative, fabricated, and subjective. They are optional. There is no fundamental order out there or in here that will in any way be damaged by their violation. Consequently, when it is difficult or inconvenient for the nihilist to comply with a value, she is likely to exercise her option to override it. It requires only a moment's reflection to appreciate the suggestion that a society of nihilists will very soon degenerate into something approximating moral anarchy.

It may be useful to put this notion of a robust moral order into evolutionary perspective. Human beings, it will be recalled, have two systems for inheriting information: genetic and cultural. Because of this happy fact our behavioral repertoire is not limited to programs governed by genes alone; we are capable of creating and learning extragenetic behavioral programs which may be transmitted by memes. Many of our learned programs for behavior have been designed, under the constraints of social realities, to counteract or override programs established by our genes, many of which would involve the use of force or deceit. We ingest learned programs in the form of moral injunctions; that is, social rules for doing some things and not others. Without these ingested rules we would behave, by default, just as our genes inform us. Now then, in order for the learned programs to override the genetic programs—as they must do regularly in order for social coherence to result—the impulses for these programs must enter into human consciousness with *at least as much force* as the genetic default programs. In other words, if moral imperatives are to override biological imperatives, then the moral imperatives must be robust; that is, they must enter into our conscious lives with all the objectivity and nonoptionality of perceived facts. This is what moral behavior is all about—I am acting morally when I am convinced that the rightness of an act is just as real as, say, the redness of blood. It makes good evolutionary sense, then, to suggest that the human brain is predisposed to regard learned rules as objective. To do so is generally adaptive.

I further suggest that this predisposition is encouraged—indeed, enabled—by the human enterprise of mythmaking. That is, myths ensure the robust quality of a moral order by enabling us to see values as being integrated with facts. When I behold a cosmos that is infused with values, then I perceive these values to be an integral part of the way things really are. And by virtue of the neurological substrates of this perception I am unlikely to engage in default behavior. The memes of a nihilistic worldview, I believe, have the effect of deconstructing these neurological conditions, thereby setting in motion the forces of amythia and social chaos. Nihilism is maladaptive.

The conclusion that nihilism is maladaptive stands in need of one important qualification. The preceding argument intends to say only that nihilism is maladaptive if it becomes widely shared in a culture over an extended period of time. Under these conditions a culture can be expected eventually to collapse into chaos. But this is not to deny nihilism an important function—that is, an adaptive one—in the short term. I have in mind the possibility that nihilism may serve as a much-needed purgative in the life of a culture whose myth has run its course. Thus nihilism may serve as a catalyst for adaptive change by deconstructing the verity of worn memes, and thereby unleashing the powers of imagination to see the world afresh. This is the view expressed in Nietzsche's imagery of the camel, the lion, and the child. The camel is the worn and burdened beast of mediocrity. The lion is the deconstructive annihilator who ravages the camel in order to make way for the new genius of the child. The revaluation of all values begins when we take a hammer to the established absolutes.

This process may be seen throughout history in the periodic emergence of skeptical thought during spells of cultural crisis. The nihilism expressed in the book of Ecclesiastes amounts to a skeptical deconstruction of the memes of the Wisdom movement, whose conventional morality had gone bankrupt. In ancient Greece the demise of traditional religion on the one hand and the bizarre extremes of speculative philosophy on the other created an atmosphere of incredulity which made the relativist doctrines of the Sophists very attractive. The social and psychological dislocations resulting from the collapse of the Greek city-state created a receptive audience for the post-Aristotelian Skeptics. And again, when feudal institutions failed and the church was in a moral shambles, Renaissance skepticism struck a responsive chord. Skepticism, then, may well be regarded as a barometer indicating the intellectual and moral climate of a culture. If the myth of a culture is itself rendered maladaptive by changing circumstances, then we may count upon an emergence of nihilism to alert us to the fact and to prepare us for fundamental changes in the life of the culture. An undercurrent of nihilism is to be found in every culture, ignored for the most part as the crackpot fulminations of marginal personalities. Under normal circumstances very few individuals in a culture will find reason to be critical of its ultimate meanings. Like geese, we humans come into the world prepared to follow the authority of the first thing that moves. We are predisposed to assimilate the memes of the myth presented to us by our culture without bothering for a justification. The normal condition of social existence is to relax one's intellectual defenses under a presumption of truth. Under normal circumstances nihilism will appear just plain irrelevant. But if the myth of a culture has reached the limits of its adaptiveness, then we may expect hypocrisies and incongruities to become increasingly evident, and as this happens the skeptics will have their audience.

This is how we should understand the emergent nihilism of the past two centuries. It tells us that Western culture as we have known it may well be coming to its last stop. Things have changed, so that the old eternal truths no longer ring true. Not that they ever *were* absolutely true, of course, but now our defenses are up and the presumption of truth has vanished, enabling us to see them for what they are: contingent caricatures masquerading as universal truths—that is, *lies*. Now, under the influence of nihilism, the lies have been detected. Their designs no longer defeat our powers of perception; they are transparent. Now the only truth we are unable to deconstruct is the truth of nihilism. But even if we could deconstruct nihilism, doing so would hardly save us from amythia. The response to contemporary nihilism is not to debunk it but to depose it, to render it uninteresting and beside the point, to resubmerge it to its rightful place as an intellectual undercurrent. Nihilism is not here to stay. It may be true enough but its truth is maladaptive. It is here, however, to condemn our worn myths and to challenge us to replace them, and to *displace it*, with an adaptive illusion, a noble lie.

As an aside—and to assuage the reader who may have gained a sense that things don't quite ring true in my argument thus far—I will attempt to clarify my own motives. I undertook the writing of this book out of concern for sustaining the natural and social systems conducive to human life—indeed, all life—on this planet. One may reasonably ask whether such a motive is consistent with the affirmation that nihilism is true. In other words, why would a confessing nihilist care one way or another about the fate of the planet? The best I am able to do with this difficult question is to admit that my own outlook may be somewhat paradoxical; that is, I would describe myself as a theoretical nihilist and an existential biophiliac. Nihilistic biophilia is hardly an intellectual movement or a school of thought, but rather a cognitive condition that one comes to by accidents of biographical circumstance and philosophical reflection.

In my own case the biophilia came first. I was fortunate enough to be raised in circumstances that gave me good reason to love my own life, and I was taught to cherish and respect the sanctity of all living beings. There wasn't a particle of nihilism anywhere on the scene—these were circumstances shaped by the certitudes of Norwegian-American Lutheranism. It was these certitudes that informed and enforced the valuing of all life and the responsibility of caring for creation. If ever I needed reasons for caring attitudes and behaviors, they were quickly supplied from a reservoir of religious tradition.

The nihilism came later, as the reservoir went dry under the heat of honest intellectual reflection. Yet a residue of care remained, a residue which has increased with age and experience and has stabilized well beyond any need of ultimate legitimations for the sanctity of life.

This assertion, however, raises another query. If the condition of nihilistic biophilia is sufficiently stable and constructive in my own life, then whence comes the urgency of writing a book designed to subvert nihilism? Am I operating out of the arrogant assumption that nihilism, like lethal weapons or classified information, is safe only in the possession of an elite class of intellectuals? So it may appear. But I prefer to think that a nihilistic orientation is culturally and historically maladaptive, despite the possibility of its being individually viable during periods of major cultural transformation. Nihilism may be tolerable and perhaps even chic for a generation or two, but only until the momentum of bygone moral certitudes begins to give way under the gravity of amythia.

THE NOBLE-LIE OPTION

If nihilism is true, then all myths are lies, all vocabularies for integrating the full range of human experience into a narrative worldview are mere contingent caricatures pretending to universal truth. Yet, I have argued, without myths human beings lack the resources to achieve personal wholeness and social coherence. Thus, we have come to the point of defending deception and self-deception as adaptive strategies for opposing the maladaptive truth of nihilism. That such a proposal can be seriously advanced reveals the acute irony of our moment in history: that which we have most deeply feared (that is, being deceived) is now presented as the ultimate source of our salvation from psychological and social chaos. The paradox of the human condition is that we are both damned and saved by deception. And the challenge emerging in our time is ultimately an aesthetic challenge. It remains for the artists, the poets, the novelists, the musicians, the filmmakers, the tricksters, and the masters of illusion to winch us toward our salvation by seducing us into an embrace with a noble lie. Nihilism disenchants the universe—it tells us that there is no objective meaning or purpose or value inherent in it. The universe just is. The challenge of a noble lie is to reenchant the universe by getting us to perceive, in spite of ourselves, that its significance is objective.

The noble-lie option introduces a third voice into the deep philosophical *Kulturkampf*. On the one hand are the nihilists saying that we can make all vocabularies used to attribute value to reality look dubious by simply taking up another vocabulary. And on the other hand we have the realists, of one persuasion or another, saying that their own vocabulary has the endorsement of reality, that things really are the way their vocabulary describes them to be. And from the wings comes a third voice to hand the lie to both nihilist and realist alike, with the assertion that adaptivity is more sublime than truth. Any vocabulary that looks bad from the point of view of survival is out of point. So let us subject all vocabularies to the adaptive standards of a noble lie.

It must be said that the noble-lie option is not entirely original, though it has been an undeveloped minority view in relation to the many variations on skepticism and realism. Plato first raised the prospect of a noble lie in the *Republic*, suggesting that a seductive fable would be expedient for getting citizens to accept a desired social order. Such a noble lie would require "a great deal of persuasion" but would " be good for making them care more for the city and one another."[14] Nietzsche does not give us a consistent position on the issue but part of him, at least, recognized the necessity of the noble lie to overcome nihilism: "There is only *one* world, and that world is false, cruel, contradictory, misleading, senseless. . . . We need lies to vanquish this reality, this 'truth,' we need lies in order to live . . . that lying is a necessity of life is itself a part of the terrifying and problematic character of existence."[15] While pragmatist philosophers are far from being explicit on the matter, it seems clear to me that the noble-lie option is implied by their subordination of truth to usefulness. Though it is a minority position in philosophy, the noble-lie option has figured prominently in the works of several literary figures, such as Joseph Conrad, Henrik Ibsen, and Eugene O'Neill. Anthony Abbott has argued that the "vital lie" theme has been the dominant one in modern drama, as playwrights have come to terms with the implications of nihilism. Characteristic of heroes in modern drama is a will to "adopt stratagems necessary for their purposes—call them 'vital lies' or 'illusions' or 'dreams.' At the heart of the matter what we call them is less important than our acknowledgment of their necessity."[16]

The remainder of this book tries to show how things might look if we took seriously the postmodern critique *and* the adaptive need for a contemporary myth. I shall begin by explaining what I mean by the term "noble lie."

The word "noble" is ambiguous. On the one hand it may mean "well bred" or "highborn," to indicate an individual or class possessing preeminent credentials. Alternatively, "noble" may mean "well meaning" or "high-minded," to describe an act or motive possessing moral excellence. When I speak of a noble lie I intend to preserve this ambiguity. We will then have two standards by which to judge the viability of a contemporary myth. A lie is noble to the extent that it has good credentials; that is, if it is plausible by the standards of the day. A lie, by contrast, is ignominious if it is implausible, farfetched, or unfathomable by contemporary standards. In other words, a noble lie is one that cannot be shown to be a lie by comparison with various other statements already received as plausible, or with what we perceive to be facts. This is not to suggest that these two tests (the coherence test and the correspondence test) are always decisive guides to verification, but they are all we have, and when a proposition satisfies them we proceed with a presumption of truth. A noble lie is a myth that cannot, at the moment, be discredited by these standards; it is one whose designs are not defeated by the designs of the coherence and correspondence tests. An ignominious lie is one that is defeated by these designs, and thereby fails to earn a presumption of truth.

If we are to construct a contemporary myth, then, it cannot be one that attempts to defeat what are already widely credited meanings. I have in mind, of course, the principles of modern science and what these principles have led us to credit as facts. The memes of a contemporary myth need not be *implied* by science—everything implied by science *ipso facto is* science—but they cannot be noble if they are *denied* by scientific meanings. Thus, for example, fundamentalist Christianity comes up as an ignominious lie because it assumes a cosmology that is defeated by the cosmology of contemporary science. This does not mean that *all* versions of the Judeo-Christian myth are ignominious lies, nor does it mean that fundamentalist Christianity has *always been* one. There may have been a time when it had noble credentials. I am saying only that it does not have them now.

I will try to be more clear. I have suggested that our survival depends on the establishment of a myth that will resubmerge the specter of nihilism, and that technically the telling of such a myth constitutes a lie. But we cannot say, surely, that any old myth will do. There are many lies that have no more promise than the maladaptive truth of nihilism. So we need to express standards for a *noble* lie. All I have suggested so far is that the first standard for nobility (the well-bred standard) is consistency with scientific cosmology. This amounts to giving the power of veto to science. The more consistent a myth's cosmological meanings with the ideas of science, the more noble the myth. If a myth integrates memes that have been discredited by science (e.g., the cosmology of creationism), then the myth is ignominious and undeserving of public recognition.

I must add that this standard of nobility does not commit us to scientific positivism—that is, the view that the only legitimate meanings are those of science. All we have committed ourselves to by this standard is the principle that meanings discredited within science are rendered unacceptable to a contemporary myth as well.

Whereas the first standard for nobility is cosmological, the second standard is moral. A noble lie must be more than merely plausible, it must be adaptive; that is, it must articulate meanings that are conducive to the simultaneous achievement of personal wholeness and social coherence; it must be therapeutic and political. A noble lie must provide individuals with the resources for achieving self-esteem by serving collective ideals, and it must provide groups with the resolve to remain focused on the needs of individuals. A noble lie presents us with a single vocabulary, one that enables individuals to expand their interests and affections into public domains, while at the same time reminding social groups that they have no legitimate purpose apart from serving particular human interests.

We can sense both the desperate need and the profound difficulty of constructing such a vocabulary by taking a quick look around. On the one hand, we find an unmistakable *need for global unity of purpose.* The unrestrained expansion of human population has put such enormous pressure on the environment that it is threatening the integrity of essential life-support systems. Population density and scarcity of resources have intensified conflicts of interests between comprehensive groups on a global scale. There is no question that these are universal problems—that is, problems that will in various ways come to affect every human being for the foreseeable future. Failure to address these problems intensively and systematically may well result in changes in the earth's natural systems that are incompatible with human survival. But no concerted effort is possible unless we devise the means of cooperation that will enable a common, universal self-understanding. We need the memes that will enable us to perceive ourselves as a single species with a shared interest in and responsibility for preserving the natural conditions for all life forms. We need a vocabulary that will help us transcend our particular differences to define ourselves and our destiny as one people committed to a unity of purpose.

Yet, at the same time, our quick look around reveals a persistent *need for individual freedom of expression.* Liberation movements of one kind or another are under way in all parts of the world. Particular human rights are being asserted in the form of movements for national liberation, ethnic and racial liberation, religious liberation, economic liberation, and liberation of gender and sexual orientation. As Richard Rorty rightly observes, people want the freedom to define their own nature and destiny and not to be subsumed under the definitions imposed by others. Individual paths to wholeness are diverse, my experiences are not yours, your story does not speak to my experience, your heroes do not inspire me, what gives you self-worth annihilates me, one size does not fit all. Without freedom of individual expression there is no possibility of personal wholeness. Universal expressions force too many victims below the line of forced altruism.

There is a perceived tension between the unmistakable need for global unity of purpose and the unmistakable need for individual freedom of expression. The difficulty of satisfying both of these needs with a single vocabulary or myth is what leads philosophers such as Rorty to declare that personal wholeness and social coherence are forever incommensurable. If a single vocabulary is imposed, it will create victims who will inevitably start up liberation movements. The power of liberation movements refutes the commensurability of public and private domains of human existence.

This doctrine of incommensurability has a certain persuasive tug to it, yet one may be allowed a different reading of liberation movements. When I consider the power of liberation movements I see a compelling demonstration of the inseparability of public and private domains of human existence. Liberation movements give us our most forceful expressions of the principle that politics and therapy are one. These movements are *essentially* both political and therapeutic. The Black Power movement of the late 1960s was avowedly political, yet it was profoundly therapeutic at the same time. I can remember being moved by news footage during this period showing Dick Gregory and Bill Cosby standing before schoolchildren leading them in the chant "Black is beautiful." The black liberation movement was a political phenomenon that gave young people the resources to find self-worth. It provided them with a single vocabulary to advance both the social coherence of the black community and the personal wholeness of individuals. Precisely the same political/therapeutic dynamic carried forward the women's movement. In fact, one of the central ideas of the women's movement was expressed in the familiar phrase "The personal is political." The lesson from liberation movements is not that universal definitions are impossible, nor is the lesson that the self-definitions of minorities are essentially private, for clearly they are not. The lesson is only that white male Eurocentric heterosexual definitions are not universal. Deconstructing the hegemony of such definitions is a necessary and salutary thing to do. But the value of this deconstructive work does not speak against an adaptive need to return to the constructive task of finding some larger definition of humanity from which we may take a unity of purpose. The white male heterosexual Eurocentric Judeo-Christian story is not everybody's story, but this fact does not necessarily entail that everybody's story cannot be ventured. Perhaps the venture will be called a lie. That's fine. Such adaptive lies are noble. And even so, it will differ only in magnitude from the lie that all African-Americans have the same experience, or that one feminist story fits all.

The moral challenge facing a noble lie is to find the memes that may unify all humans in a collective liberation movement. The noble-lie option asserts that when you deprive people of a vocabulary that integrates personal whole-ness and social coherence, you deprive them of the possibility of either. The noble-lie option dares to think that our imaginative resources for constructing a myth are not diminished by the deconstruction of foundational philosophy. The noble-lie option dares to think it is possible to do politically and therapeu-tically for all humanity what liberation movements have done for minority communities. The noble-lie option dares to think it is possible to construct a vision of things as they "really are" that will disclose to us our common nature, and that such a vision may winch us toward unity without sacrificing our diversity. This option dares to speak of nonoptional values that it is in the interests of all humans to serve, and that by our service will effect adaptive change.

Why is such a noble venture into mythmaking admitted to be a lie? I call it a lie because I have been persuaded by the postmodern critique that there are no accessible objective foundations for absolute values, that every take on ultimate realities can be shown to be contingent and caricatured, that there is no "God's eye" point of view from which anything at all can be shown to matter. Therefore, to venture into mythmaking with a design to tell every-body's story is to say what cannot be said, it is the ultimate in pretense. Yet I remain convinced, despite the truth of nihilism, that without such pretenses we cannot live.

One final point worries me. Even if a noble lie satisfies the standards of plausibility and morality, a sophisticated postmodern audience will still know it to be a lie, and if one knows a story to be a lie in advance of its telling, isn't one rendered cognitively disabled to believe it? Isn't the telling of myths (even noble ones) in a postmodern context akin to the paradox of trying to hide something from oneself? This question brings us to a third standard for nobility, the aesthetic standard. Memes are aesthetically effec-tive to the extent that an audience is contained within the frame of reality they define, to the extent that the frame succeeds in reorganizing conscious-ness. Consider, for example, how a well-crafted play or film or novel is able to get one to suspend the notion that it is "just a story." Or consider how the frame of a football game makes participants forget that it is "just a game." These experiences may be redefined in terms of story and game only when the frame is broken by the curtain or the clock. When the frame is broken, participants return to the real world. In other words, memes are aesthetically effective when they have the power to captivate, if only momentarily, the imagination of an audience. The difference between fiction and myth has to do almost entirely with the scope and resiliency of the frame. Fiction, that is, may become myth if its frame remains unbroken, if the reality of the story becomes the reality to which one returns. Fiction is enlarged into myth when its frame contains the full range of human experience. If a narrative frame satisfies the intellectual, moral, and aesthetic standards brought to it by an audience, then the question of its deconstruction will look uninteresting and irrelevant precisely because the deconstructive project will have no purchase on any of the motivational systems.

The brain is a mysterious organ, to be sure, and by what means its designs are brought to defeat will always remain one of our primary concerns. So many variables are at play in deceptive interactions that one cannot easily predict their outcomes. Moreover, each brain is unique, and what succeeds at defeating the designs of one may fail with the next. Nevertheless, when it comes to defeating the designs of nihilism with the designs of a myth, the deceiver can count on plenty of help from the dupe. That is, we are so predisposed to assimilate a mythic frame that even the skeptical designs urged upon us by nihilism can be defeated by a noble lie. "Man," said Disraeli to Bishop Wilberforce, "is a being born to believe." The nihilist doctrine of amythia is not something that can be defeated by intellectual means alone, or by moral or aesthetic means alone. But when a story is intellectually plausible, morally compelling, and aesthetically pleasing, then all three domains of human interest are gathered in a satisfying vision of the way things are. And under these conditions the nihilistic protest that this vision is "just a contingent caricature" will have all the force of "this is just a game" when the score is tied and the batter comes to the plate in the bottom of the ninth with two outs and three runners on. If nihilism has attracted an audience—as it clearly has done in contemporary Western culture—then it is only because our lies are insufficiently noble. If we can manage to tell a lie that *appears* to be objectively true, good, and beautiful, then we may be able to hide our nihilistic designs where we cannot find them.

A Federation of Meaning

The circumstances we are in and the task which we have set ourselves are reminiscent of those encountered by Plato. Plato took it upon himself to articulate a vision of everybody's story in a time when radical relativism had taken hold of the popular mind. His strategy for executing this difficult task was to "make a city in speech"; that is, to describe the ideal city, a utopia, and in doing so to show us where we have come from, what our nature is, and how we should live. I will attempt something similar in the pages ahead, although I hope with enough tentative modesty to neutralize the inherent presumption of the exercise.

I will not describe a city but rather a different kind of social reality, a federation of meaning, by which I mean a global community united by a core of memes sufficient to establish an adaptive and sustainable confluence of interests. Even as I write these words I am mindful of the many times I scoffed at the delusions of weak-minded idealists rhapsodizing about global unity with all the rigor of a Coca-Cola commercial. But now I find myself firmly among them—a curious predicament for an erstwhile cynic. It is not that I ever held the sentiment in contempt—who could disapprove of world peace?—but as a hardened realist about political affairs I could not allow myself to imagine the possibility. To what do I attribute this change of heart? For one thing, my confidence about what cannot happen in history was humbled by the amazing transformations in Eastern Europe. But in addition to historical serendipity I have been impressed by a rapid growth of cooperation in the construction of international markets and a proliferation of multinational corporations. Also, the development of information and communication technologies in the past generation has increased the feasibility of a genuine global community. But perhaps most compelling of all has been a gradual realization that if we humans fail to cooperate meaningfully on matters pertinent to energy, population, and environmental protection, we will drive ourselves into extinction. This realization, punctuated by the Earth Summit in the summer of 1992, has transformed the prospect of a coherent world order from a puerile fantasy to a firm hope. I am now able to regard those who disparage the possibility of world order as troublesome obstacles to adaptive change. That there are so many such obstacles among us and that so many of them occupy positions of power and authority are sobering facts not to be lost in a rush of optimism. Nevertheless, the possibility is now so clear and so enticing, and its alternative is so unthinkably bleak, that we may count both courage and fear as our allies. This is a *kairos* moment.

What we finally make of this moment in history will depend in no small measure on our ability to construct new means of cooperation, memes to foster both local and global confluences of interest. It will be a difficult task, but it may be said that we have already made an impressive beginning. I have in mind the emergence of *the new naturalism* as a basic vocabulary for articulating many of the fundamental elements for a global federation of meaning. By "the new naturalism" I mean, to repeat, the general outlook that has emerged along with increased interconnections between biology and the physical sciences, on the one hand, and between biology and the social sciences, on the other. This new vocabulary presents us with a compelling vision of the ways in which biological systems are dependent upon specific conditions in the inanimate world, and the ways in which psychological and social phenomena are rooted in biological systems. The new naturalism does not pretend to give us an airtight system of logically necessary truths, as did the programs of foundational philosophy. Nor is it invulnerable to the acids of nihilism. Yet it must be said that the new naturalism has more and better to say about the realities out there and in here than anything offered by traditional metaphysics and epistemology. Indeed, if anything is left for these archaic disciplines, it is only the prospect of tidying up around the edges of physics and cognitive science. It must also be said that the new naturalism is far more objective than traditional philosophical systems, for two principal reasons. First of all, the new naturalism strives for testable formulation; that is, it works hard at expressing its content in terms that may be confirmed or falsified by repeatable experimentation and observation. And second, the new naturalism is the cumulative product of independent and competitive communities of investigators rather than the brainchild of a solitary speculative genius. If it must be admitted that even the new naturalism comes in under the description of contingent caricatures (as it does), it must also be said that its caricatures are much more reliable maps of experience than those of traditional philosophy, and its results are far less dependent on social and psychological variables. The new naturalism—that is, science in general—has a taste for the kind of self-correction that has never been characteristic of philosophy. Moreover, the sciences have demonstrated an impressive and irreversible appeal across cultural boundaries, and unlike cross-cultural variants of philosophical and religious systems, they suffer little, if any, distortion or loss of content in translation. The new naturalism, it cannot be denied, is the closest human beings have ever come to constructing a universal vocabulary for describing the way things are. If we aspire to a new federation of meaning, the vocabulary of the new naturalism will be our most valuable initial asset.

Another resource already at our disposal will serve us well in the shaping of a global federation of meaning. I propose that *the logic of federalism* be employed as a structural meme to ensure that the federation of meaning will be characterized by a bedrock of fundamental consensus at the deepest levels of meaning, yet tolerant of diverse perspectives and expressions at more particular levels. It may appear at first glance that the logic of federalism is a distinctively Western meme that threatens to bias the federation of meaning in favor of provincial categories. But this is not so. There is good reason to suggest that the human brain itself operates by the logic of federalism, subsuming the particular to the general and constructing and refining meanings in a reciprocity of top-down and bottom-up mechanisms.

Plato's discussion of the ideal city in his *Republic* was driven by the principle that the fundamental purpose of a city was to address human needs. Human interests are both the source and the end of the city. If we adopt this principle, we shall see that it offers us another structural device by which to organize the following discussion—that is, according to the three domains of human interests. I have now introduced three elementary features of the federation of meaning. Its basic vocabulary will be naturalist, its basic vertical structure will be federalist, and its basic horizontal structure will be tripartite. I envision, then, a federalism of cosmology, a federalism of economy, and a federalism of morality, whose narrative integration will express a new global myth.

Federalism of Cosmology

In chapter 4 I remarked briefly on the importance of a shared cosmological perspective for achieving social coherence. When the members of a social group share a cosmology they share a cosmos, and to the extent that they do not share a cosmology they lack an essential means of cooperation. When you and I have a common cosmological perspective, our experience of the world around will be similarly organized, and we will agree in general ways about what the basic realities are and what kind of events are possible. We will also agree in general ways about what constitutes knowledge and what procedures must be followed to resolve disputes over matters of fact. When we share a cosmology we also share the elements of a rationality. The point to be taken here is a very simple one: There can be no world culture without a globally shared cosmology.

The shared cosmology of the federation of meaning will be that of the new naturalism; that is, the general perspective of modern science. This feature of the proposed federation may be received in some quarters as a proposal for dogmatic scientific positivism. It may be argued that to impose the scientific worldview on a global scale would be to visit injustice upon traditional cultures, resulting in a brutal form of scientific imperialism. That is, it appears even at this early stage of discussion that the federation of meaning may undermine diversity of experience and expression (which it professes a commitment to preserve) by attempting to homogenize the intellects of all people on earth. This is a serious criticism, and it goes directly to the heart of the proposal. If this criticism cannot be answered satisfactorily, then the proposal for a federation of meaning—or indeed *any* proposal for a coherent world order—is doomed. Whatever needs to be said about the federalism of cosmology can be lined up in response to this critique.

I will begin by agreeing that if the memes of the new naturalism were to be shared on a global scale, certain elements of traditional cultures might be expected to change radically. However, the suggestion that these changes would entail a brutal imposition of scientific imperialism assumes something unwarranted about the manner in which this federation of meaning might be promoted on a global scale. If it is envisioned that inquisitors of the new naturalism would ramble through villages exterminating everyone who professed ignorance of the second law of thermodynamics, then certainly the federation of meaning would be a demonic proposal. But nothing of the sort is being proposed. I am only trying to describe the cognitive conditions for a sustainably adaptive world culture without setting forth detailed strategies for its actualization. I concede that any number of scenarios for implementing the federation might be unacceptable. Change is always disruptive, and too much too fast can be devastating. But at the same time there may be methods of implementation that would be acceptable. I might just say that the new naturalism found its way into the mainstream of Western culture against the forces of nonscientific cosmologies, and in a manner that was neither brutal nor imperialistic. Radical changes in our cultural traditions have resulted, to be sure, and there was plenty of friction in the process, but it cannot be said fairly that the bringing of modern science to Western culture was in any way an unjust act in violation of the sanctity of traditional Judeo-Christian cosmology. The bringing of the new naturalism to traditional cultures may indeed cause some disruption, and it should not be done without sensitivity. But one must take care to prevent sensitivity to historical disruption from hardening into an argument against adaptive change.

Nor should it be assumed that the introduction of a new cosmology into a traditional culture will impair the integrity of the culture as a unique entity, in the sense that it will no longer represent a distinctive heritage. Such worries can be laid to rest by examples from various traditional cultures that have thoroughly accommodated the scientific worldview without significant loss of distinctiveness. European societies, for example, have managed to maintain distinctive traditions despite the mainstreaming of scientific cosmology. And Japan, one of the most scientifically sophisticated societies of the modern world, has not lost its uniqueness in the process of ingesting the perspectives of "Western" science. It seems quite clearly the case that when cultures are allowed to accommodate the new naturalism on their own terms, they do so with very little harm accruing either to science or to the deep traditions of the culture.

The greatest difficulties are encountered in the area of religion, when it is discovered that certain religious doctrines stand in apparent tension with scientific principles. Religious teachings always presuppose the categories and paradigms of a particular cosmology. If these categories and paradigms are gradually abandoned in favor of the vocabulary of science, then it will appear that various religious teachings are rendered false. Especially problematic are religious doctrines about the origins of the earth and the origins and nature of humanity. Such doctrines are fundamental elements of religious traditions and very often stand in direct opposition to the principles of science. When such conflicts arise in a culture faced with the influx of scientific ideas it is critically important for the intellectual leaders of the culture to find the means to resolve them. This is a process that may continue through several phases. In the initial phase it is common for the scientific enterprise to be interpreted in terms of religious categories and paradigms. But in subsequent phases of dialogue it becomes more common for religious doctrines to be simply dropped or radically reinterpreted in terms of scientific categories and paradigms. As this latter strategy comes forward, the vocabulary of the new naturalism seats itself in the cultural mainstream. I am at a loss to think of anything more essential to the movement toward a global federation of meaning than the dialogue between science and traditional cosmologies. Too often the conversations between science and religion degenerate into ignorance and are broken off in despair. And too often the lack of dialogue results in the establishment of armed camps with secularists on one side and fundamentalists on the other.

While I am on the subject I might make an argument about the place of science/religion dialogues in the process of global peace issues. Impressed by the fact that conflicts between cultures are often fueled by religious differences, many people have encouraged ecumenical conversations between leaders of religious traditions. The idea is that such dialogues may generate mutual understanding and tolerance. This strategy toward world peace may be noble enough and should not be discouraged whenever there are willing participants. But as a long-term strategy this one strikes me as fruitless and misguided. I see no long-term value in the efforts of two religious traditions to understand each other's doctrines as long as these doctrines are rooted in archaic cosmologies. How productive is it for Buddhists, say, to understand the categories and concepts of the early Christian apocalyptic worldview at a time when Christians are themselves offloading these concepts and categories? I suggest that religious leaders concentrate their efforts instead on reinterpreting their own traditions in the light of contemporary science. As this process goes forward, the vocabulary of the new naturalism will become the "better known" vocabulary in various religious traditions, at which point these different traditions will discover that they have in their new vocabulary a powerful new means of cooperation.

The question remains as to why various traditional cultures should be expected to accommodate the new naturalism. The answer is simple: Because not all cosmologies are equal, and because the new naturalism does a superior job of telling everybody's story. It is more durable than metaphysical perspectives precisely because it rejects claims to finality, inviting upon itself empirical scrutiny and falsification. And it gives us what is to date the most reliable and satisfying account of where we came from, what our nature is, and how we should live. It tells us that the universe began approximately fifteen billion years ago in a burst of energy, that the elements making up the physical universe diversified through time, that our sun (one of hundreds of billions) is just under five billion years old, that the earth and everything on it originated in the matter of stars, that life had humble beginnings on earth and diversified into millions of forms with varying complexity, that all life forms are inherently related by virtue of common chemistry and descent, that only a small minority of evolved life forms remain extant today, that life forms persist only where they are suitably adapted to their environment, that humans are a recently evolved life form, that humans are a social species endowed with large brains, that human brains are capable of formulating information that may be transmitted extragenetically to other brains, that by such transmissions of information distinctive personalities and societies are constructed, that the patterns of behavior determined by these constructions will be more or less suitably adapted to environmental conditions, and that it is possible to modify these patterns in response to changing conditions. These are just a few of the general features of the story of cosmogenesis as told by the new naturalism, a story that is filled out by thousands of specific details, many of which have been arrived at independently by a diversity of investigators, and most of which have been repeatedly confirmed by testing. What is new about the new naturalism is that the story has become more complete and coherent as scientists have recognized that the organization of matter, the organization of life, and the organization of consciousness are continuous phases of development within a singular evolutionary event.

Throughout many years of teaching courses in philosophy and religion I have seen hundreds of young adults come to the realization that the story presented to them by their Judeo-Christian traditions is, after all, not every-body's story but rather a highly contingent caricature. They come to this realization when they examine their own tradition closely and when they encounter the traditions of other cultures. When they study the Bible they conclude that it tells them less about how things really are than about the distant historical experience of a particular people. And when they take a course in anthropology or non-Western literature, or when they associate with students from Nepal and Namibia they come to realize that there are other particular peoples with their own historical experiences that have generated other myths. In other words, they come to the point of concluding that their own story is *somebody's* story. And to the extent that they grasp the contin-gency of their own story there is created in them a longing to hear something that better approximates *everybody's* story, something that does a more satisfy-ing job of describing how things really are. And in the process they discover that their friends from Nepal and Namibia share their longing. As these students—Western and non-Western alike—become more thoroughly ac-quainted with the vocabulary of the new naturalism, they find that they are able to construct a new perspective on the world and on themselves, and they are able to reinterpret their cultural traditions within the frame of their new perspective.

The new naturalism is a contingent caricature itself, and some students even get to the point of seeing it as such. But they also see that it is less contingent and less caricatured than all the other stories available to them. They come to see that the sciences *just are* the systematic attempt to minimize contingency and distortion in human accounts of the way things appear to be. The new naturalism may not be everybody's story in the absolute and final sense, but it is far and away the closest anybody has come. It is more noble.

If our survival depends on global cooperation, and if global cooperation depends on shared meanings about the way things are, and if the new natural-ism is the most adequate vocabulary of such meanings, then it follows that if human survival is a good thing, the new naturalism is worthy of accommoda-tion by every traditional culture. And of course this accommodation is exactly what we are now witnessing on a global scale.

I return now to the criticism that a federation of meaning would undermine diversity of experience and expression by attempting to homogenize the intel-lects of all people on earth. It is true that the aim of the federation of meaning is to achieve an adaptive degree of intellectual consensus, and that it might do so in the process of a global accommodation to the vocabulary of the new naturalism. But to suggest that this process would result in an oppressive and debilitating regime of scientific positivism is to assume that the scientific enter-prise is a monolith of objective and indisputable truths, which it is not. In fact, science itself may be characterized as a federalism of cosmology, such that at one level is a body of governing ideas which are virtually undisputed by the entire scientific community, but at other levels are ideas that are hotly dis-puted, and at other levels still are ideas that remain within the limits of plausibility but are not widely agreed upon. In other words, there is plenty of room within the realm of science for a wide diversity of cosmological memes. To explain more clearly what I am getting at I defer to my friend Thomas Gilbert. Gilbert describes the scientific enterprise as a huge complex of ideas which may be seen to vary with respect to their certainty or objectivity. He identifies five levels of objectivity:

> A *speculation* is any idea, however subjective, uncertain, and wild, proposed to explain a phenomenon. It is intended to loosen the grip of established notions on our thinking and chart new paths from the frontiers of knowledge into the unknown. A *conjecture* is a speculation that shows enough promise to justify testing. . . . After a conjecture has been formulated in a testable form, it becomes a *hypothesis*. A *theory* is a hypothesis that has passed at least one falsification test but not a sufficient number to shift the burden of testing from those who advocate the theory to those who question it. At some point in the testing process this shift occurs, and the theory may be called a *principle*.[17]

Gilbert goes on to say that there are relatively few principles in science. Examples in physics include the principles of thermodynamics and quantum mechanics, and in biology the principle of evolution.

I will accept Gilbert's statement concerning levels of objectivity as a description of what I mean by a federalism of cosmology. It is the set of all ideas about the way things are in the world around. Some of these ideas—that is, principles—are given greater authority because they have earned the credentials of maximum certainty. In the federation of meaning there would be a virtual global consensus at the level of principles. In this respect a homogeneity of the intellect would result, but because there are so few principles in science it would be a rather thin bedrock. Whatever public mechanisms might be devised for meme selection would give highest priority to the transmission of these ideas. As one descended on the scale of objectivity, however, less selective preference for ideas would result in greater diversity of thought and expression. At the level of speculation public mechanisms might be used to select against memes that contradict principles and prevailing theories. Accordingly, if a statement stands directly opposed to a principle of science, it should be rejected as implausible. If a statement contradicts a prevailing theory without at least as much supporting evidence as the theory itself, then it should be counted as unlikely. If a statement can be formulated as a hypothesis, then it might be considered plausible pending the outcome of testing. If a statement is consistent with principles, theories, and hypotheses but cannot be given testable formulation, then it may be regarded as tolerable but not commendable. Various theistic doctrines about the origin and destiny of the universe, for example, might enjoy not only toleration but even respect at the level of conjecture, even though creationist variations would be ruled out by virtue of violating the principle of evolution. This is only a way of saying that people who wish to employ theological paradigms should feel free to do so, but they should also respect the normative role of the new naturalism insofar as those paradigms have cosmological content.

Questions now arise about the possible mechanisms for enforcing the logic of this federalism. The prospect of "thought police" is called to mind by the mention of "selecting for" and "selecting against" ideas, and by the practice of evaluating ideas as commendable, tolerable, or implausible. So why not? A corps of thought police strikes me as a terrific idea. I wager that every person reading this book grew up in a world patrolled by thought police; that is, by teachers. As I was growing up my thinking was policed against the ideas that two fours make nine, that storks bring babies, that trees can live without water, and so on. The point is simply that the federation of meaning does not require the services of a central Inquisition, it requires only a profound commitment to nourishing the scientific enterprise and to maintaining the highest possible standards of science education. Indeed, one might insist that the highest priority of the federation of meaning is the intensive support of science education on a global scale. Those who teach science to youngsters should be offered the most generous incentives and rewarded with the most opulent praise. Their work is the foundation of the federation of meaning. There can be no global culture without a shared cosmology. To the extent that we lack common sense about the kinds of things there are in the world, how these things operate, what sorts of events are predictable and possible—to the extent that we lack a shared vocabulary for a shared cosmos, we also lack the fundamental means of global cooperation. A confluence of intellects is a confluence of interests. In the federation of meaning the alarms of cultural decline will be set off whenever a budget item threatens to overtake the line for science education.

High-quality science education will not impose an oppressive cosmological ideology. What it will do is organize the consciousness of individuals according to the logic of a federalism of ideas about the world around. Along with serious and effective science education there automatically comes the logic of federalism. That is, there comes into play a pattern of thinking that is transferable to other domains of human interest. The institution of this logic will do more for the achievement of unity and the tolerance of diversity than anything else I can imagine. When a federalism of cosmology is achieved we will possess the habits of thought required for the rest of the federation of meaning to pull itself together.

Federalism of Economy

When one considers the rapid pace at which several traditional cultures have accommodated the scientific worldview, the goal of a global federalism of cosmology appears to be a reasonable possibility. When we turn to the deep implications of the new naturalism for our political and economic options into the future, however, we see a world so radically different from our present circumstances that the possibility of actually constructing that world seems to defy the imagination. I will first attempt to describe the salient features of this new world order and then assess our prospects for getting there.

In chapter 4 I argued that an individual's curiosity motivator and hedonic motivator are interdependent, and that a corresponding interdependence may be shown to exist between the social domains of cosmology and economy. In other words, whatever the members of a social group think and believe about the world around them will influence their perception of options for an economic way of life. (A reminder: I have used the term "economy" in an unconventionally broad sense, to include the general political and economic system in which individuals compete and cooperate to secure for themselves various external means for hedonic satisfaction.) So our initial question will be this: Assuming the achievement of a global federalism of cosmology, what is implied about the economic conditions for a sustainably adaptive world culture? That is, what political and economic memes appear to be called for by the new federation of meaning?

The answer to this question will involve various assumptions about the kind of world we want to live in. There are several very different scenarios, all of which may be shown to be consistent with "a sustainably adaptive world culture." So it appears that we cannot proceed very far in shaping an economy without first declaring a few fundamental moral values. Nevertheless, we may do a better job of declaring these moral values if we first allow ourselves the benefit of more information from the sciences.

The most obvious scientific resource for thinking through issues of economy is the science of ecology. In fact, ecology and economy have a common root in the Greek *oikos*, meaning "household." Ecology is the study of interactions between the living and nonliving components of a global household. It is the study of the life-support systems of the earth and the ways in which the conditions for these systems are managed by nature. Economics is the study of the ways in which humans have involved themselves in the management of components of the global household. It has become an unfortunate convention of common sense that ecology and economy are somehow fundamentally opposed to each other—consider, for example, how ecological concern for the spotted owl has been opposed by economic concern for the jobs of loggers in the Pacific Northwest. To juxtapose ecology and economy in this way is to misunderstand both. The new federation of meaning will be a world in which human economy is commensurate with the principles of ecology.

The science of ecology is premised on the principles of biology, which tell us that life on earth can be described in terms of hierarchical organizations, where higher levels of organization are resolved in terms of lower levels. In general, then, life on earth may be described by this structural hierarchy:

biosphere

biogeographic regions

biomes

ecosystems

biotic communities

species populations

individual organisms

organ systems

organs

tissues

cells

organelles

molecules

The viability of each level in the organization of life is determined by conditions at lower levels. That is, the viability of organelles is conditioned by the integrity of molecular structures, the viability of cells is dependent on the integrity of their component organelles, the viability of tissues is dependent on the integrity of constituent cells, and so on up the ladder of organization until we come to the point where the viability of the biosphere itself is dependent on the biotic integrity of large regions of the earth's surface. Another way to express this principle is to say that higher levels enforce certain limits of viability upon lower levels. Organelles will not be viable unless molecules behave within certain limits, cells will not be viable unless organelles function within certain limits, and so on.

Eventually we come to the point of saying that certain populations of species will not be viable unless individual organisms conduct themselves within certain limits. This is the very point that brings us to the interface of ecology and economy, and to the recognition that economy ultimately answers to ecology. If human economies encourage or allow certain behaviors disruptive to the delicate balance of biological diversity within their own ecosystems, then essential life-support systems may break down, endangering the entire biotic community, humans included. An ecologically informed economy, then, is one that takes *as its very essence* the task of monitoring and regulating the cumulative impact of humans on their environment, so that this cumulative impact remains safely within ecologically sustainable limits. In other words, *politics is ecology*.

Traditional Western economic theory has been based on concepts and paradigms that are now seen to be seriously flawed from an ecological point of view. Oddly enough, even some officials of Western economies recognize this fact:

> The basic causes of our environmental troubles are complex and deeply embedded. They include: our past tendency to emphasize quantitative growth at the expense of qualitative growth; the failure of our economy to provide full accounting for the social costs of environmental pollution; the failure to take environmental factors into account as a normal and necessary part of our planning and decision-making; the inadequacy of our institutions for dealing with problems that cut across traditional political boundaries; our dependence on conveniences, without regard for their impact on the environment; and more fundamentally, our fail-

ure to perceive the environment as a totality and to understand and to recognize the fundamental interdependence of all its parts, including man himself. . . . We need new knowledge, new perceptions, new attitudes. . . . We seek nothing less than a basic reform in the way our society looks at problems and makes decisions.[18]

David Oates cites this passage in his excellent book, *Earth Rising*, in order to declare that if the passage were taken seriously it might serve as a manifesto for revolution. It is such a revolution that the federalism of economy hopes to achieve.

We have now prepared ourselves to declare some fundamental moral values to inform the political and economic memes called for by the federation of meaning. Our most fundamental value draws upon a principle inherent in the vocabulary of the new naturalism: that the ultimate goal of all organisms is to survive and to reproduce. If I may extrapolate just a bit, this value seems to imply a moral imperative to keep the cumulative impact of our species within the ecological limits consistent with our indeterminate survival. Consensus on this basic value is, I think, virtually given, but it does not take us very far. In the first place, the science of ecology is currently unable to give us precise information about what the limits of our viability are. And even if it were able, numerous factors might be independently varied to produce roughly the same "cumulative impact" of our species. These factors include the size and density of human population, the technology used to exploit resources, the efficiency with which resources are exploited, the level of consumption and waste, the measures we take to enhance environmental conservation and restoration, and so on. If the human population were sufficiently small and sparse, the species might remain within viable limits even under the reckless slash-and-burn economies typical of kinship bands. But as the population increases in size and density, then staying within limits of viability will require some combination of greater efficiency, reduced consumption, more aggressive programs for conservation and restoration, and the like. The point is that staying within ecological limits of human viability is not a simple equation. There are trade-offs to be worked out. Humans have not established a very impressive track record for working out these trade-offs in a deliberate fashion. As a species we have generally let matters run their course, choosing consequences by default and then making the best of them as they arise.

There is some concern, however, that the long-term consequences of our inaction, both in their magnitude and in their meaning, may be more than we can handle. Ecology and population biology may not be the precise sciences we wish them to be, but they are precise enough to inform us beyond reasonable doubt that current patterns of human impact are well beyond sustainable limits. Many eminent biologists are convinced that a process of mass extinction is now under way whose principal cause is the excessive impact of human beings on critical life-support systems. Some researchers project that as many as 25 percent of currently extant species will be extinct by the year 2015.[19] Continued failure to deal both globally and systematically with environmental issues is beginning to look maladaptive in the extreme. The imperative to stay within the ecological limits of human viability calls us *as a species* to address the question of our cumulative impact. Never before has there been such potential for a broad confluence of interest.

High on the agenda is the task of establishing the means of cooperation that will enable us to act decisively in this *kairos* moment. Our best and only hope lies in the construction of a global economy to reflect the federalism we find embedded in the organization of life on this planet. The imperative is to construct a federalism of economy to conform to the federalism of ecology. In its ideal form the federalism of economy would reconfigure the political map of the *world* to conform to the natural map of the *earth*, as follows:

Ecology	*Economy*
biosphere	world parliament
biogeographic regions	continental alliances
biomes	nations
ecosystems	bioregional provinces

Such an ideal may forever remain out of reach, but the creation of a unified world parliament at the highest level is becoming a real possibility. Governments are constructed to solve problems, and when problems take on global dimensions (as many have done since World War II), then a global legislative authority is very much in order. There is nothing radically new in the idea of a world federalism. The United Nations is well on the way to becoming a world parliament, but it still lacks the authority to pass and enforce laws and to compel adjudication of conflicts. It can only pass resolutions and make recommendations. It has the look and the promise of a world government but none of the powers it needs to become an effective problem-solving agency. Since 1947 the World Federalist Association (WFA) has been promoting the cause of world government as the only reasonable alternative to the global anarchy under which we now live.[20] The WFA has focused primarily on the elimination of war as the most compelling reason for establishing a world government, but in the past generation the perceived need to monitor and regulate the environmental impact of the human species has added considerably to the urgency of the idea. World federalism is a meme whose time has come. It amounts to a globalized version of the federalist system that now governs the United States. It calls for nations to give up their sovereign right to use armed force against other nations, and it provides the means by which global environmental goals may be democratically approved and enforced.

The principal obstacle to a world parliament is the meme of nationalism. The conventional wisdom of world leaders (and their followers) is that national sovereignty is the ultimate prize of the political process. But it is time that the ideal of national sovereignty be seen for what it is—a relic of the past, an ignominious lie, and a pernicious obstacle to adaptive change. In this time of great challenge and opportunity a doctrinaire defense of national sovereignty commits what Holmes Rolston III has called a "fallacy of misplaced community." There is nothing intrinsically flawed about the idea of sovereign law, but under present global circumstances we are compelled to transcend the sovereignty of nations and embrace the sovereignty of the earth. Those who worry that a global democracy would homogenize cultural or political diversity might consider instead the prospect that it would enhance and preserve diversity. Under world federalism we might find reason to be more relaxed and less defensive about our cultural differences, knowing that they are precluded by universal law from swelling into armed conflict. Under these conditions we might even find the generosity of mind required for a celebration of diversity. Nor does world federalism require that every nation reconstruct itself to conform to the paradigm of democracy. Monarchies and theocracies are consistent with world federalism, so long as nations comply with the democratic ideal at the global level of cooperation.

The trouble with sovereign nation-states is that they have proved themselves too large for local problems and too small for global problems. This condition will continue to exert simultaneous pressures in the directions of greater centralization of government to address some problems and decentralization of government to address others. The most exciting movements on the scene today are at both extremes of political activity. On the global level there is a movement toward world federalism, and on the local level many efforts are aimed at establishing bioregional provinces. The new federalism of economy will be shaped by the tension of these forces. Such a federalism might make provisions for a fair amount of freedom with respect to environmental issues. Under the guidance of ecological principles the world parliament might do no more than specify general impact goals for various bioregions, leaving those regions to decide among themselves how to trade off the variables that produce a cumulative impact. One region might opt for a more densely populated but frugal way of life, while another may prefer a sparsely populated region where per capita consumption is higher. As long as standards for protecting ecosystem integrity are met, there should be no universal bias for or against any particular definition of the good life.

The idea of world federalism has been an attractive option to many people for a long time. Yet progress toward its realization has too often been discouraging. Nations are loath to relinquish their sovereignty, and the loathing is in precisely the wrong places; namely, among those nations that occupy positions of leadership in the world. Perhaps the greatest irony of the day is that the United States is among the most unwilling to allow *its own form of government* to be universally adopted. The meme of nationalism is as firmly entrenched in the United States as it is anywhere. To see this one has only to consider the fate of a presidential candidate who would seek office on this platform: "I want to preside over the systematic dismantling of the U.S. military forces and the orderly transfer of external sovereignty to the United Nations. Moreover, I want to assist in the empowerment of the U.N. General Assembly to mandate environmental standards with which the United States must comply under force of international law." Any candidate who espoused such a program would become a laughingstock in American politics. And yet such a program is precisely what must be achieved, and rather soon. When one listens to political rhetoric and watches the surveys of political sentiment, one concludes that the prospects for a global federalism of economy are very bleak indeed. Given these prospects, it is tempting to think that the only realistic path toward political and economic reorganization on a global scale is through the blaze of some worldwide catastrophic event. Only then, in the ashes of despair, might we find the will to take decisive steps toward a federalism of economy.

And yet, despite the rhetoric and the surveys, there are unambiguous signs that world federalism is closer than we may think. The Cold War has ended, and nations that once were hostile toward the Soviet Union now find that they have a vital interest in helping to restore social coherence in that part of the world. Here is a confluence of interests that has come to replace a conflict of interests. The effort to build a lasting European coalition represents a promising strike against the meme of national sovereignty. The development of international markets and the resulting web of economic interdependence has also produced new confluences of interest. The development of communications technology has eliminated geographic barriers to cooperation. The growth of multinational corporations has created a new kind of entity, one that transcends nationalism and finds its conventions increasingly bothersome. The strain of maintaining large military forces in order to protect the meme of sovereignty is becoming an economic liability for nation after nation. The increasing awareness of global environmental problems has revealed a common interest among nations at the most basic level of material existence. And Earth Day is now an international event reminding people everywhere that we are united by the bounty and beauty of the planet. And, of course, the relentless appeal of the new naturalism is gradually transforming the conscious experience of people all over the world.

All of these developments (and more) are conspiring to assemble the elements of a new world order, even though its affirmation has not yet appeared in the rhetoric and the surveys. One day soon we may wake up to realize that the new world hoped for by world federalists has already come to pass. One day soon we may be forced to admit to ourselves that the ideal of national sovereignty, featured so prominently in political discourse and reflected so resoundingly in the popular vote, has been reduced by events to a memory, an empty meme signifying nothing. And on that day we shall find ourselves possessing the will to ratify the reality that has emerged in its place—a new federalism of economy. Such a day may come, and it may even be hastened upon us by a new moral perspective.

Federalism of Morality

In this section I shall work my way toward specifying the moral memes appropriate to a new federation of meaning. I shall follow the same formal specifications that helped me shape the federalisms of cosmology and economy; that is, I seek meanings that will satisfy an urgent need for global unity of purpose without suppressing a persistent need for individual freedom of experience and expression. It may be useful to begin with a metaethical question, a second-order inquiry. Rather than ask what are the proper standards for judging the excellence of behavior, I first ask whether there is a standard for judging the excellence of such standards. And for direction on this issue we may return to the evolutionary prehistory of the moral life.

We begin by reviewing what it means to be a living thing. I tried to say earlier that to be alive is to be motivated. Life forms may be said to vary according to the many ways in which they become aroused and seek to repair themselves to a state of equilibrium. The vagarious paths of evolution have equipped the living world with a variety of structural and strategic components that make up a rich diversity of motivational systems. Though the forms of life may vary greatly, its logic is universal: living things may be said to function well to the extent that they are able to satisfy their motivational needs, and thereby to advance their designs for survival and reproduction. In one respect, at least, all living forms are alike: We have interests that are variously defined by the details of our motivational systems. Among social animals and among species that have coevolved, the motivational systems of individual organisms are designed in such ways as to accommodate in part the interests of other individuals. In the social animals this accommodation may be described by a *principle of sociality*, or the logic by which patterns of interactive behaviors tend to optimize the distribution of motive satisfaction among members of the group. Individual organisms still seek to advance their own motivational interests, but their doing so will often coincidentally advance the interests of others as well. In the course of evolution these "optimizing" behaviors become fixed within the gene pool of a social species. As conditions change over time, these behaviors become modified to adjust for environmental disruptions to the optimal distribution of motive satisfaction. Another way of expressing this principle of sociality is to say that social animals tend toward the maintenance of confluence of interests among group members.

The various traditions of moral reasoning scattered throughout history may be seen as cultural extensions and refinements of this principle of sociality. What is so remarkably different about humans is that they attempt to compensate for disruptions to optimal satisfaction without waiting for genetic modulations of behavior—instead, they design and enforce rules for learned behaviors to override the default behaviors set by genetic rules. This should tell us something about the essential function of moral values; that is, their function is to maximize confluence of self-interests. And if the good of something has to do with performing its function well, then we have our standard for judging the excellence of moral values. That is, the most excellent moral values are those which most effectively expand confluence of self-interests among the members of a group.

This said, we are left to make three important observations about the moral life. First, moral values have both a group function and an individual function, and thus moral excellence is always to be judged in relation to a particular group and the interests of its members. Second, every group has its own boundary rules to govern who does and does not have moral standing within the group. And third, in modern society individuals typically find themselves acting as moral agents within the contexts of several different groups. In the light of these observations we begin to see the outlines of a federalism of morality consisting of concentric spheres of moral influence, each defined by its own boundary rules for membership. The model of adaptive moral reasoning discussed at the end of chapter 4 may be seen to apply independently within each of these moral communities.

The least comprehensive sphere of moral influence is the *primary group*; that is, families and circles of intimate associates. It is usually clear who has moral standing within such groups. An individual who has standing within a moral community has both rights and responsibilities with respect to other members of the group. Your rights require others in the group to respect your interests, and your responsibilities require you to respect the interests of others. Moral behaviors within a primary group are those which serve to resolve conflicts and to advance the interests of individual members, and the most excellent behaviors are those which do so in the greatest abundance. Such behaviors will be more forthcoming to the extent that an individual's interests and affections have expanded to include other members of the primary group. By this expansion the dynamics of reciprocal altruism are called into play.

At the next level of moral community are *secondary groups*. These groups may range in size and complexity from rather small organizations to large hierarchical institutions. Most of us participate in a plurality of these groups. Secondary groups are characterized by the practice of formalizing confluence of interests in terms of general purposes, specific goals, policies, procedures, and roles. Typically, moral behavior within a secondary group amounts to performing one's roles adequately. When roles are defined properly and performed well, a minimum of conflict and optimal confluence of interests will result within the secondary group. If performing well in secondary-group roles does not distribute satisfaction optimally, then the group stands in need of restructuring.

Beyond the level of secondary groups is the *comprehensive group*. Under present circumstances comprehensive groups are the many nation-states of the world, but under the new federalism of economy there will be only one comprehensive moral community, inclusive of the entire species. Comprehensive groups represent the highest level at which human beings can achieve consensus among themselves; it is at this level that the species may resolve its immense diversity into a global unity of moral purpose. The laws of a comprehensive group represent rules for behavior that are designed to minimize conflict and optimize the distribution of interest satisfaction within the species population. In general, these laws seek to advance the principle of fairness under a program of universal human rights. Moral behavior within a comprehensive group consists in one's participation in the political process of creating effective laws and in complying with them. When laws appear to be counterproductive to the principle of sociality, one may feel justified in the practice of civil disobedience as a means of reform.

We have further to go, however, for there are moral communities that transcend the boundaries of the human population. *Ecosystems, bioregions,* and the *biosphere* are moral communities just as surely as families, neighborhoods, and nations are. At these levels in the organization of life the human population is one of many interrelated species populations, and by no means the most important of them to the integrity of the whole. An ecosystem, like a family or nation, is viable to the extent that it manifests the principle of sociality; that is, to the extent that an optimal distribution of interest satisfaction is achieved across the entire biotic community. If this distribution is disrupted by any one species population, then the entire system may be endangered. If an individual family member begins to think of the family as a device to serve his exclusive interests, then he will regard the interests of other family members as irrelevant. Such a bearing within the family is inconsistent with the long-term coherence of the family. Ecosystems are no different. If humans regard the interests of nonhuman populations as less important than human interests, then they will act in ways that may endanger the whole ecosystem.

Let us remind ourselves that judgments of moral excellence are always the property of a particular moral community consisting of individuals who have motivated interests. If I never venture beyond the boundaries of my family, then it is not essential that my interests and affections extend beyond its limits. All that is essential to my moral virtue is that I regard the interests of other family members as worthy of my service. If I so value them and act accordingly, I will advance my own self-esteem interests whenever I serve the interests of my family members. It follows that there is nothing immoral about racism or ethnocentrism within the confines of a family group. As soon as I venture beyond the family, however, I enter into a larger moral community wherein the principle of sociality calls me to expand my moral valuation to include the interests of all members of the larger group. Now my racist views become immoral and I must change the scope of my affections so that I will be self-esteem motivated to address the unmet needs within the entire group. Within the boundaries of the human population there is nothing immoral about speciocentrism. Within the human moral community my bearing and behavior will be judged in relation to their service in the interests of other humans. In the larger context of an ecosystem, however, my speciocentrism becomes immoral and I am called by the principle of sociality to expand my affections to include the interests of nonhumans. In the moral community of an ecosystem I am bound to value nonhuman interests as no less sublime than human interests. And in the context of larger bioregions, and the biosphere itself I am called to expand my affections accordingly so that my self-esteem interests become contingent upon serving the interests even of distant species that may be too obscure to know about or too small to see. In the moral communities defined by ecosystems, bioregions, and the biosphere moral excellence is judged in terms of affections and consequent behaviors that serve to preserve and enhance conditions conducive to maximizing the biodiversity of these communities. To be moral in these communities means to refashion the substrates of our own behavior to accommodate the legitimate interests of nonhuman life forms.

Within the federalism of morality there is one general moral standard, expressed by the principle of sociality, which says that morally excellent behaviors are those which serve as many and diverse interests as possible. But this one standard finds applications within ever-expanding spheres of moral influence, from primary groups to the biosphere. If such a vision gives us a confusing picture of multiple moralities in constant tension, with no simple formula available for resolving the resulting moral dilemmas, then it is a confusion that we shall have to live with. Like the prefrontal lobes of the brain, we appear to be left with the difficult task of achieving harmony within a multidynamic network of independent systems. And yet we are not left without the guidance of a moral vocabulary, deserving of universal consensus, by which we may agree on how to know the good: Good *things* are known by the extent and diversity of satisfaction that result from their presence or use. Good *acts* are known by the extent and diversity of satisfaction that result from their performance. Good *persons* are known by the extent and diversity to which their interests and affections are expanded. And good *moral memes* are known by their effectiveness in making us good persons. And given such guidance, we may even see clearly what our global unity of moral purpose must be: to foster and preserve conditions for a rich diversity of life on earth.

The Contemporary Challenge

Our moment in history is a *kairos* moment, a moment rife with ambiguities of risk and promise, yet nevertheless a moment for moving forward with new ventures on a large scale. It is my belief that our *kairos* calls us to assemble a new global federation of meaning; that is, a new constellation of memes, a new myth telling us where we have come from, what our nature is, and how we should live together—a story, everybody's story, one with the courage and presumption to say how things really are and what really matters. Our challenge is nothing less than to construct a new global mentality.

There are elements of gravity and urgency in this challenge. Gravity, because if we fail we may well face the coming of a dark age, a backwash of decreasing cooperation, narrowing vision, and emerging conflicts. We may find ourselves overcome by the forces of reaction, who find in our *kairos* a call to return to the custody of the past. And there is urgency in our challenge because these forces are already among us, and they are gathering strength from the failure of our age to proffer anything more compelling than the purblind option of nihilism. We have been given a window of opportunity, poised as we are between the recently dissolved gridlock of the Cold War and the imminent prospect of incendiary face-offs between religious fundamentalisms. These fearsome hydras will be the heirs to a world bereft of meaning.

The most encouraging aspect of our challenge is that the new mentality has momentum in its favor. In fact, it has been misleading of me to suggest that there is much of anything *new* in what I have been proposing. I have tried to present in very brief outline a "federation in speech," as if it were some distant utopian ideal. But it isn't. I have proposed nothing more than an assemblage of ideas and sentiments that are already well developed and familiar. Everything is well in place. Our challenge is directed less to the production engineers than to the marketing division.

How does it happen that a new mentality comes to flourish? In the old-fashioned ways, by simultaneous efforts from the bottom up and from the top down. Bottom-up efforts may be likened to clearing and preparing the soil to receive new seeds, or whetting the appetite for a meal. Bottom-up efforts for a new mentality are those that bear on a piecemeal reorientation of human motivational systems, predisposing them to respond together when they are confronted by a new narrative integration, a new myth. Important contributions to the bottom-up efforts have been made by the debunkery of postmodernism, which has effectively deconstructed many of the old dogmas that have no place in an age of science. Even more important have been the inroads made by the new naturalism, partly as a result of better science education and partly because of the high quality of science journalism and science programs on public television. The internationalizing of markets has done much to prepare the way toward the new federation of meaning, and more extensive media coverage of world affairs has also been instrumental. The role played by the United Nations in the Gulf War and in the Somalian relief effort have established precedents to transform the world's expectations for future international crises. The heightened awareness of local and global environmental problems has also made a profound impact on the way individuals think and feel about the earth and their relations with it. Such movements and events have a cumulative effect on the organization of conscious experience, changing in important ways how and to what individuals are prepared to respond.

There is still work to be done. In the domain of education there is a need for greater consensus on what an educated person should know. This very book, I suppose, might be considered a bottom-up proposal that the core curriculum in university education should focus on cosmology, economy, and morality. In the realm of political activism there is much to do. Pressure on politicians to favor measures to strengthen the United Nations is essential. Politicians should be scolded by their constituents whenever they monger the worn shibboleths of an already defunct sovereignty. They should be taught that citizenship and patriotism are global concepts. The most important bottom-up activity has to do with the greening of habits. Environmental consciousness raising must continue until reducing, reusing, and recycling become routine, even among the wealthy. The list of bottom-up efforts goes on and on. The point of these efforts is that they produce discrete changes in each domain of human interest. They modify the substrates of an individual's cognitive, hedonic, and self-esteem motivators. They prepare the soul to hear the poet.

To describe the mentality of an age or a culture is a difficult thing to do. It involves a detailed account of how individuals perceive the world around, how they organize themselves to compete and cooperate for resources, and by what standards they judge themselves and one another. Such an account calls for an analysis of hundreds, perhaps thousands of memes. Still, in every age and culture a few core meanings figure in each of these domains of human interest and experience. These are the memes of myth, the memes that integrate cosmos, pathos, and ethos into narrative vision. As new meanings seep into the mentality of an age from the bottom up, the memes of traditional myths begin to lose their powers of integration; they become the *lesser-known objects* of interpretation rather than the *better-known means* of interpretation. Archibald MacLeish understood that when this process is complete, the end of an age has arrived:

> A world ends when its metaphor has died.
> An age becomes an age, all else beside,
> When sensuous poets in their pride invent
> Emblems for the soul's content
> That speak the meanings men will never know
> But man-imagined images can show;
> It perishes when those images, though seen,
> No longer mean.[21]

As meanings from the bottom up render old myths impotent, it is time for the sensuous poets to invent "emblems for the soul's content" and to release these images from the top down. Top-down efforts for a new mentality are those that bear on a narrative integration of the full range of human experience. The question relevant for the dawning of a new age is whether there are any images about that can gather us into a coherent mythic vision. Of course there are many new-age emblems on offer, as one expects under the conditions of amythia. And it is probably too soon to say if any of these memes will spread in the newly transformed soil with the promise of carrying us forward to a new world culture. Yet one may hope.

The myth of a new federation of meaning must be *biocentric*. That is, it will say that what matters ultimately is not the deity of theocentric myths or the humanity of anthropocentric myths but rather the conditions for a rich diversity of life forms. A biocentric myth, it should be insisted, is not misanthropic, it does not disparage or devalue human existence. Rather, it takes seriously the implications of recognizing that biodiversity is a condition of human existence. A biocentric myth will express the ultimate nature of human beings in the proposition that we are bound together with all other species in a planetary symbiosis wherein each unit of life is organized in the service of viability. The central icon of a biocentric myth is the earth, Gaia, that magnificent, bountiful, arrestingly beautiful, and divine object that is the matrix of the only life we know.

We may ask whether a biocentric myth can integrate the federalisms of cosmology, economy, and morality. Biocentrism affirms the cosmology of the new naturalism. Indeed, it takes its basic vocabulary from the sciences, adding only a narrative dimension to them. Its story is focused on the origins and development of the conditions for life as they are understood by the sciences.

In other words, the new naturalism is the normative foundation for a biocentric myth. As such, a biocentric myth can never be final; it is perpetually open to new discoveries and responds to the self-corrections of science by continuously revising itself. In fact, a biocentric myth will actively stimulate the curiosity motivator toward further explorations in efforts to learn more about the ultimate origins and conditions of life.

A biocentric myth affirms the sovereignty of the earth against the sovereignty of nations or species. It asserts that the earth has an integrity of its own, born of interacting systems, and that this integrity is the ultimate source of the good life. A biocentric narrative therefore rejects arbitrary and artificial political boundaries in favor of natural ones. The seas, the deserts, the plains, the forests, the mountains, the rivers—these are the givens of a biocentric economy. Ecology is the ultimate political and economic discipline. A biocentric myth gives political voice to the interests of nonhuman species and to the earth itself, as if it were a living being. In its affirmation that politics is ecology, a biocentric myth will assert a natural imperative for establishing global means to negotiate and enforce environmental impact limits on the hedonism of any species population, wherever excess threatens the integrity of ecosystems. This imperative calls for the creation of human institutions wherein conflicts of hedonic interests between humans may be resolved. But it also calls for resolutions of conflicts between human and nonhuman species. Such negotiations have the curious feature of casting humans in the role of speaking on behalf of the interests of nonhuman species, and any such procedures will be vulnerable to an inherent anthropocentric bias. The human species, it appears, will always have what amounts to the final word regarding the destiny of other species. There is no way around this privileged role of humanity, which implies that the destiny of nonhuman species, and ultimately the integrity of the earth itself, depend largely on the moral sensibilities of humans.

We are motivated to think well of ourselves, to make attributions of self-worth by the standards of performance given to us by our culture. By these means of cooperation our conduct is accommodated to the interests of other persons, thereby advancing the conditions of social coherence. Biocentrism transforms our moral calculi by giving us reasons to see that the principle of sociality is a principle of nature. It says that when the diversity of life increases, so does the stability and resilience of the conditions for life. Thus the interests of all living species are mutually contingent. In other words, failure to accommodate the life interests of other species may ultimately jeopardize the viability of all species. Consequently, it is in my interest to place value on the interests of every other form of life. This is the logic of reciprocal altruism taken to extremes. A biocentric myth imagines a partnership of all life forms, thereby affirming the appropriateness of extending the emotional regulators of altruistic behavior to include nonhumans. By the emotional mechanics of reciprocal altruism I will be left with a feeling of gratitude toward a fellow human who lends a hand to help me catch a rabbit for my supper. This feeling of indebtedness will predispose me to return the favor in some future interaction. Biocentrism says that I am no less indebted to the rabbit for its *being there* than I am to my kinsman for helping me to catch it. The rabbit population in the ecosystem has done just as much to benefit my interests in this case as the human population has. It says that if I fail to reciprocate vis-à-vis the rabbit population by generally protecting its collective interests—that is, by preserving its habitat—I will have done a wrong equal to that of failing to return a favor to my kinsman. Biocentric myth asserts that my attributions of self-worth should be contingent upon the extent to which my "reciprocity emotions" have expanded to include all species. We have already seen that such concepts as "brothers and sisters in Christ" and "the children of God" serve goals of social solidarity by artificially expanding kinship. The concept of interspecific partnership takes the matter far deeper in the interests of ecological stability.

Is this even remotely feasible? Are the emotions regulating altruistic behavior so plastic that they can be manipulated to include solidarity with nonhumans? It appears difficult enough to expand human affections to include conspecifics. As a child I was instructed to pray, "Dear Lord, help me to see my neighbor as myself." Seeing one's *neighbor* as oneself is so difficult to do that Judeo-Christians find themselves asking for help in the doing. How much more difficult must it be, then, to see one's neighborhood bat population as partners?

Is it feasible? We must suppose that it is. One must not underestimate the power of the arts to command the human soul and to expand its capacity to care. Certainly we recognize the expansion of affections to include dogs and cats within the moral community of the family. And we have ample evidence that many traditional cultures included plants and animals within their moral communities. But they, too, needed help in the doing. Their help came from cultural memes, and in particular from the meme of *anima mundi*—the earth as alive and sacred. Theodore Roszak has argued that the myth of *anima mundi* expresses one of the most ancient and spontaneous of human experiences. It is a universal myth that never dies, he says, but only transposes itself to new vocabularies.[22] A biocentric myth is our version of it.

The adaptive challenge of our age is to embrace once again the myth of *anima mundi* and to give it the aesthetic expression it requires in order to lead us into a new federation of meaning. The myth has been absent too long, and we have learned the hard way that the earth dies in the noxious gases of supernaturalist theologies, foundational philosophies, and positivist science. But the truth of nihilism has buried these notions at long last. And it is now for us to thank the nihilists respectfully and to send them on their way. We have a story to tell.

Biocentrism is your story and mine. It is everybody's story. It presumes to tell us how things are and which things matter. It is, nevertheless, a lie. It is a lie because it is not nature's own story, not told by the earth, not the authorized version. It is merely a tale told by humans, full of contingency and distortion, signifying hope. But it is a noble lie, one that washes down with a minimum of deception and offers up a maximum of adaptive change. And if it is well and artfully told, it will reenchant the earth and save us from the truth.

❧ *Notes* ❧

CHAPTER 1

1. For example, Exod. 34:7; Ps. 51:1–4; Prov. 6:12–19; Isa. 1:4, 59:12–15.

2. Cf. Lev. 14:1–9, 16:15–22.

3. Zech. 13:1–5.

4. Rom. 16:17; 1 Cor. 3:18, 6:9, 15:33; 2 Cor. 11:3; Gal. 3:1, 6:7; Col. 2:4, 8; 2 Thess. 2:1–12.

5. Mark 13:1–37; Matt. 24:1–36; Luke 21:1–38.

6. Cf. Mark 13:5–6, 21–22; Luke 21:8–9.

7. The signs: changing water to wine (2:1–11); healing the nobleman's son (4:46–54); healing the cripple (5:1–9); feeding the five thousand (6:1–14); walking on the water (6:15–21); healing the blind man (9:1–34); and raising Lazarus (11:1–46).

8. "Xenophanes," in *A Cultural Introduction to Philosophy*, ed. John J. McDermott (New York: Knopf, 1985), pp. 55–56.

9. Michel Despland, *The Education of Desire* (Toronto: University of Toronto Press, 1985), p. 217.

10. Plato, "Phaedo," in *The Dialogues of Plato*, trans. B. Jowett (New York: Random House, 1937), 1:468.

11. Plato, "The Republic," in Jowett, *Dialogues of Plato*, 1:646.

12. Aristotle, "Nicomachean Ethics," In *Introduction to Aristotle*, ed. Richard McKeon (New York: Modern Library, 1947), pp. 308, 309.

13. Ibid., p. 534.

14. Ibid., p. 440.

15. Epictetus, *Manual*, in McDermott, *Cultural Introduction to Philosophy*, p. 286.

16. Sextus Empiricus, *Outlines of Pyrrhonism*, in McDermott, *Cultural Introduction to Philosophy*, p. 326.

17. Ibid., p. 328.

18. Lucretius, *On the Nature of Things*, in McDermott, *Cultural Introduction to Philosophy*, p. 312.

19. Epicurus, in McDermott, *Cultural Introduction to Philosophy*, p. 309.

20. "Epicurus to Menoeceus," in McDermott, *Cultural Introduction to Philosophy*, p. 308.

21. Ignatius, "To the Ephesians," in *Early Christian Fathers,* trans. Cyril C. Richardson (Philadelphia: Westminster, 1953), p. 90.

22. Ignatius, "To the Trallians," in Richardson, *Early Christian Fathers,* p. 100.

23. Ignatius, "To the Philadelphians," in Richardson, *Early Christian Fathers,* p. 108.

24. "Letter to Diognetus," in Richardson, *Early Christian Fathers,* pp. 213, 221, 223.

25. Justin Martyr, "First Apology," in Richardson, *Early Christian Fathers,* pp. 259, 249.

26. Irenaeus, "Against Heresies," in Richardson, *Early Christian Fathers,* p. 358.

27. Ibid.

28. Tertullian, "Prescriptions Against Heretics," in S. L. Greenslade, *Early Latin Theology* (Philadelphia: Westminster, 1956), pp. 63, 41.

29. Ibid., p. 60.

30. Clement of Alexandria, "The Exhortation to the Greeks," in *Clement of Alexandria,* trans. G. W. Butterworth (Cambridge: Harvard University Press, 1960), pp. 51, 97–99.

31. Origen, "On Prayer," in *An Exhortation to Martyrdom, Prayer, and Selected Works,* trans. Rowan A. Greer (New York: Paulist Press, 1979), p. 161.

32. Augustine, "On Free Will," in *Earlier Writings,* ed. J. H. S. Burleigh (Philadelphia: Westminster, 1953), p. 200.

33. Ibid.

34. Ibid., p. 202.

35. G. R. Evans, *Augustine on Evil* (Cambridge: Cambridge University Press, 1982), p. 29.

36. Augustine, "On Trinity," in *Later Works,* ed. John Burnaby (Philadelphia: Westminster, 1955), p. 43.

37. Augustine, "On the Trinity," in *Basic Writings of St. Augustine,* ed. Whitney Oates, 2 vols. (New York: Random House, 1948), 2:748–49.

38. Sabine Baring-Gould, *The Lives of the Saints,* vol. 1 (Edinburgh: John Grant, 1914), p. 252.

39. Norman Russell and Benedicta Ward, *The Lives of the Desert Fathers: The "Historia Monarchorum in Aegypto"* (Kalamazoo: Cistercian Publications, 1981), p. 50.

40. Ibid., pp. 56–57.

41. Ibid., pp. 61–62.

42. St. Anselm, "Proslogion," in *Anselm of Canterbury,* trans. and ed. Jasper Hopkins and Herbert Richardson, 4 vols. (New York: Edwin Mellen, 1974), 1:95.

43. Ibid., p. 77.

44. St. Anselm, "De Incarnatione Verbi," in Hopkins and Richardson, *Anselm of Canterbury,* 3:13.

45. St. Anselm, "De Casu Diaboli," in Hopkins and Richardson, *Anselm of Canterbury,* 2:133, 152.

46. David Knowles, *The Evolution of Medieval Thought* (New York: Random House, 1964), p. 124.

47. William Kneale and Martha Kneale, *The Development of Logic* (Oxford: Clarendon, 1962), p. 227.

48. See *William of Sherwood's Introduction to Logic,* trans. Norman Kretzmann (Minneapolis: University of Minnesota Press, 1966), pp. 132–67, for a good example.

49. Thomas Aquinas, *Summa Theologica,* trans. John Feardon, vol. 25 (London: Blackfriars, 1969), p. 107.

50. Ibid., questions 75, 76, 77, 80.

51. W. T. Stace, ed., *The Teachings of the Mystics* (New York: New American Library, 1960), pp. 147, 163.

52. St. Teresa of Avila, *The Complete Works of Saint Teresa of Jesus,* trans. and ed. E. Allison Peers, 3 vols. (London: Sheed & Ward, 1957), 2:335.

53. *Theologia Germanica,* trans. Susanna Winkworth (New York: Pantheon, 1949), p. 126.

54. Stace, *Teachings of the Mystics,* pp. 145, 162–63, 189.

55. Meister Eckhart, *Selected Treatises and Sermons,* trans. James M. Clark and John V. Skinner (London: Fontana Library, 1963), p. 80.

56. *Theologia Germanica,* p. 186.

57. Meister Eckhart, *Meister Eckhart: A Modern Translation,* trans. Raymond Bernard Blakney (New York: Harper, 1941), p. xxiv.

58. St. Teresa of Avila, *Complete Works,* 1:120, 161.

59. Ibid., pp. 162, 161.

60. Quoted in Pierre de Nolhac, *Petrarch and the Ancient World* (Boston: Merrymount, 1907), p. 109.

61. Cicero, "De oratore," quoted in Jerrold Seigel, *Rhetoric and Philosophy in Renaissance Humanism* (Princeton: Princeton University Press, 1968), p. 6.

62. Colluccio Salutati, "Epistolario," quoted in Siegel, *Rhetoric and Philosophy,* p. 81.

63. Ibid., pp. 83–84.

64. Lorenzo Valla, "Scritti," quoted in Siegel, *Rhetoric and Philosophy,* p. 149.

65. Ibid., p. 163.

66. Erasmus, "Enchiridion Militis Christiani," in *The Essential Erasmus,* ed. and trans. John P. Dolan (New York: New American Library, 1964), pp. 51–52.

67. Ibid., pp. 28–29.

68. Erasmus, "The Praise of Folly," in *Essential Erasmus,* pp. 122, 133.

69. Michel Montaigne, "Apology for Raymond Sebond," in *The Complete Essays of Montaigne,* trans. Donald M. Frame (Stanford: Stanford University Press, 1958), p. 450.

70. Montaigne, "Of the Affection of Fathers for Their Children," in *Complete Essays,* p. 286.

71. Montaigne, "Apology for Raymond Sebond," p. 375.

72. Martin Luther, *Selections from His Writings,* ed. John Dillenberger (Garden City, N.Y.: Anchor, 1961).

73. Luther, "Two Kinds of Righteousness," in *Selections,* p. 93.

74. Luther, "Preface to Romans," in *Selections,* p. 25.

75. Luther, "Freedom of a Christian," in *Selections,* p. 72.

76. Ibid., p. 81.

77. Ibid., p. 72.

78. John Calvin, *Institutes of the Christian Religion,* trans. Ford Lewis Battles (London: SCM, 1960), p. 22.

79. Ibid., pp. 52, 55.

80. Ibid., p. 243.

81. Ibid., p. 554.

82. Ibid., pp. 69–70.

83. Ibid., p. 95.

84. Jaroslov Pelikan, *Reformation of Church and Dogma* (Chicago: University of Chicago Press, 1984), p. 265.

85. Justo L. Gonzalez, *A History of Christian Thought,* rev. ed., 3 vols. (Nashville: Abingdon, 1987), 3:182–83.

86. St. Ignatius of Loyola, from his letters, in *The Reformation,* ed. Hans J. Hillerbrand (New York: Harper & Row, 1964), p. 443.

87. Ibid., pp. 445–46.

88. Ibid., p. 448.

89. Galileo Galilei, quoted in Edwin Burtt, *The Metaphysical Foundations of Modern Science,* 2nd ed. (Garden City, N.Y.: Anchor, 1954), p. 75.

90. Galileo Galilei, "Letter to the Grand Duchess Christina," in *Readings in Christian Humanism,* ed. Joseph Shaw et al. (Minneapolis: Augsburg, 1982), p. 394.

91. Francis Bacon, "Of the Advancement of Learning," in *The Works of Francis Bacon,* ed. James Spedding et al. (New York: Hurd & Houghton, 1872), 9:97–98.

92. René Descartes, *Discourse on Method and Meditations,* trans. Laurence J. Lafleur (Indianapolis: Bobbs-Merrill, 1960), p. 75.

93. Ibid., p. 80.

94. Ibid., pp. 117–18.

95. Benedict Spinoza, "Ethics," in *The Collected Works of Spinoza,* trans. and ed. Edwin Curley (Princeton: Princeton University Press, 1985), pp. 489–90.

96. Gottfried Wilhelm von Leibniz, quoted in Benson Mates, *The Philosophy of Leibniz* (New York: Oxford University Press, 1986), p. 186.

97. John Locke, "The Conduct of the Understanding," in *The Works of John Locke,* 10 vols. (London: Thomas Tegg, 1823), 3:208, 233.

98. Antoine-Nicolas de Condorcet, "Man's Future Progress," in *The Enlightenment,* ed. Nicholas Capaldi (New York: Putnam, 1967), pp. 291–92.

99. Voltaire, *Philosophical Dictionary,* ed. and trans. Theodore Besterman (Baltimore: Penguin, 1971), p. 359.

100. Roland Stromberg, *An Intellectual History of Modern Europe* (New York: Appleton-Century-Crofts, 1966), p. 210.

101. Arthur Schopenhauer, *The World as Will and Idea,* in *Schopenhauer: Selections,* ed. D. H. Parker (New York: Scribner, 1956), p. 60.

102. Ibid., pp. 275–76.

103. Søren Kierkegaard, "The Journals," in *A Kierkegaard Anthology,* ed. Robert Bretall (New York: Modern Library, 1946), p. 10.

104. Kierkegaard, "The Present Age," in *Kierkegaard Anthology,* pp. 264–65.

105. Kierkegaard, "That Individual," in *Existentialism from Dostoevsky to Sartre,* ed. Walter Kaufmann (New York: Meridian, 1956), p. 93.

106. Kierkegaard, "Present Age," p. 261.

107. Friedrich Nietzsche, "The Antichrist," in *The Portable Nietzsche,* ed. Walter Kaufmann (New York: Viking, 1968), p. 576.

108. Nietzsche, "The Gay Science," in *Portable Nietzsche,* p. 449.

109. Nietzsche, "The Antichrist," in *Portable Nietzsche,* p. 613.

110. Nietzsche, "Gay Science," p. 449.

111. Jean-Paul Sartre, "Existentialism Is a Humanism," in Kaufmann, *Existentialism from Dostoevsky to Sartre,* p. 304.

112. Ibid., p. 295.

113. Ibid., p. 288.

114. Ibid., pp. 307–28.

115. Bertrand Russell, "The Philosophy of Logical Atomism," in *Readings in Twentieth-Century Philosophy,* ed. William Alston and George Nakhnikian (New York: Free Press, 1963), p. 374.

116. Ludwig Wittgenstein, *Tractatus Logico-Philosophicus,* in *Historical Introduction to Philosophy,* ed. Albert Hakim (New York: Macmillan, 1987), p. 677, 676.

117. Rudolf Carnap, "Philosophy and Logical Syntax," in Alston and Nakhnikian, *Readings in Twentieth-Century Philosophy,* pp. 432–33.

118. Ludwig Wittgenstein, *Philosophical Investigations,* trans. G. E. M. Anscombe, 3rd ed. (New York: Macmillan, 1958), p. 8e.

119. Ibid., pp. 47e, 103e.

120. Sigmund Freud, *Civilization and Its Discontents,* trans. James Strachey (New York: Norton, 1961), p. 28.

121. B. F. Skinner, *About Behaviorism* (New York: Knopf, 1974), p. 14.

122. Ibid., p. 10.

123. Ibid., p. 16.

124. A. H. Maslow, *Toward a Psychology of Being,* 2nd ed. (New York: Van Nostrand, 1968), p. 190.

125. Ibid., p. 25.

126. Ibid., p. 203.

127. Ibid., p. 115.

128. Robert Nisbet, *History of the Idea of Progress* (New York: Basic Books, 1980).

129. Georges Sorel, *The Illusions of Progress,* trans. John Stanley and Charlotte Stanley (Berkeley: University of California Press, 1969), p. xlv.

130. Reinhold Niebuhr, *The Nature and Destiny of Man,* 2 vols. (New York: Scribner, 1941), 1:252.

131. Ibid., p. 96.

132. Reinhold Niebuhr, "Ten Years That Shook My World," *Christian Century,* April 26, 1939.

133. Niebuhr, *Nature and Destiny of Man,* 1:255, 17.

134. Karl Marx, "Toward the Critique of Hegel's *Philosophy of Right,*" in Karl

Marx and Friedrich Engels, *Basic Writings on Politics and Philosophy,* ed. Lewis
S. Feuer (Garden City, N.Y.: Anchor, 1959), p. 263.

135. Paul Kurtz, "Humanism and the Moral Revolution," in *The Humanist
Alternative,* ed. Paul Kurtz (Buffalo, N.Y.: Prometheus, 1973), p. 50.

136. Corliss Lamont, *Humanism as a Philosophy* (New York: Philosophical
Library, 1949), pp. 120, 133.

137. Walter T. Stace, "Man Against Darkness," *Atlantic,* September 1948,
p. 54.

138. Ibid., p. 57.

139. George Mosse, *The Crisis of German Ideology* (New York: Universal
Library, 1964), p. 292.

140. Joachim Fest, *The Face of the Third Reich* (New York: Pantheon, 1970),
p. 83.

141. Ibid., p. 299.

142. Robert Jay Lifton, *The Nazi Doctors* (New York: Basic Books, 1986), p.
18.

143. Ibid., p. 16.

144. Ibid., p. 74.

145. Ibid., pp. 426–27.

CHAPTER 2

1. This principle assumes that cross-cultural studies will reveal the presence of
a bias against deception in non-Western cultures as well. What little I know of
non-Western traditions supports this assumption. One thinks, for example, of the
central role of maya (illusion) in Hindu traditions. However this may be, biological arguments of the sort I am about to develop must stand on their own merits
and not take their substance primarily from demonstrations of cross-cultural universals or the lack thereof. In any event, I will leave it to the experts in cultural
anthropology to strengthen or weaken my case from their own perspectives.

2. Irvin Rock, *An Introduction to Perception* (New York: Macmillan, 1975),
p. 24.

3. J. Z. Young, *Philosophy and the Brain* (New York: Oxford University
Press, 1987), p. 28.

4. William H. Calvin, *The Cerebral Symphony* (New York: Bantam, 1990).

5. The concept of schemas presented here has certain affinities with theoreti-
cal constructs used by various investigators. I have been particularly influenced by
Donald Hebb's "cell assemblies"(*The Organization of Behavior* [New York: John
Wiley, 1949]); by John Z. Young's "programs" (*Programs of the Brain* [New York:
Oxford University Press, 1978]); and by the concept of "schemata" presented by
both Jean Piaget (*The Construction of Reality in the Child* [New York: Basic
Books, 1971]) and by David Rumelhart ("Schemata: The Building Blocks of
Cognition," in *Theoretical Issues in Reading Comprehension,* ed. R. J. Spiro, B.
C. Bruce, and W. F. Brewer [Hillsdale, N.J.: Lawrence Erlbaum, 1980]).

6. Stanley Coren, Clare Porac, and Lawrence M. Ward, *Sensation and Perception* (New York: Academic Press, 1979), pp. 85–88, 330.

7. Calvin, *Cerebral Symphony,* pp. 238–41.

8. Rumelhart, "Schemata," p. 37.

9. Helen Keller, *The Story of My Life* (New York: Doubleday-Page, 1903), p. 23.

10. Ibid., p. 24.

11. J. D. Bransford and M. K. Johnson, quoted in Rumelhart, "Schemata," p. 48.

12. Claire F. Michaels and Claudio Carello, *Direct Perception* (Englewood Cliffs, N.J.: Prentice-Hall, 1981), p. 81.

13. Robert Sekuler and Randolph Blake, *Perception* (New York: Knopf, 1985), pp. 422–23.

14. Coren et al., *Sensation and Perception,* pp. 399, 400.

15. Sekuler and Blake, *Perception,* p. 428.

16. Coren et al., *Sensation and Perception,* p. 277–78.

17. Ibid., p. 425.

18. Ibid., p. 431.

19. Ursula Goodenough, "Deception by Pathogens," *American Scientist* 79 (July–August 1991): 344–55.

20. R. T. Damian, "Molecular Mimicry: Parasite Evasion and Host Defense," in *Molecular Mimicry,* ed. M. B. A. Oldstone (Berlin: Springer-Verlag, 1989), p. 102.

21. Wolfgang Wickler, *Mimicry in Plants and Animals* (New York: World University Library, 1968), pp. 40–45.

22. H. E. Hinton, "Natural Deception," in *Illusion in Nature and Art,* ed. R. L. Gregory and E. H. Gombrich (New York: Scribner, 1973), p. 121.

23. Wickler, *Mimicry in Plants and Animals,* p. 61.

24. Ibid., pp. 165–66.

25. Hinton, "Natural Deception," p. 130.

26. Wickler, *Mimicry in Plants and Animals,* p. 64.

27. James L. Gould and Carol Grant Gould, *Sexual Selection* (New York: Scientific American Library, 1989), pp. 228–29.

28. Ibid., p. 217.

29. Wickler, *Mimicry in Plants and Animals,* pp. 179, 195.

30. Charles A. Munn, "Birds That 'Cry Wolf,' " *Nature* 319 (January 9, 1986):143.

31. Tex Sordahl, "The American Avocet (*Recurvirostra americana*) as a Paradigm for Adult Automimicry," *Evolutionary Ecology* 2 (1988): 189.

32. Tex Sordahl, "Evolutionary Aspects of Avian Distraction Display," in *Deception: Perspectives on Human and Nonhuman Deceit,* ed. Robert W. Mitchell and Nicholas S. Thompson (Albany: State University of New York Press, 1986), pp. 87–112.

33. Von G. Rüppell, "A Lie as a Directed Message of the Arctic Fox," in Mitchell and Thompson, *Deception,* pp. 177–81.

34. Robert W. Mitchell and Nicholas S. Thompson, "Deception in Play Between Dogs and People," in Mitchell and Thompson, *Deception,* pp. 193–204.

35. Maxine Morris, "Large Scale Deception: Deceit in Captive Elephants?" in Mitchell and Thompson, *Deception,* pp. 183–91.

36. Frans de Waal, "Deception in the Natural Communication of Chimpanzees," in Mitchell and Thompson, *Deception,* p. 228.

37. Richard W. Byrne and Andrew Whiten, "The Thinking Primate's Guide to Deception," *New Scientist* 116 (December 1987):55.

38. De Waal, "Deception," p. 230.

39. H. Lyn Miles, "How Can I Tell a Lie? Apes, Language, and the Problem of Deception," in Mitchell and Thompson, *Deception,* pp. 245–66.

40. Theodosius Dobzhansky, "Nothing in Biology Makes Sense Except in the Light of Evolution," *The American Biology Teacher* 35 (1973):125.

CHAPTER 3

1. David Hume, *A Treatise of Human Nature,* ed. P. H. Nidditch (New York: Oxford University Press, 1978), p. 251.

2. Ibid., p. 252.

3. Konrad Lorenz, *Behind the Mirror: A Search for a Natural History of Human Knowledge* (New York: Harcourt Brace Jovanovich, 1977), p. 27.

4. J. Z. Young, *Philosophy and the Brain* (New York: Oxford University Press, 1987), p. 28.

5. J. Z. Young, *An Introduction to the Study of Man* (New York: Oxford University Press, 1971), pp. 634–35.

6. Young, *Philosophy and the Brain,* p. 5.

7. Ibid., pp. 180–81.

8. Seymour Epstein, "The Unconscious, the Preconscious, and the Self-concept," in *Psychological Perspectives on the Self,* ed. J. Suls and A. G. Greenwald (Hillsdale, N.J.: Lawrence Erlbaum, 1983), 2:236.

9. Ibid., p. 237.

10. Dorothy Rogers, *Life-Span Human Development* (Monterey, Calif.: Brooks/Cole, 1982), p. 80.

11. Howard Gardner, *Developmental Psychology* (Boston: Little, Brown, 1982), p. 195.

12. Roy F. Baumeister, *Identity: Cultural Change and the Struggle for Self* (New York: Oxford University Press, 1986), p. 178.

13. Morris Rosenberg, *Conceiving the Self* (New York: Basic Books, 1979), p. 9.

14. Howard B. Kaplan, *Self-attitudes and Deviant Behavior* (Pacific Palisades, Calif.: Goodyear, 1975), p. 10.

15. Gordon Allport, *Pattern and Growth in Personality* (New York: Holt, Rinehart & Winston, 1961), pp. 55–56.

16. See Rosenberg, *Conceiving the Self,* pp. 54–57, for a brief review.

17. Donald T. Stuss and D. Frank Benson, *The Frontal Lobes* (New York: Raven, 1986), p. 248.

18. For a review of philosophical arguments against the possibility of self-deception see Alfred Mele, "Recent Work on Self-Deception," *American Philosophical Quarterly* 24 (January 1987):1–17; also, Mike W. Martin, ed,. *Self-*

Deception and Self-Understanding (Lawrence: University Press of Kansas, 1985), esp. pp. 222–83.

19. T. S. Champlin, "Self-Deception: A Reflexive Dilemma," *Philosophy* (1977):283.

20. Robert Trivers, *Social Evolution* (Menlo Park, Calif.: Benjamin/Cummings, 1985), pp. 415–20.

21. Ludwig von Bertalanffy, *General Systems Theory* (New York: Braziller, 1968), p. 215.

22. Frank W. Abagnale, Jr., with Stan Redding, *Catch Me if You Can* (New York: Grosset & Dunlap, 1980), p. 130.

23. Mark L. Knapp, *Essentials of Nonverbal Communication* (New York: Holt, Rinehart & Winston, 1980).

24. Irving Goffman, *The Presentation of Self in Everyday Life* (Garden City, N.Y.: Doubleday, 1959), p. 67.

25. William Broad and Nicholas Wade, *Betrayers of the Truth* (New York: Simon & Schuster, 1982), pp. 38–52.

26. Goffman, *Presentation of Self,* p. 4.

27. Ronny E. Turner, Charles Edgley, and Glen Olmstead, "Information Control in Conversations: Honesty Is Not Always the Best Policy," *Kansas Journal of Sociology* 11, no. 1 (1975):72.

28. Trivers, *Social Evolution,* p. 395.

29. Quoted in Mark L. Knapp and Mark E. Comadena, "Telling It Like It Isn't: A Review of Theory and Research on Deceptive Communications," *Human Communications Research* (Spring 1979):271.

30. For a discussion of these defenses see Paul Ekman, *Telling Lies: Clues to Deceit in the Marketplace, Politics and Marriage* (New York: Norton, 1985).

31. Turner et al., "Information Control in Conversations," p. 69.

32. Anthony Greenwald, "The Totalitarian Ego: Fabrication and Revision of Personal History," *American Psychologist* 35, no. 7 (1980):603.

33. C. R. Snyder, "Reality Negotiation: From Excuses to Hope and Beyond," *Journal of Social and Clinical Psychology* 8, no. 2 (1989):136.

34. Greenwald, "Totalitarian Ego," p. 605.

35. Broad and Wade, *Betrayers of the Truth,* p. 113.

36. Ibid., p. 114.

37. Quoted in John Caughey, *Imaginary Social Worlds* (Lincoln: University of Nebraska Press, 1984), pp. 159–60.

38. Ibid., pp. 167, 186.

39. Norman N. Holland, *The Dynamics of Literary Response* (New York: Norton, 1975), p. 75.

40. Arnold M. Ludwig, *The Importance of Lying* (Springfield, Ill.: Charles C Thomas, 1965), pp. 179–80.

41. Shelley E. Taylor, *Positive Illusions: Creative Self-deception and the Healthy Mind* (New York: Basic Books, 1989), p. xi.

42. Ibid., p. 11.

43. Greenwald, "Totalitarian Ego," p. 607.

44. Ibid., p. 605.

45. Taylor, *Positive Illusions,* pp. 29–32. See also Martin Seligman, *Learned Optimism* (New York: Knopf, 1991), for a thorough discussion of the many benefits attending the habit of making positive attibutions of self-worth.

46. Sissela Bok, *Secrets: On the Ethics of Concealment and Revelation* (New York: Pantheon, 1982), pp. 10–14.

47. Erving Goffman, *Asylums: Essays on the Social Situation of Mental Patients and Other Inmates* (Garden City, N.Y.: Anchor, 1961), p. 14.

48. I. Wallace, D. Wallechinsky, A. Wallace, and S. Wallace, *The Book of Lists #2* (New York: Bantam, 1980), quoted in C. R. Snyder, Raymond Higgins, and Rita J. Stucky, *Excuses: Masquerades in Search of Grace* (New York: Wiley, 1983), p. 169.

49. Snyder et al., *Excuses,* p. 47. The following discussion draws extensively on this excellent book.

50. Delroy L. Paulhus and Peter Suedfeld, "A Dynamic Model of Self-Deception," in *Self-Deception: An Adaptive Mechanism?* ed. Joan S. Lockard and Delroy L. Paulhus (Englewood Cliffs, N.J.: Prentice-Hall, 1988), p. 133.

51. Quoted in Snyder et al., *Excuses,* p. 49.

52. C. M. Parkes, "What Becomes of Redundant World Models? A Contribution to the Study of Adaptation to Change," *British Journal of Medical Psychology* 48 (1975):132.

53. Seymour Epstein, "Controversial Issues in Emotion Theory," *Review of Personality and Social Psychology: Emotions, Relationships, and Health,* ed. P. Shaver (Beverly Hills, Calif.: Sage, 1984), p. 65.

54. Ronnie Janoff-Bulman and Christine Timko, "Coping with Traumatic Life Events," in *Coping with Negative Life Events,* ed. C. R. Snyder and Carol E. Ford (New York: Plenum, 1987), p. 142.

55. Elisabeth Kübler-Ross, *On Death and Dying* (New York: Macmillan, 1969), p. 39.

56. Avery D. Weisman, *On Dying and Denying* (New York: Behavioral Publications, 1972), p. 104.

57. Mardi Horowitz, "Psychological Response to Serious Life Events," in *The Denial of Stress,* ed. Shlomo Breznitz (New York: International Universities Press, 1983), quoted in Daniel Goleman, *Vital Lies, Simple Truths* (New York: Simon & Schuster, 1985), p. 52.

58. Patrick Cooke, "They Cried Until They Could Not See," *New York Times Magazine,* June 23, 1991, p. 25.

59. Morris Eagle, "Psychoanalysis and Self-Deception," in Lockhard and Paulhus, *Self-Deception,* p. 82.

60. For a review of the literature, see Linda S. Perloff, "Social Comparisons and Illusions of Invulnerability to Negative Life Events," in Snyder and Ford, *Coping with Negative Life Events,* pp. 217–42.

61. Ibid., pp. 218–19.

62. Ronnie Janoff-Bulman, "The Benefits of Illusions, the Threat of Disillusionment, and the Limitations of Inaccuracy," in *Journal of Social and Clinical Psychology* 8, no. 2 (1989):160–61.

63. Perloff, "Social Comparisons," pp. 221–22.

64. John T. Partington and Catherine Grant, "Imaginary Playmates and Other Useful Fantasies," in *Play in Animals and Humans,* ed. Peter K. Smith (Oxford: Basil Blackwell, 1984), p. 221.

65. Caughey, *Imaginary Social Worlds,* pp. 148–50.

66. A. Shurcliff, "Judged Humor, Arousal, and the Relief Theory," *Journal of Personality and Social Psychology* 8 (1968):360–63.

67. Avner Ziv, *Personality and Sense of Humor* (New York: Springer, 1984), pp. 53, 58.

68. Heinz Hartmann, *Ego Psychology and the Problem of Adaptation* (New York: International Universities Press, 1939), p. 64.

69. Reuben Fine, *A History of Psychoanalysis* (New York: Columbia University Press, 1979), p. 296.

70. See Randolph Nesse, "The Evolution of Psychodynamic Mechanisms," in *The Adapted Mind: Evolutionary Psychology and the Generation of Culture,* ed. J. Barkow, L. Cosmides, and J. Tooby, pp. 601–24 (New York: Oxford University Press, 1992).

71. Eugene d'Aquili, "Mystical States and the Experience of God: A Model of the Neuropsychological Substrate," paper presented at the annual meeting of the Institute on Religion in an Age of Science, Star Island, N.H., August 1991.

72. Charles V. Ford, Bryan H. King, and Marc H. Hollander, "Lies and Liars: Psychiatric Aspects of Prevarication," *American Journal of Psychiatry* 145 (May 1988):556.

73. Theodore Millon, *Disorders of Personality: DSM-III, Axis II* (New York: Wiley, 1981), chaps. 12–14.

74. Snyder, "Reality Negotiation," p. 151.

CHAPTER 4

1. Richard D. Alexander, *The Biology of Moral Systems* (New York: Aldine De Gruyter, 1987), p. 34.

2. David P. Barash, *Sociobiology and Behavior,* 2nd ed. (New York: Elsevier, 1982), p. 74.

3. Ibid., p. 115.

4. Robert Axelrod and W. D. Hamilton, "The Evolution of Cooperation," *Science* 211 (1981):1390–96.

5. Robert Trivers, *Social Evolution* (Menlo Park, Calif.: Benjamin/Cummings, 1985), p. 388.

6. For an apt description of chimp social life, see Frans de Waal, *Chimpanzee Politics* (New York: Harper & Row, 1982).

7. Richard Dawkins, *The Selfish Gene* (New York: Oxford University Press, 1976), p. 206.

8. Elman R. Service, *Profiles in Ethnology,* 3rd ed. (New York: Harper & Row, 1978).

9. Allen W. Johnson and Timothy Earle, *The Evolution of Human Societies* (Stanford: Stanford University Press, 1987), p. 19.

10. Elman R. Service, *Primitive Social Organization* (New York: Random House, 1962), p. 113.

11. Ibid., p. 117.

12. Karl Polanyi, *Primitive, Archaic, and Modern Economies,* ed. George Dalton (Garden City, N.Y.: Anchor, 1968), pp. 139–74.

13. Leslie A. White, *The Concept of Cultural Systems* (New York: Colombia University Press, 1975), p. 166.

14. Loyal D. Rue, *Amythia: Crisis in the Natural History of Western Culture* (Tuscaloosa: University of Alabama Press, 1989), chap. 4.

15. Ibid.

16. Ibid., pp. 86–87.

17. The work of Myrdene Anderson among the Saami of Lapland is a rare and excellent example of the kind of work that needs doing. See Myrdene Anderson, "Cultural Concatenation of Deceit and Secrecy," in *Deception: Perspectives in Human and Nonhuman Deceit,* ed. Robert W. Mitchell and Nicholas S. Thompson, pp. 323–48 (Albany: State University of New York Press, 1986).

18. C. H. Cooley, "On Primary Groups," in *Sociology: The Classic Statements,* ed. Marcello Truzzi (New York: Random House, 1971), p. 279.

19. Richard D. Alexander, *Darwinism and Human Affairs* (Seattle: University of Washington Press, 1979), p. 135.

20. Phyllis Rose, *Parallel Lives* (New York: Knopf, 1984), p. 7.

21. Robert M. Liebert, Rita Wicks Poulos and Gloria Strauss Marmor, *Developmental Psychology,* 2nd ed. (Englewood Cliffs, N.J.: Prentice-Hall, 1977), p. 322.

22. Ibid., p. 323.

23. This has been a very sketchy sample of deceits used to influence the moral compliance of children. An exhaustive treatment would require its own book. Robert B. Cialdini has surveyed various deceptive strategies employed by "compliance professionals," many of which strategies have common applications within familial interactions. Interested readers should consult his *Influence: The New Psychology of Modern Persuasion* (New York: Quill, 1984).

24. Erving Goffman, *Frame Analysis* (Boston: Northeastern University Press, 1986), p. 86.

25. Paul Blumberg, *The Predatory Society: Deception in the American Marketplace* (New York: Oxford University Press, 1989).

26. Cialdini, *Influence,* p. 171.

27. Blumberg, *Predatory Society,* pp. 41, 70–71.

28. Ibid., p. 213.

29. Donna Woolfolk Cross, *Mediaspeak: How Television Makes Up Your Mind* (New York: Coward-McCann, 1983), pp. 26, 35.

30. William H. Whyte, *The Organization Man* (New York: Simon & Schuster, 1956).

31. Quoted in Blumberg, *Predatory Society,* p. 199.

32. Cialdini, *Influence,* pp. 102–103.

33. Cross, *Mediaspeak,* p. 16.

34. Blumberg, *Predatory Society,* p. 224.

35. Sun Tzu, *The Art of War,* trans. Samuel B. Griffith (Oxford: Clarendon, 1963), p. 66.

36. Donal J. Sexton, "The Theory and Psychology of Military Deception," in Mitchell and Thompson, *Deception,* p. 353.

37. *New York Times,* February 28, 1991.

38. The best guide to this literature is the bibliography in David A. Charters and Maurice A. J. Tugwell, eds., *Deception Operations* (London: Brassey's, 1990), pp. 407–14.

39. Edward Jay Epstein, *Deception: The Invisible War Between the KGB and the CIA* (New York: Simon & Schuster, 1989), pp. 22–29.

40. Justin Martyr, *First Apology* (Edinburgh: John Grant, 1912), pp. 52–72.

41. Michael Ruse, "Creation Science: The Ultimate Fraud," in *Philosophy of Biology,* ed. Michael Ruse, pp. 329–36 (New York: Macmillan, 1989).

42. Keith Nickle, *The Synoptic Gospels* (Atlanta: John Knox Press, 1980), pp. 98–108.

43. Matt. 12:38–39, Mark 8:11, Luke 11:16.

44. Robin Lane Fox, *Pagans and Christians* (New York: Knopf, 1987), p. 442.

45. Quoted in Paul N. McCloskey, Jr., *Truth and Untruth: Political Deceit in America* (New York: Simon & Schuster, 1972), p. 73.

46. Nicolò Machiavelli, "Discourses on Titus Livius," in *The Prince,* ed. Robert M. Adams (New York: Norton, 1977), p. 177.

47. Cross, *Mediaspeak,* pp. 168, 179.

48. Montague Kern, *30-Second Politics: Political Advertising in the Eighties* (New York: Praeger, 1989), p. 26.

49. James MacGregor Burns, *Leadership* (New York: Harper & Row, 1978), p. 434.

50. F. G. Bailey, *The Prevalence of Deceit* (Ithaca, N.Y.: Cornell University Press, 1991), p. 29.

51. F. G. Bailey, *Humbuggery and Manipulation: The Art of Leadership* (Ithaca, N.Y.: Cornell University Press, 1988), p. 29.

52. Ibid., p. 90.

53. Garrison Keillor, *We Are Still Married* (New York: Viking, 1989), p. xix.

54. William J. Barnds, *The Right to Know, to Withhold, and to Lie* (New York: Council on Religion and International Affairs, 1969), p. 30.

55. Bailey, *Prevalence of Deceit,* p. 72.

56. Michael Kammen, *Selvages and Biases* (Ithaca, N.Y.: Cornell University Press, 1987), p. 55.

57. Quoted in Andrew Ward, "The Role of Multiculturalism in Education," in *Contemporary Philosophy* 14 (May/June 1992):9.

58. Samuel Butler, *Erewhon Revisited* (New York: Modern Library, 1933), p. 468.

59. Quoted in C. V. Wedgwood, *Truth and Opinion* (New York: Macmillan, 1960), p. 102.

60. Carol Kammen and Michael Kammen, "Uses and Abuses of the Past: A Bifocal Perspective," in M. Kammen, *Selvages and Biases,* pp. 282–303.

61. Cf. Acts 9 with Ezek. 1–2.

62. Alan F. Segal, *Paul the Convert* (New Haven: Yale University Press, 1990), p. 15.

63. Paul Johnson, *A History of Christianity* (New York: Atheneum, 1980), pp. 35–44.

64. Peter Brown, *The Cult of the Saints* (Chicago: University of Chicago Press, 1981), pp. 9, 12.

65. Jonathan Sumption, *Pilgrimage: An Image of Mediaeval Religion* (Totowa, N.J.: Rowman & Littlefield, 1975), pp. 39, 41.

66. Victor Turner and Edith Turner, *Image and Pilgrimage in Christian Culture* (New York: Columbia University Press, 1978), p. 189.

67. Quoted in Justo L. Gonzalez, *A History of Christian Thought* (Nashville: Abingdon, 1987), 1:179.

68. Martin Luther, "Commentary of Galatians," in *Selections from His Writings,* ed. John Dillenberger (Garden City, N.Y.: Anchor, 1961), p. 128.

CHAPTER 5

1. Mary Louise Pratt, "Humanities for the Future," in *The Politics of Liberal Education,* ed. Darryl J. Gless and Barbara Herrnstein Smith (Durham, N.C.: Duke University Press, 1992), p. 14.

2. Johnnella E. Butler, "The Difficult Dialogue of Curriculum Transformation: Ethnic Studies and Women's Studies," in *Transforming the Curriculum,* ed. Johnnella E. Butler and John C. Walter (Albany: State University of New York Press, 1991), p. 10.

3. William J. Bennett, *To Reclaim a Legacy* (Washington, D.C.: National Endowment for the Humanities, 1984), p. 3.

4. Ibid., pp. 29–30.

5. Allan Bloom, *The Closing of the American Mind* (New York: Simon & Schuster, 1987), p. 346.

6. Ibid., p. 187.

7. Ibid., p. 380.

8. Quoted in James W. Hall and Barbara L. Kevles, eds., *In Opposition to Core Curriculum* (Westport, Conn.: Greenwood, 1982), p. 7.

9. Benjamin Barber, "The Philosophical Despot: Allan Bloom's Elitist Agenda," in *Essays on "The Closing of the American Mind,"* ed. Robert L. Stone (Chicago: Chicago Review Press, 1989), p. 86.

10. Richard Rorty, *Contingency, Irony, and Solidarity* (New York: Cambridge University Press, 1989), p. xv.

11. Jacques Derrida, *Writing and Difference,* trans. Allan Bass (Chicago: University of Chicago Press, 1987), pp. 79–80.

12. Rorty, *Contingency, Irony, and Solidarity,* p. 8.

13. E. O. Wilson, *On Human Nature* (New York: Bantam, 1978), pp. 2–3.

14. Plato, *The Republic of Plato,* trans. Allan Bloom (New York: Basic Books, 1968), pp. 94–95.

15. Friedrich Nietzsche, *The Will to Power,* trans. Walter Kaufmann (New York: Random House, 1967), p. 451.

16. Anthony S. Abbott, *The Vital Lie* (Tuscaloosa: University of Alabama Press, 1989), p. 5.

17. Thomas L. Gilbert, "The Dynamics of Human Destiny," paper presented at the 39th Annual Conference of the Institute on Religion in an Age of Science, Star Island, N.H., July 27, 1992.

18. Council on Environmental Quality, quoted in David Oates, *Earth Rising: Ecological Belief in an Age of Science* (Corvallis: Oregon State University Press, 1989), p. 14.

19. Kenton Miller, Walter Reid, and Charles Barber, "Deforestation and Species Loss," in *Preserving the Global Environment,* ed. Jessica Tuchman Mathews (New York: Norton, 1991), p. 79.

20. Benjamin B. Ferencz and Ken Keyes, Jr., *Planethood* (Coos Bay, Oreg.: Love Line Books, 1991).

21. Archibald MacLeish, "Hypocrite Auteur," in *Collected Poems, 1917–1952* (Boston: Houghton Mifflin, 1952), pp. 173–74.

22. Theodore Roszak, *The Voice of the Earth* (New York: Simon & Schuster, 1992), pp. 136–37.

Selected Bibliography

Aaron, Richard. 1955. *John Locke*. Oxford: Clarendon.

Abagnale, Frank W., Jr., with Stan Redding. 1980. *Catch Me if You Can*. New York: Grosset & Dunlap.

Abbott, Anthony S. 1989. *The Vital Lie: Reality and Illusion in Modern Drama*. Tuscaloosa: University of Alabama Press.

Abelard, Peter. 1933. *The Letters of Abelard and Heloise*. Ed. C. K. Scott-Moncrieff. New York: Knopf.

Abramson, L. Y., and L. B. Alloy. 1981. "Depression, Non-Depression, *Journal of Experimental Psychology* 110: 436–47.

Alexander, E., Jr. 1987. "A Study of Scientific Self-Deception." *Surgical Neurology* 28: 403–4.

Alexander, Richard D. 1979. *Darwinism and Human Affairs*. Seattle: University of Washington Press.

——. 1987. *The Biology of Moral Systems*. New York: Aldine de Gruyter.

Alloy, L. B., L. Y. Abramson, and D. Viscusi. 1981. "Induced Mood and the Illusion of Control." *Journal of Personality and Social Psychology* 41:1129–40.

Allport, Gordon. 1961. *Pattern and Growth in Personality*. New York: Holt, Rinehart & Winston.

Alpern, Matthew, Merle Lawrence, and David Wolsk. 1967. *Sensory Processes*. Belmont, Calif.: Wadsworth.

Alston, William, and George Nakhnikian, eds. 1963. *Readings in Twentieth-Century Philosophy*. New York: Free Press.

Anderson, Myrdene. 1986. "Cultural Concatenation of Deceit and Secrecy." In *Deception: Perspectives on Human and Nonhuman Deceit,* ed. Robert W. Mitchell and Nicholas S. Thompson. Albany: State University of New York Press.

Anderson, Walter Truett. 1987. *To Govern Evolution: Further Adventures of the Political Animal*. Boston: Harcourt Brace Jovanovich.

Anselm, St. 1974–76. *Anselm of Canterbury*. Ed. and trans. Jasper Hopkins and Herbert Richardson. 4 vols. 2nd ed. New York: Edwin Mellen.

Aoki, Chiye, and Philip Siekevitz. 1988. "Plasticity in Brain Development." *Scientific American* 259:56–64.

Aquinas, St. Thomas. 1964–75. *Summa Theologica*. Trans. Thomas Gilby. 60 vols. London: Blackfriars.

324 / Selected Bibliography

————. 1975. *On the Truth of the Catholic Faith: Summa Contra Gentiles*. Trans. Anton C. Pegis. 4 vols. New York: Doubleday.

Arak, Anthony. 1984. "Sneaky Breeders." In *Producers and Scroungers: Strategies of Exploitation and Parasitism*, ed. C. J. Barnard. New York: Chapman & Hall.

Arendt, Hannah. 1969. "Lying in Politics: Reflections on the Pentagon Papers." In *Crisis of the Republic*, ed. Hannah Arendt. New York: Harcourt Brace Jovanovich.

Armstrong, J. A. 1979. "Biotic Pollination Mechanisms in the Australian Flora— A Review." *New Zealand Journal of Botany* 17:467–508.

Arnheim, Rudolf. 1969. *Visual Thinking*. Berkeley: University of California Press.

————. 1974. *Art and Visual Perception: A Psychology of the Creative Eye*. Rev. ed. Berkeley: University of California Press.

Arterton, F. Christopher. 1984. *Media Politics: The News Strategies of Presidential Campaigns*. Lexington, Mass.: Lexington Books.

Atkinson, John W. 1964. *An Introduction to Motivation*. Princeton: Van Nostrand.

Auerbach, Erich. 1968. *Mimesis: The Representation of Reality in Western Literature*. Trans. Willard R. Trask. Princeton: Princeton University Press.

Augustine. 1909. *The City of God*. 2 vols. Trans. John Healey. Edinburgh: John Grant.

————. 1948. *Basic Writings of St. Augustine*. Ed. Whitney J. Oats. 2 vols. New York: Random House.

————. 1953. *Earlier Writings*. Ed. J. H. S. Burleigh. Philadelphia: Westminster.

————. 1955. *Later Works*. Ed. John Burnaby. Philadelphia: Westminster.

————. 1961. *Confessions*. Trans. R. S. Pine-Coffin. Baltimore: Penguin.

Averick, Leah S. 1976. "Cop and Blow or 'A Taste of Honey.' " *Transactional Analysis Journal* 6:15–17.

Axelrod, Robert. 1984. *The Evolution of Cooperation*. New York: Basic Books.

Axelrod, Robert, and W. D. Hamilton. 1981. "The Evolution of Cooperation." *Science* 211: 1390–96.

Bach, Kent. 1981. "An Analysis of Self-Deception." *Philosophy and Phenomenological Research* 41:351–70.

Bach, Richard. 1979. *Illusions: The Adventures of a Reluctant Messiah*. New York: Delacorte.

Badcock, C. R. 1980. *The Psychoanalysis of Culture*. Oxford: Basil Blackwell.

————. 1986. *The Problem of Altruism: Freudian-Darwinian Solutions*. Oxford: Basil Blackwell.

Bahmanyar, S., J. Srinivasappa, P. Calali, R. S. Fujinami, et al. 1987. "Antigenic Mimicry Between Measles Virus and Human T Lymphocytes." *Journal of Infectous Diseases* 156:526–27.

Bailey, F. G. 1988. *Humbuggery and Manipulation: The Art of Leadership*. Ithaca, N.Y.: Cornell University Press.

————. 1991. *The Prevalence of Deceit*. Ithaca, N.Y.: Cornell University Press.

Baker, Samm S. 1971. *The Permissible Lie: The Inside Truth About Advertising*. Boston: Beacon.

Barash, David P. 1982. *Sociobiology and Behavior*. 2nd ed. New York: Elsevier.

Baring-Gould, Rev. Sabine. 1914. *The Lives of the Saints*. 16 vols. Edinburg: John Grant.

Barlow, H. B., and J. D. Mollon, eds. 1982. *The Senses*. Cambridge Texts in the Physiological Sciences, no. 3. Cambridge: Cambridge University Press.

Barnard, C. J., ed. 1984. *Producers and Scroungers: Strategies of Exploitation and Parasitism*. New York: Chapman & Hall.

Barnds, William J. 1969. *The Right to Know, to Withhold, and to Lie*. New York: Council on Religion and International Affairs.

Barnes, Deborah M. 1988. "AIDS Virus Coat Activates T Cells." *Science* 242 (October): 515.

Baron, Robert J. 1987. *The Cerebral Computer*. Hillsdale, N.J.: Lawrence Erlbaum.

Barrett, C. K. 1960. *The Gospel According to St. John*. London: S.P.C.K.

Bartley, S. Howard. 1969. *Principles of Perception*. 2nd ed. New York: Harper & Row.

Basso, Ellen B. 1987. *In Favor of Deceit: A Study of Tricksters in an Amazonian Society*. Tucson: University of Arizona Press.

Baumeister, Roy F. 1986. *Identity: Cultural Change and the Struggle for Self*. New York: Oxford University Press.

———. 1987. "How the Self Became a Problem: A Psychological Review of Historical Research." *Journal of Personality and Social Psychology* 52:163–76.

———. 1989. "The Optimal Margin of Illusion." *Journal of Social and Clinical Psychology* 8:176–89.

Baumeister, Roy F., Dianne M. Tice, and Debra C. Hutton. 1989. "Self-Presentational Motivations and Personality Differences in Self-Esteem." *Journal of Personality* 57:547–79.

Bayard, P., and L. Monjour. 1987. "Features of Mimicry in *Plasmodium Falciparum*." *Annales de Parasitologie Humaine et Comparée* 62:276–78.

Becker, Ernest. 1973. *The Denial of Death*. New York: Free Press.

Bell, Richard H., ed. 1978. *The Grammar of the Heart*. New York: Harper & Row.

Benedict, St., Abbot of Monte Cassino. 1981. *The Rule of Saint Benedict*. Ed. Timothy Fry. Collegeville, Minn.: Liturgical Press.

Bennett, William J. 1984. *To Reclaim a Legacy: A Report on the Humanities in Higher Education*. Washington D.C.: National Endowment for the Humanities.

Bentall, R. P. 1990. "The Illusion of Reality: A Review and Integretion of Psychological Research on Hallucinations." *Psychological Bulletin* 107:82–95.

Berger, Peter. 1961. *The Precarious Vision: A Sociologist Looks at Social Fictions and Christian Faith*. Garden City, N.Y.: Doubleday.

Berrios, G. E., and P. Brook. 1984. "Visual Hallucinations and Sensory Delusions in the Elderly." *British Journal of Psychiatry* 144:662–64.

Bertalanffy, Ludwig von. 1968. *General Systems Theory*. New York: Braziller.

Betts, Richard K. 1982. *Surprise Attack: Lessons for Defense Planning*. Washington, D.C.: Brookings.

Beuken, William, Sean Freyne, and Anton Weiler, eds. 1988. *Truth and Its Victims*. Philadelphia: Fortress Press.

Bierstedt, Robert. 1963. "The Ethics of Cognitive Communication." *Journal of Communication* 13 (September): 199–203.

Bitterman, M. E. 1988. "Creative Deception (A Letter to the Editor)." *Science* 239 (March): 1360.

Blanshard, Paul. 1958. *American Freedom and Catholic Power.* 2nd ed. Boston: Beacon.

Bloch, Maurice, ed. 1975. *Political Language and Oratory in Traditional Society.* New York: Academic Press.

Bloom, Allan. 1987. *The Closing of the American Mind.* New York: Simon & Schuster.

Bloom, Harold. 1973. *The Anxiety of Influence: A Theory of Poetry.* New York: Oxford University Press.

Blum, Larry. 1973. "Deceiving, Hurting, and Using." In *Philosophy and Personal Relations,* ed. Alan Monefiore. London: Routledge & Kegan Paul.

Blumberg, H. H. 1972. "Communication of Interpersonal Evaluations." *Journal of Personality and Social Psychology* 23:157–62.

Blumberg, Paul. 1989. *The Predatory Society: Deception in the American Marketplace.* New York: Oxford University Press.

Bochenski, I. M. 1970. *A History of Formal Logic.* Trans. Ivo Thomas. 2nd ed. New York: Chelsea.

Boehner, Philotheus. 1952. *Medieval Logic.* Manchester: Manchester University Press.

Bok, Sissela. 1979. *Lying: Moral Choice in Public Life.* New York: Vintage.

———. 1980. "The Self Deceived." *Social Science Information* 19:923–35.

———. 1982. *Secrets: On the Ethics of Concealment and Revelation.* New York: Pantheon.

Bolinger, Dwight L. 1980. *Language, the Loaded Weapon: The Use and Abuse of Language Today.* New York: Longman.

Bolles, Robert C. 1975. *Theory of Motivation.* 2nd ed. New York: Harper & Row.

Bower, B. 1989. "Deceptive Successes in Young Children." *Science News* 135 (June): 343.

Bower, G. H. 1981. "Mood and Memory." *American Psychologist* 36:129–48.

Bowyer, J. Barton. 1980. *Cheating.* New York: St. Martin's Press.

Boyd, J. F. 1986. "Polymyositis, Molecular Mimicry, and Autoimmunity." *Lancet* 2 (October 4): 808.

Boyd, Robert. 1985. *Culture and the Evolutionary Process.* Chicago: University of Chicago Press.

Brams, Steven J. 1977. "Deception in 2×2 Games." *Journal of Peace Science* 2:171–204.

Brams, Steven J., and Frank C. Zagare. 1977. "Deception in Simple Voting Games." *Social Science Research* 6:257–72.

———. 1981. "Double Deception: Two Against One in Three-Person Games." *Theory and Decision* 13 (March): 81–90.

Breckinridge, Scott D. 1986. *The CIA and the U.S. Intelligence System.* Boulder, Colo.: Westview.

Brembeck, Winston L., and William S. Howell. 1976. *Persuasion: A Means of Social Influence*. 2nd ed. Englewood Cliffs, N.J.: Prentice-Hall.

Brewin, C. 1985. "Depression and Causal Attributions: What Is Their Relation?" *Psychological Bulletin* 2:297–309.

Bridgstock, Martin. 1982. "A Sociological Approach to Fraud in Science." *Australian and New Zealand Journal of Sociology* 18 (November): 364–83.

Brinton, Alan. 1983. "St. Augustine and the Problem of Deception in Religious Persuasion." *Religious Studies* 19 (December): 437–50.

Broad, William, and Nicholas Wade. 1982. *Betrayers of the Truth*. New York: Simon & Schuster.

Brophy, Jere E. 1977. *Child Development and Socialization*. Chicago: Science Research Associates.

Brower, Lincoln P., ed. 1988. *Mimicry and the Evolutionary Process*. Chicago: University of Chicago Press.

Brower, Lincoln P., J. v. Z. Brower, and C. T. Collins. 1963. "Experimental Studies of Mimicry 7." *Zoologica* 48:65–84.

Brown, Jonathon D. 1986. "Evaluations of Self and Others: Self-Enhancement Biases in Social Judgements." *Social Cognition* 4:353–76.

Brown, Jonathon D., and Judith M. Siegel. 1988. "Attributions for Negative Life Events and Depression: The Role of Perceived Control." *Journal of Personality and Social Psychology* 54:316–22.

Brown, Peter. 1981. *The Cult of the Saints*. Chicago: University of Chicago Press.

Brown, Robert McAfee. 1985. "Paid Informers, Deception, and Lies." *Christian Century* 102:1027–30.

Bühler, Karl-Ernst. 1984. "Unwahrheit und Täuschung, Grunddimensionen menschlicher Existenz: Zum Problem des Unbewußten." [Untruth and self-deception as fundamental dimensions of human existence: The problem of the unconscious]. *Fortschritte der Neurologie, Psychiatrie* 52 (February): 35–40.

Bultmann, Rudolf. 1971. *The Gospel of John*. Trans. G. R. Beasley-Murry. Philadelphia: Westminster.

Burns, James MacGregor. 1978. *Leadership*. New York: Harper & Row.

Burtt, Edwin A. 1954. *The Metaphysical Foundations of Modern Science*. 2nd ed. Garden City, N.Y.: Anchor.

Butler, Johnnella E., and John C. Walter, eds. 1991. *Transforming the Curriculum: Ethnic Studies and Women's Studies*. Albany: State University of New York Press.

Butler, Samuel. 1933. *Erewhon Revisited*. New York: Modern Library.

Butterworth, G. W., trans. 1960. *Clement of Alexandria*. Cambridge: Harvard University Press.

Buttigieg, Joseph A., ed. 1987. *Criticism Without Boundaries: Directions and Crosscurrents in Postmodern Critical Theory*. Notre Dame: University of Notre Dame Press.

Buttrick, George Arthur, ed. 1962. *The Interpreter's Dictionary of the Bible*. 4 vols. Nashville: Abingdon.

Byrne, Richard W., and Andrew Whiten. 1987. "A Thinking Primate's Guide to Deception." *New Scientist* 116 (December): 54–57.

———, eds. 1988. *Machiavellian Intelligence*. New York: Oxford University Press.

Calvin, John. 1960. *Institutes of the Christian Religion*. Trans. Ford Lewis Battles. London: SCM.

Calvin, William H. 1990. *The Cerebral Symphony*. New York: Bantam.

Campbell, J. D., and P. J. Fairley. 1985. "Effects of Self-Esteem, Hypothetical Explanations, and Verbalization of Expectancies on Future Performance." *Journal of Personality and Social Psychology* 48:1097–111.

Capaldi, Nicholas. 1979. *The Art of Deception*. Buffalo, N.Y.: Prometheus.

Carr, Karen L. 1992. *The Banalization of Nihilism: Twentieth-Century Responses to Meaninglessness*. Albany: State University of New York Press.

Caughey, John. 1984. *Imaginary Social Worlds*. Lincoln: University of Nebraska Press.

Chadwick, Henry. 1966. *Early Christian Thought and the Classical Tradition*. New York: Oxford University Press.

Champlin, T. S. 1977. "Self-Deception: A Reflexive Dilemma." *Philosophy* 52:281–99.

Changeux, Jean-Pierre. 1985. *Neuronal Man: The Biology of Mind*. Trans. Laurence Garey. New York: Pantheon.

Charters, David A., and Maurice A. J. Tugwell, eds. 1990. *Deception Operations: Studies in the East-West Context*. London: Brassey's.

Cheney, Dorothy, Robert Seyfarth, and Barbara Smuts. 1986. "Social Relationships and Social Cognition in Nonhuman Primates." *Science* 234:1361–65.·

Churchland, Patricia Smith. 1986. *Neurophilosophy: Toward a Unified Science of the Mind-Brain*. Cambridge: MIT Press.

Cialdini, Robert B. 1984. *Influence: The New Psychology of Modern Persuasion*. New York: Quill.

Cirino, Robert. 1972. *Don't Blame the People: How the News Media Use Bias, Distortion, and Censorship to Manipulate Public Opinion*. New York: Vintage.

Clausewitz, Karl Von. 1984. *On War*. Ed. and trans. Michael Howard and Peter Paret. Rev. ed. Princeton: Princeton University Press.

Cleveland, S. E., E. E. Reitman, and C. Bentinck. 1963. "Therapeutic Effectiveness of Sensory Deprivation." *Archives of General Psychiatry* 8:51–56.

Cohen, Avner, and Marcelo Dascal, eds. 1989. *The Institution of Philosophy: A Discipline in Crisis?* La Salle, Ill.: Open Court.

Coleman, William E. 1984. "Where the Action Isn't: Toward a Rhetoric of Illusion." *Etc.* 41:278–85.

Comer, N. L., L. Madow, and J. J. Dixon. 1967. "Observations of Sensory Deprivation in a Life-Threatening Situation." *American Journal of Psychiatry* 124:164–69.

Connell, J. P. 1985. "A New Multidimensional Measure of Children's Perception of Control." *Child Development* 56:1018–41.

Conway, M., and M. Ross. 1984. "Getting What You Want by Revising What You Had." *Journal of Personality and Social Psychology* 47:738–48.

Cooke, Patrick. 1991. "They Cried Until They Could Not See." *New York Times Magazine*, June 23.

Coon, Carleton S. 1971. *The Hunting Peoples*. Boston: Little, Brown.

Copleston, Frederick. 1950. *A History of Philosophy*. 7 vols. Westminster, Md.: Newman Press.

Coren, Stanley, Clare Porac, and Lawrence M. Ward. 1979. *Sensation and Perception*. New York: Academic Press.

Cormier, Stephen M. 1986. *Basic Processes of Learning, Cognition, and Motivation*. Hillsdale, N.J.: Lawrence Erlbaum.

Coyne, J. C., and I. H. Gotlib. 1983. "The Role of Cognition in Depression: A Critical Appraisal." *Psychological Bulletin* 94:472–505.

Cox, F. E. G., ed. 1982. *Modern Parasitology: A Textbook of Parasitology*. Oxford: Blackwell Scientific.

Crites, Stephen. 1979. "The Aesthetics of Self-Deception." *Soundings* 62:107–29.

Cross, Donna Woolfolk. 1983. *Mediaspeak: How Television Makes Up Your Mind*. New York: Coward-McCann.

Cunningham, Alastair J. 1978. *Understanding Immunology*. New York: Academic Press.

Cunningham, Michael. 1972. *Intelligence: Its Organization and Development*. New York: Academic Press.

Cupitt, Don. 1981. *Taking Leave of God*. New York: Crossroads.

———. 1989. *Radicals and the Future of the Church*. London: SCM.

Damian, R. T. 1979. "Molecular Mimicry in Biological Adaptation." In *Host-Parasite Interfaces*, ed. B. B. Nickol. New York: Academic Press.

———. 1989. "Molecular Mimicry: Parasite Evasion and Host Defense." In *Molecular Mimicry*, ed. M. B. A. Oldstone. Berlin: Springer-Verlag.

Dance, K. A., and N. A. Kuiper. 1987. "Self-Schemata, Social Roles, and a Self-Worth Contingency Model of Depression." *Motivation andEmotion* 11: 251–68.

Dang, C. V. 1986. "Polymyositis and Molecular Mimicry." *Lancet* 2 (October): 975.

Daniel, Donald C., and Katherine L. Herbig, eds. 1981. *Strategic Military Deception*. New York: Pergamon.

d'Aquili, Eugene. 1991. "Mystical States and the Experience of God: A Model of the Neuropsychological Substrate." Paper presented at the annual meeting of the Institute on Religion in an Age of Science, Star Island, N.H., August.

Darwin, Charles. 1984. *The Various Contrivances by Which Orchids Are Fertilized by Insects*. 2nd ed. Chicago: University of Chicago Press.

Davis, Joel. 1984. *Endorphins*. Garden City, N.Y.: Doubleday.

Dawkins, Richard. 1976. *The Selfish Gene*. New York: Oxford University Press.

Décarreaux, Jean. 1964. *Monks and Civilization*. Trans. Charlotte Haldane. London: George Allen & Unwin.

Deci, Edward L. 1975. *Intrinsic Motivation*. New York: Plenum.

Delia, Jesse G. 1971. "Rhetoric in the Nazi Mind: Hitler's Theory of Persuasion." *Southern Speech Communications Journal* 37 (Winter): 136–49.

DeMonbreun, B. G., and W. E. Craighead. 1977. "Distortion of Perception and

Recall of Positive and Neutral Feedback in Depression."*Cognitive Therapy and Research* 1:311–29.

Demorest, Amy, et al. 1984. "Words Speak Louder than Actions: Understanding Deliberately False Remarks." *Child Development* 55 (August): 1527–34.

DePaulo, Bella M., Keith Lanier, and Tracy Davis. 1983. "Detecting the Deceit of the Motivated Liar." *Journal of Personality and Social Psychology* 45 (November):1096–1103.

DePaulo, Bella M., and Robert Rosenthal. 1979. "Telling Lies." *Journal of Personality and Social Psychology* 37:1713–22.

Derrida, Jacques. 1987. *Writing and Difference*. Trans. Allan Bass. Chicago: University of Chicago Press.

Descartes, René. 1960. *Discourse on Method and Meditations*. Trans. Laurence J. Lafleur. Indianapolis: Bobbs-Merrill.

Despland, Michel. 1985. *The Education of Desire*. Toronto: University of Toronto Press.

DeVane, William Clyde. 1965. *Higher Education in Twentieth-Century America*. Cambridge: Harvard University Press.

Devlin, Judith. 1987. *The Superstitious Mind*. New Haven: Yale University Press.

de Waal, Frans. 1982. *Chimpanzee Politics: Power and Sex Among Apes*. New York: Harper & Row.

———. 1986. "Deception in the Natural Communication of Chimpanzees." In *Deception: Perspectives on Human and Nonhuman Deceit,* ed. Robert W. Mitchell and Nicholas S. Thompson. Albany: State University of New York Press.

Dobzhansky, Theodosius. 1973. *Genetic Diversity and Human Equality*. New York: Basic Books.

———. "Nothing in Biology Makes Sense Except in the Light of Evolution." *The American Biology Teacher* 35 (1973):125–29.

Dodd, Charles Harold. 1968. *The Interpretation of the Fourth Gospel*. Cambridge: Cambridge University Press.

Donald, Merlin. 1991. *Origins of the Modern Mind: Three Stages in the Evolution of Culture and Cognition*. Cambridge: Harvard University Press.

Donaldson, Margaret. 1979. *Children's Minds*. New York: Norton.

Douglas, W., and K. Gibbons. 1983. "Inadequacy of Voice Recognition as a Demonstration of Self-Deception." *Journal of Personality and Social Psychology* 44:589–92.

Dunphy, Dexter C. 1972. *The Primary Group: A Handbook for Analysis and Field Research*. New York: Meredith.

Eagle, Morris. 1988. "Psychoanalysis and Self-Deception." In *Self Deception: An Adaptive Mechanism?* ed. Joan S. Lockard and Delroy L. Paulhus. Englewood Cliffs, N.J.: Prentice-Hall.

Eck, Marcel. 1970. *Lies and Truth*. Trans. Bernard Murchland. New York: Macmillan.

Eco, Umberto. 1976. *Theory of Semiotics*. Bloomington: Indiana University Press.

Edelman, Gerald M. 1987. *Neural Darwinism: The Theory of Neuronal Group Selection*. New York: Basic Books.

Edelman, Gerald M., W. Einar Gall, and W. Maxwell Cowan, eds. 1984. *Dynamic Aspects of Neocortical Function*. New York: Wiley.

Edelman, Murray J. 1964. "Politics as Symbolic Action." In *The Symbolic Uses of Politics*. Urbana: University of Illinois Press.

Edelson, Marshall. 1988. *Psychoanalysis: A Theory in Crisis*. Chicago: University of Chicago Press.

Edwards, Philip. 1978. "Shakespeare and the Healing Power of Deceit." *Shakespeare Survey* 31:115–25.

Ekman, Paul. 1985. *Telling Lies: Clues to Deceit in the Marketplace, Politics, and Marriage*. New York: Norton.

Ekman, Paul, Wallace V. Friesen, and Klaus R. Scherer. 1976. "Body Movement and Voice Pitch in Deceptive Interaction." *Semiotica* 16:23–27.

Ellis, H. C., R. L.Thomas, A. D. McFarland, and J. W. Lane. 1985. "Emotional Mood States and Retrieval in Episodic Memory." *Journal of Experimental Psychology: Learning, Memory, and Cognition* 11:363–70.

Ellul, Jacques. 1965. *Propaganda: The Formation of Men's Attitudes*. New York: Knopf.

———. 1981. "The Ethics of Propaganda." *Communication* 6:159–76.

Elster, Jon. 1983. *Sour Grapes: Studies in the Subversion of Rationality*. Cambridge: Cambridge University Press.

———. 1985. *The Multiple Self*. Cambridge: Cambridge University Press.

Epstein, Edward Jay. 1989. *Deception: The Invisible War Between the KGB and the CIA*. New York: Simon & Schuster.

Epstein, Seymour. 1983. "The Unconscious, the Preconscious, and the Self-Concept." In *Psychological Perspectives on the Self*, ed. J. Suls and A. G. Greenwald, vol. 2. Hillsdale, N.J.: Lawrence Erlbaum.

———. 1984. "Controversial Issues in Emotion Theory." In *Review of Personality and Social Psychology: Emotions, Relationships, and Health*, ed. P. Shaver. Beverly Hills, Calif.: Sage.

Erasmus. 1964. *The Essential Erasmus*. Ed. and trans. by John P. Dolan. New York: New American Library.

Essock, Susan M., Michael T. McGuire, and Barbara Hooper. 1988. "Self-Deception in Social Support Networks." In *Self-Deception: An Adaptive Mechanism?*, ed. Joan S. Lockard and Delroy L. Paulhus. Englewood Cliffs, N.J.: Prentice-Hall.

Evans, G. R. 1978. *Anselm and Talking About God*. New York: Oxford University Press.

———. 1982. *Augustine on Evil*. Cambridge: Cambridge University Press.

Felson, R. B. 1981. "Ambiguity and Bias in the Self-Concept." *Social Psychology Quarterly* 44:64–69.

———. 1984. "The Effect of Self-Appraisals of Ability on Academic Performance." *Journal of Personality and Social Psychology* 47:944–52.

Feltwell, John. 1986. *The Natural History of Butterflies*. New York: Facts on File.

Ferencz, Benjamin B., and Ken Keyes, Jr. 1991. *Planethood: The Key to Your Future*. Coos Bay, Oreg.: Love Line Books.

Fest, Joachim. 1970. *The Face of the Third Reich*. New York: Pantheon.

Fine, Reuben. 1979. *A History of Psychoanalysis*. New York: Columbia University Press.

Fingarette, Herbert. 1969. *Self-Deception*. London: Routledge & Kegan Paul.

Fiske, S. T., and S. E. Taylor. 1984. *Social Cognition*. Reading, Mass.: Addison-Wesley.

Flavell, J. H. 1986. "The Development of Children's Knowledge About the Appearance-Reality Distinction." *American Psychologist* 41:418–25.

Fogden, Michael, and Patricia Fogden. 1974. *Animals and Their Colors*. New York: Crown.

Ford, Charles V., Bryan H. King, and Marc H. Hollander. 1988. "Lies and Liars: Psychiatric Aspects of Prevarication." *American Journal of Psychiatry* 145 (May):554–62.

Fowles, John. 1966. *The Magus*. Boston: Little, Brown.

Fox, Robin Lane. 1987. *Pagans and Christians*. New York: Knopf.

Freedman, J. 1978. *Happy People: What Happiness Is, Who Has It, and Why*. New York: Harcourt Brace Jovanovich.

Frend, W. H. C. 1967. *Martyrdom and Persecution in the Early Church: A Study of a Conflict from the Maccabees to Donatus*. Garden City, N.Y.: Anchor.

Freud, Anna. 1966. *The Ego and the Mechanisms of Defense*. 2nd ed. New York: International Universities Press.

Freud, Sigmund. 1961. *Civilization and Its Discontents*. Trans. James Strachey. New York: Norton.

Frisby, John P. 1979. *Seeing: Illusion, Brain and Mind*. Oxford: Oxford University Press.

Fry, R. L., R. E. Vlietstra, R. H. Anderson, C. Kawai, and M. Tynan. 1988. "The Problem of Deception Within Medical Science." *International Jounal of Cardiology* 18 (February): 123–24.

Fugita, Stephen S., Mark C. Hogrebe, and Kenneth N. Wexley. 1980. "Perceptions of Deception: Perceived Expertise in Detecting Deception, Successfulness of Deception and Nonverbal Cues." *Personality and Social Psychology Bulletin* 6 (December): 637–43.

Fuster, Joaquin M. 1989. *The Prefrontal Cortex: Anatomy, Physiology, and Neuropsychology of the Frontal Lobe*. 2nd ed. New York: Raven.

Gardner, Howard. 1982. *Developmental Psychology*. 2nd ed. Boston: Little, Brown.

———. 1982. *Art, Mind, and Brain*. New York: Basic Books.

Gardner, Lloyd C. 1970. *Architects of Illusion: Men and Ideas in American Foreign Policy, 1941–1949*. Chicago: Quadrangle.

Gazzaniga, Michael S., and Colin Blakemore, eds. 1975. *Handbook of Psychology*. New York: Academic Press.

Geis, Michael L. 1987. *The Language of Politics*. New York: Springer-Verlag.

Gellner, Ernest. 1970. "Concepts and Society." In *Rationality*, ed. Bryan R. Wilson. Oxford: Basil Blackwell.

Germond, Jack W., and Jules Witcover. 1981. *Blue Smoke and Mirrors: How Reagan Won and Why Carter Lost the Election of 1980*. NewYork: Viking.

Gibson, James Jerome. 1950. *The Perception of the Visual World*. Boston: Houghton Mifflin.

Gilbert, Daniel T., and Joel Cooper. 1985. "Social Psychological Strategies of Self-Deception." In *Self-Deception and Self-Understanding: New Essays in Philosophy and Psychology*, ed. Mike Martin. Lawrence: University Press of Kansas.

Gilbert, Thomas L. 1992. "The Dynamics of Human Destiny." Paper presented at the 39th Annual Conference of the Institute on Religion in an Age of Science, Star Island, N.H., July 27.

Gilson, Etienne. 1956. *The Christian Philosophy of St. Thomas Aquinas*. New York: Random House.

Girard, René. 1965. *Desire, Deceit, and the Novel*. Trans. Y. Freccoro. Baltimore: Johns Hopkins University Press.

Gless, Darryl J., and Barbara Herrnstein Smith, eds. 1992. *The Politics of Liberal Education*. Durham, N.C.: Duke University Press.

Goffman, Erving. 1959. *The Presentation of Self in Everyday Life*. Garden City, N.Y.: Anchor.

———. 1967. *Interaction Ritual: Essays in Face-to-Face Behavior*. Garden City, N.Y.: Anchor.

———. 1986. *Frame Analysis: An Essay on the Organization of Experience*. Boston: Northeastern University Press.

Goldstein, Jeffrey H., and Paul E. McGhee, eds. 1972. *The Psychology of Humor: Theoretical Perspectives and Empirical Issues*. New York: Academic Press.

Goleman, Daniel. 1985. *Vital Lies, Simple Truths: The Psychology of Self-Deception*. New York: Simon & Schuster.

———. 1987. "Who Are You Kidding?" *Psychology Today* 21 (March): 24–30.

Golin, S., T. Terrell, and B. Johnson. 1977. "Depression and the Illusion of Control." *Journal of Abnormal Psychology* 86:440–42.

Golin, S., T. Terrell, J. Weitz, and P. L. Drost. 1977. "The Illusion of Control Among Depressed Patients." *Journal of Abnormal Psychology* 88:454–57.

Gombrich, E. H. 1969. *Art and Illusion*. 2nd ed. Princeton: Princeton University Press.

Gombrich, E. H., Julian Hochberg, and Max Black. 1972. *Art, Perception, and Reality*. Baltimore: John Hopkins University Press.

Gonzalez, Justo L. 1987. *A History of Christian Thought*. Rev. ed. 3 vols. Nashville: Abingdon.

Goodenough, Ursula. 1991. "Deception by Pathogens." *American Scientist* 79 (July–August): 344–55.

Goodin, Robert E. 1980. *Manipulatory Politics*. New Haven: Yale University Press.

Gordon, Ian E. 1989. *Theories of Visual Perception*. Chichester: Wiley.

Gould, James L., and Carol Grant Gould. 1989. *Sexual Selection*. New York: Scientific American Library.

Gould, Stephen Jay. 1983. *Hen's Teeth and Horses' Toes*. New York: Norton.

Grant, Susan. 1984. *Beauty and the Beast: The Coevolution of Plants and Animals*. New York: Scribner.

Green, S. K., and A. E. Gross. 1979. "Self-Serving Biases in Implicit Evaluations." *Personality and Social Psychology Bulletin* 5:214–17.

Greenberg, Irwin. 1982. "The Role of Deception in Decision Theory." *Journal of Conflict Resolution* 26 (March): 139–56.

Greenslade, S. L. 1956. *Early Latin Theology*. Philadelphia: Westminster.

Greenwald, Anthony G. 1980. "The Totalitarian Ego: Fabrication and Revision of Personal History." *American Psychologist* 35, no. 7: 603–18.

Greenwood, Davydd J., and William A. Stini. 1977. *Nature, Culture, and Human History: A Bio-Cultural Introduction to Anthropology*. New York: Harper & Row.

Gregory, Anita. 1980. "Why Do Scientists Engage in Fraud?" *Parapsychology Review* 11:1–6.

Gregory, R. L. 1970. *The Intelligent Eye*. New York: McGraw-Hill.

————. 1973. *Eye and Brain: The Psychology of Seeing*. 2nd ed. New York: McGraw-Hill.

Gregory, R. L., and E. H. Gombrich, eds. 1973. *Illusion in Nature and Art*. New York: Scribner.

Grossman, Michael Baruch, and Martha Joynt Kumar. 1981. *Portraying the President: The White House and the News Media*. Baltimore: John Hopkins University Press.

Gur, Ruben C., and Harold A. Sackeim. 1979. "Self-Deception: A Concept in Search of a Phenomenon." *Journal of Personality and Social Psychology* 37:147–69.

Haight, M. R. 1980. *A Study of Self-Deception*. Atlantic Highlands, N.J.: Humanities Press.

Haiman, Franklyn S. 1958. "Democratic Ethics and the Hidden Persuaders." *Quarterly Journal of Speech* 44 (December): 385–92.

Hakim, Albert, ed. 1987. *Historical Introduction to Philosophy*. New York: Macmillan.

Hall, Calvin S., and Lindzey Gardner. 1970. *Theories of Personality*. 2nd ed. New York: Wiley.

Hall, James W., and Barbara L. Kevles, eds. 1982. *In Opposition to Core Curriculum: Alternative Models for Undergraduate Education*. Westport, Conn.: Greenwood.

Haney, William V. 1979. *Communication and Interpersonal Relations*. 4th ed. Homewood, Ill.: Irwin.

Hanson, Karen. 1986. *The Self Imagined*. New York: Routledge & Kegan Paul.

Harrison, Alan. 1989. *The Irish Trickster*. Sheffield: Sheffield Academic Press for the Folklore Society.

Hartmann, Heinz. 1939. *Ego Psychology and the Problem of Adaptation*. New York: International Universities Press.

Hebb, Donald. 1949. *The Organization of Behavior*. New York: John Wiley.

Hebb, Donald. 1982. *The Conceptual Nervous System*. Ed. Henry A. Buchtel. Oxford: Pergamon.

Heidegger, Martin. 1978. *Martin Heidegger: Basic Writings*. Ed. David Farrell. London: Routledge.

Heilbrun, A. B., Jr., R. S. Diller, and V. S. Dodson. 1986. "Defensive Projection and Paranoid Delusions." *Journal of Psychiatric Research* 20:161–73.

Heilveil, Ira. 1976. "Deception and Pupil Size." *Journal of Clinical Psychology* 32:675–76.

Heinze, Ruth-Inge. 1985. "Consciousness and Self-Deception: The Art of Undeceiving." *Saybrook Review* 5:11–27.

Hellman, Nathan. 1983. "Bach on Self-Deception." *Philosophy and Phenomenological Research* 44 (September): 113–20.

Henry, D. P. 1972. *Medieval Logic and Metaphysics: A Modern Introduction*. London: Hutchinson.

Hewstone, Miles, ed. 1983. *Attribution Theory: Social and Functional Extensions*. Oxford: Basil Blackwell.

Hiebert, Ray, et al., eds. 1975. *The Political Image Merchants: Strategies for the Seventies*. 2nd ed. Washington, D.C.: Acropolis Books.

Hiley, David R. 1988. *Philosophy in Question: Essays on a Pyrrhonian Theme*. Chicago: University of Chicago Press.

Hillerbrand, Hans J., ed. 1964. *The Reformation*. New York: Harper & Row.

Hirsch, E. D., Jr. 1987. *Cultural Literacy: What Every American Needs to Know*. Boston: Houghton Mifflin.

Hochberg, Julian E. 1978. *Perception*. 2nd ed. Englewood Cliffs, N.J.: Prentice-Hall.

Hock, P. H., and J. Zubin, eds. 1965. *Psychopathology of Perception*. New York: Grune & Stratton.

Holland, Norman N. 1975. *The Dynamics of Literary Response*. New York: Norton.
———. 1982. *Laughing: A Psychology of Humor*. Ithaca, N.Y.: Cornell University Press.

Hood, Leroy E., Irving L. Weissman, and William B. Wood. 1978. *Immunology*. Menlo Park, Calif.: Benjamin/Cummings.

Hooke, Robert. 1983. *How To Tell the Liars from the Statisticians*. New York: Marcel Dekker.

Hopper, Robert, and Robert A. Bell. 1984. "Broadening the Deception Construct." *Quarterly Journal of Speech* 70 (August): 288–302.

Horvath, Frank. 1979. "Effect of Different Motivational Instructions on Detection of Deception with the Psychological Stress Evaluator and the Galvanic Skin Response." *Journal of Applied Psychology* 64:323–30.

Hume, David. 1978. *A Treatise of Human Nature*. Ed. P. H. Nidditch. New York: Oxford University Press.

Huxley, J. R. 1986. "A Possible Explanation for the Symbolic Nature of Language." *Journal of Theoretical Biology* 123 (December): 321–24.

Hyman, Ray. 1989. "The Psychology of Deception." *Annual Review of Psychology* 40:133–54.

Isen, A. M., and B. Means. 1983. "The Influence of Positive Affect on Decision-Making Strategy." *Social Cognition* 2:18–31.

Isen, A. M., and R. Patrick. 1983. "The Effects of Positive Feelings on Risk-Taking: When the Chips Are Down." *Organizational Behavior and Human Performance* 31:194–202.

Janoff-Bulman, Ronnie. 1989. "The Benefits of Illusions, the Threat of Disillusionment, and the Limitations of Inaccuracy." *Journal of Social and Clinical Psychology* 8, no. 2: 160–61.

Janoff-Bulman, Ronnie, and Christine Timko. 1987. "Coping with Traumatic Life Events." In *Coping with Negative Life Events*, ed. C. R. Snyder and Carol E. Ford. New York: Plenum.

Jaroff, Leon. 1988. "Fighting Against Flimflam." *Time*, June 13, pp. 70–72.

Johannesen, Richard L. 1967. *Ethics and Pursuasion: Selected Readings*. New York: Random House.

———. 1983. *Ethics in Human Communication*. 2nd ed. Prospect Heights, Ill.: Waveland Press.

Johnson, Allen W., and Timothy Earle. 1987. *The Evolution of Human Societies: From Foraging Group to Agrarian State*. Stanford: Stanford University Press.

Johnson, J. E., and A. Tversky. 1983. "Affect Generalization and the Perception of Risk." *Journal of Personality and Social Psychology* 29:710–18.

Johnson, M. K., C. L. Raye, H. J. Foley, and M. A. Foley. 1981. "Cognitive Operations and Decision Bias in Reality Monitoring." *American Journal of Psychology* 94:37–64.

Johnson, M. K., C. L. Raye, A. Y. Wang, and T. H. Taylor. 1979. "Fact and Fantasy: The Roles of Accuracy and Variability in Confusing Imaginations with Perceptual Experiences." *Journal of Experimental Psychology: Human Learning and Memory* 5:229–40.

Johnson, M. K., T. H. Taylor, and C. L. Raye. 1977. "Fact and Fantasy: The Effects of Internally Generated Events on the Apparent Frequency of Externally Generated Events." *Memory and Cognition* 5:116–22.

Johnson, Paul. 1980. *A History of Christianity*. New York: Atheneum.

Jones, W. T. 1969–75. *A History of Western Philosophy*. 2nd ed. 5 vols. New York: Harcourt Brace Jovanovich.

Jung, John. 1978. *Understanding Human Motivation: A Cognitive Approach*. New York: Macmillan.

Justin Martyr. 1912. *First Apology*. Edinburgh: John Grant.

Kaluger, George, and Meriem Fair Kaluger. 1979. *Human Development: The Span of Life*. St. Louis: C. V. Mosby.

Kammen, Michael. 1987. *Selvages and Biases: The Fabric of History in American Culture*. Ithaca, N.Y.: Cornell University Press.

Kandel, Eric R. 1976. *Cellular Basis of Behavior*. San Francisco: W. H. Freeman.

Kaplan, Howard B. 1975. *Self-Attitudes and Deviant Behavior*. Pacific Palisades, Calif.: Goodyear.

Katz, Steven T., ed. 1978. *Mysticism and Philosophical Analysis*. New York: Oxford University Press.

Kaufmann, Walter, ed. 1956. *Existentialism from Dostoevsky to Sartre*. New York: Meridian.

Kavka, S. J. 1987. "Deception." *Postgraduate Medicine* 82 (September): 73–74.

Kaye, John. 1912. *The First Apology of Justin Martyr*. Edinburgh: John Grant.

Keillor, Garrison. 1989. *We Are Still Married*. New York: Viking.

Keller, Helen. 1903. *The Story of My Life*. New York: Doubleday-Page.

Kelley, Carl F. 1977. *Meister Eckhart on Divine Knowledge*. New Haven: Yale University Press.

Kennedy, C. R. 1984. "Host-Parasite Interrelationships." In *Producers and Scroungers: Strategies of Exploitation and Parasitism*, ed. C. J. Barnard. New York: Chapman & Hall.

Kennedy, John M. 1974. *A Psychology of Picture Perception*. San Francisco: Jossey-Bass.

Kern, Montague. 1989. *30-Second Politics: Political Advertising in the Eighties*. New York: Praeger.

Kerr, Clark. 1991. *The Great Transformation in Higher Education: 1960–1980*. Albany: State University of New York Press.

Kerr, Philip, ed. 1990. *The Penguin Book of Lies*. New York: Viking.

Kety, S. S. 1974. "From Irrationality to Reason." *American Journal of Psychiatry* 131:957–62.

Key, Wilson Bryan. 1973. *Subliminal Seduction: Ad Media's Manipulation of a Not So Innocent America*. Englewood Cliffs, N.J.: Prentice-Hall.

———. 1976. *Media Sexploitation*. Englewood Cliffs, N.J.: Prentice-Hall.

———. 1980. *The Clam-Plate Orgy and Other Subliminal Techniques for Manipulating Your Behavior*. Englewood Cliffs, N.J.: Prentice-Hall.

Kieckhefer, Richard. 1984. "John Tauler." In *An Introduction to the Medieval Mystics of Europe*, ed. Paul Szarmach. Albany: State University of New York Press.

Kierkegaard, Søren. 1946. *A Kierkagaard Anthology*. Ed. Robert Bretall. New York: Modern Library.

Klein, Allen. 1989. *The Healing Power of Humor*. Los Angeles: Jeremy P. Tarcher.

Knapp, Mark L. 1980. *Essentials of Nonverbal Communication*. New York: Holt, Rinehart & Winston.

Knapp, Mark L., and Mark E. Comadena. 1979. "Telling It Like It Isn't: A Review of Theory and Research on Deceptive Communications." *Human Communication Research* 5 (Spring): 270–85.

Kneale, William, and Martha Kneale. 1962. *The Development of Logic*. Oxford: Clarendon.

Knowles, David. 1964. *The Evolution of Medieval Thought*. New York: Random House.

———. 1969. *Christian Monasticism*. New York: McGraw-Hill.

Koepping, Klaus-Peter. 1985. "Absurdity and Hidden Truth: Cunning Intelligence and Grotesque Body Images as Manifestations of the Trickster." *History of Religions* 24:191–214.

Kohn, Alexander. 1986. *False Prophets: Fraud and Error in Science and Medicine.* New York: Basil Blackwell.

Kottak, Conrad Phillip. 1987. *Cultural Anthropology.* 4th ed. New York: Random House.

Kraemer, Ross S. 1988. *Maenads, Martyrs, Matrons, Monastics.* Philadelphia: Fortress Press.

Kraut, Robert E., and Donald Poe. 1980. "Behavioral Roots of Person Perception: The Deception Judgements of Customs Inspectors and Laymen." *Journal of Personality and Social Psychology* 39:784–98.

Krebs, J. R., and N. B. Davies. 1978. *Behavioural Ecology: An Evolutionary Approach.* Oxford: Blackwell Scientific.

Kreitler, Hans, and Shulamith Kreitler. 1976. *Cognitive Orientation and Behavior.* New York: Springer.

Kretzmann, Norman, Anthony Kenny, and Jan Pinborg, eds. 1982. *The Cambridge History of Later Medieval Philosophy.* New York: Cambridge University Press.

Kübler-Ross, Elizabeth. 1969. *On Death and Dying.* New York: Macmillan.

Kurtz, Paul. 1973. *The Humanist Alternative.* Buffalo, N.Y.: Prometheus.

———. 1986. *The Transcendental Temptation.* Buffalo, N.Y.: Prometheus.

Kysar, Robert. 1976. *John, the Mavrick Gospel.* Atlanta: John Knox Press.

Lamont, Corliss. 1949. *Humanism as a Philosophy.* New York: Philosophical Library.

Langer, E. J. 1975. "The Illusion of Control." *Journal of Personality and Social Psychology* 32:311–28.

Larson, Charles U. 1983. *Persuasion: Reception and Responsibility.* 4th ed. Belmont, Calif.: Wadsworth.

Lavin, M. 1987. "Mutilation, Deception, and Sex Changes." *Journal of Medical Ethics* 13 (June): 86–91.

Lawrence, C. H. 1984. *Medieval Monasticism.* New York: Longman.

Lazarus, R. S. "The Costs and Benefits of Denial." In *Denial of Stress,* ed. S. Brenitz. New York: International Universities Press.

Leavy, Stanley A. 1988. *The Image of God: A Psychoanalysist's View.* New Haven: Yale University Press.

Lee, D. E. 1987. "The Self-Deception of the Self-Destructive." *Perceptual Motor Skills* 65 (December): 975–89.

Lefcourt, H. M. 1973. "The Function of the Illusions of Control and Freedom." *American Psychologist* (May): 417–25.

Leff, Gordon. 1958. *Medieval Thought: St. Augustine to Ockham.* Baltimore: Penguin.

Lehman, David. 1991. *Signs of the Times: Deconstruction and the Fall of Paul de Man.* New York: Poseidon.

Leibniz, G. W. 1981. *New Essays on Human Understanding.* Ed. and trans. Peter Remnant and Jonathan Bennett. New York: Cambridge University Press.

Lenz, William E. 1985. *Fast Talk and Flush Times: The Confidence Man as a Literary Convention.* Columbia: University of Missouri Press.

Lettieri, R. J. 1983. "Consciousness, Self-Deception, and Psychotherapy: An Analogue Study." *Imagination, Cognition, and Personality* 3:83–97.

Levine, David O. 1986. *The American College and the Culture of Aspiration, 1915–1940.* Ithaca, N.Y.: Cornell University Press.

Levine, Lawrence W. 1988. *Highbrow/Lowbrow: The Emergence of Cultural Hierarchy in America.* Cambridge: Harvard University Press.

Lewicki, Pawel. 1984. "Self-Schema and Social Information Processing." *Journal of Personality and Social Psychology* 47:1177–90.

Lewin, Roger. 1987. "Do Animals Read Minds, Tell Lies?" *Science* 238 (December): 1350–51.

———. 1989. "How Females Entrap Males." *Science* 243 (March): 1289.

Lewinsohn, P. M., W. Mischel, W. Chaplin, and R. Barton. 1980. "Social Competence and Depression: The Role of Illusory Self-Perceptions." *Journal of Abnormal Psychology* 89:203–12.

Lewis, Michael, Catherine Stanger, and Margaret W. Sullivan. 1989. "Deception in 3-Year-Olds." *Developmental Psychology* 25:439–43.

Liddell Hart, B. H. 1954. *Strategy.* New York: Praeger.

Liebert, Robert M., Rita Wicks Poulos, and Gloria Strauss Marmor. 1977. *Developmental Psychology.* 2nd ed. Englewood Cliffs, N.J.: Prentice-Hall.

Lifton, Robert Jay. 1986. *The Nazi Doctors: Medical Killing and the Psychology of Genocide.* New York: Basic Books.

Lindskold, Svenn, and Pamela S. Walters. 1983. "Categories forAcceptability of Lies." *Journal of Social Psychology* 120 (June): 129–36.

LineBarger, Paul M. A. 1948. *Psychological Warfare.* Washington, D.C.: Infantry Journal Press.

Lipowski, Z. J. 1967. "Delirium, Clouding of Consciousness, and Confusion." *Journal of Nervous and Mental Disease* 145:227–55.

Livingstone, Margaret S. 1988. "Art, Illusion, and the Visual System." *Scientific American* 259 (January): 78–85.

Lockard, Joan S., Barbara C. Kirkevold, and Douglas F. Kalk. 1980. "Cost-Benefit Indexes of Deception in Nonviolent Crime." *Bulletin of the Psychonomic Society* 16: 303–6.

Lockard, Joan S., and Delroy L. Paulhus, eds. 1988. *Self-Deception: An Adaptive Mechanism?* Englewood Cliffs, N.J.: Prentice-Hall.

Locke, John. 1823. *The Works of John Locke.* 10 vols. London: Thomas Tegg.

Lorenz, Konrad. 1977. *Behind the Mirror: A Search for a Natural History of Human Knowledge.* New York: Harcourt Brace Jovanovich.

Lowenthal, Leo, and Norbert Guterman. 1970. *Prophets of Deceit.* 2nd ed. Palo Alto, Calif.: Pacific Books.

Luckiesh, M. 1965. *Visual Illusions: Their Causes, Characteristics and Applications.* New York: Dover.

Ludwig, Arnold M. 1965. *The Importance of Lying.* Springfield, Ill.: Charles C Thomas.

Lugo, James O., and Gerald L. Hershey. 1974. *Human Development: A Psychological Approach to the Psychology of Individual Growth.* New York: Macmillan.

Lukacs, John. 1968. *Historical Consciousness: Or the Remembered Past*. New York: Harper & Row.

Lundgren, David C., Virginia H. Jergens, and Jay L. Gibson. 1980. "Marital Relationships, Evaluations of Spouse and Self, and Anxiety." *Journal of Psychology* 106:227–40.

Luther, Martin. 1961. *Selections from His Writings*. Ed. John Dillenberger. Garden City, N.Y.: Anchor.

Machiavelli, Nicolò. 1977. *The Prince*. Ed. Robert M. Adams. New York: Norton.

MacLeish, Archibald. 1952. "Hypocrite Auteur." In *Collected Poems, 1917–1952*. Boston: Houghton Mifflin.

Magee, Bryan. 1983. *The Philosophy of Schopenhauer*. New York: Oxford University Press.

Maher, B. 1974. "Delusional Thinking and Perceptual Disorder." *Journal of Individual Psychology* 30:98–113.

Mahler, Margaret S., Fred Pine, and Anni Bergman. 1975. *The Psychological Birth of the Human Infant*. New York: Basic Books.

Mahoney, Michael J. 1988. "Self-Deception In Science." *Origins Research* 11:1–2, 6–7, 10.

Maier, Richard A., and Lavrakas, Paul J. 1976. "Lying Behavior and Evaluation of Lies." *Perceptual and Motor Skills* 42:575–81.

Manstead, Anthony S., H. L. Wagner, and C. J. MacDonald. 1986. "Deceptive and Nondeceptive Communications: Sending Experience, Modality, and Individual Abilities." *Journal of Nonverbal Behavior* 10:147–67.

Margolis, Joseph. 1991. *The Truth About Relativism*. Cambridge, Mass.: Basil Blackwell.

Markus, H. 1977. "Self-Schemata and Processing Information About the Self." *Journal of Personality and Social Psychology* 35:63–78.

Markus, H., and Nurius, P. 1986. "Possible Selves." *American Psychologist* 41:954–69.

Martin, Mike W. 1986. *Self-Deception and Morality*. Lawrence: University Press of Kansas.

——, ed. 1985. *Self-Deception and Self-Understanding: New Essays in Philosophy and Psychology*. Lawrence: University Press of Kansas.

Marx, Karl, and Friedrich Engels. 1959. *Basic Writings on Politics and Philosophy*. Ed. Lewis S. Feuer. Garden City, N.Y.: Anchor.

Maslow, A. H. 1968. *Toward a Psychology of Being*. 2nd ed. New York: Van Nostrand.

Matas, M., and A. Marriot. 1987. "The Girl Who Cried Wolf: Pseudologia Phantastica and Sexual Abuse." *Canadian Journal of Psychiatry* 32 (May): 305–9.

Materson, James F. 1988. *The Search for the Real Self*. New York: Free Press.

Mates, Benson. 1986. *The Philosophy of Leibniz*. New York: Oxford University Press.

Mathews, Jessica Tuchman, ed. 1991. *Preserving the Global Environment: The Challenge of Shared Leadership*. New York: Norton.

Mavrodes, George I. 1978. "Real v. Deceptive Mystical Experiences." In *Mysticism and Philosophical Analysis*, ed. Steven T. Katz. New York: Oxford University Press.

Mayer, Milton. 1955. *They Thought They Were Free: The Germans, 1933–35.* Chicago: University of Chicago Press.

McCloskey, Paul N., Jr. 1972. *Truth and Untruth: Political Deceit in America.* New York: Simon & Schuster.

McDermott, John J., ed. 1985. *A Cultural Introduction to Philosophy.* New York: Knopf.

McGaffin, William, and Erwin Knoll. 1968. *Anything but the Truth: The Credibility Gap—How News Is Managed in Washington.* New York: Putnam.

McGehee, Ralph. 1983. *Deadly Deceits: My Twenty-five Years in the CIA.* New York: Sheridan Square.

McGhee, Paul E. 1979. *Humor: Its Origin and Development.* San Francisco: W. H. Freeman.

McGinn, Bernard, ed. 1986. *Meister Eckhart, Teacher and Preacher.* Mahwah, N.J.: Paulist Press.

McKeon, Richard. 1957. "Communication, Truth, and Society." *Ethics* 67:89–99.

———, ed. 1947. *Introduction to Aristotle.* New York: Modern Library.

McLaughlin, Brian P., and Amelie Oskenberg Rorty, eds. 1988. *Perspectives on Self-Deception.* Berkeley: University of California Press.

Meister, Eckhart. 1941. *Meister Eckhart: A Modern Translation.* Trans. Raymond Bernard Blakney. New York: Harper.

———. 1963. *Selected Treatises and Sermons.* Trans. James M. Clark and John V. Skinner. London: Fontana Library.

———. 1981. *The Essential Sermons, Commentaries, Treatises and Defense.* Trans. Edmund Colledge and Bernard McGinn. Ramsey, N.J.: Paulist Press.

Mele, Alfred. 1987a. *Irrationality: An Essay on Akrasia, Self-Deception, and Self-Control.* New York: Oxford University Press.

———. 1987b. "Recent Work on Self-Deception." *American Philosophical Quarterly* 24 (January): 1–17.

Mettrick, D. F., and S. S. Desser, eds. 1982. *Parasites, Their World and Ours.* New York: Elsevier Science.

Michaels, Claire F., and Claudia Carello. 1981. *Direct Perception.* Englewood Cliffs, N.J.: Prentice-Hall.

Miles, H. Lyn. 1986. "How Can I Tell A Lie? Apes, Language, and the Problem of Deception." In *Deception: Perspectives on Human and Nonhuman Deceit*, ed. Robert W. Mitchell and Nicholas S. Thompson. Albany: State University of New York Press.

Miller, D. T. 1976. "Ego Involvement and Attributions for Success and Failure." *Journal of Personality and Social Psychology* 34:901–6.

Miller, D. T., and M. Ross. 1975. "Self-Serving Biases in Attribution of Causality: Fact or Fiction?" *Psychological Bulletin* 82:213–25.

Miller, Robert. 1991. *Cortico-Hippocampal Interplay and the Representation of Contexts in the Brain.* New York: Springer-Verlag.

Millham, Jim, and Richard W. Kellogg. 1980. "Need for Social Approval: Impression Management or Self-Deception?" *Journal of Research in Personality* 14:445–57.

Millon, Theodore. 1981. *Disorders of Personality: DSM-III, Axis II*. New York: Wiley.

Minnich, Elizabeth Kamarck. 1985. "Why Not Lie?" *Soundings* 68:493–509.

Mischel, W., E. B. Ebbeson, and A. M. Zeiss. 1976. "Determinants of Selective Memory About the Self." *Journal of Consulting and Clinical Psychology* 44:92–103.

Mitchell, Robert W., and Nicholas S. Thompson. 1986. "Deception in Play Between Dogs and People." In *Deception: Perspectives on Human and Nonhuman Deceit,* ed. Robert W. Mitchell and Nicholas S. Thompson. Albany: State University of New York Press.

———, eds. 1986. *Deception: Perspectives on Human and Nonhuman Deceit.* Albany: State University of New York Press.

Montaigne, Michel. 1958. *The Complete Essays of Montaigne*. Trans. Donald M. Frame. Stanford: Stanford University Press.

Monts, J. Kenneth, Louis A. Zurcher, Jr., and Rudy V. Nydegger. 1977. "Interpersonal Self-Deception and Personality Correlates." *Journal of Social Psychology* 103:91–99.

Moore, Sonia. 1984. *The Stanislavski System: The Professional Training of an Actor*. 2nd ed. New York: Viking.

Morris, Maxine. 1986. "Large-Scale Deception: Deceit in Captive Elephants?" In *Deception: Perspectives on Human and Nonhuman Deceit,* ed. Robert W. Mitchell and Nicholas S. Thompson. Albany: State University of New York Press.

Mosse, George. 1964. *The Crisis of German Ideology*. New York: Universal Library.

———, ed. 1968. *Nazi Culture*. New York: Universal Library.

Mourant, John A. 1964. *Introduction to the Philosophy of Saint Augustine*. University Park: Pennsylvania State University Press.

Moustakas, Clark E. 1962. "Honesty, Idiocy, and Manipulation." *Journal of Humanistic Psychology* 2 (Fall): 1–15.

Mueller, Conrad G. 1965. *Sensory Psychology*. Englewood Cliffs, N.J.: Prentice-Hall.

Munn, Charles A. 1986. "Birds that 'Cry Wolf.' " *Nature* 319 (January): 143–45.

Murdoch, Iris. 1977. *The Fire and the Sun: Why Plato Banished the Artists*. Oxford: Clarendon.

Murphy, Kevin R. 1987. "Detecting Infrequent Deception." *Journal of Applied Psychology* 72 (November): 611–14.

Natale, Jo Anna. 1988. "Are You Open to Suggestions?" *Psychology Today* 22 (September): 28–30.

Nesse, Randolph. 1992. "The Evolution of Psychodynamic Mechanisms." In *Psychology and the Generation of Culture,* ed. J. Barkow, L. Cosmides, and J. Tooby, pp. 601–24. New York: Oxford University Press.

Nickle, Keith F. 1980. *The Synoptic Gospels*. Atlanta: John Knox Press.

Nickol, Brent B., ed. 1979. *Host-Parasite Interfaces*. New York: Academic Press.

Nicolai, Jürgen. 1974. "Mimicry in Parasitic Birds." *Scientific American* 231 (October): 92–98.

Niditch, Susan. 1987. *Underdogs and Tricksters: A Prelude to Biblical Folklore.* San Francisco: Harper & Row.

Niebuhr, Reinhold. 1939. "Ten Years That Shook My World." *Christian Century,* April 26.

———. 1941–43. *The Nature and Destiny of Man.* 2 vols. New York: Scribner.

Nietzsche, Friedrich. 1967. *The Will to Power.* Trans. Walter Kaufmann. New York: Random House.

———. 1968. *The Portable Nietzsche.* Ed. Walter Kaufman. New York: Viking.

———. 1974. *The Gay Science.* Trans. Walter Kaufmann. New York: Random House.

Nisbet, Robert. 1980. *History of the Idea of Progress.* New York: Basic Books.

Nitecki, M. H., ed. 1983. *Coevolution.* Chicago: University of Chicago Press.

Nolhac, Pierre de. 1907. *Petrarch and the Ancient World.* Boston: Merrymount.

Novak, Michael. 1974. *Choosing Our King: Powerful Symbols in Presidential Politics.* New York: Macmillian.

Nussbaum, Martha. 1983. "Fictions of the Soul." *Philosophy and Literature* 17:145–61.

Oates, David. 1989. *Earth Rising: Ecological Belief in an Age of Science.* Corvallis: Oregon State University Press.

Odum, Eugene P. 1989. *Ecology and Our Endangered Life-Support Systems.* Sunderland, Mass.: Sinauer.

Oddie, G. J., and R. W. Perrett. 1986. "Truth Telling and Fatal Illness." *New Zealand Medical Journal* 99:759–61.

O'Hair, Henry D., Michael J. Cody, and Margret L. McLaughlin. 1981. "Prepared Lies, Spontaneous Lies, Machiavellianism, and Nonverbal Communication." *Human Communication Research* 7:325–39.

Oldstone, M. B. 1987. "Molecular Mimicry and Autoimmune Disease." *Cell* 50 (September): 819–20.

———, ed. 1989. *Molecular Mimicry: Cross-Reactivity Between Microbes and Host Proteins as a Cause of Autoimmunity.* New York: Springer-Verlag.

Oldstone, Michael B. A., and Abner L. Notkins, eds. 1986. *Concepts in Viral Pathogenesis II.* New York: Springer-Verlag.

Olson, Jerry C., and Philip A. Dover. 1978. "Cognitive Effects of Deceptive Advertising." *Journal of Marketing Research* 15 (February): 29–38.

Olson, Philip. 1970. *The Study of Modern Society: Perspectives from Classic Sociology.* New York: Random House.

Origen. 1979. *An Exhortation to Martyrdom, Prayer, and Selected Works.* Trans. Rowan A. Greer. New York: Paulist Press.

Ornstein, Robert, and Paul Ehrlich. 1990. *New World, New Mind: Moving Toward Conscious Evolution.* New York: Simon & Schuster.

Ostrovsky, Victor, and Claire Hoy. 1991. *By Way of Deception.* New York: St. Martin's Paperbacks.

Otte, D. 1974. "Effects and Functions in the Evolution of Signalling Systems." *Annual Review of Ecology and Systematics* 5:385–417.

———. 1975. "On the Role of Intraspecific Deception." *American Naturalist* 109:239–42.

Owen, Dennis Frank. 1982. *Camouflage and Mimicry*. Chicago: University of Chicago Press.

Packard, Vance. 1957. *The Hidden Persuaders*. New York: McKay.

Parenti, Michael. 1980. *Democracy for the Few*. 3rd ed. New York: St. Martin's Press.

Parkes, C. M. 1975. "What Becomes of Redundant World Models? A Contribution to the Study of Adaptation to Change." *British Journal of Medical Psychology* 48(2):131–37.

Partington, John T., and Catherine Grant. 1984. "Imaginary Playmates and Other Useful Fantasies." In *Play in Animals and Humans*, ed. Peter K. Smith. Oxford: Basil Blackwell.

Patterson, James T. 1987. *The Dread Disease: Cancer and Modern American Culture*. Cambridge: Harvard University Press.

Patterson, Thomas E. 1980. *The Mass Media Election: How Americans Choose Their President*. New York: Praeger.

Pelikan, Jaroslav. 1984. *Reformation of Church and Dogma*. Chicago: University of Chicago Press.

Pelton, Robert D. 1980. *The Trickster in West Africa: Myth, Irony, and Sacred Delight*. Berkeley: University of California Press.

Pfeiffer, John E. 1977. *The Emergence of Society: A Prehistory of the Establishment*. New York: McGraw-Hill.

Phillips, D. Z. 1988. *Faith After Foundationalism*. New York: Routledge.

Piaget, Jean. 1971. *The Construction of Reality in the Child*. New York: Basic Books.

Pieper, Josef. 1960. *Scholasticism: Personalities and Problems of Medieval Philosophy*. New York: Pantheon.

Plato. 1937. *The Dialogues of Plato*. Trans. Benjamin Jowett. 2 vols. New York: Random House.

———. 1968. *The Republic of Plato*. Trans. Allan Bloom. New York: Basic Books.

Polanyi, Karl. 1968. *Primitive, Archaic, and Modern Economies: Essays of Karl Polanyi*. Ed. George Dalton. Garden City, N.Y.: Anchor.

Pope, William R., and Donelson R. Forsyth. 1986. "Judgements of Deceptive Communications: A Multidimensional Analysis." *Bulletin of the Psychonomic Society* 24 (November): 435–36.

Popkin, Richard. 1979. *The History of Scepticism from Erasmus to Spinoza*. Berkeley: University of California Press.

Portmann, Adolf. 1959. *Animal Camouflage*. Trans. A. J. Pomerans. Ann Arbor: University of Michigan Press.

Preston, Ivan. 1975. *The Great American Blow-up: Puffery in Advertising and Selling*. Madison: University of Wisconsin Press.

Price, Peter W. 1980. *Evolutionary Biology of Parasites*. Princeton: Princeton University Press.

Prickett, Stephen. 1986. *Words and the Word*. Cambridge: Cambridge University Press.

Randi, James. 1982. *Flim-Flam!* Buffalo, N.Y.: Prometheus.

Richardson, Cyril C., trans. 1953. *Early Christian Fathers*. Philadelphia: Westminster.

Riggio, Ronald E., and Howard S. Friedman. 1983. "Individual Differences and Cues to Deception." *Journal of Personality and Social Psychology* 45 (October): 899–915.

Rock, Irvin. 1975. *An Introduction to Perception*. New York: Macmillan.

Rogers, Dorothy. 1982. *Life-Span Human Development*. Monterey, Calif.: Brooks/ Cole.

Rogers, Richard, ed. 1988. *Clinical Assessment of Malingering and Deception*. New York: Guilford.

Rorty, Amélie O. 1980. "Self-Deception, Akrasia, and Irrationality." *Social Science Information* 19:905–22.

Rorty, Richard. 1989. *Contingency, Irony, and Solidarity*. New York: Cambridge University Press.

Rose, Phyllis. 1984. *Parallel Lives*. New York: Knopf.

Rose, Richard. 1988. *The Postmodern President: The White House Meets the World*. Chatham, N.J.: Chatham House.

Rosenberg, Morris. 1979. *Conceiving the Self*. New York: Basic Books.

Rosenkilde, Carl E. 1983. *Functions of the Prefrontal Cortex: Behavioral Investigations Using Ablation and Electrophysiological Techniques in Rats, Cats, Dogs, and Monkeys*. Uppsala: Almqvist & Wiksell.

Rosenstock-Heussy, Eugene. 1970. *Speech and Reality*. Norwich, Vt.: Argo.

Rostand, Jean. 1960. *Error and Deception in Science*. New York: Basic Books.

Roszak, Theodore. 1992. *The Voice of the Earth*. New York: Simon & Schuster.

Rowland, Christopher. 1985. *Christian Origins: From Messianic Movement to Christian Religion*. Minneapolis: Augsburg.

Rudolph, Frederick. 1977. *Curriculum: A History of the American Undergraduate Course of Study Since 1636*. San Francisco: Jossey-Bass.

Rue, Loyal D. 1989. *Amythia: Crisis in the Natural History of Western Culture*. Tuscaloosa: University of Alabama Press.

Rumelhart, David. 1980. "Schemata: The Building Blocks of Cognition." In *Theoretical Issues in Reading Comprehension*, ed. R. J. Spiro, B. C. Bruce, and W. F. Brewer. Hillsdale, N.J.: Lawrence Erlbaum.

Rumelhart, David E., James L. McClelland, and the PDDP Research Group. 1986. *Parallel Distributive Processing*. 2 vols. Cambridge: MIT Press.

Rüppell, Von G. 1986. "A Lie as a Directed Message of the Arctic Fox." In *Deception: Perspectives on Human and Nonhuman Deceit*, ed. Robert W. Mitchell and Nicholas S. Thompson. Albany: State University of New York Press.

Ruse, Michael, ed. 1989. *Philosophy of Biology*. New York: Macmillan.

Russell, Norman, and Benedicta Ward, trans. 1981. *The Lives of the Desert Fathers: The Historia Monachorum in Aegypto*. Kalamazoo: Cistercian Publications.

Sackeim, H. A. 1983. "Self-Deception, Self-Esteem, and Depression: The Adaptive Value of Lying to Oneself." In *Empirical Studies of Psychoanalytical Theories*, ed. J. Masling. Vol. 1. Hillsdale, N.J.: Analytic Press.

Sackeim, H. A., and R. C. Gur. 1978. "Self-Deception, Self-Confrontation, and Consciousness." In *Consciousness and Self-Regulation: Advances in Research and Theory*, ed. Gary E. Schwartz and David Shapiro, vol. 2. New York: Plenum.

———. 1979. "Self-Deception, Other-Deception, and Self-Reported Psychopathology." *Journal of Consulting and Clinical Psychology* 47:213–15.

Samstag, Nicholas. 1966. *How Business Is Bamboozled by the Ad Boys*. New York: Heineman.

Sarbin, T. R. 1981. "On Self-Deception." *Sciences* 364:220–35.

Sargant, William. 1957. *Battle for the Mind: A Physiology of Conversion and Brainwashing*. New York: Doubleday.

Sayers, William B. 1989. "The Lighter Side of Lying." *Parents*, June.

Schaefer, T., and N. Bernick. 1965. "Sensory Deprivation and Its Effects on Perception." In *Psychopathology of Perception*, ed. P. H. Hock and J. Zubin. New York: Grune & Stratton.

Scharfenberg, Joachim. 1988. *Sigmund Freud and His Critique of Religion*. Trans. O. C. Dean. Philadelphia: Fortress Press.

Schlenker, B., ed. 1985. *The Self and Social Life*. New York: McGraw-Hill.

Schopenhauer, Arthur. 1956. *Schopenhauer: Selections*. Ed. D. H. Parker. New York: Scribner.

Schrank, Jeffrey. 1975. *Deception Detection*. Boston: Beacon.

Schumaker, John F. 1990. *Wings of Illusion: The Origin, Nature and Future of Paranormal Belief*. Buffalo, N.Y.: Prometheus.

Schweitzer, Sydney C. 1979. *Winning with Deception and Bluff*. Englewood Cliffs, N.J.: Prentice-Hall.

Segal, Alan F. 1990. *Paul the Convert: The Apostolate and Apostasy of Saul the Pharisee*. New Haven: Yale University Press.

Seigel, Jerrold. 1968. *Rhetoric and Philosophy in Renaissance Humanism*. Princeton: Princeton University Press.

Sekuler, Robert, and Randolph Blake. 1985. *Perception*. New York: Knopf.

Seligman, Martin E. P. 1991. *Learned Optimism*. New York: Knopf.

Service, Elman R. 1962. *Primitive Social Organization: An Evolutionary Perspective*. New York: Random House.

———. 1978. *Profiles in Ethnology*. 3rd ed. New York: Harper & Row.

Sexton, Donal J. 1986. "The Theory and Psychology of Military Deception." In *Deception: Perspectives on Human and Nonhuman Deceit*, ed. Robert W. Mitchell and Nicholas S. Thompson. Albany: State University of New York Press.

Shapiro, A. K. 1964. "Factors Contributing to the Placebo Effect: Their Implications for Psychotherapy." *American Journal of Psychotherapy* 18:73–88.

Shaw, Joseph, et al., eds. 1982. *Readings in Christian Humanism*. Minneapolis: Augsburg.

Shaw, Marvin E. 1981. *Group Dynamics: The Psychology of Small Group Behavior.* 3rd ed. New York: McGraw-Hill.

Shimp, Terence, and Ivan L. Preston. 1981. "Deceptive and Nondeceptive Consequences of Evaluative Advertising." *Journal of Marketing* 45:22–32.

Shrauger, J. S. 1972. "Self-Esteem and Reactions to Being Observed by Others." *Journal of Personality and Social Psychology* 23:192–200.

Shurcliff, A. 1968. "Judged Humor, Arousal, and the Relief Theory." *Journal of Personality and Social Psychology* 8:360–63.

Singer, Jerome L. 1973. *The Child's World of Make-Believe: Experimental Studies of Imaginative Play.* New York: Academic Press.

Sisson, Robert F. 1980. "Deception: Formula for Survival." *National Geographic* 157 (March): 394–415.

Sitton, Sarah C., and Susan T. Griffin. 1981. "Detection of Deception from Clients' Eye Contact Patterns." *Journal of Counseling Psychology* 28:269–71.

Skinner, B. F. 1974. *About Behaviorism.* New York: Knopf.

Slade, Peter D., and Richard P. Bentall. 1988. *Sensory Deception: A Scientific Analysis of Hallucination.* Baltimore: John Hopkins University Press.

Slatkin, M., and D. J. Futuyma. 1983. *Coevolution.* Sunderland, Mass.: Sinauer.

Sloan, Tod S. 1987. *Deciding: Self-Deception in Life Choices.* New York: Methuen.

Smith, Peter B., ed. 1980. *Small Groups and Personal Change.* London: Methuen.

Snyder, C. R. 1989. "Reality Negotiation: From Excuses to Hope and Beyond." *Journal of Social and Clinical Psychology* 8, no. 2: 136.

Snyder, C. R., Raymond L. Higgins, and Rita J. Stucky. 1983. *Excuses: Masquerades in Search of Grace.* New York: Wiley.

Snyder, C. R., and Carol E. Ford, eds. 1987. *Coping with Negative Life Events.* New York: Plenum.

Snyder, Mark. 1987. *Public Appearances/Private Realities: The Psychology of Self-Monitoring.* New York: W. H. Freeman.

Snyter, C. Michael, and Judith P. Allik. 1981. "The Fakability of the Personal Orientation Dimensions: Evidence for a Lie Profile." *Journal of Personality Assessment* 45 (October): 533–38.

Sordahl, Tex. 1986. "Evolutionary Aspects of Avian Distraction Display." In *Deception: Perspectives on Human and Nonhuman Deceit,* ed. Robert W. Mitchell and Nicholas S. Thompson. Albany: State University of New York Press.

———. 1988. "The American Avocet (*Recurvirostra americana*) as a Paradigm for Adult Automimicry." *Evolutionary Ecology* 2:189–96.

Sorel, Georges. 1969. *The Illusions of Progress.* Trans. John Stanley and Charlotte Stanley. Berkeley: University of California Press.

Spedding, James, et al., eds. 1872. *The Works of Francis Bacon.* New York: Hurd & Houghton.

Spero, Robert. 1980. *The Duping of the American Voter: Dishonesty and Deception in Presidential Television Advertising.* New York: Lippincott & Crowell.

Spinoza, Benedict. 1985. *The Collected Works of Spinoza.* Ed. and trans. Edwin Curley. Princeton: Princeton University Press.

Spiro, R. J., B. C. Bruce, and W. F. Brewer, eds. 1980. *Theoretical Issues in Reading Comprehension*. Hillsdale, N.J.: Lawrence Erlbaum.

Stace, Walter T. 1948. "Man Against Darkness." *Atlantic*, September.

———, ed. 1960. *The Teachings of the Mystics*. New York: New American Library.

Starkie, Walter. 1957. *The Road to Santiago: Pilgrims of St. James*. New York: Dutton.

Stebbins, R. A. 1975. "Putting People On: Deception of Our Fellow Man in Everyday Life." *Sociology and Social Research* 59:189–200.

Steward, Julian H. 1955. *Theory of Culture Change: The Methodology of Multilinear Evolution*. Urbana: University of Illinois Press.

———. 1977. *Evolution and Ecology: Essays on Social Transformation by Julian H. Steward*. Ed. Jane C. Steward and Robert F. Murphy. Urbana: University of Illinois Press.

Stockwell, John R. 1978. *In Search of Enemies: A CIA Story*. New York: Norton.

Stone, Robert L., ed. 1989. *Essays on "The Closing of the American Mind."* Chicago: Chicago Review Press.

Stoutamire, W. P. 1974. "Australian Terrestrial Orchids, Thynid Wasps, and Pseudocopulation." *American Orchid Society Bulletin* 43:13–18.

Stromberg, Roland. 1966. *An Intellectual History of Modern Europe*. New York: Appleton-Century-Crofts.

Stuss, Donald T., and D. Frank Benson. 1986. *The Frontal Lobes*. New York: Raven.

Sumption, Jonathan. 1975. *Pilgrimage: An Image of Mediaeval Religion*. Totowa, N.J.: Rowman & Littlefield.

Sun Tzu. 1963. *The Art of War*. Trans. Samuel B. Griffith. Oxford: Clarendon.

Sussman, Barry. 1988. *What Americans Think and Why Politicians Ignore Them*. New York: Simon & Schuster.

Swann, W. B., Jr. 1984. "Quest for Accuracy in Person Perception: A Matter of Pragmatics." *Psychological Review* 91:457–77.

Swann, W. B., Jr., and C. A. Hill. 1982. "When Our Identities Are Mistaken: Reaffirming Self-Conceptions Through Social Interaction." *Journal of Personality and Social Psychology* 43:59–66.

Swann, W. B., Jr., and S. J. Read. 1981a. "Acquiring Self-Knowledge: The Search for Feedback That Fits." *Journal of Personality and Social Psychology* 41: 1119–28.

———. 1981b. "Self-Verification Processes: How We Sustain Our Self-Conceptions." *Journal of Experimental Psychology* 17:351–70.

Swidler, Leonard. 1990. *After the Absolute: The Dialogical Future of Religious Reflection*. Minneapolis: Fortress Press.

Swimme, Brian, and Thomas Berry. 1992. *The Universe Story*. San Francisco: HarperCollins.

Sykes, Charles J. 1988. *ProfScam: Professors and the Demise of Higher Education*. Washington, D.C.: Regnery Gateway.

Szarmach, Paul E., ed. 1984. *An Introduction to the Medieval Mystics of Europe*. Albany: State University of New York Press.

Taylor, Mark C. 1984. *Erring: A Postmodern A/Theology*. Chicago: University of Chicago Press.

Taylor, Shelley E. 1989. *Positive Illusions: Creative Self-Deception and the Healthy Mind*. New York: Basic Books.

Taylor, Shelley E., and J. Brown. 1988. "Illusion and Well-Being: A Social Psychological Perspective on Mental Health." *Psychological Bulletin* 103:193–210.

Taylor, Shelley E., Rebecca L. Collins, Laurie A. Skokan, and Lisa G. Aspinwall. 1989. "Maintaining Positive Illusions in the Face of Negative Information: Getting the Facts Without Letting Them Get to You." *Journal of Social and Clinical Psychology* 8:114–29.

Teresa of Avila, St. 1957. *The Complete Works of Saint Teresa of Jesus*. Ed. and trans. E. Allison Peers. 3 vols. London: Sheed & Ward.

Theologia Germanica. 1949. Trans. Susan Winkworth. New York: Pantheon.

Tiger, Lionel. 1979. *Optimism: The Biology of Hope*. New York: Simon & Schuster.

Tillinghast, Pardon E. 1972. *The Specious Past: Historians and Others*. Reading, Mass.: Addison-Wesley.

Toates, Frederick. 1986. *Motivational Systems*. New York: Cambridge University Press.

Tobin, Frank. 1986. *Meister Eckhart: Thought and Language*. Philadelphia: University of Pennsylvania Press.

Trager, William. 1986. *Living Together: The Biology of Animal Parasitism*. New York: Plenum.

Trivers, Robert. 1985. *Social Evolution*. Menlo Park, Calif.: Benjamin/Cummings.

Trivers, Robert, and Huey P. Newton. 1982. "The Crash of Flight 90: Doomed by Self-Deception?" *Science Digest* 90 (November): 66–67, 111.

Truzzi, Marcello, ed. 1971. *Sociology: The Classic Statements*. New York: Random House.

Turner, Ronny E., Charles Edgley, and Glen Olmstead. 1975. "Information Control in Conversations: Honesty Is Not Always the Best Policy." *Kansas Journal of Sociology* 11, no. 1: 69–89.

Turner, Victor, and Edith Turner. 1978. *Image and Pilgrimage in Christian Culture: Anthropological Perspectives*. New York: Columbia University Press.

Utthal, William. 1981. *A Taxonomy of Visual Processes*. Hillsdale, N.J.: Lawrence Erlbaum.

Vane-Wright, R. I. 1976. "A Unified Classification of Mimetic Resemblances." *Biological Journal of the Linnean Society* 8:25–56.

Van Voorhis, Wesley C., and Harvey Eisen. 1989. "A Surface Antigen of *Trypanosoma cruzi* That Mimics Mammalian Nervous Tissue." *Journal of Experimental Medicine* 169:641–52.

Vaughan, C. 1988. "Hawks Stoop with a Group to Increase Hunting Success." *Science News* 133 (April): 222.

Voltaire. 1971. *Philosophical Dictionary*. Ed. and trans. Theodore Besterman. Baltimore: Penguin.

Ward, Andrew. 1992. "The Role of Multiculturalism in Education." *Contemporary Philosophy* 14 (May/June): 9.

Wardle, Miriam G., and David S. Gloss. 1982. "Effects of Lying and Conformity on Decision-Making Behavior." *Psychological Reports* 51 (December): 871–77.

Warner, Richard. 1976. "Deception in Shamanism and Psychiatry." *Transnational Mental Health Research Newsletter* 18:2, 6–12.

———. 1980. "Deception and Self-Deception in Shamanism and Psychiatry." *International Journal of Social Psychiatry* 26:41–52.

Watson, Peter. 1978. *War on the Mind: The Military Uses and Abuses of Psychology*. New York: Basic Books.

Watylawick, Paul. 1976. *How Real Is Real?* New York: Random House.

Webley, Paul, and Margaret Burke. 1984. "Children's Understanding of Motives for Deception." *European Journal of Social Psychology* 14:455–58.

Wedgwood, C. V. 1960. *Truth and Opinion: Historical Essays*. New York: Macmillan.

Weinstein, N. D. 1980. "Unrealistic Optimism About Future Life Events." *Journal of Personality and Social Psychology* 39:806–20.

———. 1982. "Unrealistic Optimism About Susceptibility to Health Problems." *Journal of Behavioral Medicine* 5:441–60.

Weinstein, N. D., and E. Lachendro. 1982. "Egocentrism as a Source of Unrealistic Optimism." *Personality and Social Psychology Bulletin* 8:195–200.

Weisman, Avery D. 1972. *On Dying and Denying*. New York: Behavioral Publications.

Weiss, Mark L., and Alan E. Mann. 1985. *Human Biology and Behavior: An Anthropological Perspective*. 4th ed. Boston: Little, Brown.

Welles, Jim. 1981. "The Sociobiology of Self-Deception." *Human Ethology Newsletter* 3 (February): 14–19.

Whaley, B. 1969. *Strategem: Deception and Surprise in War*. Cambridge: MIT Center for International Studies.

White, Leslie A. 1959. *The Evolution of Culture: The Development of Civilization to the Fall of Rome*. New York: McGraw-Hill.

———. 1975. *The Concept of Cultural Systems: A Key to Understanding Tribes and Nations*. New York: Columbia University Press.

Whiten, Andrew, and Richard W. Byrne. 1988. "Tactical Deception in Primates." *Behavioral and Brain Sciences* 11:233–73.

Whyte, William H. 1956. *The Organization Man*. New York: Simon & Schuster.

Wickler, Wolfgang. 1965. "Mimicry and the Evolution of Animal Communication." *Nature* 208:519–21.

———. 1968. *Mimicry in Plants and Animals*. Trans. R. D. Martin. New York: World University Library.

Wilding, J. M. 1982. *Perception: From Sense to Object*. London: Hutchinson.

Wilkinson, Simon R. 1986. " 'Pretend Illness': An Analysis of One Phase in the Development of Illness Behavior." *Family Systems Medicine* 4:376–84.

William of Sherwood. 1966. *William of Sherwood's Introduction to Logic*. Trans. Norman Kretzmann. Minneapolis: University of Minnesota Press.

Wilson, E. O. 1978. *On Human Nature*. New York: Bantam.

———. 1980. *The Insect Societies*. Cambridge: Harvard University Press.

Wise, David. 1973. *The Politics of Lying: Government Deception, Secrecy, and Power*. New York: Random House.

Wise, David, and Thomas B. Ross. 1967. *The Espionage Establishment*. New York: Random House.

Wittgenstein, Ludwig. 1958. *Philosophical Investigations*. Trans. G. E. M. Anscombe. 3rd ed. New York: Macmillan.

———. 1980. *Culture and Value*. Trans. Peter Winch. Ed. G. H. von Wright. Chicago: University of Chicago Press.

Wolk, Robert L., and Arthur Henley. 1970. *The Right to Lie: A Psychological Guide to the Uses of Deceit in Everyday Life*. New York: Wyden.

Woodruff, Guy, and David Premack. 1979. "Intentional Communication in the Chimpanzee: The Development of Deception." *Cognition* 7:333–62.

Woodward, Bob. 1987. *Veil: The Secret Wars of the CIA*. New York: Simon & Schuster.

Workman, Herbert B. 1913. *The Evolution of the Monastic Ideal*. London: Epworth.

Young, John Z. 1971. *An Introduction to the Study of Man*. New York: Oxford University Press.

———. 1978. *Programs of the Brain*. New York: Oxford University Press.

———. 1987. *Philosophy and the Brain*. New York: Oxford University Press.

Zagorin, Perez. 1990. *Ways of Lying: Dissimulation, Persecution, and Conformity in Early Modern Europe*. Cambridge: Harvard University Press.

Ziv, Avner. 1984. *Personality and Sense of Humor*. New York: Springer.

⊂⊃ *Index* ⊂⊃